A REFRESHING AND RETHINKING RETRIEVAL
OF GREEK THINKING

New Studies in Phenomenology and Hermeneutics

Kenneth Maly, General Editor

New Studies in Phenomenology and Hermeneutics aims to open up new approaches to classical issues in phenomenology and hermeneutics. Thus its intentions are the following: to further the work of Edmund Husserl, Maurice Merleau-Ponty, and Martin Heidegger – as well as that of Paul Ricoeur, Hans-Georg Gadamer, and Emmanuel Levinas; to enhance phenomenological thinking today by means of insightful interpretations of texts in phenomenology as they inform current issues in philosophical study; to inquire into the role of interpretation in phenomenological thinking; to take seriously Husserl's term *phenomenology* as "a science which is intended to supply the basic instrument for a rigorously scientific philosophy and, in its consequent application, to make possible a methodical reform of all the sciences"; to take up Heidegger's claim that "what is own to phenomenology, as a philosophical 'direction,' does not rest in being real. Higher than reality stands *possibility*. Understanding phenomenology consists solely in grasping it as possibility"; to practice phenomenology as "underway," as "the *praxis* of the self-showing of the matter for thinking," as "entering into the movement of enactment-thinking."

The commitment of this book series is also to provide English translations of significant works from other languages. In summary, **New Studies in Phenomenology and Hermeneutics** intends to provide a forum for a full and fresh thinking and rethinking of the way of phenomenology and interpretive phenomenology, that is, hermeneutics.

For a list of books published in this series, see page 343.

A REFRESHING AND RETHINKING RETRIEVAL OF GREEK THINKING

Kenneth Maly

UNIVERSITY OF TORONTO PRESS
Toronto Buffalo London

ISBN 978-1-4875-5607-5 (cloth)   ISBN 978-1-4875-5609-9 (EPUB)
                                  ISBN 978-1-4875-5608-2 (PDF)

New Studies in Phenomenology and Hermeneutics

Library and Archives Canada Cataloguing in Publication

Title: A refreshing and rethinking retrieval of Greek thinking /
    Kenneth Maly.
Names: Maly, Kenneth, author.
Series: New studies in phenomenology and hermeneutics (Toronto, Ont.)
Description: Series statement: New studies in phenomenology and
    hermeneutics | Includes bibliographical references and index.
Identifiers: Canadiana (print) 20230566871 | Canadiana (ebook)
    20230566901 | ISBN 9781487556075 (cloth) |
    ISBN 9781487556099 (EPUB) | ISBN 9781487556082 (PDF)
Subjects: LCSH: Philosophy, Ancient.
Classification: LCC B111 .M35 2024 | DDC 180 – dc23

Cover design: Alexa Love
Cover image: iStock.com/Spyros

We wish to acknowledge the land on which the University of Toronto
Press operates. This land is the traditional territory of the Wendat, the
Anishnaabeg, the Haudenosaunee, the Métis, and the Mississaugas of the
Credit First Nation.

University of Toronto Press acknowledges the financial support of the
Government of Canada, the Canada Council for the Arts, and the Ontario
Arts Council, an agency of the Government of Ontario, for its publishing
activities.

Canada Council   Conseil des Arts
for the Arts   du Canada

ONTARIO ARTS COUNCIL
CONSEIL DES ARTS DE L'ONTARIO

an Ontario government agency
un organisme du gouvernement de l'Ontario

Funded by the   Financé par le
Government   gouvernement   Canadä
of Canada   du Canada

We could not know his stunning head,
wherein the eyes ripened like apples. And yet
his torso still glows, like a candelabrum,
in which his gaze, however dimmed,
persists and glistens. Else the bow of his breast
could not blind you, nor, in the gentle coiling
of the loins, could a smile reach into that center
which carried fertility.

Else this stone would stand disfigured and stunted
under the limpid slump of the shoulders …
and would not flicker so,
like the hides of beasts of prey;
and would not be bursting at the seams
like a star: for there is there no pose
that does not see you.
You must change your life.
– Rainer Maria Rilke,
"Archaïscher Torso Apollos"

At bottom the only courage that is demanded of us is to
have the courage for the most strange, the most singular,
the most inexplicable that we may encounter.
– Rainer Maria Rilke

Poetry … purges from our inward sight the film of familiarity
which obscures from us the wonder of our being.
– Percy Bysshe Shelley

One thing I have learned in a long life is that all our science,
measured against reality, is primitive and childlike … Everything
is energy, and there is nothing more to say.
– Albert Einstein

All of us are prisoners of our early indoctrinations,
for it is hard, very nearly impossible,
to shake off one's earliest training.

– Robert Heinlein

It is not ill fate that has sent you on this pathway
but rather the powers of what is fitting and in accord:
For it lies off the beaten track of humans.

– Parmenides

Do not imagine, think, or deliberate,
Meditate, act, but be at rest,
With an object do not be concerned.

– Tilopa

The alterations of the spiritual and the material tides … filled me
with admiration and reverence. A small boy begins by being unable
to explain the unexplainable, but when he grows old he often looks
away from what cannot be explained. I am grateful that fate has
preserved me from this form of blindness.

If I know what I shall find, I do not want to find it.
Uncertainty is the salt of life.

– Erwin Chargaff

Contents

4 Bringing the Book to a Close   289

Suggestions, Guidelines

Dear Reader, I am aware that this book is not orthodox scholarship. Its style and way of unfolding break the chains of the usual paradigm. It has a certain freedom, in which thinking forges new pathways. Given its uniqueness, I offer some guidelines while you read and work with it.

Experience. We cannot come to know what is at the heart of this writing project without experience. And experience is never totally definable. Experience cannot be measured or calculated. Heidegger insists on experience as primary in his pursuit. Here are a few examples of how Heidegger sees the need for experience (what is in bold here is mine): For both languages (the original and the translation) the translator is "intrinsically bound to the language and **the experience** of its deep sway [*das Wesen*]" (GA 5:328).

> With that, what is meant by *Unverborgenheit* ... what we are to think with the name αληθεια **is not yet experienced**, let alone held fast in a rigorous thinking. (GA 54:16–17)

> In Fragment I, 28, the goddess says: "**but it is necessary for you to experience everything**." (GA 15:406)

> The awakening to Ereignis/enowning **must be experienced, it cannot be proven**. The question came with a certain contradiction, lying in the fact that **thinking is supposed to be the experiencing** of the

> matter itself … insofar as **experiencing is nothing mystical**, not an act of spiritual enlightenment, but rather the entry into dwelling in Ereignis/enowning … the **awakening to Ereignis/enowning remains something that must be experienced** … (GA 14:63–4)

It is about lived experience, direct and concrete experience. And could lead to a transformation in our thinking.

Using everyday language, we can say that philosophy is generally thought of as an intellectual exercise with a certain kind of vocabulary. A university degree becomes the qualification for this kind of work. We tend to busy ourselves in finding cogent arguments in a kind of book knowledge. Heidegger calls this "scholarship," which he then distinguishes from thinking. It is as if we take a philosophy book off the shelf, enjoy reading it and activating the intellect, and then put the book back on the shelf and "return to living our lives." To **experience** is something else.

* **Poi-etic language**. Whatever the thrust of this writing is, it is to a great extent elusive and poi-etic. If we seek a summary of what Heidegger finally means in the form of propositional sentences, we will be frustrated, and perhaps disappointed. Poi-etic saying is non-conceptual and calls for *doing thinking, along the way*. Having an experience with the thinking-saying.

David Bohm says that we are "often able to overcome this tendency toward fragmentation by using language in a freer, more informal, and 'poetic' way." I call this poi-etic language.

What is the reason for the hyphen? The word comes from the Greek *poiesis* (ποίησις), which in turn stems from the verb *poieo* (ποιέω). The words ποίησις-ποιέω-ποιητικός do indeed refer to the art of poetry and what we mean to say with the word *poetic*, for example, "that is poetic language." But ποιέω also says: I do, make, gather, create, celebrate, produce, or bring about. So ποίησις has two meanings: One, poetry, poem. Two, creating, making, bringing forth. The hyphen (a) keeps fresh our understanding that what is going on here is more than "poetic" and (b) gives our thinking-saying a space for staying open to what the word says-shows in the second sense.

Aristotle has a powerful example of how the word *poi-etic* is a fitting coinage of a word. In *De Anima* (III, 5, 430a 15–17) he speaks of a *mind* (νοῦς, *nous*) that makes-gathers-brings about all things (πάντα ποιεῖν, *panta poiein*), aka "poi-etic mind" (*nous poi-etikos*, νοῦς ποιητικός). It is obvious that this use of the word ποιητικός cannot simply be translated as "poetic" in our language! In order to say what the Greek word says-shows, the "new" word *poi-etic* fits very well.[1]

How can we apply poi-etic language on a practical level? It is virtually impossible to avoid the usual subject-verb-object structure, but we can allow our saying to break free of this structure in small ways. Sometimes we write as if it *is* poetry. Less static and closed, more dynamic and opening. Verbal forms rather than nouns. The most important way to move into poi-etic saying is to constantly remind ourselves that our saying is dynamic.

Language, then, is a poi-etic saying rather than logical-propositional. Connotation rather than denotation. Dynamic rather than static. Inexhaustible rather than definite. Open-ended rather than defining. And saying is a showing. To summarize, our usual language explains and defines, whereas poi-etic language says and in saying shows. Something is gathered or created or emerges in poi-etic saying, something that includes the "poetic" but goes beyond that.

* **Coining new words**. Indeed, I have coined several new words. These are called neologisms. In Heidegger scholarship there is at times a tendency to disparage neologisms. I, on the other hand, find the use of neologisms very positive and even necessary or "called for," in order to grasp what is being said and to understand what Heidegger is really getting at.

Languages are **living languages**. This means that new words emerge as language deals with new experiences and new things that happen in the world. To wit: such "neologisms" as internet, surfing, laptop, cyberspace, beatnik, meme, nerd, twitter, spam. The same thing happens when we dig into new possibilities for thinking. Here are some of the words that I "coin" in order to get a sense of things that is "better" than what the dictionary offers: the dynamic **one-ing** instead of uniting into a static one, the dynamic **minding** instead of mind as a static unity, experiencing the **no-way-out** instead of logical dilemma, **no-thing** instead of nothing.

* **Repetitions**. The many repetitions in this book are deliberate. They belong to the poi-etic way of saying, which is central to the book. I urge the reader to take each repetition seriously.

Heidegger himself often uses repetitions. Traditionally tautology belongs to logic, but in Heidegger's way of thinking and writing, tautology is "saying the same" as a way of seeing something new in each repetition. I am reminded of Gertrude Stein's "A rose is a rose is a rose." The same holds true when Heidegger says that the many names for the same dynamic is a richness and a sign of the power of the dynamic itself.

* **Mirrorings and encirclings.** In the context of the aforementioned items having to do with language – poi-etic language, coining new words, repetitions – the following elements of this book mirror and encircle one another:

- Buddhism
- Daoism
- Bohm and quantum physics
- Heidegger's quest
- The refreshing, rethinking retrieval of Greek philosophy, especially early Greek thinking

Whereas the experience and thinking and saying within each of these elements show aspects that are unique to each one, they share a common thread. Their mirroring of this common thread helps us in our coming-to-know what is at stake. As each encircles the others and the non-dual dynamic wholeness of it all, we find beacons of light that show us the way. It is a circle dance rather than a forward march. The circle has no corners or stop signs, that is, periods. This encircling is not regular or organized. It is not driven or deliberate. It turns back rather than moving in one direction.

Given the forces at work in this project, the manner in which these elements mirror and encircle one another is specific to our project.

* **Coming back to the original.** Quite often I have chosen to include the original German alongside the English. Among other things, this is a reminder never to lose sight of the original German and how it necessarily informs the English translation. This is necessary – especially in the case of Heidegger's German – even if the reader does not know German.

These guidelines are gentle reminders, words of caution, pointers, tips. You are your own guiding light.

* **A Technical Matter: References to Heidegger's** *Gesamtausgabe.* References in the text and notes are to the various volumes of the *Gesamtausgabe*, as follows: GA followed by the volume number and then the page number – for example, GA 8:17.

All the translations of Heidegger's German are my own. I have allowed myself a bit of freedom that I would not allow if I were doing an "official" translation for publication. For this reason – among others – you will often find the German words in the text in brackets within quotations and otherwise in parentheses. Within quotations from Heidegger, parentheses are his, while brackets are mine.

You will find full bibliographical information in the Bibliography at the end of the book.

Preamble: Telling the Story of This Book

*This Preamble grew out of a lengthy dialogue with a close friend. It took place at the very beginning of the COVID pandemic. Not knowing who would live and who would die, I decided that it was important to put into writing what my project as a whole entails, in case I would not get the chance to finish the writing. This includes (a) opening minds up to the experience of dao, buddha mind, the field of quantum physics, Heidegger's being/beyng – aka the non-dual dynamic of radiant emptiness, and (b) finding this part of the way things are, including us, as totally natural **within** our own Western tradition. This involves above all a fresh look at what got lost in early Greek thinking, along with the effort to retrieve that.*

Can you describe the purpose of this book on Greek philosophy?

The fullness of what the Greeks thought and said – what Nietzsche called the "high-spirited conversation (*Geistergespräch*)" – got covered over almost immediately after the Greek "golden age." First, for more than one thousand years CE, Western philosophy had only Latin translations of Aristotle. The original Greek texts had been preserved in the Arabic world, above all in Toledo, Spain. They were discovered by Western Christian thinkers around the middle of the thirteenth century. Along with the original Greek versions of the texts that were already known about, new texts by Aristotle were discovered, texts that the Western world at the time did not have. Only then did the Western, mostly Christian, philosophers start to deal with Greek philosophy in the original.

This lack of access to the original Greek texts, and the dominant filter of Christianity, made what the Greeks originally thought and said virtually unavailable. At a time when only Latin translations were available and were filtered through Christianity, direct and honest access to Greek thinking did not happen. Until now. Until first Nietzsche and then Heidegger opened the door.

Second, as a consequence of this already existing miscomprehension of the Greeks, efforts to translate from the original Greek – in all Western languages, including German and English – did not always try to retrieve what the Greeks really thought and said. Rather they dutifully translated from the Greek using the vocabulary and grammar of the *then current Western philosophy*, precisely *not* going back to the Greeks. In this way they hid access to the richness of the original or originary thinking-saying by the Greek thinkers. I along with Nietzsche and Heidegger call these "mistranslations."

My purpose here is to uncover and retrieve what the Greeks thought, along with what was necessarily left unthought. This happened within the filter of Christianity and the mistranslations into English that followed in the seventeenth and eighteenth centuries – motivated in part by the dominance of rationalism. (In this book you will find many examples of this "retrieval," for you to check out.)

When and how did this project begin?

If you had asked me this question a few years ago, I would have said that the idea came to me in the early 2000s. But … in October 2019 I was in La Crosse, Wisconsin, where I still have a few boxes of files stored. While I was going through these boxes, I discovered a note written in 1989, where I outlined very briefly my intention to pursue such a project as the one that I am now fully into. Then, lo and behold!, I found a folder with the first one hundred pages of a draft for this same project. It was dated 1992, and I had forgotten entirely that it existed! (It turns out that much of this very early version was unusable now: Much has changed in the intervening years, including me.)

Describing the how is a bit more complicated. Several conditions came together in my life, both professional and personal, which at least on one level make up the conditions by which this book simply had to get written.

One, I had learned enough classical Greek at the university to be able, along the way, to question the English and German translations of the Greek texts.

Two, this was aided and supported by my enthusiasm for Heidegger's thinking, which has never abated despite the whole rigmarole surrounding (a) sometimes misreading Heidegger through the lens of deconstruction and (b) being waylaid by fascination with Heidegger's involvement in German politics in the 1930s.

Three, in that context, I was inspired, fascinated, and challenged by how Heidegger worked with the Greek texts. I will tap into just one example here – we will delve into this question more than once in this book. The Greek word ἀλήθεια has traditionally and almost always been translated into German as *die Wahrheit* and into English as *truth*. With these translations we have *reduced* what the Greek word says, to something like truth as correctness – in logic and sentence structure and propositions. This move simply hides or covers over what the Greeks wanted to say about the dynamic of ἀλήθεια – which went far beyond the logical or propositional.

Literally, ἀ-λήθεια (λήθη, with the *alpha-primitivum*) says "not-hiding" or "not-in-hiding" or "coming out of hiding" as in disclosure or non-concealment or emergence (from hiding). This new and fresher translation is so clearly *not* saying anything about logic and syntax or propositions. Rather it immediately opens our thinking to the dynamic of showing the way things are *and how they reveal themselves prior to and apart from logical and propositional truth as "correctness."*

Heidegger is saying to me and to every reader: Look at this. Do you see how the word ἀλήθεια says so much more than the "truth" of logic and propositions? Check this out for yourself.

Four – and this condition somehow arches over all the conditions that I have described so far – Heidegger has taught and guided me in the wonderful and essential work of the philosopher to be careful with words and how they are used, to not be reckless in using them, to tend to words as they show the way things are. Simply put: To take care of words.

In *Sein und Zeit* Heidegger addresses our work as philosophers:

> When we apply such pieces of evidence [e.g., regarding the Greek word ἀλήθεια and how it got translated], we must guard against unrestrained word mysticism; at the same time, however, it is **the business of philosophy to preserve the force of the most elemental words** [the bold is mine] ... so that "common sense" does not reduce them to incomprehensibility. (GA 2:291)

Elemental words are those words that say and show the way things are and what is most central to meaningful human existence. We dare not reduce them, as if they have nothing to say, thus never questioning them in their full and deep sway as words that "say" rather than define.

So, for the above reasons, I am excited about this project: working with the Greek texts and offering some ways of refreshing the translations of the Greek texts and thereby moving closer to what the Greeks actually experienced, thought, and said.

Note: The checking is not done by a kind of one-to-one comparison of the Greek word to the word in translation. Rather it is done "from the future," from what is in front of us as we do this work – what "confronts" us. We check the fitness of the words in translation by measuring them against what is to be thought, what calls for thinking. And by interpreting in translation, we come up to what is being said in the Greek and how the new translation is a fresher way to say-show what the Greek thinkers were about, as they preserved the force of the most elemental words.

The fifth condition is my own work as professor of philosophy at the University of Wisconsin–La Crosse, where I ended up teaching a course in Greek philosophy approximately thirty times. Heeding Heidegger's warning not to automatically "know" what the Greeks were thinking by using the available translations, I decided not to translate many of the key words, but rather to leave them in Greek. And I decided to leave them in Greek font: λόγος instead of *logos*, ἀλήθεια instead of *aletheia*, ἐνέργεια instead of *energeia*. And I had the students learn the Greek alphabet. Without anticipating the result, it became clear that this strategy worked! First of all, the students enjoyed this task of learning the Greek alphabet and working with these key words in Greek. Second, it provided a distance from any automatic understanding of what the words were saying – for example, λόγος = logic. And the students were excited to actually think what the Greek word says instead of using the "obvious" English word in translation. This turned out to be important: not only opening the mind to something fresher, but also learning to think in Greek.

What are the important experiences that have brought you to this point in your life, where this writing project becomes a culmination of your many years of teaching, translating, thinking?

First, let me say that the path on which my life and life's work has taken me is clearer in hindsight than it was in the going of the way. I suppose that this is natural, or?

Born and raised on a farm, I had to learn how to be practical. That used to be the only way to survive and thrive on a farm. You don't sleep in. You have chores to do, and you don't have the choice not to do them. (At least with my father!)

Having lived closer to the land and closer to the survival mode – than city folks, as we called them – it is hard for us to forget our roots. We share a kind of honesty with ourselves that automatically keeps up with us – at least for part of the journey. Whatever we do and try to achieve, it has to be grounded and stay genuine. What is purely logical or abstract doesn't cut it. It is more about experience – what we see with our own eyes and how things really happen – than about theory. Of course, it is also about learning to think critically about this domain of experience.

When I was fourteen, I left the farm to go to a Catholic seminary in Ohio. When I was twenty-two, I left the seminary and eventually went to graduate school at Duquesne University in Pittsburgh. Then in 1979 I got my first full-time position, teaching at the

University of Wisconsin–La Crosse. I retired from there in December 2005.

While I was teaching in La Crosse, my wife and I chose to live in the country and to raise our children "on the land." It so happened that we bought our milk unpasteurized from a neighbour, Paul. Often when I stopped to get milk, he and I would chat about farming. And one day I asked him about the corn that was still standing in the field, and why he had not yet cut it for silage.[1] Paul nodded a little, looked off into the distance, and then said: "Yes, the farm magazines say that it should be cut now, based on scientists and their fancy research." Then looking at me with a mischievous grin, he said: "But they don't feed the cows, I do!" Experience trumps abstract theory.

With that, I turn to the question: Why *this* book? And what experiences have brought me to this point? I think that I was born into "it," namely a set of conditions whereby I, in my own quiet way, found myself on the cusp between two worlds or two models of how humans see and understand the way things are – in the outer world, in our own inner life, and in the whole universe. For now, let me call them the "old model" and the "new model" within Western thinking. (In part 1-i, I describe what is going on in these two ways in a more "philosophical" wording. There I will rename them the traditional-inherited (TI) and the refreshing-retrieving (RR) ways in Western thinking.)

The "old model," the traditional, inherited ways. The traditional Western world view that has been dominant for the past three centuries or more values – that is, holds for true – the following patterns or paradigms, as what is exclusively true or "more" true.

The world is made up of independent, static substances.
Things appear as solid, "objective," substantial particles.
Rationalistic science, mathematical proofs, Cartesian dualism count.
Western philosophers and scientists have traditionally tried to think what reality is as it is "on its own," separate from our experience of it.
We are accustomed to see the world as independent, static, external objects.

The world that we have inherited from the nineteenth century
is mechanical-mechanistic and divisible and is based on an
unconditional faith in objective reality.
We learned to celebrate quantifying and to glorify what can be
measured or calculated.
The empirical is king: quantified, hardened, measurable,
calculable, standardized.
Body and soul-mind are understood as separate, and the way
to understand the world is through concepts.
Language is definitional, analytical, and abstract.

These many words mirror the inherited ways. Let me try to
open up beyond what these descriptors of the "old model" say, by
putting them into words that form the framework of this book on
refreshing, rethinking retrieval of Greek philosophy.
The "old" model focuses on:

- the either-or separation of **dualism**, rather than the non-dual
  "unity" or oneness – even better, the dynamic oneness or one-ing
  as dynamic,[2]
- rational-intellectual **conceptualization** as the dominant mode of
  thinking, rather than a thinking emerging from concrete lived
  experience,
- what is **static, independent**, solid, hardened, rather than the ever-
  changing dynamic of the way things are, the changing conditions
  that come together to shape what is and to keep changing the way
  things are,
- the almost exclusive dominance of the **quantitative, rational**
  description of things in the world.

The "new model," new and fresh openings. Meanwhile, however,
another way has been emerging in Western thinking for several
generations now. This way of seeing the world is more open-ended,
more creative, more dynamic.

The world is made up of dynamic, generative fields.
Things appear as intertwined relationships, in a kind of
synergistic wholeness, an always already belonging together.

Nothing of what is is dead matter, but a living presence.
This world is a harmonious creating where all things interact
   with all other things in a coherent dynamic and non-dual
   whole. Everything but everything is entangled.
In its nonduality, this dynamic wholeness or oneness dissolves
   the duality of subject–object, of observer–observed.
This wholeness is indivisible, rich connectedness. It is self-
   organizing. It is a non-dual dynamic – a oneness or a one-
   ing – in which the phenomenon is entwined.
This world is always changing and in process, involving a
   transforming, and metamorphosis and always unfolding –
   there is no static result. Nothing static, no beginning, no end.
The way to knowing the world and things in this fresh manner
   is through direct experience – non-conceptually.
The mysterious aspects of connectedness and oneness in
   coherence are valued.
The dynamic of the mind is awareness, holistic knowing,
   experiencing.
Mind is not isolated or separate but is always in touch with
   other minds and with the world, the way things are.
Mind is non-dually one with everything, in intuitive knowing.
Things are not either-or but both-and – relational, that is, they
   are what they are depending on a bunch of conditions.

The new ways or fresh openings include both ways:

- the either-or separation of dualism, *within* the **non-dual dynamic** –
  a oneness or one-ing – in which the phenomenon is entwined,
- rational-intellectual conceptualization as the dominant mode
  of thinking, *within* a thinking emerging from **non-conceptual,
  concrete lived experience,**
- what is static, solid, hardened, independent, *within* the **ever-
  changing dynamic** of the way things are, the changing conditions
  that come together to shape what is,
- the quantitative, rational description of things in the world, *within*
  the **immeasurable** that is in everything but is itself not anything,
  no-thing. Mind in Buddhism, the *dao* in Daoism, the energy field
  of quantum physics, and the **emptiness** in Buddhism. What the

Greeks wanted to say with *physis, logos, aletheia*. And what I call
the non-dual dynamic of radiant emptiness. And what Heidegger
calls beyng-Ereignis (*Sein-Seyn-Ereignis*).

Note: I use these words of Heidegger here for the first time. They
will appear a couple more times here in the Preamble. These
words play a big part in our understanding of how Heidegger's
thinking opens up to the non-dual dynamic of radiant emptiness,
also named buddha mind, *dao*, the field of energy or the quantum potential of quantum physics – and then in the key Greek
words that open up this same dynamic in early Greek thinking.
(Since these words of Heidegger are key words throughout this
book, I will focus on them directly in the Interlude that follows
this Preamble.)

*Can you explain more what the words **old** and **new** mean here?*

Good question. The terms are obviously relative.

1. What I call here "old" are the traditional ways we have inherited
    in the West. But relative to what came before the onset of this
    world view, those ways were once "new" and thus still today
    often viewed as part of "the modern period."[3]
2. What I call here "new" are the ways of thinking are new *in the
    West*, having emerged more recently in the West. They are a kind
    of new opening onto the world and how we understand ourselves
    in that world. This is mirrored in the term "new physics" as
    opposed to the "old," classical physics of Galileo and Newton.
3. But a part of what happens in the "new" physics and quantum
    mechanics and relativity theory hearkens back to very "old" ways
    in Asian thinking, for example, Daoism and Buddhism. And to
    the ways in which the Greek thinkers saw the way things are.
    Here we are trying to retrieve these "old" ways of Greek thinking.
    Thus what the "new" ways in the West open up is a way of
    seeing the way things are that is quite similar to the "old" ways
    of Buddhism and Daoism **and** – as we will see in this project of
    thinking – already there in Western thinking, especially with the
    early Greek thinkers. Remember that Thales lived in Ionia in Asia

Minor between ca. 625 BCE and ca. 546 BCE, that the Buddha was
born in ancient India while Thales was alive, in 564 BCE, and that
the *Daodejing*[4] was written around this time as well. It is evident,
then, that early Greek thinking was contemporaneous with both
Buddhist and Daoist teachings and ways of life.
4. Buddhism was clearly on the minds of Albert Einstein,[5] Erwin
Schrödinger,[6] Niels Bohr,[7] and Anton Zeilinger.[8] Also, in the book
The Quantum and the Lotus,[9] Matthieu Ricard and Trinh Xuan
Thuan have a conversation about the significant connections
between the teachings of Buddhism and the recent discoveries in
quantum physics. Given how the "new" physics resonates with
the "old" Buddhism, what I call here the "new ways" is in some
sense a remembering of the "old" ways in Buddhism and early
Greek thinking.

You mention here quantum physics and Buddhism.[10] *How do they fit
into your project with Greek philosophy?*

Let me try to explain. There is a kind of encircling going on. Within
this encircling, I propose the following image: Roughly 2,500 years
ago, the Buddha and Buddhism began with a world view and way
of thinking and experience of mind that is non-dual as it works
beyond just humans, mind that is no-thing, has no form and is
above all dynamic. Not static. One could say that human mind
is one with the beyond-human mind. At about the same time,
early Greek thinkers were working with a similar view of the way
things are. This way of early Greek thinking and saying got hidden
and covered over rather soon afterwards. This dimension of early
Greek thinking is what we are called upon to "retrieve." Note that
the Asians did not lose sight of this experience of the way things
are, whereas the West did lose sight.

In a sense, the "new" quantum physics has carved a new
road that is taking Western science and thinking back to what
the Buddhists have been practising and teaching for these many
centuries – and what Western thinking had forgotten. In other
words, Buddhism shows what quantum physics has rediscov-
ered: the way things are and a way of thinking and doing that is

more inclusive, that is non-dualistic and not static, that is more experience than conceptual, and that teaches the dynamic of emptiness: spacious, empty like space and awareness beyond form. Within the past century, quantum physics and quantum potential, relativity, and entanglement have led to a world view that resonates with that of Buddhism. As I have just shown, running through the literature and writings of these scientists is a thread of Buddhism.[11]

This book will show that the world view that is in "old" Buddhism and Daoism and in the "new" quantum physics is also present in Greek philosophy. A thread runs through Greek thinking that is similar to Buddhist teachings and that mirrors some of the core discoveries of quantum physics. This thread got covered over. First in later Greek philosophy. Then as a result of the filter of Christianity. Then by the dualistic metaphysics and the dualistic rationalism and calculability of things from modern philosophy and science. This covering over was exacerbated or partly caused by terrible mistranslations of the Greek texts. Guided by Heidegger's thinking, I want to refresh, rethink, and retrieve these "old" Greek ways of thinking and saying.

Can you say more about these three ways (now including Daoism) and how they motivate your work?

Yes. The intermeshing of Buddhism, Daoism, and quantum physics intrigues me. And finding a similar view and way of thinking in Greek philosophy (a) makes me happy and (b) is somehow useful. You could say that the goal of this writing includes completing the quartet: Asian thinking (especially Buddhism and Daoism); some key aspects of today's science, especially quantum physics with the quantum potential and entanglement that is core to it;[12] Heidegger's lifelong pursuit; *and early Greek thinking*!

Let me explain. Towards the end of the nineteenth century, physics opened up a road that led to fresh insights, changing our understanding of the way things are and of the world, including our own place within this new dynamic. Its name is quantum physics.

In the process of reflecting on these new ways of seeing, scientists as well as thinkers noticed that these new Western ideas and awarenesses somehow aligned with "old" Eastern ways of thinking and seeing the way things are in the world.

This for me enriching and exciting project is intended to show how these same ideas, which we find in contemporary physics and in Buddhism and Daoism, are also to be found in the writings of Greek thinkers. It is my sense that uncovering these aspects of Greek thinking – bringing them out of hiding – will be useful and beneficial to us today. Finding these words and thoughts – (a) within our own historical unfolding and (b) as expressed by Western thinkers at roughly the same time as Buddhism – will shed light on how things "started" in the early days of Western thinking. This light was first shed by Nietzsche and grew brighter as Heidegger turned to the early Greeks. Heidegger's work opens up the possibility that I, after Heidegger, can engage in this writing project. This light provides a fresh and radiant way of seeing the world and of living well. From Rilke's "Archaic Torso of Apollo" at the front of this book:

> Else this stone ... would not be bursting at the seams
> like a star: for there is there no pose
> that does not see you.
> You must change your life.

From Albert Einstein:

> We see a universe marvelously arranged, obeying certain laws, but we understand the laws only dimly. Our limited minds cannot grasp the mysterious force that sways the constellations. I am fascinated by Spinoza's pantheism. I admire even more his contributions to modern thought ... [including] the soul and the body as one, not as two separate things.[13]

> The scientist's religious feeling takes the form of a rapturous amazement of the harmony of natural law, which reveals an intelligence of such superiority that, compared with it, all the systematic thinking and acting of human beings is an utterly insignificant reflection.[14]

Buddhism has the characteristics of what would be expected in a cosmic religion for the future: It transcends a personal God, avoids dogmas and theology; it covers both the natural and the spiritual; and it is based on a religious sense aspiring from the experience of all things, natural and spiritual, as a meaningful unity.[15]

You said earlier that "the immeasurable that is in everything but is itself not anything, no-thing … [like] mind in Buddhism, dao in Daoism, the energy field of quantum physics, and the emptiness in Buddhism" – somehow names what is at the core of what belongs to the "old" ways in Asian thinking as well as to the "new" ways of thinking in quantum mechanics. What makes you focus so much on these ways?

First, let me make clear that this intertwining is background to the primary goal of opening up Greek thinking to a new richness. What I say here – about the "immeasurable" – helps us grasp what is at stake in our retrieving reading of Greek thinking.

Let me describe what I am getting at. Throughout the whole of history there have been individuals – and sometimes entire societies – that have known a kind of timeless wisdom. "Known" here in the sense of holding, understanding, and experiencing that wisdom.

I will try to say what I mean by this "timeless wisdom." It is my own version. It ties into what some call "perennial wisdom." My intention here is to put into words what has been to a large extent absent in our Western culture and thinking for many centuries now, something that Asian ways of thinking and doing have kept alive since the time of the Buddha. And something that has emerged as possibility from within quantum physics and relativity. And something that *belongs at the core of early Greek philosophy*. It was there in the early Greek ways of thinking but got lost through the filter of Christianity, through the dominance of rational dualistic thinking in the modern period, and through mistranslation of the Greek texts.

Let me play with the words "timeless wisdom." **Wisdom** here means both understanding and experiencing. One could say this way of thinking and experiencing is transforming. In my book *Five*

Groundbreaking Moments in Heidegger's Thinking I tried to show how Heidegger's quest was always to find and then say a thinking that is experiential, non-conceptual, non-dual – a thinking that above all changes us.

Timeless here says a dynamic and an awareness that is lasting, imperishable, abiding-enduring, and "biding" in the sense of trustworthy. This timeless wisdom is, then, not a thing or no-thing, not a concept but beyond concepts, non-dual and not encounterable in comparing. It is emptiness – what I call "the non-dual dynamic of radiant emptiness." It is undifferentiated formlessness, even as it manifests different states of the non-dual dynamic or interdependent conditions by which "dualistic" things/beings-concepts emerge within a non-dual whole, beyond parts.

This timeless wisdom is known indirectly and said poi-etically. It is more spacious. Since it is no-thing and non-conceptual, we in our awareness might say "is as is" or "as such." This "is as is" or "as such" can be named the unmanifest field or the dynamic of emptiness.

We can say that mind in Buddhism is unconditioned as in "beyond all conditions." That the *dao* of Daoism is unconditioned. That quantum physics pushes the envelope in this direction when Bohm calls it "the immeasurable." And that we will find the same dynamic at work in Greek thinking.

Mind and awareness mirror this non-dually. We in our knowing awareness participate in the "as such." This enriches us. We find our bliss and deep meaning in realizing and living it.

This non-dual dynamic of the "as such" is at our core within the enveloping wholeness of what is. It is like the ocean in its depth, not the waves. It goes beyond ourselves. Even though it is often named a supreme being, phenomenologically it is beyond even this limiting identity. Certainly it is beyond all dogmas and beliefs. We could call it boundless. And it is natural to us humans.

It is not easy to pin all of these words down …

I am aware of that. And I agree. I might even call what I have just tried to say a kind of meandering. But I am confident that everyone can feel something of this spacious, timeless, non-sensuous and non-dual dynamic. And many of us realize that we have had an experience of this "as such."

When Heidegger directs our knowing awareness to the region where this dynamic lies, he says that we experience something like it in times of grief, ecstasy, and boredom – moments when we experience a state of awareness without moorings, without something familiar to hold on to. Even though we today do not spend much of our aware time in this state – and we tend to dismiss it because it is immeasurable – it is a natural state.

It is similar to the state of mind with LSD or the state of awareness when skydiving. But those states are externally induced. We can come to this state more naturally. Even though it is uncommon, it is a natural state.

So maybe it is not a case of pinning it down but rather of opening mind's awareness to what is more vast than we usually know, to an open expanse in which we do not usually dwell.

How does this timeless awareness fit into your project in this book?

A very good question! First, let me say that I want to focus on this "timeless wisdom" – by way of "wandering" amid word-images that can open us up to what is going on in "just is" – as a kind of background awareness.

Now to your question. With these poi-etic images in mind, let me focus on the project of this book. A bit earlier I listed four "new" ways that provide a fresh opening. I now present these four ways specifically as markers for when we focus on the retrieval and how to do it (part 2); I will then go directly to the key words of Greek philosophy and to the texts themselves (part 3). These markers open up the sayings of Greek philosophy that got covered over and hidden:

- the **non-dual**, which encompasses the either-or separation of dualism, as it *holds and embeds it in* the non-dual dynamic – a oneness or a one-ing,

- the **non-conceptual**, which encompasses the rational-intellectual conceptualization as the dominant mode of thinking, as it *holds and embeds it in* a thinking emerging from concrete lived experience,
- the **becoming**, which encompasses what is static, solid, hardened, independent, as it *holds and embeds it in* the ever-changing *dynamic* of the way things are, the changing conditions that come together to shape what is,
- **emptiness**, which encompasses the quantitative, rational description of things in the world, as it *holds and embeds it in* the immeasurable that is in everything but is itself not anything, no-thing – whose names are beyng-Ereignis (Heidegger), mind and emptiness (Buddhism), *dao* (Daoism), and the immeasurable field of energy, also known as the quantum potential (Bohm).

When we get to the actual work of reading and retranslating the Greek texts and words (part 4), these are the four markers by which we will do that, as we try to open up to a fresh reading and saying of what the Greeks said.

***

A little secret, hidden here at the end of the Preamble. How can we get a first *feel* for this non-dual dynamic of radiant emptiness? Then, how can we more fully *experience* this dynamic? Finally, how can we *say* it, after getting the feel for it and after some sense of the experience?

As I see it, Heidegger was continually in pursuit of the dynamic of no-form and no-thing beyng-Ereignis, especially how we gain access to it. A very precious moment in this searching happens at the beginning of a dialogue in *Feldweg-Gespräche (1944–45)* (GA:77:205–6). The dialogue is titled "Evening Conversation in a Prisoner of War Camp in Russia between a Younger and an Older [Soldier]." What is exciting about this conversation is how it (a) starts from the "form" of the forest that provides the space for the awareness, then (b) moves to the "formless" spaciousness as such, expansive awareness of the inexhaustible no-thing – named in the "spaciousness of the forests" that "swings into a hidden distance." Finally, (c) who are we within this formless vastness? Notably, the last two parts of the conversation presented here take place as awarenesses and sayings from within the formless. Then, of course, how to say it?

Y = Younger Soldier; O = Older Soldier

Y: *When we marched to our workplace this morning, something healing suddenly came over me from the rustling sound of the spacious [expansive, vast] forest. Throughout the whole day, I have been thinking about what this healing thing could be based on.*

O: *Perhaps it is the inexhaustible of the enveloping vastness that is around us in these forests of Russia.*

Y: *You are doubtless thinking that the spaciousness that prevails in the vastness brings us something liberating.*

O: *I do not mean only the spacious in the vastness, but also that such vastness leads us out and away [from ourselves].*

Y: *The spaciousness of the forests swings into a hidden distance, but at the same time returns to us without ending with us.*

O: *It is almost as if, from within the open yet veiled expanse, nothing could ever break in and put itself in the way of our being [Wesen, what is own to us] and blocks its course. Thus, nothing encounters [us] that bends our being back to itself and encloses it in a narrowness through which it becomes rebellious within itself.*

Y: *The vastness brings us to the objectless [the formless no-thing] and at the same time saves us from disintegrating into it. It [the vastness] releases our being into the open and at the same time gathers it into the simple, as if its lingering abiding is pure arrival to which we are admitted.*

O: *Such vastness makes us free. It frees us, even as here, between the walls of these barracks behind the barbed wire, we constantly bump up against objects, scraping ourselves against them.*

1. What are the names to say this no-thing and formless dynamic, which we experience?

    On the level of form:
    - *the rustling sound of the spacious [expansive, vast] forest,*
    - *the inexhaustible of the enveloping vastness in the forests,*
    - *emerging in the hidden distance.*

    On the level of no-form:
    - *the inexhaustible of the enveloping vastness,*
    - *the spaciousness that prevails in the vastness,*
    - *the vastness that leads us out of and away from – beyond – ourselves,*
    - *the open yet veiled expanse,*
    - *the vastness that brings us to the objectless formlessness,*
    - *the lingering abiding of the vastness.*

2. How does the no-form and no-thing spaciousness-vastness work on and with us?

    - *by coming over us in its wholeness (the core meaning of healing),*
    - *by opening us up to something that liberates us from our separateness and duality,*
    - *by leading us out of and away from ourselves,*
    - *by protecting us from what gets in the way of this opening beyond our separate self, namely that which would bend our being back to itself and enclose it in a narrowness through which it becomes rebellious within itself (i.e., the rebellious ego-subject trying to protect itself),*
    - *by releasing our being into the open and at the same time gathering it into the simple.*

3. How can we **say** this work that the no-form dynamic of spaciousness and vastness is engaged in?

    - *The dynamic of spaciousness liberates us.*
    - *It leads us out of ourselves without ending in us, i.e., the non-dual dynamic of no-form spaciousness-vastness.*
    - *It brings us to the objectless, no-thing and no-form dynamic of being-emptiness, beyond dualism and conceptualization, at the same time saving us from disintegrating into it. That is, we as humans become one with the no-form spaciousness without undoing the non-dual dynamic. This is beyond concept.*

- *In its lingering abiding, it is pure arrival to which we are admitted. It comes to us in a non-dual dynamic.*
- *As inexhaustible, it envelops us.*

The spaciousness-vastness of the no-form **dynamic** takes us beyond ourselves. We are one-ing with this beyond of spaciousness, to that which is objectless, namely no-thing and no-form. It releases our being into the open. And we are the flashpoint for this "arrival, admitted into it, healed by it." We respond to the claim laid upon us by the dynamic of the spaciousness-vastness, in our uniqueness as the flashpoint for *the spaciousness that prevails in the vastness* and for standing awarely in the *inexhaustible*.

Buddhism calls it mind. Daoism calls it *dao*. Quantum physics calls it the non-linear dynamics of the field or the field of energy aka the quantum potential. Heidegger calls it beyng, to which he gives many names. Beyng or the non-dual dynamic of radiant emptiness, called here inexhaustible spaciousness-vastness, *is not* even as it functions, is *no-thing* even as it is at-work and is experienceable by us humans. And it is this dimension-dynamic in the words of Greek thinking that got covered over and hidden, and we aim here to uncover this no-form no-thing dynamic in a retrieval.

We will return directly to this question of the "how" at the end of the book: how to experience, how to know, and how to say the non-dual dynamic of radiant emptiness.

Reminder: This Preamble was prepared prior to the bulk of the book. It mirrors how I thought of this writing project *before* it was actually written. In this sense it is preliminary and as such simply a guidepost. I decided to leave this preliminary character stand.

A REFRESHING AND RETHINKING RETRIEVAL
OF GREEK THINKING

Interlude: Heidegger's Words *Da-sein* and *Sein-Seyn-Ereignis*

Since Heidegger – especially with these words – plays a significant role in this book, I will take a moment to focus on these key words. For those readers who are new to Heidegger, a basic understanding is useful. (Note that the other words that mirror what is being retrieved in early Greek thinking – *dao*, buddha mind, and the immeasurable, no-thing energy field of quantum physics – will be dealt with along the way.) I suggest that you, the reader, read through this Interlude, to get an initial appreciation for what these ways say-show. And then, as you continue reading, perhaps you will feel the urge to come back here and look these pages over again, to get a deeper and richer understanding of what is at stake in these, Heidegger's key words.

Dasein, Da-sein. For our purposes you can ignore the difference. At one point Heidegger started to hyphenate the word. And he told a colleague of mine, in a private conversation, that the word could always be read with the hyphen, whether or not it appears in his writings that way.

First the **da**. In ordinary German *da* means "here" or "there." In Heidegger's thinking the word *da* indicates the "open expanse" in which one finds oneself. Being "there" means being open to or being "there" in that open region. Thus *da* always has an *ecstatic* character.

Second, **Dasein**. In ordinary German *Dasein* means "entity" or "existence." In Heidegger's thinking, from *Sein und Zeit* onward, it is a way of saying (1) being-in-the-world and (2) being in the opening-out (expanse) in which being itself emerges – or in which beings emerge as the very unfolding or emerging. (In more "usual" English, this phenomenon might be called "the process of coming forth," as in: The wildflower's bud comes forth into bloom – emerges, unfolds, in its coming forth.) Thus, *Dasein* is the word for human existence *in its ownmost and most proper way of being*, that is, standing-out in the opening expanse (of being itself – what Heidegger will later call *Seyn/beyng*). As such, the word *Dasein* describes the fundamental comportment or relationship that "humans" have – to the world and then to being as emerging – as "ec-static." This names the fundamental shift, in Heidegger's thinking, away from subjectivity and its objectifying, *to* the always already relatedness in the non-dual dynamic of no-thing and no-form "being" that cannot be objectified.

The word *Dasein* does not appear so often here in this book. If and when it does appear, it is without italics, because it has become an English word. More central to the movement in this book are the words that I use again and again: being-beyng-Ereignis, or just two of them: beyng/Ereignis. Since they are such key words for this book, I will now explain how to understand them.

Sein and **Seyn**. As far as I can tell, Heidegger's unusual spelling of the German word **Seyn** first appeared in print in 1962, when the Bremen lectures from 1949 were published. But what the distinction really means was somewhat difficult to decipher until the publication of *Beiträge zur Philosophie (Vom Ereignis)* in 1989, in which he makes this distinction thematic. It is there that he explains this word **Seyn/beyng** and what he wants to accomplish with this spelling.

***

a. How to Understand Seyn/beyng

Remember that *Beiträge* was written in 1936–7 and hidden in a drawer until its publication in 1989. (Some call it his second major work, after *Sein und Zeit,* and I agree.) Why did Heidegger choose to keep this important work in the closet, so to speak?

It is my understanding that the "leap" that *Beiträge* invites us to make requires from "colleagues in thinking" a lot of preparation. Without this preparation, what he was trying to say in *Beiträge* would get lost. It was therefore Heidegger's wish that people read and process his lecture courses first. In the epilogue to *Beiträge,* F.-W. von Herrmann explains Heidegger's directive in this regard:

> The reason that this large, pathfinding manuscript was not published at the beginning of the publication of the *Gesamtausgabe* but only four-teen years thereafter is Heidegger's directive for the publication of his *Gesamtausgabe,* which was particularly important to him. According to that directive, publication of the manuscripts planned for the third and fourth divisions could begin only after the lecture courses in the second division were published.[1] He explained this decision with the remark that knowledge and appropriating study of the lecture texts are a necessary prerequisite for understanding the unpublished writings, especially those from the 1930s and the first half of the 1940s. (GA 65:512–13)

In *Beiträge* Heidegger uses the word **das Sein** to refer to the being of metaphysics, that is, being as other than beings but somehow still thought in terms of beings (the ontological difference). Thus, even though the question of being is about no-thing – thus other than or over against beings – the word lent itself to the limited view of something static and separate-independent, and above all was often taken to be itself a being (often taken as a highest being, what some call God). Using this word, it was hard for thinking to separate being – formless and not a thing – from beings, phenomena, things with form. This led Heidegger to name the question as that of *Seyn,* which I translate with the word *beyng.*

He uses the word **das Seyn** to gain access or open up a dynamic that no longer thinks in terms of beings (forms). To think *Seyn* is to think beyng without beings (no-form), to think without reference to or hold on to beings. Beyng is not thought from beings, but rather from within the deep sway of beyng as disclosing, as emerging, as clearing-opening. These are all ways of saying the no-thing no-form non-dual dynamic of what this book is addressing.

One might say that the word *being* was "mediated" through or in its relationship to beings – and that the word *beyng* is, as it were, unmediated. Note that mediation here implies a duality, whereas the non-mediated implies "it itself" or an at-oneness. And note that the thinking said in *Seyn* is not based on conceptualizing or rational discourse. Opening to beyng-Ereignis involves *experience and a poi-etic saying*.

Note that, whereas Heidegger makes this distinction very clearly in *Beiträge*, he himself is not always consistent in his usage. However, once we know the distinction between *Sein* and *Seyn*, we are able to think *Seyn*, even when the word that Heidegger has used is *Sein*. A prime example of this is towards the end of 1962 essay "*Zeit und Sein*," where Heidegger shows that with the thinking of Ereignis we retrieve the oldest of the old, named *aletheia*. He says there that the task of that essay was "to think being [*Sein*] into what is own to it, from within and out of Ereignis, without considering the relation of being to beings." This means, he says, "thinking being [*Sein*] without considering metaphysics" (GA 14:29). When one thinks about the thinkable and the sayable in this essay, it is clear that, when Heidegger wrote "thinking being [*Sein*] without considering metaphysics," he could have used *Seyn* instead of *Sein*.

There is a short text from which we can get a good idea (a) of how to understand what *Seyn/beyng* is saying-showing and (b) of the wager that we undertake, given that there is no proof for this pathway. After presentation of the text from the lecture "*Das Ding*" in *Vorträge und Aufsätze* (GA 7:184–7) is "A Letter to a Young Student," dated 18 June 1950. I will now quote from this letter, apropos the (a) and (b) just mentioned, namely: how to understand how beyng works and then how to take into account the fact that where this pathway goes has no logical proof.

While reading this letter, you will notice that sometimes Heidegger writes "*Sein*" in quotation marks, indicating that here he is no longer speaking of being-*Sein*. It seems to me that there are other places where he could have used quotation marks. Given the dynamic of the "thinkable" here, I propose that you read *Seyn/ beyng* whenever you see "being" in quotation marks and some- times when it is not. Now, quoting the letter:

> You ask: From where does the thinking of being receive its directive?
>
> You will not take "being" [beyng?] as an object nor thinking as a mere activity of a subject. Thinking that is at the basis of the lecture (*Das Ding*) is not a mere representation of something existent [or at- hand]. "Being" [beyng?] is by no means identical with reality [objectiv- ity, *Wirklichkeit*] or with the real thing that has just been observed. Nor is being [beyng?] in any way set against no-longer-being and not-yet- being; these two themselves belong to the deep sway [*Wesen*] of being [beyng?]. (GA 7:184)[2]

- *Here Heidegger alludes to the timelessness of beyng. For it is within beyng in its no-form and no-time and no-where that things manifest.*

> In the thinking of being [beyng?], it will never be that only something real is presented and this taken as *the* true. To think "being" ["*Sein*," beyng?] means to be in accord with the claim of what is own to it. The accordance emanates from the claim and is released back to it. The accordance is a stepping back in the face of the claim and thus an enter- ing into its language. (GA 7:185)

- *We are being claimed by and responding to beyng itself. Beings that are over against being are not determinative in this dynamic. The word* **Seyn/beyng** *says this!*
- *For sure this "being" is nothing like the being belonging to the ontological difference. Heidegger sought long and hard to find a word that could say this not-like-the-other-being. Here he says "being" (in quotation marks), which mirrors what the word* **Seyn/ beyng** *says.*

On all this, from within a lengthy gathering and constant testing, the accordance *especially* must pay attention to the ear, in order to hear a claim of being [beyng?]. But in this very process it can mishear. The possibility of going astray is at its greatest with this thinking. This thinking can never be proven in the way that mathematical knowing can. But it is also not arbitrary, but bound into the deep-swaying affordance of being [*Wesensgeschick des Seins* {Seyn: beyng?}] – but never binding as a statement, rather simply a possible occasion to go the way of accordance and to do this in the full gathering of thoughtfulness on the being [beyng] that has *already* come to language. (GA 7:185)

One of the strange experiences I have with my lecture is that people inquire of my thinking as to where it receives its directive from, as if this question is only necessary in relation to this thinking. On the other hand, no one ever thinks of asking: where did Plato get the directive to think of being as ἰδέα, where did Kant get the directive to think of being as the transcendental of objectivity, as a position (gravity)?

But perhaps one day the answer to these questions can be derived precisely from those attempts at thinking which, like mine, are wide-open arbitrariness.

Nor can I provide you with an identity badge with the help of which what I have said could be conveniently identified at any time as consistent with "reality."

Everything here is a path of the examining hearing accordance. Way is always in danger of becoming a rogue way. Going down such paths requires practice in the going. Practice requires craftsmanship. Stay on the way in genuine need and learn the craft of thinking unswervingly, yet erring. (GA 7:186–7)

My suggestions for dealing with all this are (a) to know the distinction between *Sein* and *Seyn* as Heidegger makes it in *Beiträge* and as I have tried to say-show it here and (b) to be aware that the word *Sein* was central to Heidegger's pursuit from the very beginning, where sometimes something of what *Seyn* says was more hidden than at other times and (c) decide for yourself how to read those instances of *Sein* that are ambiguous, given that there is no logical proof for all of this.

b. How to Understand Ereignis

Ereignis. Perhaps the most difficult of all these words to translate. And I leave it mostly untranslated in this writing. I do this primarily because, in using the word *Ereignis*, Heidegger's thinking takes us deeper into the question with which it is dealing all the time, such that the *German* word unfolds deeper than and beyond anything that it "usually" means in German. Thus, the translator has first to think all the way into what the *German* word is saying – only to be faced with the question: What does it mean in English? In a sense *Ereignis* is a *singulare tantum*, that is, simply untranslatable – as are *dao* and *logos*.

Let us take a moment to understand what is at stake here, before we go to possible translations of Ereignis – which we have already surmised is impossible to translate! We have inherited a world view in which things are separate and not interconnected, static and not in movement. The gist of this book is to show how "things" are not in isolation from other things. A "thing" in itself is not anything! Things/beings do not stand alone. *And* things/beings are never separate from the no-thing no-form dynamic of beyng/Ereignis, aka the non-dual dynamic of radiant emptiness.

The way things are is interdependent and dynamic – and "one." *Dao*, buddha mind, the no-thing no-form energy field or the quantum potential of quantum physics and Heidegger's beyng-Ereignis are all in pursuit of experiencing, thinking, and saying the non-dual and non-physical dynamic that is there within – and sustains – whatever manifests as things/beings.

All of these words show this non-physical no-form no-thing dynamic by and in which "things" are more like conditions coming together than independent, static beings. This is the dynamic that Ereignis is meant to say.

I want now to offer some word-images from Heidegger, in order to flesh out what is happening here. In 1947 Heidegger wrote what I will call a "poem" (better said: thinking poetically) titled *Aus der Erfahrung des Denkens* (From within the Experience of Thinking). It appears in the book of the same title (GA 13:75–86). At the core of this text are ten pages, each of which begins with a poi-etic description of something in the natural world, followed by four lines of thinking – still in part poi-etic, but less so. Here I will present five of those first lines of poi-etic descriptions of something in the natural world.

When the early morning light waxes silently over the mountains ...

Wenn das frühe Morgenlicht still über den Bergen wächst ...

When in pre-summer scattered daffodils, hidden in the meadow, bloom and the mountain rose glows under the maple tree ...

Wenn im Vorsommer vereinzelte Narzissen verborgen in der Wiese blühen und die Bergrose unter dem Ahorn leuchtet ...

When the mountain stream tells of its falls over the boulders in the stillness of the nights ...

Wenn der Bergbach in der Stille der Nächte von seinen Stürzen über die Felsblöcke erzählt ...

When the bells ring and ring from the slopes of the high valley over which the herds slowly move ...

Wenn es von den Hängen des Hochtales, darüber langsam die Herden ziehen, glockt und glockt ...

When the evening light, falling somewhere in the forest, showers its trunks with gold ...

Wenn das Abendlicht, irgendwo im Wald einfallend, seine Stämme umgoldet ...

Note that in each of the five lines of poetry several conditions come together to make one experience. Morning light and mountains; daffodils, meadow, mountain rose, and maple tree; mountain stream, boulders and stillness of the night; bells, slopes, high valley, herds; evening light, forest, trunks, gold. Then note the verbs: waxes, blooms and glows, tells, rings and slowly moves, falls and showers with gold. All of these conditions create a mood as a non-conceptual, non-dual-one dynamic as they say or hint at – in between the words, as it were – that non-dual and no-thing formless and radiant emptiness. Then, we humans have the unique ability to *experience* what the word-images say-show. Finally, we humans are the ones who can *say all of this*.

Our experience gathers all these word-images and conditions into the *one* experience. Heidegger's Ereignis says-shows this gathering, this belonging together of all these conditions, a mutual belonging. Each condition is own to all the others, as well as own to itself in the one-ing.

c. The History of the Word *Ereignis* and Its Cognates

In his *Deutsches Wörterbuch*[3] Herrmann Paul writes that into the eighteenth century *ereignen* appeared along with the forms *ereigen*, *eräugnen* and *eräugen*. And in the eighteenth century this original meaning was still alive and "is used in instances where now it is no longer possible." The word *Ereignis* is a later development, following the use of the words *Ereignung* and *Eräugnung*. The word *Ereignis* follows on the word *eignen*, the verb form stemming from the adjective *eigen* (under the word *ereignen*).

In Paul's dictionary the word *eignen* is listed within the entry for *eigen*. *Eignen* means *eigen sein*. In English we can use the same translation for both these German wordings: befitting, fitting for, being fit (under the word *eignen*). Here Paul says that the word *eignen* means "*tauglich sein*": being suitable or fitting. Under the word *tauglich* Paul says "*geeignet sein*": fitting or something that is "own" to. Gathering, *eignen* means: to own, suit, be fitting to, befit; to have to do with, appertain, belong to, inhere in.

So now we come to the root word for all of this: the adjective *eigen*. Along with the usual meanings that are used today – *eigen-own* as belonging to in the sense of possessing: my own money, all that I own – is the meaning of "own to" as belonging to the essence of something (*zu seinem Wesen gehöriges*). To come into one's own as in to fulfil one's potential, that is, what is own to a person. (See OED under *own*.) Gathering, *eigen* in German means: own, proper to, as in "to make one's own," here "to make own the belonging-together." It is in this sense that we can talk about Ereignis in terms of own or owning or enowning.

Super-interesting is to find out (OED) that the English word *own* is "cognate with Old Frisian *ēgen*, *ēin*, Old Saxon *ēgan* (Middle Low German *ēgen*), Middle Dutch *ēghin*, *eighen* (Dutch *eigen*)." Note that the first thing Paul says in his long entry for the word *eigen* is "Old High German *eigan* [English *own*]." (After you have listened to a number of dialects in Austria or Bavaria in Germany – or *any* Swiss dialect! – it is easy to understand how the "h" disappears in the slurring dialect ... and then how the "g" somehow also disappears.)

Just as the German adjective *eigen* becomes the verb *eignen*, so too does the English adjective *own* become *owning, owning-to, enowning*. Question: When Paul says "where now it is no longer possible," he is referring to the various word-images I have gathered here. Does that mean that the usual translation of *Ereignis* as event, happening, incidence, occurrence has taken over? Hiding the originary saying of Ereignis as enowning, owning-over-to? Perhaps.

Heidegger wants to bring all of this together in the word *Ereignis*. Heidegger makes clear that the *eigen* part of the word says "own," while the *er-* part of the word says something like "enabling," "bringing into the condition of," "welling up": bringing into its own, coming into one's own, the very action by which this own (to humans, to things, to beyng, and then to owning-to and owning-over of conditions one to the other) is enacted in thinking Ereignis. Ereignis names the enabling and enacting character of this owning-to and owning-over. In this context, as we were translating *Beiträge zur Philosophie (Vom Ereignis)*, Parvis Emad and I translated *Ereignis* as "enowning."

Ereignis is the joining together of humans and beyng in a belonging-together that befits humans and beyng for each other in what is own to each one as well as to the belonging-together. Ereignis is the self-oscillating of this "en-owning" or belonging-together. Ereignis is both the impetus for beyng to emerge and the withdrawal that keeps hidden. Certain English words intimate something of this: appropriating, fitting, and befitting.

Note that Ereignis is a name for all that Heidegger aspired to when using the word *being* – later *beyng* – as he is pursuing the "question of being." And the no-thing dynamic that the word and thinking call for is a dynamic that is no-thing, formless, non-dual – within which phenomena and things emerge, phenomena that have form and exist in a world of duality.

(Note that this book focuses more on the non-dual dynamic of beyng or radiant emptiness than on phenomena and things, for the simple reason that we today are way more familiar with things having form than with what this work of thinking aspires to gain access to, namely the non-dual and formless dynamic of radiant emptiness – akin to buddha mind, *dao*, the immeasurable field of energy of quantum physics – and beyng as Ereignis. But remember: The goal here is to find this same "non-dual and formless dynamic of radiant emptiness" in Greek philosophy!)

Already in 1976 Heidegger scholar and translator Albert Hofstadter suggested saying Ereignis as "enownment."[4] That was pre-deconstruction, and most serious Heidegger scholars at the time took Hofstadter's word seriously, as he was perhaps the translator *par excellence* of Heidegger into English. He grounded this decision in the knowledge that Heidegger wanted *ereignen* to say its connection to *eigen*: own: to make one's own, to be own to, the owning work as such.[5]

Hofstadter refers to Heidegger's saying how we must simply experience this *eignen*, must experience how human Dasein and being are "en-owned" (*ge-eignet*) to each other. Ereignis-enowning is the letting-belong-together, the one befitting the other, of being and time, humans and being. To explain this, Hofstadter states:

At the center of *das Ereignis* is "own," [and] the most literal possible translation of *das Ereignis* ... en-, -own, and -ment: enownment ... the

> letting-be-own-to-one-another ... the letting be married of any two or more ... Enownment is not their belonging, but what lets their belonging be.[6]

This "own" has nothing to do with owning-as-possession and everything to do with the work or dynamic by which the different conditions are brought into belonging to and with one another and are helped to realize themselves and one another in realizing this non-dual belonging.[7]

We could perhaps say what is happening in Ereignis as "the dynamic of owning." Enowning is the gathering of each into its own. In *Beiträge*, Ereignis says beyng's enowning call to Da-sein (the enowning throw of beyng) and enowned Da-sein's throwing open this dynamic. In section 133 of *Beiträge* Heidegger writes:

> Beyng needs man in order to hold sway; and man belongs to beyng, so that he can accomplish his utmost destiny as Da-sein. (GA 65:177)

As I wrote in my book *Heidegger's Possibility*, "The thinking that thinks enowning (the enowning throw of being to Da-sein and, thus enowned, Da-sein's throwing open the enowning throw, all of that together making up 'enowning as such,' 'the midpoint that is enowning') manifests the way things are in this dynamic."[8] I would now use the word *beyng* rather than *being*. And I would now stress the no-thing no-form non-dual-one, inseparable dynamic.

Reminder: The dynamic enowning-Ereignis is no-thing whatsoever even as it radiates, is no-thing whatsoever even as it is dynamically at work, is no-thing whatsoever even as we can experience "it."

The non-dual dynamic of Dasein-being is implicitly said in *Sein und Zeit*. But, as Heidegger says there, the grammar and syntax were not available to pursue it. In *Sein und Zeit*, published in 1927? Until *Beiträge*, written between 1936 and 1938?

Even in *Beiträge* he makes clear that these words and this thinking are preparatory. Even if this thinking is preparatory, it is already and still thinking. Does "preparatory" say waiting until beyng grants to us to think-say it? Is that what gets said then in the retrieval of the early Greeks? With a kind of reticence I ask: Is Heidegger trying to say it there, in *Beiträge*?

Let me close this section with a key quotation from Heidegger and a significant "correction" to what *Ereignis* ultimately says for Heidegger:

> *"Ereignis"* – the word that I used earlier
> – is too easily misunderstood,
> as if it only means "happening-event" [*Geschehnis*].
> *"Eignen"* [*Eignis*] – gazingly letting-belong
> in the clearing of the fourfold
> – owning-crossing-over [owning-over-to, *übereignen*]
> – full owning [owning-all-the-way, *vereignen*]. (GA 81:47)

Heidegger died in 1976. This quotation belongs to one of the last things that he wrote. Here he explains how the word *Ereignis* was "too easily misunderstood." Thus here, towards the end of his life, he shapes the question of all questions by focusing on the *eignen* part of the word. This emphasizes belonging-together, the one befitting the other, of things/beings and the no-thing no-form dynamic. This dynamic, this belonging, this dynamic of belonging – one befitting the other – is, as it were, his last way of saying beyng-Ereignis.

What can we take from this "announcement"?

- that this dynamic is non-dual, no-thing, itself formless;
- that it is for sure not the being of metaphysics;
- that it carries the emptiness akin to buddha mind and *dao*;
- that it names the immeasurable in all aspects of its non-dual dynamic;
- that it says-shows the radiant emptiness of beyng;
- that the word *Eignis* says this better than his earlier word *Ereignis* or *Er-eignis*.

I suggest that the quotation just presented – I will call this the *"Eignen"* [*Eignis*] quotation – requires a deep and fundamental reassessment of Heidegger's lifework, reassessing what has been bandied around ever since *Beiträge* was first published in 1989 – including the decision to create a second translation of *Beiträge*, in which the word *Ereignis* is translated as "event." With the "*Eignen*" [*Eignis*] quotation, the door to translating *Ereignis* as "event" is simply closed. It is important that we be true to Heidegger's call and see our work as moving forward rather than backward, into the future that is coming-unto-us.

Shaking Up the Established Views

Part 1 is a series of vignettes that open our view to this project as a whole. It is written in a language that is intended to reach intelligent and fresh minds who do not necessarily have a philosophical training. It is my wish that this book be read and appreciated by – and useful to – the many thoughtful people who seek deeper meaning for their lives.

These vignettes include: personal reflections, a first look at how to understand what the Greeks offered, what refreshing retrieval means, a first look at the kind of language and wording that is called for, issues of translation, the core theme of change, and the dynamic (not static). And an overview of the traditional-inherited way of thinking and the more hidden way of thinking that is less logical, as it says the dynamic of intertwining conditions that touch on the formless non-dual dynamic that I call radiant emptiness.

In this context you will find brief forays into Heidegger on technique, Nietzsche's view of the early Greeks, and William Broad's using the "other" side of Greek thinking about the Oracle of Delphi. Finally, there are isolated examples of "retrieving" what the Greeks experienced, thought, and said (Socrates and logos-mythos-ergo, Nietzsche's reading of Thales, and Heidegger's reading of Aristotle's **Metaphysics, Book Θ**)*. The forays mentioned in this paragraph are glimpses into what will become central in part 3.*

Part 1 invites the reader to move through these pages more like a dance than a field march.

a. A First Look: What Is at Stake

As I will try to show, especially in part 3, early Greek philosophy carries a stimulating experience of the way things are as intuitive (less conceptual), dynamic, fluid, fluent, changing (by no means static), in a kind of deep, non-dual dynamic of interdependent conditions (beyond all dualism) – all of this within a telling dynamic of radiant emptiness (no-thing, open-ended and without boundaries). All of this is above all concrete, that is, an experience.

To a large extent this view of the way things are existed simultaneously in Asian thinking, for example, in Buddhism and Daoism, and in Greek philosophy. The difference is this: Whereas this thread was never lost in Asian thinking and is carried into the present day, in the West and already in the later Greeks, Western philosophy started to move away from this view of the way things are – and eventually, with Christianity, covered over and hid this rich dimension in early Greek thinking. When exactly this happened is hard to locate. But somewhere along the road, after the high point of Greek thinking, the early Greek experience got reduced to something more rigidly logical, to a fixed and rigid system, to a more calculative-analytical thought – to what Heidegger names metaphysics. Over time, this more limited and defined view, for example, the dominance of rationalism and substance metaphysics, has determined the range of Western thinking – less mystery, less cryptic, a kind of sterilizing. This reduction falsifies the richer unfolding of the human mind and experience and hides a lot of what we can experience naturally.

The book you hold in your hands wants to retrieve this fresh way of seeing the way things are, for example, there in early Greek thinking but lost and covered over, in part from the Christian filter, then from rationalism, and finally from mistranslations. We can say that after early Greek thinking thrived in its openness to all possibility, this fresh way was abandoned and never retrieved. The language required for this effort goes beyond the ordinary, traditional language of Greek philosophy.

The question now becomes: Is this project about Greek philosophy as a whole or "just" early Greek philosophy, that is, thinking before Socrates? It is my conviction that this thread runs through all of Greek philosophy, including Socrates, Plato, and Aristotle. From my own experience and conviction, Greek philosophy – from Thales all the way through Aristotle – is far richer and more alive than we know and can ever imagine. There is a thread running throughout Greek thinking that is more about experience, less dualistic, and more non-conceptual, and, above all, that deals with dynamic emptiness. That is, in all things as they are, this thread goes beyond things-substances-form and *is* the no-form, no-thing, and non-dual dynamic of emptiness within which all things manifest themselves. The dramatic interplay of *logos-mythos-ergon* in the Socratic dialogues,[1] Plato's *chora* in the *Timaeus*,[2] and Heidegger's rethinking of *dynamis-energeia-entelecheia* in Aristotle's *Metaphysics, Book Θ*, all exemplify this thread.

Thus, one can say that, whereas the primary focus of this book is on early Greek thinking, often called pre-Socratic, the thrust of the retrieval applies to all of Greek philosophy. For this reason I have decided not to add the word *early* to the title of the book. That said, to do justice to Plato and Aristotle in these matters would require a whole book in itself.

I invite you, the reader, to come along with me and to check it out for yourselves. This is an invitation to open to this possibility, to go along with the thinking, and to check everything out in your own world-experience-thinking. Given our history, it is not always easy to be aware of this dynamic and of how to say-show what is going on.

How, then, to get there? Not just by understanding Greek philosophy with the intellect, but by genuinely awakening to the process itself, in experience and in ourselves. By not reducing Greek philosophy to what we can know rationally or analytically but letting early Greek thinking open up to a dynamic that is itself formless and without boundaries (another name for emptiness). By not limiting ourselves to the traditional translations and interpretations of the Greek thinkers but looking for something fresher.

Above all, we will do this uncovering and retrieving by looking closely at key words from early Greek thinkers (part 3).

What does it mean to refresh, rethink, and retrieve early Greek philosophy? Let me count the ways:

1. Inspired by Heidegger's work, by opening up to the possibility that a "return" to Greek thinking can help us reach into a **domain** that was there in early Greek thinking but has been closed off since the Greeks – for example, with the dominant interpretation of the Greeks via Christianity, with emphasis on the theoretical and the rational, and with the dominance of the empirical and measurable.
2. By taking Greek thinking **in its own right**, at a time when the understanding of the way things are was not yet reduced to a dualistic metaphysics and to super-conceptual constructs of how we see the world and the way things are.
3. By understanding that my **translations of the Greek texts** use words that reveal, say, and show a *truer* rendition of what the early Greeks thought and said. Truer than the one that mirrors (a) Christian philosophy and (b) realism-idealism and (c) an analytical and theoretical understanding. The possibility and viability of this "way" will become clear as we go the way of this writing project.
4. By paying close attention to the part of Greek philosophy that does not just *study* meaning but seeks to *experience* **meaning**. There are several ways to say this: experiential rather than abstract, concretely lived rather than conceptual-theoretical – engaged thinking and lived experience.

    Let me offer two examples of this experiential dimension in Greek philosophy:
    • **Socrates** uses dialogue as a practice of philosophy. For Socrates the dialogue was a way of life. *It was his practice!* The goal was self-knowledge and wisdom. What we learn in the dialogue changes us, we are to put it into practice. When we are doing philosophy, there is a dynamic at work in our mind. The energetic that is at work for Socrates leads to a transformation from ignorance to wisdom and then active engagement in

life. This "action" aspect of *experience* is named ἔργον-*ergon* in Socrates.

Another dimension in Socrates is μῦθος-mythos. For Socrates *mythos* is *not* fairy tale or myth as generally understood, but rather that dimension of life that is non-transparent, the hidden element as such. That is, beyond concepts and logic, honouring the hidden dimension of radiant emptiness.

And of course λόγος-*logos*. For Socrates λόγος is more than just logic or a rational account. It includes both language and dialogue *and* the element of gathering that is there in the Greek word. For Socrates λόγος says speech-gathering-thought. Not so much logic or discourse, but more dialogue in which thoughts are gathered.[3]

In a broad way of speaking, this dramatic interplay of *logos-mythos-ergon* in Socrates strongly implies – says –

- the **non-dual dynamic** – a oneness or a one-ing – that is entwined in the way things are,
- the central role of *ergon* or non-conceptual, concrete lived experience,
- the **ever-changing dynamic** of the way things are, that is, the changing conditions that come together to shape the way things are, which cannot be experienced-grasped logically or conceptually, and
- the role of *mythos* or the **immeasurable** that is itself not anything (no-thing), that is at work in everything, and that we can experience.
- **Heraclitus** – as obscure as his thinking and the stuff of his thinking is – experienced both thinking and the stuff of thinking as inseparable from living. There is the story of how someone walked past his dwelling and saw Heraclitus warming himself by the fire. And Heraclitus is said to have said: Come in, here too the gods are present.

In Fragment B101 Heraclitus says it this way: "I sought out myself." I inquired within. I looked for to find myself. I looked for meaning within myself, that is, how to live my life. Not as subjective ego, but as the flashpoint in which knowing awareness lets be revealed the non-dual at-one dynamic no-thing unfolding: λόγος. (Fragment B50: "If you listen, not to me but [heeding] λόγος, it is wisdom to agree that all is one.") Not by intellectual or conceptual inquiring, but intuitively and in a "lived" way. All together: experience.

In this same vein, Heraclitus says that ψυχή/*psyche* – the flashpoint in us where this lived experience happens in us – cannot be fathomed, so deep is it (Fragment B45). *Psyche* is hard to fathom and the core of living at the same time. And way more than "soul." (The word ψυχή/*psyche* is one of the seven key words in early Greek thinking that I deal with in part 3, where we will address the fact that all of the existing translations of ψυχή miss the boat.)

5. By looking to see how the new, fresh themes – alternative to the traditional-inherited reading – emerge in the more originary sayings of the Greek words and the more originary translations:
   - ongoing dynamic movement rather than static
   - interdependent conditions rather than independent substances
   - the German word *Bedingung* (English: "condition") as the no-form and no-thing dynamic within which things (*Dinge*) emerge. *Be-dingungen,* that is, as conditions for "things"
   - non-dual way of things rather than dualism
   - non-conceptual thinking, beyond the conceptual
   - the no-thing and non-existing dynamic within which things emerge and to which they return – also known as radiant emptiness.

6. By being careful how we hear and use language. The Greek thinkers had a deep love of language and cared for and tended to language. Heidegger: "… the ultimate business of philosophy is to preserve the *power of the elemental words* in which Dasein expresses itself from being bulldozed into unintelligibility through common [vulgar] sense." (GA 2:291).

From a language that is merely defining, denotative, conceptual, dualistic to a language that is poi-etic, a poi-etic saying that shows the indeterminacy of emptiness and its generative power. Poi-etic language that says-shows.

7. By accepting the invitation to follow along as I try to let unfold a particular way of reading, saying, and translating words of early Greek thinking. Coming along and seeing if this way resonates with you and how the words "say" in the fresh retrieval. While retrieving the fuller saying in the Greek words, by allowing language and the word to say more than what is in the books, that is, living with awareness, leading to direct experience – from conceptual intelligence to clear awareness, from knowledge to intuitive wisdom.

    What awakens in you, the reader and hearer? Use this starter for your own inquiry in the non-reducible Greek philosophy. I am writing this book from a deep inner drive, my calling, what is own to me. This belongs to my living fully. I invite you to try it.

8. Finally, it is about a certain excitement. Just do it! Be lit up! A kind of jump-out-of-the-bed-to-meet-the-day momentum. For me, what counts here is the joyful effort in writing this book. May you enjoy the same joyful effort in following up. Good or bad? That does not matter and is not the point. Giving birth is what counts. Perhaps the early Greek thinkers were also enjoying this richness.

b. The Starting: Movement and Change

- *Smell the new grass growing, smell the freshly mown grass.*
- *Savour the first sip of a cold Czech beer.*
- *Marvel at the night sky when the moon is not there and when streetlights do not dim the stars.*
- *Hear the stunning silence of a silent forest.*
- *Gently touch a baby's skin.*
- *Feel that we are alive. Know that the world is alive.*

The seeds for this book were sown many years ago. As I already mentioned, I taught Greek philosophy at the University of

Wisconsin–La Crosse for almost thirty years. Each September I faced a set of twenty-five to forty new faces, most of them eager to experience what they had heard from other students about my course. First, that the teacher was super-passionate about this stuff. Second, that they would have to learn the Greek alphabet, which was exciting for them. Third, that this course would open their eyes to a new, fresh reading of the Greeks. Fourth, that some of their peers had discovered that they would be invited to think along with the teacher – and that their thinking would be taken seriously. Finally, that the invitation to learn stuff in this class was an invitation to learn and to think for the sheer joy of it all. An invitation, as Rilke says, to "change your life."

I spent much of my life as a "professional" philosopher reading and studying and teaching twentieth-century phenomenology, especially Martin Heidegger. Reading and thinking with Heidegger opened my eyes to the fact that many translations are poor translations, in part because they hide much of the power in the original thinking. Translations often hide the true and deeper sense of what the Greeks wanted to say. And in doing this, the translation limits the dynamic movement-change inherent in the original words. If we take the Greek words seriously, in their own right, a fresh and new perspective of the Greeks emerges.

What was most exciting for my students was to be shown that translations are a bit unsteady (in line with the Latin proverb *omnis comparatio claudicat*: Every comparison limps) and that they themselves could learn to see this and could experience the sheer joy of those new openings into what the Greek words say.

This joyful work of teaching Greek philosophy changed my life, and it often changed the students' lives. Over the years several students have told me how this course transformed their way of seeing the world. That their own engagement in thinking transformed their own lives. They learned to see how movement and change are at the centre of our lives *and* experienced the change in their own lives in the process.

So let us start with change.

My reading of Heidegger in the original German – as well as studying and practising Buddhism – led me to the awareness-insight that everything in our known world is always changing. There is nothing standing still at the beginning and nothing stand-ing still at the end. In a radical sense there *is* no beginning and no end. What belongs intrinsically to things, to the way things are in their core aspect, is change, process, unfolding. Everything in the world changes, is always changing. (Change, impermanence, is key to any Buddhist practice.)

Sitting on a tree stump in the woods outside my former home in western Wisconsin – or in one of the many beautiful green spaces in Prague, where I lived for two years, or in Vienna, where I now live – I can almost *see* changing as it happens. In the spring the fat buds seem ready to explode into flowers or leaves – and sometimes do explode! Sometimes in the fall, immediately after the right kind of frost, the many coloured leaves drop so fast that you imagine their blocking your view beyond them. Snow and water and ice and steam and clouds, ever changing.

Parmenides is usually seen as the philosopher *par excellence* of static being, the world as unchanging "reality." We usually see Par-menides as the philosophy of "being" and Heraclitus as the phi-losopher of "becoming." In part 3 we will focus on the key words in Parmenides that say-show change and movement. He is *also* and above all a philosopher of change!

Aristotle belongs here as well. Much of how we read Aristotle – especially when we see the traditional-inherited ways of trans-lating *dynamis-energeia-entelecheia* in Aristotle's *Metaphysics, Book* Θ – says static potential and static result. First is *dynamis* (static potential), then is movement-*kinesis* that "changes potential into actuality" or static result or completed thing.

Guided by Heidegger's rethinking of these words, we come to a very different insight, namely, the sturdy thread of dynamic, expe-riential, non-dual concrete movement and change, *throughout*!

There is much in Aristotle about the way things are whereby philosophers can readily "reduce" things to independent, static substances – understood conceptually and abstractly. For sure, this more logical and abstract thread is there in Aristotle. But the thread of dynamic, experiential, non-dual concrete movement and change is there as well. The way things are is always at-work: ἐνέργεια, ἐν+ἔργον (*energeia, en-ergon*) and never a static "before" or "after" *any* movement.

Finally, for Aristotle ethics is a practice learned in experience (practical wisdom in what we today call his "virtue ethics") and is carried out amid changing conditions. What he calls moderation or "the mean between two extremes" can also be called "deciding what to do depending on the various intertwining conditions."

I do not argue that the traditional interpretation and translation is not there in Aristotle. But this "retrieved Aristotle" is *also* there, and strongly so. (I will go into more detail later, in section f.)

The traditional interpretation of Greek philosophy – which sees primarily static and independent substances, infinite-unchangeable principle, a highest being – limits what the Greeks were saying, thus limiting the possibilities of thinking and then living in an expanding world of movement-change. And, whereas the seeds for this traditional interpretation are there in Greek philosophy, the Greeks also thought and said in another, fresher way. This fresher way is what we are focusing on in this project.

This little section was motivated by students who called or sent me letters, to confirm that after taking my course in Greek philosophy, they had incorporated a deep sense of movement and change at the centre of their lives.

In this context I ask: If you really think about it, what is the highest calling for a teacher? It is not to provide answers and solutions that the students can simply drop into their backpacks and "take home," without doing any thinking and without being critical, instead just taking someone else's word for it. The teacher has the golden opportunity – indeed, the obligation – to stimulate and provoke students' own thinking. The task of the teacher, says Heidegger, is to "let learn." What better contribution can a person make to the world than showing and enacting and guiding as much excellence as possible, showing and practising respect – for self, for others, and for texts – and showing and bringing happiness to the world? To have the chance do this as a teacher of young minds is a gift beyond compare.

I write this book with the hope that it excites you, provokes you, and brings you to engage in thinking. There is no greater joy in teaching.

c. The Two Ways of Thinking

The one way – that we know so well – has been dominant in Western thinking and doing for several centuries. It is now time to experience the other way, which in some sense is "fresh." *Both* are central to who we are.

Looking out the window of the train, admiring and relishing the Czech and then the German countryside, I am reading *If You Want to Write* by Brenda Ueland, first published in 1938.[4] Reading a line in the book, I get inspired to work on this book. There she writes: "everybody is talented, original and has something important to say."

I have something important to share about – but more essentially *from* – Greek philosophy. For a long time now the translators' and many of culture's filters have hidden – may I say suppressed? – the richness in the original Greek texts.

As I already said, in my classes at the University of Wisconsin and a couple of other universities, I took these Greek words back to their origins, trying to retrieve their originary meaning. In this book I want to share this process. I want to look at some of the key words in Greek philosophy and release them, to roll them like marbles in the palm of my hand, to feel the words. I invite you along on this ride and ask simply that you check these things out. Think: Fresh!

In part 3 I will look at ten key Greek words in greater detail. Here I want to whet your appetite. Put a few of these Greek words into play, play with them. For instance, *logos* means-says many things – and not just "logic." *Mythos* means-says "the non-transparent-withdrawing-hiding" while things reveal themselves – and not fairy tales or phantasies or "myths." *Empeiria* means-says experience (I emphasize: not the empirical of empirical science), and *energeia* means "being-at-work" – in *ergon* – and dare not be translated simply as "actuality" that is complete and taken as a static "end result." These English words have their origins in Greek philosophy, but the traditional translations betray those origins. In a sense, we no longer hear what the Greeks truly said.

I do not mean true, as in true or false. I mean true to the way things are, mind's heeding the phenomena and language's saying what they "truly" are – and not laying some definition or concept on the way things are, thereby reducing their power to say what is true beyond or "more than" definition. Definitions are useful, but in the big questions of life and the universe definitions limit rather than open up. We are after how the Greeks "truly" said.

The challenge is to go beyond definitions, to let the Greek words say the "so much more" than what we normally know about them, something definitions cannot do. This challenge will come up again and again. Take the central and key issues of life and death: love, grief, sadness, friendship, ecstasy. We can – and even must – have definitions for such words. But no definition can encompass all that happens in love, in grief, in friendship.

Death. In a small hospital in Norfolk, Nebraska, my father is lying in a coma. He will be in this coma for two weeks, before dying on 3 July 1984. My mother and all ten of his children, plus in-laws, are there – standing watch. How do you describe that experience? How can you "define" what is happening during this time? And try to "define" your own experience of mortality: that you will also die?

Why is this fresh look important? In part because the world is in trouble. Yes, the trouble of black and white thinking that abounds today. Yes, the danger that the science that is empirical and rationalistic is often taken for the only truth. Yes, the trouble of environmental degradation and the danger to the planet that lies therein. Yes, overpopulation. Yes, the trouble of power-seeking partisan politics. But there is another, underlying trouble: the trouble our civilization is in because it sees the world or "the way things are" as a bunch of static and independent entities – monads, in the literal sense. (When I use the marker "the way things are," I intend it as a constant reminder that "the way things are" is not determined or totally known by reason and intellect and is for sure not the same thing as "reality." There is no "reality" as such.)

You may ask: What is wrong with this dominant view of the world? Our civilization has made many advancements precisely by isolating entities and cells. There is nothing wrong with this view of the world. It is useful and it works. The question is: Can life be *reduced to* what is available in this world view? For me the answer is No. On a deeper level, the fullness of our lives and existence is much more than a collection of isolated, reducible, and predictable events or things. We live in a world pregnant with possibility, change, novelty and complex webs of meaning, webs that cannot be reduced to or captured by isolationist ways of thinking. Rereading rehearing rethinking and resaying – retrieving what Greek thinking says – can help us know and experience this opening.

Heidegger has helped us think how these two ways of thinking can be thought. He names them the calculating way of thinking and the meditative-minding way of thinking. Here I share with the reader what I wrote in my book *Five Groundbreaking Moments in Heidegger's Thinking*:

Gelassenheit or the Memorial Address

In October 1955 Heidegger gave a Memorial Address in his home city of Meßkirch, Germany, titled *Gelassenheit** (GA 16). In that address he speaks of the domination of calculating thinking (*das rechnende Denken*) and what is today almost absent, namely the counter-dynamic: mindful or minding thinking (*das besinnliche*

---

* Numbers in parentheses in this section refer to this German text.

Nachdenken and then *das besinnliche Denken*). This mindful or mind-ing thinking hints at the thinking that belongs to this "other" way of thinking and saying. Here Heidegger uses a language that hints at and "starts" this enriching opening for thinking.

We today – as in 1955 – are confronted with the domination of calculating thinking in the extreme form that it takes in the techni-cal world that dominates today. Note that this is not about technol-ogy, but about the mindset of technicity.[5] Calculating thinking is trapped in the "jaws of planning and computation, of organization and automatic operations" (522). And "the world now appears as an object that calculating thinking attacks, which nothing should be able to resist any longer" (523).

Calculating thinking is planning, investigating, researching, set-ting up of a business or industry. Calculating thinking rushes from one opportunity to the next. It never relaxes, never comes to mindfulness.

In the form of modern technicity, calculating thinking has a hidden power to determine how humans are connected to the way things are (to what is). This form of calculating thinking controls-rules-commands the whole planet. It subdues, controls, and steers. Its pow-ers bind-chain-trammel, transmigrate-press-forth, and beset-besiege.[6]

But there is another way to think:

> *Minding thinking.* When we come to know what is own to us as humans, namely that we are thinking beings, we become minding beings. We are oriented to think. Minding thinking is careful, pondering, contemplat-ing thinking [*nachdenken*] of the sense of things, which is at work in everything that is. (520)

> This minding thinking [*das besinnliche Denken*] requires a greater effort … a longer preparation … a more subtle care-diligence … And it must also be able to wait, just as the farmer [has to wait] to see whether the seed sprouts and grows to maturity [becomes ripe]. (520)

Minding thinking or careful minding dwells with what is near. It asks: What way of being lies behind technicity? What belongs in a deep way to what is, to the way things are? It "demands from us that we do not remain one-sidedly stuck in an idea-conception and that we do not keep rushing on a single track in a conceptual direction" (526). It asks: Is there something else besides calculating thinking and the mindset of technicity that is own to humans? Can minding thinking open out onto "thing" as phenomenon inseparable from the no-thing, non-dual dynamic of radiant emptiness? And then: What is this dynamic emptiness? And how does it look and how do we learn to think-say it?

We can allow ourselves to be slaves to the dominant way of thinking that is rationalism or technicity. Or we can do something else. Heidegger:

> We can use technical objects as they were meant to be used. But we can at the same time let these [technical] objects just be and not intrude on us in our inner and ownmost being. We can say "yes" to the unavoidable usage of technical objects, and at the same time we can say "no," insofar as we keep them from claiming us totally and thus bending out of shape, confusing-unhinging, and finally demolishing what is ownmost to us. (527)

Heidegger calls for two ways: One, releasement to the things (*die Gelassenheit zu den Dingen*). This lets us see things as more than technical. Not denouncing or wanting to destroy what is technical in things, but to see the "more than," to experience things in the richness of things in their flourishing, as what is own to things – as phenomena inseparable from something that is vaster, while hidden. Heidegger will name this: beyng as enowning. I name it also as radiant emptiness.

Two, openness for the mystery (*die Offenheit für das Geheimnis*). When we become aware that in the technical world (the world of technicity) there still dwells a hidden sense, this lets both of these strategies show how, what comes forth to us, in things, is intimately connected to the hidden. What shows itself, emerges ... and simultaneously withdraws.

About these two ways:

> Releasement to the things and openness to the mystery belong together. They preserve for us the possibility to stay in the world in a totally other

> way. They promise us a new ground and soil on which we can stand
> within the world of technicity and, unthreatened by it, can endure. (528)

Gathering the saying within these words, we see some of the aspects that go beyond our understanding of the chronological "beginning" with the Greeks – as we have come to understand them – to another, fresh beginning, aka the "starting," as what gets things started for our thinking. This way is not conceptual-intellectual, dualistic, or static. And we have, naturally, a first inkling of how the non-dual, inseparable phenomenon gets thought in Heidegger: Nothing is thrown out or removed. The question becomes: How can we think the "starting" of another beginning, as it introduces another, transforming way of thinking – from within our traditional, inherited paradigm, to which technicity belongs – to a new opening as thinking opens our seeing and hearing to things beyond their being technical objects?

This address is an example of how Heidegger explores the whole of thinking, always pushing thinking and language to the edges of what is possible and bringing thinking around to the widest and deepest dynamic of what is own to humans, own to things, and own to radiant emptiness or beyng – inseparably. And there is still some way to go. I propose that looking at and thinking through the non-dual thinking of inseparable phenomena and non-conceptual language offers enriching possibilities in our quest.

This opening to meditative-minding thinking, to releasement to the things, and to the openness of mystery will accompany us as a guidepost all the way through this writing project.

From here to the Greeks. As we look through the openings into what the Greek words say originarily, we ask: Why is this fresh look at Greek philosophy important? First, it opens the door to a more honest and richer reading of Greek texts. Second, it is more true to what the Greeks said. Third, it opens up how the origins of Western philosophy see the world differently from our "received" paradigm ... and invites us to greater awareness and even greater joy!

Heidegger above all showed us the way here. And this is my invitation to the reader – my challenge, my provocation – not that you believe me, but that you take the time and energy to think along with me on this path, to check everything out in your own experience and with your own critical mind. Using a fresh look at the Greek words themselves for clues.

Today, we often turn to Asian religious, cultural. and philosophical traditions – such as Buddhism, Daoism and Hinduism – to discover how things are interdependent and always dynamically in motion, changing, with a respect for the hidden and the mystery and the way of releasement. And we are inspired by the openings in quantum physics, as well as in the world view, comportment, and teachings of the indigenous peoples in North America.

In all of this we see a turn away from the "traditional" rationalistic and logical way of thinking and away from seeing the way things are as merely static, independent, and conceptualizable. This turn away can be seen in many popular books and movies, for example, the Force in *Star Wars* and the magical world that is alive in *Lord of the Rings* and *Harry Potter and the Philosopher's Stone*. Surely this turn mirrors and responds to a longing within us that is deeply human. To what is that longing attracted?

What I want to share with you, for your own honest appraisal, is that the seeds for what attracts us to Asian thinking and to the challenge to thinking that comes from quantum physics and Indigenous ways of being – and to these stories-movies – are generative in Greek thinking.

The story I will tell in this book is about another way of thinking-reading Greek philosophy, one that is carried along with but hidden within the traditional reading of Greek philosophy, that is, seeing "the way things are" as independent and static substances. We need to refresh our thinking, to see how "the way things are" is an ongoing interdependent co-emerging of a set of conditions (*Be-ding-ungen*) and how our awareness – also called "mind" – is intertwined with that.

Following Heidegger's lead and inspired by this possibility, **I find this refreshment of thinking solidly present in Greek**

philosophy. I want to share my insights with you. I will do this by working and playing with the key Greek words themselves. As they come to us today in the original Greek texts (part 3).

d. Entering the Way

In Latin class many years ago, my teacher gave us a Latin saying at the beginning of every class, which we had to learn by heart. One day the saying went: *Repetitio est mater studiorum*. Repetition is the mother of studies. The saying is a bit boring, until I look up the word *studium* in the thesaurus. One of many words listed as a translation of the Latin *studium* is: *pondering*. Borrowing that word, the saying now goes: Repetition is the mother of ponderings. Or: Repetition is the mother of learnings.

As you may have noticed, I repeat myself. This is deliberate. Repetition is a cousin to "tautology." I do not shy away from repetition or tautology. I welcome it. For in repeating, we learn to ponder. This is an invitation to think creatively, while sustained and grounded by Greek words and their original saying.

This book is a series of invitations.

First, it invites you, the reader, to check out the observation that in our epoch we have limited how we see the world, such that we don't see the all of it any more. And we think that our limited and limiting constructs are all that there is and are "real." The dominant paradigm today is both that things are seen as independent and static substances and that concepts are taken to be somehow separate from the world and themselves static as well. This mode of thinking is reductionist, dualistic, mechanistic, calculative, rationalistic. By eliminating or pushing away a more inclusive, rounder, richer way of seeing the world, we have weakened our understanding and position in the world. It is imbalanced.

Second, it invites you, the reader, to imagine and then to enact what has been pushed to the side, for example, the way of seeing a world that is less abstract and less logical, that is non-dual, interdependent, and dynamic – more experiential, more in tune with subtleties of life and the world. Opening out to the intuitive, experiential way that goes *beyond* calculative thinking to a minding thinking that balances things out. Redressing a balance. Rejoining the hidden powers of the mind, which have power precisely in their hiddenness.

This is not a call to eliminate the way of thinking we have inherited, but rather a call to balance. Balancing it out with an "other" – often hidden and unknown to us – way of seeing, experiencing, thinking, saying the way things are. Returning, rejoicing, retrieving. And perhaps more essential?

Third, it invites you, the reader, to see how this "return" is not into irrationality or into some form of voodoo mysticism. Rather, the hidden powers of the mind – to open out to the hidden dynamic – belong precisely to what is most natural to us. We are naturally not just rational-logical beings. We are naturally not just thinkers of the black-and-white, without subtlety or refinement in our thinking and in the world we want to understand. This return or enrichment or rounding-out is not about being lost in the clouds or something "mystical" – which would then "by definition" be something that is opposed to the rational – but rather includes the rational and calculative within its dynamic, in non-dual fashion.

It is a full-fledged balance. It is an unfolding dynamic of what we one day want to know non-dually. It will enrich our lives. It will be "more" natural than the reductionist way of seeing things, which excludes an essential part of mind and of the world.

Finally, this book invites you to turn to the Greek philosophers –

- most prominently, the early Greek thinkers before Socrates, where the richness of retrieval is most pronounced, but also
- in an extremely abbreviated way, the major Greek thinkers Socrates-Plato-Aristotle – where this retrieval yields rich openings.

In both cases we take a new look at the words used by these Greek thinkers. We come to know how much richer their original words were – and are – than the mediocre translations that have come down to us. In their original richness, so many of the Greek words tell of the intuitive along with the rational, of change and the no-thing dynamic that is involved in everything, of how things exist for what they are as conditions within dynamic change and how the hidden dimensions of the mind and of the changing world are "natural."

One way to catch a glimpse of this "natural" intuitive awareness, which shows-mirrors this no-thing dynamic of radiant emptiness that is involved in everything, is to focus on experiences that show this while also showing the limits of rational definition. There are a number of human experiences that can help us see (a) how we have learned to limit our understanding of them by defining too much and (b) what possibilities there are for a refreshing knowing that comes from these experiences.

These experiences include love, grief, ecstasy, friendship – and even boredom. We can start with what we can know and say explicitly about these experiences, but we necessarily reach a point where we "do not know." The Greeks honoured this space, honoured the balance that happens when human thinking lets this space in on an equal basis – honoured the power and truth of the heart.

And we learn this by heeding the words in their originary meanings and in their nuances.

Let us look at how two of these experiences – love and friendship – (a) do indeed offer something we can latch onto in order to "define" or analyse what they are, but (b) are undefinable in what is "true" to them. First, friendship. Friendship is about … honesty, loyalty, generosity … But can you ever fully define friendship, however long our list of adjectives is? At the edge of what we can define – where the hidden dimensions start to show themselves – is where the naturally occurring rebalancing takes place, when we allow the hidden powers of the mind, as well as the hidden aspects of what is ultimately not totally knowable, to flourish.

Second, love. We have learned to define love. We have learned to make lists of what all belongs to love. We have even learned how to define several kinds of love:

- *philia* or the love of friends. This is sometimes referred to as "mental" love, because it seemingly has nothing to do with the body.

But that is too limiting. *Philia* is the love of comrades, the love that belongs to familiarity and loyalty. As in Phila-delphia: City of Brotherly Love.

- *agape* or the deep love of holding dear, sometimes thought of as "unconditional love." Sometimes in the New Testament this is called "charity," including the element of self-sacrifice that belongs to Christian charity. It is perhaps the most giving of self of all the forms of love.
- *eros* or the love that is about attraction, about being drawn with one's whole being to something or someone noble and elevated. The real meaning of *eros* in Greek philosophy may indeed involve the kind of attraction that we today mean when we talk of sex and passion and erotic connection: lust. But this kind of "eros" is too limiting to say everything that the Greek word says. It is passionate primarily in the sense of one's "passion for music" or "passion for running." Even as physical attraction belongs to *eros* in this sense, *eros* points to and shows much more. By itself, physical attraction barely taps into the rich meanings of the Greek word.

  When I check around in my various dictionaries (you can do this yourself) I get: Eros is romantic love and desire, sensual love. But in its deeper meaning it is about attraction, the forces of attraction, being drawn to the noble and elevated in a noble and deep way. It is about bonds and bonding. And somewhere Socrates talks of the erotic attraction to the Good.

How do we gain access to these deeper meanings – at least to the problem of translations that have "reduced" the meaning of the original Greek word?

I hope that you find this journey as exciting as I do. And I hope that it will transform you too!

Mine is perhaps an ambitious project, that is, to show how the truth has been hidden from our eyes. To show that we have come to see the world in this reductionist, inert, dualistic way, but there is a way out. The exciting thing is that this way out is already there with the "ancient" Greeks. Come think along with me and I will show you how they can help us come to see this alternative path to a richer and more fulfilling life of the mind.

Do not believe me. Check it out for yourself.

e. Beacons to Guide Us

Exploring. We often study Greek philosophy for the answers it provided and may still provide us. Greek philosophy is certainly not void of answers, sometimes even straightforward ones. But it is also about questioning the way things are and about how thinking happens, **especially in early Greek philosophy**. Sometimes those issues are addressed explicitly, sometimes implicitly. Greek philosophy is not a set of simple answers. For sure its answers are often less definitive than what we may want today. Rather than answers, early Greek philosophy is a network of generative questions – questions that inspire concern and call for the engagement of an open mind, thinking that points to the intuitive beyond conceptual thinking.

One often reads statements like "the Greeks tried to find the fundamentals of nature or reality, and they found 'them' in the four physical elements of earth, air, fire, and water." Thales was for water, and Heraclitus was for fire, and so on. I argue that there is no evidence in the original texts that this was their search or their expectation. For one thing, there is no evidence that, when Thales said "All is water," he meant only the physicality of water.

Rather, they were exploring. They took joy in the mind's activity, which led to a sense of dignity as humans. Rather than looking for – or "finding" – answers or solutions, they took delight in the very exploration. Making sense of what comes our way, what appears in front of us, does not necessarily mean finding a definition or a definitive answer. We make sense of a lot of things by coming to know them better, by increasing our awareness and by applying our critical thinking skills, lest we get lost in our own confusions and disturbances. What is called for is an experience-based critical thinking.

Stephen Hawking said somewhere: Make sense of what you see ... and wonder about what makes the universe exist. Be curious. He did not say: Find the final answer, so that you can pack up and go home and watch television.

Life shows the power of change and unfolding rather than the neatness of static unity or concepts. Greek philosophy never intended to describe the way things "are" ... and then to stop – as if thinking and beings could ever be reduced to a "finished" product or thought. That would be a dead tradition, implying a certainty that would then have to be defended ... or merely reinterpreted. Mine is a call for us to rethink the dominance in the world around us of *that* science and rationalism that seeks certainty, with its strongly held conviction that this kind of science has "the answers" to everything.

Rather, all thinking is finite and embodied in the flesh, thus a "living tradition," if you will. Thinking is alive, and all that is alive changes. Rather than a stifling tradition, Greek philosophy is a vigorous opening into how the big questions touch us. This philosophy does not reach for a "final" result; rather, it is a quest, an exploration. Philosophy as done by the Greeks is not a theory or a set of theories; it is a *practice*.

We engage one another in thinking, moving away from security and certainty and towards openings and revelations. We strive for the ongoingness of genuine thinking.

In his book *The Great Work of Your Life*, Stephen Cope writes:

> But for now, here's an experiment. Stop reading for a minute, and ask yourself these questions: Am I living fully right now? Am I bringing forth everything I can bring forth? Am I digging down into that ineffable inner treasure-house that I know is in there? That trove of genius? Am I living my life's calling? Am I willing to go to any lengths to offer my genius to the world?[7]

It is in this spirit that I found myself compelled to write this book.

A new beginning. I am moved to be part of a new beginning at a time when the world poses real dangers to our ability to think – there is so much to consume, and such a dramatic shift to computer images, verbal and non-verbal. Consumerism and the love of the internet can override and hide our natural capacities for understanding, can diminish our awareness – our capacity to think. And now with AI on the brink of bursting through and upsetting or outdoing everything ... the kind of thinking called for here is so important. My question is: Can AI ever get to the non-dual dynamic of radiant emptiness, to that which is no-thing but is at work, to that "gaze" of mind that belongs to this "other" – new in the West, old in the East? I have my doubts.

At the same time there are so many fresh possibilities. How can we hold on as the bullet train of consciousness speeds up, as the mind's eye, pinballing through quick journeys, threatens to turn us into passive beings – so much to take in, so fast ... a cutting off from the natural world – not being able to slow down?

I want to celebrate the vastness of the natural, to see rich possibilities in our world of experience and in how we think. Doing so calls for a renewal, a refreshing way of experiencing life, thinking, and the way we and all things are. We are not abandoning old patterns but opening ourselves to new experiences, which can/will retrieve "old" experiences. If we unfetter our reading of the Greeks from mistranslations, misinterpretations, and rote regurgitation, we find that they hold a key to being open to this new experience.

What I present here in this book is a rereading and rehearing of the texts of early Greek thinking, an opening to the refreshing possibilities of this retrieval. This revisioning offers a path from a world cast in stone – "the real world" – to the undefined and undefinable, boundless space of being.

To what might this way of thinking and reading lead? It might shed light beyond our current system, helping us to see the light. But more than that, it is our heritage. It is natural to us. We do it because it is who we are as humans who work, have families, dance, sing, write poetry, and think. This kind of joy is our birthright. Let us reclaim it.

The big questions. Attracted to the joyful work of philosophy, we are excited by the questions of core thinking. Even academics who flatten Greek philosophy, either through common and accepted but misguided wisdom about the texts or by producing mistranslations – even they agree that Greek philosophers dealt creatively with a few core questions:

- **the way things are**
  (metaphysics and ontology ... the nature of reality ... the origin of things ... the stuff of the universe),
- **how we are to live**
  (ethics ... striving for excellence ... developing the mind ... reaching for the highest human potential), and
- **the nature and scope of knowledge**
  (epistemology ... the question of true or certain knowledge ... how we know what we know).

I wanted my students to enjoy Greek philosophy. I wanted it to spark their natural gift for seeing beyond theories and concepts, for grappling with big questions as if they and not Thales or Anaximander were asking them. I wanted them to have the feeling that this reading and engaged thinking mirrored who they are. I wanted them to feel the joy and magic in being aware like this.

I remember well those moments in the classroom when, after heartily engaging in the questions and in the language of the Greeks, now and again one or another of the students showed full awe on their faces. Their astonishment was palpable, and so was their joy. These moments made teaching ecstatic.

For this, the freshness of Heidegger's thinking was my inspiration and guide.

Philosophy as engagement, enactment. Thinking is more than a form of mental gymnastics. Thinking is more than an intellectual game we put back on the shelf when we "return to" "actual living." We must retrieve Greek words and sayings and thinking for their possibilities – possibilities that engage us and demand action, from word to deed. One without the other might be good scholarship, but that's not good philosophy. It is not good thinking. It is not good living.

Engagement with Greek philosophy in its fullness is a necessary and useful component of the refreshing revisioning that is called for. Thinking without wisdom is short-sighted. Theory and abstraction without engagement is empty.

The Greeks. Who were the Greeks? And what did they put on the table, to experience, think, and say? Thales, Anaximander, Xenophanes, Heraclitus, Parmenides, Pythagoras, Anaxagoras, Empedocles, Democritus?[8]

What made the early Greeks the first *thinkers*? What happened in that "golden age" in Greece? Nietzsche's creative language in *Philosophy in the Tragic Age of the Greeks* offers some insights:

> The Greeks knew how to begin at the proper time ... to begin in bliss [*Glück*], in mature vigour, from within a passionate exhilaration of courageous and victorious maturity ... An uncompromising imperative holds sway between their thinking and their character. They are devoid of conventionality, for in their day there was no philosophical or academic professionalism. All of them stand magnificently alone as the only ones of their time whose lives were devoted *to insight alone* [italics mine]. They all possessed the wholesome energy of the ancients, in which they excelled all who came after in finding their own style and in developing this, through a complete transformation, to the finest and greatest detail ... continuing the high conversation in the mind [*das hohe Geistesgespräch*].
>
> Thus all of them [the early Greek thinkers] form ... the republic of creative minds ... There is a steely necessity that binds a philosopher to a genuine culture ... in a healthy and genuine culture ... they had life in lavish abundance before their eyes.[9]

- *Beginning in* **bliss, beyond any convention,** *the early Greek thinkers did their thing: dwelling in* **insight alone, standing magnificently alone,** *experiencing* **complete transformation, being creative minds,** *living a life with a* **lavish abundance of mind activity.**
- *This led to a* **courageous and non-compromising imperative,** *a passionate exhilaration,* **within the wholesome energy of the ancients.**

Part of my endeavour in this writing is to show how, after and despite centuries of misunderstanding, early Greek thinking remains fundamental to our lives today. How it opens up new possibilities for thinking and for living. I want to share with you, the reader, how it is possible for us to retrieve this possibility, from within Greek words and thinking. We do not need to turn to other cultures and narratives to find this. There is nothing wrong with turning to Asian thinking – to Buddhism, Daoism, Hinduism, Jainism – to find enriching possibilities. It can be very helpful. And they have some wisdom and strategies for developing the mind that even the Greeks did not have – witness Tibetan Buddhism. But here I want to share the joy of finding this other possibility within our own Western modes, from the very beginning of Western philosophy to what quantum physics shows, to what this move fore-shows.

The constructs and interpretive translations that we inherit and bring to the study of Greek philosophers can render us constitutionally unable to understand them fully. Our received understanding colours our apprehension of what the Greeks are really saying. Our received dualities of body-mind, matter-spirit, and body-soul – even humans-divinities – are barriers to a full, nuanced appreciation of Greek thinking. Contemporary physics has put the lie to our construct of a universe ordered with independent, static particles. Recently, when scientists discovered the Higgs boson particle, some astute ones commented that it was not a "particle" in any usual sense, but more a "field," an "influence," or a "dynamic."[10] The filters through which we think have not caught up with this new awareness, an awareness anticipated millennia ago by the Greeks.

While it is intuitively obvious that what is empirically measurable is not necessarily "more real" than that which is not so readily available – think of death, loss, and grief, and of the meanderings of love, both emotional and spiritual – our modern bias towards the quantifiable or the categorical is quite entrenched. Instead of laying this "later" template onto the "earlier" Greek thinking and language, we need to retrieve the *originary* Greek thinking as it shows in and of itself, with its own bearing on the way things are. We open the doors to what is possible.

As you will see in this book, poor translations that are read through the lens of modern biases have led to understandings of the Greek thinkers that bear little resemblance to the nuanced discoveries that the Greeks made about the big questions of metaphysics, ontology, ethics, and epistemology. Simply put: Poor translations close doors rather than open them.

We dare not "read back" into the Greek texts that which later misinterpretations have preprogrammed our eyes to see and our ears to hear.

Note: I do not offer these meanderings as "scientific proof." Rather I invite you the reader to read, hear, think along with – and make your own assessment. Be open to what I try to show, check it out both in thought and in experience, and then decide! In the end it is up to you!

The question of translation. The motivation to do the hard work of re-visioning Greek philosophy can be found only in a solid understanding of how far our received constructs about the Greeks have strayed from the actual texts. Some of that distance from the Greek texts can be attributed to intentional deception by particular scholars pursuing their own agendas: rationalists' hijacking of the word *logos*, for instance. Some of that distance comes from ignorance. Some of it stems from the filter of Christianity and the "Age of Reason." In any case, those "sins" against Greek thinking are many, but most of them can be readily identified and debunked. More insidious are the layers upon layers of translation – from the original Greek to Latin and then to English – that have corrupted our understanding of Greek thought. Yes, modern scholarship has returned to the original Greek texts, but too often the new translations confirm contemporary bias and support received constructs, rather than carefully attempting to understand what the original thinker was saying. (In part 3 we will dig into this matter with exuberance.)

We have all seen humour based on mistranslation. Take Steinbeck's most famous novel, *The Grapes of Wrath*. Translate it into another language, for example, French: *Raisins de la colère*. Translate that translation back to English, and the tale of the Joads becomes *Angry Raisins*! There's wisdom in such humour, wisdom that can be applied to the Greeks: we must take great care with what the Greek words say for which we have no English equivalent.

It is useful, sometimes, to leave the word in Greek.

One of the most important words that we need to look at is *logos* (λόγος). In Latin, it means *ratio*; in French, *raison*; in English, "reason" or "logic." Each of those translations is an approximation, and each of those approximations brings with it ideas that are not adequate to the Greek λόγος, since it leaves important subtleties – that are indeed part of λόγος – covered over.

So do not be surprised that in this focus on the Greeks I spend a lot of time with *logos*. Rather, λόγος, for *that* form of the word is open to more possibility.

How should we hear λόγος in the English language? The semantic frameworks we have been handed would suggest the following meanings:

- reason or logic
- speech-speaking
- gathering or speech-gathering-thought
- intellectual account
- plea or opinion
- reasoned discourse or argument.

I contend that we should hear the word λόγος "also" as logic or rational. But in no way is this sufficient for the word. I suggest that we open ourselves to hearing λόγος as "gathering" ... or "gathering thought" ... or "thoughtful gathering" ... or, perhaps, or "speech-gathering thought." (Much more on λόγος in part 3.)

This is the kind of gathering, of enfolding and unfolding, at the heart of λόγος. There are many other words that require a similar approach. We will deal with those as they come along.

Translation does exist and we will not get rid of it, even if we wanted to. Nor should we. Translation is necessary to the human mind. But a perfect translation is impossible, and thus translation is at most viable.

Translation is a kind of pledge, a promise. The translator ponders the words in both languages, trying to find the word that fits best. Very often this word is not the word that appears in the lexicon of either language or in the typical two-language dictionary. And when the translator has found the word that says what the original text "wants to say," she or he takes a kind of pledge: that the chosen translation is a viable way to say what is being said in the original text. The dictionary cannot be the arbiter of this pledge. Rather the measure must be the matter itself and the saying of the said – or the said in the saying.

Translations, then, retain an honest questionableness. Since there can never be an "objective," one-to-one translation, or an "absolutely accurate" translation, there is room for thoughtful dialogue. No one can claim that his or her translation is the "only one possible," but hopefully one's best effort to be both *true* to the original text – taking into account the possibly inexpressible nuance of the original – and *free from* the inevitable errors brought by a too-easy association in the new language with its existing and worn-out words.

It is a difficult task: to work past our biases and then apprehend the possibility in what the Greek might have been trying to say. A gap necessarily exists between the original and the translation, a gap containing space for the inexpressible in the original text.

It is our joyful work here to explore that gap.

f. First Glimpses

In this section I present a brief look or glimpse at five places in Greek philosophy, in order to show how the traditional-inherited (TI) translations are not completely accurate. These glimpses are offered to help us "cut our teeth" on this whole project of retrieving Greek thinking. Check these out, to see if they activate your critical acumen in comprehending how the usual translations camouflage what the Greeks thought and said. These places are:

1. What does Thales want to say with his statement "All is water"?
2. What does the Greek word ψυχή-*psyche* want to say in Greek thinking, all the way from Heraclitus to Aristotle?
3. How are we to understand Aristotle's four "causes"?
4. What is Aristotle saying about the way things are with the words *dynamis* and *energeia* and *kinesis*, the movement from "potential" to "actual"?
5. How does Heidegger gather up the issue in his "retrieval" of what these three words say-show in Aristotle?

Thales on water. Taking Nietzsche as our guide, we see how Thales did *not* ask the metaphysical question about the one thing that makes up the universe or the way things are and then answer it with: Water. Rather, Thales was exploring a new way to see the world. Water is an image for flowing, changing (water, ice, steam, clouds … all about movement and change).

Let us hear Nietzsche from *Philosophy in the Tragic Age of the Greeks*:[11]*

> Greek philosophy seems to begin with an absurd notion, with the prop-osition that water is the origin and womb of all things … Had he said "water turns into earth," we should have but a scientific hypothesis, a wrong one but difficult to disprove. But he went beyond the scientific … Thales did not overcome the low level of empirical insight prevalent in his time. What he did was to pass beyond its horizon … What drove him … was … to see [just how] "all things are one." (38–9)

Not the one thing that is the basis of the universe. Not an abstract notion. Not looking for a fundament on which to build a theory of everything. Not "the thinking that calculates and measures" but a thinking that is "propelled by … the power of creative imagination" (40).

---

* Unless otherwise noted, all numbers in parentheses in sections f and g refer to this text.

Thales's thinking is one that does not move within the realm of superstition, of fable, of the gods. It is rather a thinking that deals directly with the way things are and what is "naturally so."

> Thales is a creative master who began to see into the depths of nature without the help of fantastic fable. (42)

Thus, rather than being a quest of empirical science and for proof and certainty, it is philosophical thinking. For Nietzsche, the philosopher

> is ever on the scent of those things that are most worth knowing, the great and the important insights ... The philosopher seeks to hear within himself the echoes of the world symphony and to re-project it ... He grasps for it in order to get hold of his own enchantment ... Thus, Thales had seen the oneness of all that is [the way things are and not as a static unity!], but when he went to communicate it, he found himself talking about water! (44)

For Nietzsche, Thales's word *water* is a marker, an image, not a metaphysical "reality." The magnificence of the image of water is that it mirrors movement, change, dynamic unfolding. First, "all is water" says that all is non-dually one – and then the oneness of all phenomena is "like water," changing, becoming, dynamic. This is far from the metaphysical unity that Western philosophical scholarship has attributed to Thales – and today tries either to defend as "realism" or to debunk as the illusion of "absolute truth." Neither view understands the power of Thales's insight.

Considering all this, it is inappropriate – and perhaps folly – to reduce Thales to a proto-scientist or proto-philosopher who was looking for a "theory of everything" or the one fundamental "thing" that makes up the physical universe. You could say that he went "way beyond that"!

(Note that the next section takes up Nietzsche's reading of Greek philosophy in fuller detail.)

The Greek word *psyche* (ψυχή). It was inappropriately translated into Latin as *anima* and into English as *soul* (German: *Seele*). If we begin with Aristotle's words "ψυχή is the principle of life of any living being," we need to be cautious.

Our traditional notion of soul is less than ψυχή. Plato said that the psyche is "not-so-connected" to the body, and Aristotle said that the psyche is "significantly-if-not-essentially-connected" to the body. And the Scholastics varied, depending on whether they were more within the tradition of Plato–Plotinus or that of Aristotle–Aquinas. But for sure, when considering the Greek ψυχή, the Christian overlay in Scholastic philosophy named *anima* or *soul* as more important than the body and the essence of the human being. And the Scholastic soul has no movement in it.

But are these interpretations sound, and how much so? Heraclitus, Fragment B45, says: "You will not find the boundaries of ψυχή, even if you go down all roads, so deep-unfathomable is its λόγος."

And Fragment B115: "Φυχή has a λόγος that, from within and out of itself, becomes ever richer."

What is ψυχή whose boundaries cannot be found? And what is ψυχή that is ever-growing? Some commentaries on Heraclitus even suggest that ψυχή is not only soul but also self. But whatever Heraclitus is saying about ψυχή, it has nothing to do with the self as we know it. And it cannot be limited or reduced to the human soul, Christian or otherwise.

When I would discuss this with my students, most of them – mostly those with some kind of Christian background – were sure they had a "soul." There were always a few who said that the soul – as understood in the Judeo-Christian context or the context of German Idealism – does not exist. But of course they were not so sure about ψυχή in Heraclitus! One student joked: Heraclitus's ψυχή-*psyche* is so amorphous that we hardly know what it is if it does exist! Again, with them and with us, it is about exploration, not about finding for certain.

When I check my *Online Etymology Dictionary*, I find that the Greek ψυχή is "animating spirit." The word refers etymologically to breath (ψυχή) and to breathing, blowing (ψύχειν). But then it tells us that the Greek word ψυχή says: "the soul, mind, spirit; breath; life, one's life, the invisible animating principle or entity which occupies and directs the physical body."[12] But what if the human *psyche*, as the principle of human life, is more like the dynamic ongoing awareness of the mind? What if both Heraclitus and Aristotle were thinking psyche more as "mind" – not as the mind-*Geist* that makes up our intellect and that knows and is known by epistemology, but as mind as awareness, minding mind? Who studies *this* ψυχή?

When I look at the entry for *psyche* in *Greek Philosophical Terms: A Historical Lexicon*,[13] and when I excavate the hidden treasures in what is generally a more traditional reading of the Greek words, I find that the word *psyche* is very rich and not at all limited to soul or self or even mind – the psychological sense of the term in the early twentieth century. To wit, in Peters's words *psyche*:

- is the breath of life, vital principle ...
- is for Homer the "breath of life" ... that escapes, normally, from the mouth of the dying hero ... closely associated with motion ...
- is for Plato a way that is more akin to the pre-Socratic motif of *kinesis*: In the *Timaeus* it is the *psyche tou pantos*: psyche of the all ... vitalizing and governing matter, as one of its main functions.

Ψυχή, then – as breath of life or movement – says something about how "the way things are" in living beings and in life itself is about change and movement.

Can one say that ψυχή is the "whole of human life-*living*" – as opposed to the human being who is dead? Once *psyche* is thought as a dynamic that goes beyond breathing, it takes on the meaning of movement, in perception or otherwise. "Otherwise" here means that perhaps *psyche* can also mean what gathers and sustains movement in everything, a kind of *logos* or harmony-equilibrium.

At this point in our pursuit, I mean primarily not to "define" or even to know precisely what *psyche* is and does (its function), **but rather to put into doubt our usual conception of *psyche*.** With this turn, something important happens: We open our minds and thinking to new possibility, and we see that there is more to it: more than soul-self, more than something that inheres in humans, more than our usual understandings. (We will take up this question of the ψυχή in part 3, where the central question is the non-dual dynamic of radiant emptiness.)

Aristotle's "causes." Perhaps the most exciting foray in this new and enriching way of reading Greek philosophy emerges when we look at Aristotle. Here I offer a quick glimpse into the possibilities that emerge when we take Aristotle's Greek for what it says from itself, rather than from the many overlays and coverings from the history of Western philosophy post-Aristotle, and above all when we go underneath the usual English translations of Aristotle. We do this by relistening to the Greek text and retranslating the words. This we do "from within the word in the Greek" and what thinking calls for in this retrieval. (Here I am guided by Jacob Klein.[14])

What happens when we look at Aristotle's notions of matter and form (also known as potentiality and actuality, especially in the Latin of the Scholastics)? Let us look at the first two of the four "causes" that inhere in everything that exists. Aristotle's thinking always started with what was there, concretely and in experience – and then thought it back to what must be its "causes." But the Greek word for "cause" here is αἴτιον-*aition*. This has little to do with the traditional, current notion of cause in "causality" or cause and effect. Surely our current notion is quite useful in many ways. But does it **say** what the Greek word αἴτια says? αἴτιον comes from the Greek word αἴτιος. Checking several Greek–English dictionaries, I find these words: cause, mother, motive, reason; ground, motive, antecedent; responsible for; activating, actuating, borne in upon, conducive, contributing, motivating, precipitating; instrumental.

So αἴτιον says so much more than cause! For starters, we can say that, for what is there in front of us, for the way things are – concretely and experientially there – αἴτια are aspects or conditions of phenomena or things. These "causes" are not anything solidly or physically there that "cause" anything, but rather those aspects or conditions of a thing that are responsible for it, that activate it, that are conducive and instrumental – the "mothers" of things. Our way of naming this dynamic is: What are the causes?

Gathering, the Greek word αἴτιov says much more than cause. Aristotle's four "causes" (αἴτια) are four kinds of responsibility or conditions by which to understand things in the world. We could say that they make up four conditions that are brought to bear when anything exists or comes to exist.

The first two conditions by which things are and by which we understand them are matter and form. These together make up hylomorphism – from the Greek words ὕλη-*hyle* and μορφή-*morphe*. *Hyle* is usually said to be "matter" and sometimes "prime matter." But it is not anything material or physical at all, in itself, because it only manifests as "matter" when it is together with "form."

So … ὕλη-*hyle* as one of these "causes" is not really any *thing*. Rather it underlies the form of any *thing*. It has no properties and cannot exist by itself. So then what is it? It is a condition by which this energy of *hyle* is dynamically striving towards some form. As such, it is a condition of movement and change. It is dynamic, never static. It is "empty of form," which says "not any thing," or: no-thing. And it as such is no-form.

When this condition manifests together with "form," then there is something. But that something is itself always in motion, in action. Rather than being defined as "material" and "formal" causes, the conditions for the possibility of anything to be include (a) *hyle*, the dynamic potential always in action towards joining the form by which it is something, and (b) *morphe*, the form or shape that something has. And this formless and no-thing dynamic continues in the "formed."

We can get a better understanding of what is at issue here if we turn to Aristotle's words on another level. Aristotle says that whenever we study something that is – a brick house, a tree, a human being – we cannot know it directly. We can only know it, as we say, by analogy. It is "like" something. But it is not a separate and independent thing at all. It may be one of the conditions by which things come to be, but to call it an independent "thing" is …

well, not true! It never exists separately. And it is certainly not something individual or discrete.

Δύναμις-ἐνέργεια-ἐντελέχεια (*dynamis-energeia-entelecheia*). At another point in his writings, Aristotle uses a whole new set of words to describe this phenomenon. He looks at things – empirically, that is, in "experience" – and says there is some dynamic as the condition for things "within which" phenomena appear. This he calls in Greek δύναμις/*dynamis*, which we normally translate as "potency" or "potentiality." And traditionally we hear in this word a name for something that is merely potential, something that is quietly and passively waiting to be acted upon, with no power of its own and not dynamic at all! Sometimes called *materia prima*?

But this *dynamis*, itself in movement-dynamic, is nothing passive and nothing material-physical! Its no-thing and no-form "condition" does not wait passively to be acted upon. It is always already "in action," anticipating, filled with pregnant possibility that is already at work in δύναμις.

In the traditional interpretation of Aristotle here, when this passive "potency" gets acted upon, it becomes something – a tree, a building, a glass. And this something is then "actual," which traditionally means having reached its result and then being static. Aristotle's word for this actuality is *energeia* (ἐνέργεια). In the received, traditional sense, something moves from potentiality to actuality and then stands there in its ἐντελέχεια or completedness, that is, has reached its goal and is now static. But this is not the way things are, and Aristotle knew that!

Let us take a tree as an example. When we look at an oak tree, we say that the "potentiality" of oak tree is in the acorn and that when it sprouts and then is a seedling and then a young sapling … it is on its way to becoming an oak. And at one point it becomes an oak tree. But then our usual thinking thinks that the oak tree is now there, complete and "actual" – completed and static. But the Greek words do not say this. Rather they say that the tree is always "being-at-work" (*en*-ergon) in becoming an oak tree. It is always changing, in motion: always at-work.

Far from a metaphysics of substance and things standing alone, statically, Aristotle's words focus on the dynamic quality of everything, from beginning to end – or we might say "always" or without end or "timelessly." Normally we think that once something has come to exist for what it is – even the tree – then it has reached completion and is somehow a "result." Without meaning to, we then often think that this result is now "again" a static independent substance.

This traditional way of reading Aristotle – to a large part "caused" by translations that are limiting – is about some *thing* waiting some *where*, passively, until it is acted upon and then becoming something by being acted upon. And that something is again a static result.

But taking the Greek words at face value – remembering what is at the core of the Greek words themselves – these are two conditions that are brought to bear in the coming to be of any *thing* and in our understanding of that coming to be. And the Greek words tell us something like this: For everything that is and that we want to understand, there are these two conditions ... and both of them are in action, at-work, from the beginning (and is there ever then a real "beginning"?) to the end (and is there then ever an "end"?). Everything is always dynamic, in movement, at work.

Here I want to expand on and go further into the issue of translation of *dynamis-energeia-entelecheia*. I invite the reader to join me in looking at several passages in Aristotle's *Metaphysics, Book Θ*, in order to study how the English translations affect the reading and interpretation of Aristotle on these crucial matters.[15] This new reading of Aristotle on *dynamis-energeia-entelecheia* is important, for several reasons:

a. It shows clearly a reading-retrieval of this core "teaching" by Aristotle that most people are not aware of.
b. It is a prime example of how Heidegger works in his retrieving of Greek philosophy.
c. It upends our traditional-inherited understanding of Greek philosophy, which *puts Aristotle squarely within metaphysics*, that is,

belonging in the first beginning according to Heidegger – where, at least in part, Aristotle *does not* belong!
d. If there is any theme or text (with key words) in this project that (a) demonstrates a text in Greek philosophy that history has misread and mistranslated for a very long time – precisely the way of thinking that we have inherited and that needs a fresh rethinking – and (b) shows so directly and so clearly the power and necessity of this refreshing, rethinking retrieval … this is it!

The question in this section of Aristotle's *Metaphysics* is the τέλος-goal of things or of movement. The central question here is movement-κίνησις. When observing a phenomenon or thing, where and how does it begin (δύναμις)? Of what does the "actuality" of a phenomenon or thing consist (ἐνέργεια)? How can we understand the movement (κίνησις) of the transition from potentiality to actuality? And finally: When the whole process comes to an end – when the movement has reached its goal (τέλος) – what is reached and what is this reaching? Is the end or goal an end station – an end where there is no longer anything in movement, in action, in process? Or not? And what can we know of the phenomenon or thing at this "end"? This is the question of the Greek word ἐντελέχεια. "Literally" ἐντελέχεια says being-in-the-end or goal: ἐν-τέλος-ἔχειν or ἔχειν in τέλος, being in the goal.

The traditional interpretation, handed down to us through the Scholastics and into the modern period of philosophy, is roughly this: κίνησις-movement takes place only in the transition or crossing from δύναμις to ενέργεια or ἐντελέχεια. Movement takes place only in the crossing from potentiality to actuality or completedness. It is rather simple. If movement is only in the transition, then the "from where" (δύναμις) and the "to where" (ἐνέργεια) are not in movement – in the one case a static "not yet" and in the other a static result. But how can δύναμις be reduced to passive potentiality?

A more precise reading of Aristotle calls for a new rendering of these components, which will show that *all three* are dynamic and active – not only κίνησις but also δύναμις, as well as ἐνέργεια-ἐντελέχεια. Heidegger's reading and translating of these key points in Aristotle's metaphysics move within this dynamic. And it is based on going back to the Greek texts, to see what *they* said and thought, that is, not determined by how these texts were translated into Latin and later into English in the seventeenth and eighteenth centuries.

What Heidegger's reading of Aristotle opens up is the "but": But, when Aristotle calls ἐντελέχεια a movement, then what? The inherited reading of Aristotle ignores this "ἐντελέχεια as movement" and explains that movement can "only" be in the κίνησις and not in actuality (ἐνέργεια). Such an interpretation or reading has to see ἐνέργεια as a result that is completed, thus no longer in movement.

But when we take what in Aristotle is said and meant – "so obviously" – in a fresh way, when we look at it anew, when we rethink it, based on hearing the word anew and away from the inherited translations – then (a) movement is not limited to the κίνησις of the crossing but is a part of the entire dynamic from δύναμις to ἐντελέχεια, (b) δύναμις is never inert, passive potentiality, but always an inborn active tendency, (c) ἐνέργεια is not the name for a finished actuality that from now on stands "without movement," but continues to work and to unfold, and (d) ἐντελέχεια is in no way a finished completeness, but an ongoing being-at-work in the τέλος. Thus (e) ἐνέργεια and ἐντελέχεια are phenomenologically the same, and all three of them (δύναμις ἐνέργεια ἐντελέχεια) are always and a continually active and dynamic movement: they are all of them always "at-work," that is, dynamically and in movement.[16] I suggest that δύναμις is a name for the no-form no-thing dynamic of radiant emptiness.

Joe Sachs[17] writes a remarkable paragraph about translating Aristotle into English, which applies singularly to the translation of *dynamis-energeia-entelecheia* in Book Θ of Aristotle's *Metaphysics:*

At all the most crucial places, the usual translations of Aristotle abandon English and move toward Latin. They do this because earlier translations did the same. Those earlier translators did so because their principal access to Aristotle's meaning was through Latin commentaries. The result is jargon, but that seems not to make most of the professional scholars uncomfortable; after all, by perpetuating such inaccessible English texts, they create a demand for interpreters that only they can fill. I have criticized the current state of Aristotle-translating at length in the introduction to a recent translation of my own. There it seemed necessary to explain to those familiar with other translations the many departures they were about to encounter. Here a briefer justification may suffice: My aim is to give you in translation an experience as close as I can make it to reading the original. The original is written not for specialists but for generally educated people of any sort who are willing to think hard. Where Aristotle exploits the resources of the Greek language to capture his meaning, the translation will be in bad English; where he departs from Greek usage to coin new words and novel ways of saying things, the translation will be in worse English. From the point of view of a classicist, a good English translation of a classical author is one that finds, for every word or phrase in the original, some equivalent expression that reads smoothly in our language. This may be a good practice with some kinds of writing, but philosophic meaning cannot be captured in habitual uses of language. The point of view of a professional philosopher may, however, pay too much heed to the linguistic choices that have become habitual in modern philosophy and in the secondary literature, at the expense of faithfulness to the original.[18]

(I would say that – in connection with Klein's important essay, with Heidegger's putting existing translations of Aristotle into question, and with Klein's own overall understanding of Greek and of Aristotle – Sachs revolutionized the translation and study of Aristotle in English. Sachs went on to translate many texts of Aristotle, including *Metaphysics*, *Physics*, *Nichomachean Ethics*, and *De Anima*. These translations are the backbone for retranslating Aristotle into English and thus **retrieving the thought in Aristotle's "said."** Turning now to the words of Aristotle, I will present a few texts from his *Metaphysics* and show where and how this fresh and "less Latin" way of translating Aristotle fits in with what Heidegger calls the "return" to the Greeks.)

Please keep in mind the difference between dynamic movement and static potential or static completedness, between concrete

thinghood and static substance, between *entelecheia* as being active within the end/*telos* and *entelecheia* as *telos* in static completedness, between ἐνέργεια as being-at-work and ἐνέργεια as "complete reality." Note here the startling juxtaposition of the traditional-inherited (TI) translation and the (RR) refreshing-retrieving translation.
    I summarize here:

TI: "Potentiality" (δύναμις) is "passive, inert, static potentiality."
    "Actuality" (ἐνέργεια) is derived from "activity" and has the
    meaning of "complete reality" or points to the completed reality
    (ἐντελέχεια). When complete(d), it is static, a static "result."
RR: The formless δύναμις is just that: dynamic, moving and never
    static. The *telos*/end is being-at-work (ἐνέργεια). Thus what
    we usually think of as the end – as complete and done, with
    nothing happening or in movement – is simply not what
    Aristotle says: ἐνέργεια is not some static result. The activity of
    things forms a **continuous state of being-at-work** (ἐν+ἔργον or
    ἐνέργεια). And this being-at-work (dynamic unfolding) con-
    tinues in the end. This is what Aristotle means by ἐντελέχεια:
    a **being unceasingly at-work in the τέλος/end**. The end is still
    dynamically unfolding.

Let us now look at several passages from Aristotle:

1. **1045b32 δύναμις-dynamis ... ἐντελέχεια: being-at-work-in-telos
   ... ἔργον: at-work.**
      The traditional translations use such words as (passive)
   "potency" and "complete reality" or "actuality" or
   "completedness." But Sachs translates this passage this way:

      but in another way in virtue of potency and complete being-at-
      work and of a doing-something.

   I note here that Sachs does not open up δύναμις-*dynamis* as
   much as I see possible. *Dynamis* is nothing passive. It is also not
   material. Rather it is a dynamic of possibility that belongs to
   everything.

2. **1047a30 (ἐνέργεια: *energeia*) connected to ἐντελέχεια: being-at-work-in-*telos*.**
   The traditional translations use such words as "actuality" (ἐνέργεια), which is connected to "completedness" or "complete reality" (ἐντελέχεια). But Sachs translates this passage this way:

> The phrase being-at-work [ἐνέργεια], which is designed to converge in meaning with being-at-work-staying-complete [ἐντελέχεια], comes to apply to other things from belonging especially to movements.

In his glossary Sachs writes that *energeia* is being-at-work. There he says:

> Activity comes to sight first as motion, but Aristotle's central thought is that all being is being-at-work ... Since the end and completion of any genuine being is its being-at-work, the meaning of the word [ἐνέργεια] converges (1047a 30–1, 1050a 22–4) with that of following: **Being-at-work-staying-itself** (ἐντελέχεια). A fusion of the idea of completeness with that of continuity or persistence. Aristotle invents the word by combining ἐντελες (complete, full grown) with ἔχειν (= ἕξις, to be a certain way by the continuing effort of holding on to that condition), while at the same time punning on ἐνδελέχεια (persistence) by inserting τέλος (completion) This is a three-ring circus of a word, at the heart of everything in Aristotle's thinking, including the definition of motion. Its power to carry meaning depends on the working together of all the things Aristotle has packed into it. Some commentators explain it as meaning being-at-the-end, which misses the point entirely, and it is usually translated as "actuality," a word that refers to anything, however trivial, incidental, transient, or static, that happens to be the case, so that everything is lost in translation, just at the spot where understanding could begin.[19]

3. **1050a21 τὸ γὰρ ἔργον τέλος, ἡ δὲ ἐνέργεια τὸ ἔργον, διὸ καὶ τοὔνομα ἐνέργεια λέγεται κατὰ τὸ ἔργον καὶ συντείνει ϖρὸς τὴν ἐντελέχειαν.**
   The traditional translations use such words as "actuality" having the meaning of "complete reality." But Sachs translates this passage this way:

For the end [τέλος] is work [ἔργον], and the work is a being-at-work [ἐνέργεια], and this is why the phrase being-at-work [ἐνέργεια] is meant by reference to work and extends to being-at-work-staying-complete [ἐντελέχεια].

Sachs explains:

That is, beings do not just happen to perform strings of isolated deeds, but their activity forms a **continuous state of being-at-work**, in which they achieve the completion that makes them what they are. Aristotle is arguing that the very thinghood of a thing is not what might be hidden inside it, but a definite way of **being unceasingly at-work**, that makes it a thing at all and the kind of thing it is.[20]

Once again, notice how, all along, the traditional-inherited translations use words that are static and disconnecting:

- δύναμις: passive potentiality, "mere" potency (no indication of anything "dynamic" or a "being-in-movement" as part of its being).
- ἐνέργεια: actuality, static result, complete reality.
- ἐντελέχεια: complete, static reality, completedness.

What Sachs does in his translations is pretty much turn everything upside down.

Gathering Heidegger's retrieval. Let me finish our reading of Aristotle in translation here by hearing how Heidegger gathers the issue, as he "retrieves" what Aristotle says about δύναμις and ἐνέργεια and ἐντελέχεια as names for being and "ways of being-in-movement." The "starting" for this mindful thinking comes from the final pages of Heidegger's *Aristoteles, Metaphysik Θ 1–3. Von Wesen und Wirklichkeit der Kraft* (GA 33).* To start, I quote Heidegger:

[T]he right way of distinguishing δύναμις and ἐνέργεια can only happen with an earlier and continual adhering to κίνησις. What does that

---

* Numbers in parentheses in this section refer to this text.

mean? Nothing less than: the presence of capability [δύναμις as *Vermögen*] as such, in the same way as actively being-at-work [ἐνέργεια as *Wirklichkeit*], in the sense of carrying-it-out [*Vollzug*] are *ways of being-in-movement* [*Weisen des In-Bewegung-seins*]. (216)

As a kind of gathering – comparing the various traditional translations of Aristotle with the "retrieving" translations of Sachs and inspired by Heidegger's groundbreaking work on thinking and translating (or translating and thinking) Aristotle – I now do a reading-commentary of, and a meditative interpretation of, the last pages of Heidegger's *Aristoteles, Metaphysik Θ 1–3* (216–24). I paraphrase, with Heidegger's own words in quotation marks:

1. As one of the manifold ways of saying being, the interactive dynamic of δύναμις-κίνησις-ἐνέργεια (= ἐντελέχεια) merges in a rich inseparable dynamic. (Reminder of the non-dual inseparable way of being as beyng as Ereignis as non-dual dynamic of radiant emptiness.)
2. What holds these three together in their inseparability is κίνησις, movement. And then δύναμις and ἐνέργεια (= ἐντελέχεια) show, each in its own way, an always ongoing dynamic of being-in-movement. All is movement, dynamic at-oneness. For example, as Heidegger says above, "the right way of distinguishing δύναμις and ἐνέργεια can only happen with an earlier and continual adhering to κίνησις." That is, both δύναμις and ἐνέργεια "are *ways of being-in-movement*" (216).
3. The dynamic of δύναμις is called "the starting moment [*Hinausführen*, leading out] of the power [*Vermögen*, capability] itself into that to which it, as itself power, surges" (218). Heidegger gives the example of a runner in the 100-metre race. Right before the race, the runner is on the starting blocks, poised to run. We might say that the runner is not yet in motion, but we see the loose open hands, the fingers touching the ground almost pushing off. The face and eyes are tensed towards what lies ahead.

    The runner is poised to start running. This poise is already filled with readiness. So one can say that the runner's pose is far removed from a pose without movement, the runner's pose is an active anticipation "away from the position." I might say that the runner is in active anticipation. Its way of being is as full preparedness and as leading-out (as the dynamic "starting").

(I have provided a summary of what Heidegger describes in much fuller detail in GA 33:217–18. What Heidegger does in this passage is an excellent example of phenomenological seeing and interpretation or laying out – of a *dynamic* and not something static at all.)

4. We are called to think Aristotle's words here "beyond any abstract deliberation." We are called to think-say "what is said by bringing it forth from out of what shows itself to the truly philosophizing look-glance" (221). The true philosophical look is to the phenomenon, which becomes manifest in *empeiria*: experience. This is non-conceptual.

5. Ἐνέργεια says: being-at-work (*am-Werke-sein*). That is its way of being. Its way of being is being-in-movement as the ongoing dynamic of actualizing.

6. Ἐντελέχεια says: holding itself in staying complete (*Sich-in-Fertigkeit-halten*). Holding itself adroit and ready. (Sachs: being-at-work-staying-complete.) Here movement shows itself "as that whereby something is in motion [in full gear], something is at work, something is going on, happening" (218).

   The dynamic of movement is everywhere. Everything is inseparably interconnected, that is, a dynamic onefold or one-ing. We do not say this conceptually or dualistically. Rather we heed what shows itself and learn how to think and say it.

   This is the inseparable intertwining of δύναμις and ενέργεια, held together by κίνησις-movement, that is, in such a way that all three are of one piece as the non-dual inseparable *dynamic* of beyng or radiant emptiness.

7. If we hear all of these words as saying beyng, then we highlight how these words do not name things, beings, or concepts. Rather they say the no-thing non-dual dynamic of radiant emptiness. One could say that the movement that inheres in all three words *is* the non-dual dynamic of radiant emptiness, also sayable as beyng as Ereignis, *dao*, buddha mind, and the quantum potential of quantum physics.

g. The Example of Nietzsche

I am not alone nor the first to offer an invitation to reread – rehear – the texts of the ancient Greeks. Of course, I get my motivation from Heidegger's work with the Greeks. But even before him – and in his own way – Nietzsche reclaimed the life of early Greek thinking, from Thales to Heraclitus, in *Philosophy in the Tragic Age of the Greeks*. He rejected the inherited way of reading the Greeks that was practised in the nineteenth century. Rather than seeing Thales, Anaxagoras, Anaximander, and Heraclitus as primitive metaphysicians trying to discover and name the one material element that the universe is made of, Nietzsche heard something else in the words of these early Greek thinkers. He read and heard about dynamic unfolding, about the excitement of questioning without demanding answers.

Nietzsche did not see the work of these thinkers as independent attempts at finding a unified theory of the way things are – earth, water, air, fire – a "unified theory of everything." Instead, he saw in these thinkers a recognition that "the way things are" is a dynamic unfolding, that the world we experience is more than a world of static substances. A simple word for this dynamic is *change* – and not merely static being – the dynamic of interdependent conditions and not merely independent things/beings. And nowhere is there a highest being or highest unchanging principle.

Nietzsche offered a thinking path that had largely been ignored: the understanding of "the way things are" as a dynamic unfolding or becoming. This is at the core of his mantra "eternal recurrence of the same." With that the question of "the way things are" becomes more open-ended.

Nietzsche's insight was the recognition that the "are" in the "the way things are" is not static: It is a becoming. As I see it, for 2,500 years now, dynamic unfolding has been the thread that moves through almost all early Greek thinking – at least in some form or other and for some part of their inquiry.

Nietzsche challenges us above all to see that this rereading and rethinking retrieval is not an abstract exercise. It is not something that we do for a while, then put back on the shelf, in order then to live our lives. Greek philosophy demands something from us. Experience and change. Thinking is at the same time a doing, and it changes us. We dare not hide behind abstractions because we fear dealing with the way things are or become – or because we fear engaging with the world. Nietzsche's truth – my truth – is not a dogma but rather an engagement in developing the mind, activating mind-energy that goes beyond mere academic exercise. (Here I am reminded again of Rilke's poem on Apollo's torso, namely that hidden within the torso and emerging from it is the challenge: You must change your life.)

Philosophy in the Tragic Age of the Greeks invites us[21] to move away from the received-inherited-traditional way of thinking about the way things are – usually called "reality" – towards a fresh and open way of thinking and seeing the way things are in their widest reach, which includes the possibility that the "being" of things/beings-phenomena is non-physical, non-dual, dynamic emptiness as an opening-freeing. It is a rejection of thinking as mental gymnastics; it is instead thinking as conscious, critical awareness. It is a rejection of reality as static substance, that is, as the *one* reality that is an unchanging foundation. Rather it is the way things are *as* a dynamic unfolding and enfolding, a simultaneous emerging and disappearing. Like the sun, emerging in the morning and disappearing in the evening. Like an acorn, emerging as the oak tree … being at work as an oak tree and never reaching a "final, completedness" of oak tree.

Seeing the dynamic aspect of the way things are in the widest range points thinking towards the no-thing, non-dual dynamic of radiant emptiness. Empty of form, things, and concepts, it is a freeing and opening to all possibility – emptiness within which things manifest non-dually.

Traditionally we take these early Greek texts as incomplete or failed attempts at order, at neatly arranged and argued logic. We fail to see what they really are: not-so-neat, non-linear dialogical inquiry – they might even be legitimately tautological. Our task, Nietzsche tells us, is to recognize that these Greek texts, although remote in time, challenge us in our experience today – each thinker with his or her own way of saying, neither primitive nor incomplete. Certainly there are gaps and repetitions at times, relative to today's style of writing. But a carefully arranged, logical order of thinking is not their aim.

Rather, the early Greek thinkers – often misleadingly named the "pre-Socratics" – engaged in a conversation about serious matters, intended to expand our ability to think, our ability to stay with the question. It is a thinking that honours the true complexity of the matter. It goes beyond the everyday, the readily available. Nietzsche's engagement with the early Greeks challenges us to transform our thinking, to move from the obvious to the unmanifest, to pass to the less well known.

***

Excursus: What does Nietzsche want to say with the word *tragic* in *Philosophy in the Tragic Age of the Greeks*? While that word appears in the title of the earlier work *Philosophy in the Tragic Age of the Greeks* (1871), he addresses this question in detail in another writing, *The Birth of Tragedy* (1873).[22]*

The word *tragedy* literally means "goat song." And while there are a few favourite theories, no one knows for certain the connection between "goat song" and what the Greeks meant by tragedy. Nietzsche extrapolates the "goat song" or "tragedy" from its role as the chorus in Greek theatre. And contrary to what the word means today, *tragic* is something beneficial, good, joyful, as it opens humans to a dimension that goes beyond the moralistic and the "too ordered" world of intellectual abstraction. Or as Nietzsche says: "What killed tragedy … [is] Socratic morality, dialectic, the satisfaction and serenity of the theoretical man" (3–4). Let us look at this paragraph in its entirety:

> What does the *tragic* myth mean precisely for the Greeks of the best, strongest, and bravest age? What about that tremendous phenomenon

---

* All numbers in parentheses in this excursus refer to this text.

of the Dionysian? And what about what was born out of the Dionysian – tragedy. And by contrast, what are we to make of what killed
tragedy – Socratic morality, dialectic, the satisfaction and serenity of the
theoretical man? (3–4)

Then Nietzsche adds: "Where then must tragedy have come from?
Perhaps out of *joy*, out of power, out of overflowing health, out of
overwhelming fullness?" (6). So what is Nietzsche saying with the
words *tragic* and *tragedy*?

I will now present a number of quotations from *The Birth of Tragedy*, with the intention of letting emerge a fuller picture of what
Nietzsche "wants to say." (My annotations appear after the quotations, in italics.)

[The Apollonian and Dionysian eventually] appear paired up with each
other and, as this pair, finally produce Attic tragedy, as much a Dionysian as an Apollonian work of art. (11)

- *The Apollonian and Dionysian belong together in order to produce and
  have tragedy.*

We suspect that the birth of tragedy cannot be explained either from the
high estimation of the moral intelligence of the masses or from the idea
of the spectator without a play. (27)

- *What tragedy is cannot be gleaned from what Nietzsche calls "Socratic
  morality." Note that for Nietzsche Socrates represents a limiting morality and too much rational dialectic (the theoretical spectator), thus
  coming after the tragic age of the Greeks. Nietzsche says that Socrates
  holds "that nature can be rationally understood" (59). Following Sallis's
  insights in* **Being and Logos: Reading the Platonic Dialogues**, *I deal
  with a Socrates who is different from Nietzsche's Socrates.*

I believe that the civilized Greek [*der griechische Culturmensch*] felt
himself lifted up [*aufgehoben*] by the sight of the chorus of satyrs, and
the next effect of Dionysian tragedy is that the state and society, in

general the gap between man and man, give way to an invincible feeling of unity, which leads back to the heart of nature. The metaphysical consolation – with which, as I am immediately indicating here, every true tragedy leaves us, that, in spite of all the transformations in phenomena, at the bottom of everything life is indestructibly powerful and delightful. (28)

- *The German words that Nietzsche uses here – **der griechische Culturmensch** and **aufgehoben** – have a double meaning. The Greek person is **either** "too civilized" (as in bland or too agreeable) and is then reversed by the sight of the chorus of satyrs **or** well-bred and enlightened and thus "lifted up." Knowing Nietzsche's irony, I suspect he means the former. In either case, tragedy takes this human being beyond what is normally there.*
- *Here Nietzsche names it the Dionysian tragedy, stressing how it is the Dionysian that brings the tragic to the fore.*
- *With the "invincible feeling of unity, which leads back to the heart of nature," thinking moves beyond the dialectical and theoretical – beyond to the lived, to the feeling of a non-dual and dynamic one-ing. This is what the Dionysian adds to the Apollonian, necessary for the rebirth of tragedy.*
- *"Every true tragedy leaves us" with an "indestructibly powerful and delightful [**lustvoll**, zestful, passionate, sensual] life "at the bottom of everything." We could say that this is the intoxification that the Dionysian brings. Tragedy takes place **only when** this is added to the Apollonian.*

[T]he poet [of the tragic chorus] is only a poet because of the fact that he sees himself surrounded by shapes which live and act in front of him and into whose innermost being he gazes. (31)

- *The poet is only a poet – and speaks poi-etically – when surrounded by "shapes that live and act," that is, a lived, concretely intuitive experience.*
- *The poet gazes into what is most "own" to the living and acting of these "shapes" on stage, that is, humans. This is also nothing theoretical, dialectical, or moral. It is **life** in experience.*

At this point we are concerned with the question whether the power whose opposition broke tragedy has sufficient force for all time to hinder the artistic reawakening of tragedy and the tragic world view. If the old tragedy was derailed by the dialectical drive for knowledge and for the optimism of science, we might have to infer from this fact an eternal struggle between *the theoretical* and *the tragic world view*, and only after the spirit of science is taken right to its limits and its claim to universal validity destroyed by the proof of those limits would it be possible to hope for a re-birth of tragedy. (59)

- *The power named here is the Apollonian in isolation.*
- *We can hope for the rebirth of tragedy only when the dialectical and the isolated-theoretical **again** meet up with the "feeling of unity, which leads back to the heart of nature" with its "overwhelming fullness" and "indestructibly powerful and delightful" life.*

If only it can now understand how to keep learning continuously from a single people, the Greeks … when have we needed these most eminent of mentors more than now, when we are experiencing *the rebirth of tragedy* …? (69)

Yes, my friends, believe with me in the Dionysian life and in the re-birth of tragedy. The age of the Socratic man is over: crown yourselves with ivy, take the thyrsus stalk in your hand, and don't be amazed when tigers and panthers lie down fawning at your feet. Only now you must dare to be tragic men … You are to lead the Dionysian celebratory procession and have faith in the miracles of your god! (71)

In the total effect of tragedy the Dionysian regains its superiority once more. Tragedy ends with a tone which never could resound from the realm of Apollonian art. (75)

[W]e have to keep hold of those leaders who illuminate the way for us, the Greeks. Up to now, in order to purify our aesthetic awareness, we have borrowed from them both of those images of the gods [Apollo and Dyonysos], each of whom rules over his own specific artistic realm, and by considering Greek tragedy, we came to an awareness of their mutual contact and intensification.

To us the downfall of Greek tragedy must appear to have occurred through a remarkable tearing apart of both of these primordial artistic drives, an event which was accompanied by a degeneration and transformation of the character of the Greek people ...

That downfall of tragedy was at the same time the downfall of myth. Up to that point the Greeks were instinctively compelled to tie everything they lived through immediately to their myths ... in a certain sense, to be timeless. In this stream of the timeless, however, the state and art both plunged equally, in order to find in it rest from the weight and greed of the moment. (79–80)

- *Each of the Apollonian and the Dionysian "rules over his own specific artistic realm, and by considering Greek tragedy, we came to an **awareness of their mutual contact and intensification**." The two entwined as one is the emergence of the tragic, in its joy!*
- *We see myth here as the non-transparent. Hidden or indirectly and poi-etically revealed.*

For now we understand what it means in tragedy to want to keep looking and at the same time to yearn for something beyond what we see ... That striving for the infinite, the wing beat of longing, associated with the highest delight in clearly perceived reality, reminds us that in both states we must recognize a Dionysian phenomenon, which always reveals to us all over again the playful cracking apart and destruction of the world of the individual as the discharge of primordial delight. (83)

- *"something beyond what we see": the mythic, the Dionysian, the non-conceptually lived.*
- *"the playful cracking apart and destruction of the world ... as the discharge of primordial delight": opening out beyond the traditional-inherited (TI) way of being to the playful, primordial delight. In what? In the non-dual dynamic of radiant emptiness!*

Nietzsche finds in tragedy the marriage of the Apollonian and the Dionysian. For the Apollonian, the dream is illusion – we are in control. The Apollonian is the principle of order: "nothing in excess" and "know thyself" – the sayings that are inscribed on the temple of Apollo at Delphi. The Apollonian is the elevation of the transparent world over the no-way-out. By contrast, the Dionysian is the primordial – unencompassable for the Apollonian order of things. The opposite of control, the Dionysian is loose abandonment. Dionysos was, after all, the god of wine and intoxication. Put succinctly: Both the Apollonian and the Dionysian are needed to fully express what the human being is, the way things are, the ecstatic Dionysian along with the Apollonian order. Apollonian order that ignores the Dionysian is no more helpful for understanding than the Dionysian that becomes barbaric without the balance of the Apollonian – a loss, rather than a transcendence, of self.

And there is more: The non-transparent dimension is also manifest within the Apollonian, which denotes not only order and arrangement and control but also music and poetry – the latter two hardly reducible to the rationality that is often associated with the Apollonian. In *The Birth of Tragedy*, Nietzsche contrasts the Apollonian and Dionysian but also identifies the dynamic tension between the two: Neither is itself when not in tension with the other. Think, perhaps, of the yin and yang circle: Hidden within the white, ordered and control side of the circle – and emerging within it – is the black, intuitive, experiential, and not-so-rational side of the mind. Also, the yin-yang of transparent and nebulous. Let us see where this thinking takes us … from yin-yang or left-brain-right-brain thinking to …?

In the next chapter, on the Delphic Oracle, we are reminded that, as part of the temple to the god Apollo, there is an emblem of the god Dionysos – on the temple itself!

Inspired by Nietzsche's opening the door to the tragic that is "beyond" what convention says about the moral, the dialectical, and the theoretical, I want to look at possibility hidden within his words, words that haunt us.

We know that, for Nietzsche, Greek tragedy sang about "*ekstasis*" or "standing outside oneself." Today we use the word *ecstasy* to refer to an "aha!" experience, including perhaps a kind of out-of-body or trance-like experience; or, in religions, to a spiritual experience of expanded consciousness. (It is also slang for the drug MDMA.) But in its origin and etymology it means, literally, standing outside oneself, going beyond the usual self-limitation.

Nietzsche's opening of the tragic mirrors a stepping outside oneself, an effacing of self, an entrée to a different way of being. To experience tragedy is to be enchanted beyond what is civilized, to stand outside one's "self," to experience a non-personal and nothing "beyond." Through tragedy, we are transported to the human condition as such; the "mine" is gone as tragedy takes us beyond this body and that which is "here" – in simple terms, beyond beings to being as such, to the "just is." Tragedy as stepping-outside-self takes us to being as emptiness, the radiant emptiness that in its freeing opens up all possibility. Emptiness is possibility. This is the journey of the struggling hero, who steps out beyond the conformity of society to enter into a strange land, a place beyond a purely personal way of being – or simply "beyond."

This strange place is in no way initially graspable. It is not transparent to reason. Thus the Greeks called it ἀπορία or ἀ-πορία – "a-poria" – literally "no way out." Dilemma, query, puzzle, perplexity. For Nietzsche and for us, it is an invitation to remain in that perplexity, or, picking up on a theme from Heidegger, to stay in the no-way-out, to remain open to an experience filled with the non-transparent. In this undeniably dynamic gathering, called tragedy, there is something that cannot be easily categorized, that cannot be made static with transparent logic. Nietzsche invites us to keep our eyes open to the dynamic gathering that haunts us in this no-way-out. He invites us to stay with it, become at home with it. He invites us to seek out and honour that which seems estranging. This no-way-out comes from being itself, from the dynamic unfolding (the "freeing empty") that is in, with, and beyond all things. We need to dwell in this utter openness, dynamically in tragic tension within the one-ing of enfolding and unfolding, of the Apollonian and Dionysian. End of excursus.

***

Nietzsche begins *Philosophy in the Tragic Age of the Greeks** by telling us that we love our engaged great thinkers "because of their
ways and the nature of their intentions," while we who come after
often "find their one great mistake" (23). Those who follow the
great thinkers write mere commentaries. Thus "whoever rejoices
in great human beings will also rejoice in philosophical systems,
even if they are completely erroneous" (23). This means that the
originary thinking of the early Greek philosophers includes more
than just theories or concepts or even metaphysical notions.

And a voice tells Nietzsche ... and us: "So this has existed –
once, at least – and is therefore a possibility, this way of life, this
way of looking at the human scene" (23) – and, I might add, this
way of looking at the way things are. Nietzsche's intention, then,
is to retell the story of these early philosophers – meant to be a
beginning

> toward the recovery and re-creation of certain ancient names, so that
> the polyphony of Greek nature at long last may resound once more. The
> task is to bring to light what we must ever love and honour and what
> no subsequent enlightenment can take away: great individual human
> beings. (24)

Because their work includes passion and possibility, great thinkers perform a higher function than merely constructing concepts
and definitions – higher than a definitive knowing about the way
things are, as in "all is water, all is fire, all is air, or all is mind."

The usual notions of "the unity of everything" or concepts and
definitions do not justify philosophy. For Nietzsche, the Greeks
"have once and for all *justified* philosophy simply by having
engaged in it, and engaged in it more fully than any other people"
(28). It is not that the Greeks are necessarily the "one and only,"
but rather that their way of doing philosophy can show us a way
of thinking that is fresher than what we have inherited over the

---

* Unless otherwise noted, numbers in parentheses in this section refer to this text.

centuries, as the Greeks were translated into Latin and then many other languages, and then as the enriching and elemental words were reduced to concepts that belong to later ages rather than to Greek philosophy itself. I argue that returning to the Greeks enriches our thinking today, from within the Greek words and their originary saying, as they are "applied," that is, as their enactment in our hands.

For Nietzsche, the Greeks knew how to begin: "in the midst of good fortune, at the peak of mature manhood, as a pursuit springing from the ardent joyousness of courageous and victorious maturity" (28). Again, passion and possibility trump the battening down of hatches and the nailing down of definitions. The latter, this derived mode of thinking – which we have inherited and which has closed off our thinking from rich possibility – loses sight of "the magnificent, profound mythology of the Greeks" and has "reduced it to the physical trivialities of sun, lightning, storm and mist which originally gave rise to it" (30).

The Greeks did not invent the elements of philosophy and science, but they "tackled the job of so fulfilling, enhancing, elevating and purifying" these elements that they invented "the archetypes of philosophic thought" (31). Archetypes: primal images. This thinking is of the strictest necessity devoted to insight alone: There is no need to justify such activity. It is devoid of conventionality, requiring only open, creative minds. While real thinking, the hard work of doing philosophy, is accomplished in magnificent solitude, it is at the same time a "high-spirited conversation [*das hohe Geistergespräch*]" (32).

Nietzsche wants to tell the story of this high-spirited conversation, this profound dialogue of the mind on its highest level. My intention in this book is to remember Nietzsche and his journey in telling this story, and then to carry Nietzsche's intentions beyond even the steps that he took. Nietzsche here is a springboard that takes us further into this profound dialogue, in a way that he did not – and perhaps could not – do in 1871. We today have experiences and thinking that point to new possibilities for exploring the way things are, possibilities that were not yet available when Nietzsche attempted his history of ancient Greek philosophy.

As I have said earlier, it is sad that there is so little extant of what these early Greek thinkers thought and said and wrote – not one of their works has come to us in complete form. It is possible, if not likely, that any one of these early Greek thinkers – Parmenides, Heraclitus, Anaximander – was as major a philosopher for history as Plato and Aristotle were; but as it stands, we have complete texts of Plato and Aristotle, while from these early Greek thinkers we have ... only fragments.

But perhaps we can unearth inklings of how early philosophical thought was at one with engaged living. Can we find hints of how philosophical thought took place wholly within living human beings? Were there moments of pure insight gatherings of the dynamic interplay of the Apollonian and the Dionysian – rather than the separateness of many sides, for example, Thales's water, or Heraclitus's fire and becoming versus Parmenides's "static" being? Surely these early Greek thinkers were not the crude metaphysicians we have come to know them as. And they were not the idealists or realists that we have come to see them as, by our having read "our" idealism-realism *back into* their work, centuries after they did their thinking.

If we dwell for a moment in the dualistic thinking, which too many of us find most comfortable, we interpret Nietzsche's rendition of the Dionysian–Apollonian as something like this: wild orgiastic frenzy and then order; the promise of life and vitality overcome by the god of distance; excess–rapture overlaid with moderation. The night and the day, the dynamic and the static, fusion and individuation, boundlessness and lawful order, receptivity and lucidity, chaotic overflowing and subjugation.

But there is another approach, an approach Nietzsche hinted at in both *The Birth of Tragedy* and *Philosophy in the Tragic Age of the Greeks*. The early Greeks were trying to think through and to express a dynamic balance of the Apollonian and the Dionysian, a non-dualistic dance. Not an either-or but a both-and.

Can we find this interweaving of *mythos* and *logos* – of dark and light, of rapture and measure? Can we read the Greeks afresh, with an openness that lets emerge a vibrant interplay of duelling yet inseparable currents? The early Greeks had this balance and saw the dangers of imbalance. In the ensuing centuries, an imbalance emerged: towards the rational, towards order, towards social convention, towards the separation of all things from all other things – abandoning the dynamic unfolding that is essential to them.

If we can see how the *daimon*, or inner voice, was about anarchy and the natural order of things, then we retain the dance of balance of the two, of μύθος and λόγος, of the Dionysian and the Apollonian. The movement from within μύθος to λόγος was the great Greek impulse, but eventually we lost sight of the sustaining unmanifest dynamic μύθος within which the order-shaping λόγος emerged.

There is something ineffable in the μύθος, something a-poretic. There is a wonder at the invisible and the hidden. And mind, in its awareness, stays attuned to this, even as we, with our usual language and grammar, gather thinking into a kind of order, into the transparency of daylight.

Philosophical thinking began with the Greeks in a kind of non-dual interbeing of poles: the rational and the non-rational, the eternal and the mortal, knowledge and ignorance. This non-rational, mortal ignorance or not-knowing is a constitutive element of the world. It names ambiguity, indeterminacy – reason's limitation or boundary.

Hannah Arendt suggested that the ineffable names questions and issues that escape human knowledge but haunt human reason. Heidegger said that the spoken word is determined by the ineffable.

Philosophy in the Tragic Age of the Greeks was published posthumously. Nietzsche abandoned the work in favour of his *Untimely Meditations*. That wasn't unusual behaviour for him: having been trained as a philologist (i.e., a critical reader of classical Greek and Latin texts in their original languages), Nietzsche was nothing if not eclectic. His outlines and notes for *Philosophy in the Tragic Age of the Greeks* included chapters on more philosophers, including Socrates. This section of my book is no substitute for the original material. The first portions of both *The Birth of Tragedy* and *Philosophy in the*

Tragic Age of the Greeks contain many useful insights: ideas that help us understand the Greeks as well as, more importantly, notions of how to approach the Greeks, how to see and hear with eyes and ears uncluttered by inherited biases:

> Philosophy is distinguished from science by its selectivity and its discrimination of the unusual, the astonishing, the difficult and the divine ... Philosophical thinking ... is ever on the scent of those things which are most worth knowing, the great and the important ... The philosopher seeks to hear within himself the echoes of the world symphony and to re-project them in the form of concepts ... He grasps for [thinking] in order to get hold of his own enchantment, in order to perpetuate it. (43–4)

Note that Nietzsche did not carry his groundbreaking insight all the way. By the time he came to Parmenides, he saw only "ice": sheer unchanging-static being. We now can carry the baton of movement-change farther than Nietzsche did. Indeed, the thread of understanding the way things are as dynamic and interdependent runs through all of Greek philosophy.

h. The Oracle of Delphi

Why is the Oracle of Delphi so important for this book? For two reasons that are central to its narrative. First, this book offers the standard explanation in the modern era for how the Greeks became people of reason, how they set aside all things mystical and mythical so as to rely on reason alone. This interpretation of things was solidified when in the seventeenth century the then current understanding of *logos* as reason or rational account (French: *raison*; Latin: *ratio*) was read back into the Greek texts, all the way from Heraclitus to Aristotle. (We will show this in detail when we look carefully at the key Greek words in part 3.) Second, this book reflects the importance of taking into account the centrality of the intuitive and non-conceptual for the early Greek thinkers.

In *The Oracle: The Lost Secrets and Hidden Messages of Ancient Delphi*,[23]* William Broad explains how for the past several centuries we Westerners have "found" (i.e., traced) our current reliance on the rational "back there" in the Greeks. He tells how, during his undergraduate studies in ancient Greek philosophy and mythology – and especially in his graduate studies in the history of science – he saw the Greeks as "my heroes, these fierce rationalists" (4). Drawn to the story of the Oracle of Delphi and its various interpretations over the years, he learned that the Greeks "also revered the occult" (4).

Broad's book retrieves this "other" side of Greek thinking by telling the story of how an archaeologist working alongside a geologist (or a geologist working with an archaeologist) showed scientifically that the Oracle was factually and historically dealing with the hidden, that which is not revealed to rational discourse. In a sense Broad tells the story of "retrieving" a fuller and more originary and richer balance in the Greek world, by reincorporating the Oracle of Delphi. In other words, Broad brings the two threads together.

Once we have told this story in detail, we can then see how a similar "retrieval" is called for in reading the texts from Thales through Aristotle. Just as with the Oracle of Delphi, the dominant and now traditional reading of the Greek texts has been done through the lens of rational science, empirical and-or sense-based knowledge.

The dominant traditional way of understanding the Greeks over the past three hundred years. Here I want to call the tradition an "overreaching" – that is, going too far in one direction, and doing so by overlooking or passing over a prominent thread in Greek thinking and the Greek way of life. Broad shows the path to this overreach (I paraphrase here): Beginning with the modern science of Galileo and Newton and then flowing over into Descartes and *cogito ergo sum*, the bulk of today's tradition wants rationality and the science that goes with it to be everything. The striving here is for certainty, a certainty that can be achieved only by overlooking

---

* Numbers in parentheses in this section are from this book.

or eliminating those dimensions that are not open to certainty or black-and-white interpretation. The tradition wants clarity, even transparency. A kind of mathematical certainty. And to a large extent the tradition that dominates today has come to expect this in *all* realms, going beyond science, into economics, psychology, technology, and eventually even philosophy. Or philosophy first of all? Cracks are beginning to be seen, but we have a ways to go to find the vital balance or equilibrium that is called for.

Broad shows how this dedication to the rational and to thinking with certainty indeed existed for the Greeks. "But their genius had another side, one of occult impulses and procedures far removed from the world of reason" (13). They took into account what went beyond human conceptual understanding.

Here, too, is an intriguing comparison between the Apollonian and the Dionysian. Apollo stood for order and reason, for "the god's victory over the powers of darkness" (27). This is all okay. But when Broad gazed on the ruins of the temple, he found that the temple at Delphi, which we know was dedicated to the god Apollo, also had a side dedicated to Dionysos! That's right. The west side of the temple was clearly dedicated to Dionysos, a god who – according to many scholars of Greek thinking and of the Greek world – was the counterpole to Apollo, a Dionysian frenzy, on the west side of the temple facing the setting sun and the night (5).

Apollo "helped forge the bonds of civilization. Dionysus loosened them ... The two gods were one" (40–1).

What the Oracle of Delphi did, what she stood for, and why this was so important. The oracle's importance ranged from being a social catalyst, a kind of voice for enlightened society, to developing an inner sense of what is true and good. Her voice carried from Athens to the Greek colonies around the Mediterranean Sea to Egypt. Its influence spanned the sixth century BCE through to the death of Alexander in 323 BCE and that of Aristotle in 322 BCE. The Oracle of Delphi is a key component in Socrates's telling the story of his lifework in *The Apology*.

What did the Oracle do? There is a lot we do not know about the Oracle of Delphi, but a lot we do know. We know there was an underground cavern near the southwest corner of the temple at Delphi, dedicated to Apollo – and, as we now know, dedicated to Dionysos as well. We know that one or several women from the surrounding region were chosen to be the voice of the Oracle. We know that for almost one thousand years this oracle was considered by all levels of society to be an important source for decisions, for wisdom, for giving information. We know that the oracle's voice was heeded. Above all, we know that the oracle was revered for speaking from a dimension that was precisely not rational and not transparent – thus, from the occult or the hidden. As such, it mirrored the *mythos* to go along with the *logos*.

Listen to Heraclitus (Fragment B93):

> The sublime, whose place for intimating saying is at Delphi, neither only discloses nor only conceals, but rather hints [gives signs, portends, points to, intimates].[24]

Hinting rather than knowing for sure. Concretely, we know that the Oracle played a significant role for politicians and military leaders when they needed to make important decisions. It may have played a role for normal citizens making decisions about their lives. And we know that – following Heraclitus's words about "hinting" – the one asking a question of the Delphic Oracle was challenged to interpret in concrete and-or practical terms what the Oracle said in hints, that is, indirectly or in accord with the *mythos* that tells of what is hidden or nontransparent.

There are things that we do not know, as well as things that are not so important for this book. It does not matter here whether one calls the voice divine, that is, from the god or gods. It does not matter whether there was just one woman at a time or a "team" of women who served as the voice of the Oracle. What matters is that it was honoured as a voice from the *mythos* or the hidden and non-transparent.

Broad's book tells an exciting story. First, the story of the many authors of that time who took it as a given that the spokeswoman sitting in the cavern breathed in a gas that was in some sense hallucinatory. This opened her mind or awareness and allowed her access to a space otherwise hidden and unknowable. These authors included Plutarch, Euripides, Pausanias, and Herodotus.

Second, the story of the various scientific excavations at the temple – for example, those conducted by Victorian researchers, who had developed a sudden interest in the mystic and occult. By the end of the nineteenth century, interest had flared on both sides of the Atlantic. In Boston at the time the banker James Loeb took an interest in excavating Delphi and learning more. (It was Loeb who founded the Loeb Classical Library, to this day a trove of bilingual Greek–English texts.)

Broad tells of the race between the French and the Americans to arrange permission from the Greek government to excavate the site at Delphi. In the end, the French won. Broad tells us that their wish was to prove that gases emerging naturally from the fissures in the rock were the cause of the mind-altering that allowed the voice of the oracle to reach deeper into the hidden than a human mind can normally do. Yet their conclusion was just the opposite of what they wished.

They concluded that there was no fault through which gases from the earth could come. This led to several theories. One, that the priests used the women's voices of the Oracle to gain political power. Another, that the priests induced an altered state of consciousness by human-made means, and kept this fact hidden from the Greek society at the time. Yet another, that the priests simply stood behind the women sitting in the cavern and whispered the "answer" to the question that had been posed to the Oracle; the female voice simply repeated the answer whispered to them.

Yet, many people still wanted to believe in the mystic dimension of the Oracle.

Third, then, is the exciting story of how the balance was redressed by the geologist Jelle de Boer and the archaeologist John Hale. Together they were able to see things that the French archaeologists did not see or understand – or saw and chose not to report? – namely, that there was a strong and scientifically based likelihood that there were fissures in the rock that made up the walls of the underground chamber and that gases could have emerged from the fissures, gases that led to altered states of consciousness for those breathing that air.

One conclusion that can be drawn here is quite important to this book. That is, even though Western science has many successes to its name and even though it counts as among the major advancements of Western civilization, it needs to revere the limits of its reach. It did not do this over the past 150 years regarding the Oracle of Delphi. And the rationalism that underpinned the reductionist way of science did indeed overreach. And it was science itself, in the work of de Boer and Hale, that corrected the missteps of earlier scientific endeavours.

This tells us yet again how quickly the eyes can take on lenses not of their own making. Human cultural values and psychology can influence what we think of as "objective" and "value-free" science. I remind the reader of the epigram at the beginning of this book by the science fiction author Robert Heinlein: "All of us are prisoners of our early indoctrinations, for it is hard, very nearly impossible, to shake off one's earliest training." If we are open-minded and bold in our thinking action, we have a chance to redress this imbalance.

What Broad calls the "Mystic Clue." Broad remembers his question to philosophy that lingered long after his undergraduate days studying under David Hull at the University of Wisconsin. Broad: "He challenged a basic tenet of modern science – that the march of progress would reveal a seamless web of knowledge in which investigators linked one theory and discipline to another, mapping out networks of intellectual ties and ultimately reducing the complexities of life to simple laws of physics" (28). Science's construct that "the universe was, in essence, a giant machine that researchers were rapidly breaking down into increasingly small bits and explaining very nicely in the language of mathematics" (28) – this construct did not hold water for Hull.

Now, years later and after the work done by de Boer and Hale, Broad has come to see that there was "a furious international debate" that "pitted staunch defenders of expansive science against those who argued that – in its current state of development, and perhaps forever – it failed to explain some of the world's most important features and possibilities, including all manner of things psychic and spiritual" (229).

Broad:

> Most fundamentally, de Boer and his colleagues questioned the heavy metaphysical responsibilities that contemporary science had thrust onto the foundation of the scientific process known as reduction ... Reduction is the process by which scientists find points of investigative entry into natural systems that would otherwise get impenetrably complex. During reduction, scientists break nature into its constituent parts, moving down through the complex hierarchy of matter to focus on levels where interactions are more fundamental and mechanisms easier to understand ... Where reduction gets divisive is when its supporters claim that its realm *includes not just physics and the other sciences but enormous swaths of metaphysical territory as well*, as they have done intermittently in the course of the twentieth century and with increasing bravado in recent decades, to the point that *their assertions are now frequently seen as the conventional wisdom* ... Its champions claim that reduction's many successes show that *the nature of ultimate reality is completely physical*, that nothing exists beyond elemental forces and physical objects and their properties. By whatever name, it is an act of faith rooted in materialism. (230–1, italics mine)

The door that opened for de Boer and Hale went beyond the normal purview of science. They re-established scientifically the conclusion that there were fissures in the rock, that these fissures would have emitted gases, and that these gases would have been mind-altering:

> The finding suggested that science – the most powerful institution of our day, a discipline rooted in the illuminating power of human reason – sheds a very strong but narrow light that can leave many intriguing questions and possibilities lurking in the shadows, including ones often associated with mysticism. It [the finding] did not prove them, of course ... But, contrary to the claims of reductive naturalists, the finding did not rule them out either. (242)

> Science might try to plumb mysticism ... but never grasp its truths. (244)

Gathering thoughts. This story of the Oracle of Delphi is one of several examples for the key wish that I have, namely to let readers see and understand the richness of our own thinking heritage. I wish to show that, within the origins of Western thinking, there resides the dynamic that we need today, namely that dualism is not at the core of the "way things are" and that there are phenomena and dynamics that rationalism and metaphysics cannot get to or handle. We can, of course, learn from other traditions, for example, from some Asian ways of thinking and from Native American ways of thinking. But we carry something essential for us today in our own history as well, above all in early Greek thinking.

What is that dynamic? For some time now we have been living in a world that is out of balance. Too much rationalism. Too fierce with the rational. Too reductionist. Too calculating and calculative. Not science as such, but the science that overreaches. These areas of "too much" have killed the dynamic balance that is called for.

The dynamic balance was there in the beginning of Greek philosophy. For some reason the tradition took a gigantic step away from the balance and towards one-sided calculative reason. This "step away" is mirrored in the English translations of the Greek done in the seventeenth and eighteenth centuries. (In part 3 of this book I will delve into this issue by focusing on key Greek words and how they say "more than" our traditional and usual translations.)

Excessive rationalism is actually not reasonable; indeed, ironically, it is a bit in conflict with reason. Science itself must contend with this seeming paradox, namely that its own "rational" approach is perhaps not adequate for seeing, knowing and saying "truly" the way things are – or all of "the way things are" – and is itself not so "rational"! When science is reduced to the rationalistic and reductionist, it tends to come up with – end up with – a kind of materialism that is not worthy of science. And of course a kind of dualism. (Note: I am not talking about "science," but rather about a specific way of science.)

When we make distinctions, when we analyse, when we define the parts in great detail, we sometimes lose sight of the coherent and dynamic whole. Both are needed, so how do we get to this interactive, non-dual state of the world and of the mind?

This is about dynamic wholes, that is, wholes that are in movement and interactive interchange – a dynamic of non-dual at-oneness. This whole embraces both the analytic and the synthetic, both the detailed and specific and the broader and more flexible, that which shows itself in experience and cannot be reduced to the calculative-rational, or simply to substances as metaphysics sees them. The broader way of seeing is necessarily more vague, less calculable, more hidden and withdrawing from view – more encompassing but less directly graspable.

Using the words *mythos* and *logos*: Traditionally, the ordering part of *logos* names who we are, fits us better, is more central to us culturally – but it needs the balance of *mythos*. Now, the question is: Is *mythos* more essential than *logos*? It would seem not. Given the rounding that the two together provide, *mythos-logos* becomes more essential! And then the question is: How do we move from the limiting, ordering *logos* to a wider sense of *logos* as gathering, and then to *mythos* and the hidden-non-transparent, the revelation that is needed to find the balance?

Mythos is *logos*, *logos* is *mythos*, *mythos* and *logos* inseparable …

Our goal, then, is ambivalence – not in our usual sense of the word, "ambivalent" as in inconclusive, mixed, hesitant, clouded, fuzzy, vague, unclear in the face of an either-or. Rather, ambi-valent in an encompassing manner that opens up what the word really says: strong (*valere*, as in valiant, valour) in both (*ambi*) – that is, the both-and: both the scientific "logos" and the non-transparent hidden "mythos."

i. Word Images as Guideposts and Openings

This section shows some of the approaches I took in Greek philosophy class to open up minds to see possibilities for experiencing, thinking, and saying the way things are. The word images are meant as

a. naming the "one" side that we know all too well: rational, ordered, measurable, knowable in concepts

b. openings to the "other" side, that is, aspects that often got covered over in Western philosophy and metaphysics: the indirect, the concrete, lived experience, intuition

c. openings to experiencing and seeing the both-and of these differing dimensions of the way things are and of how we think and say them.

What makes this a whole is the non-dual intertwining dynamic of the various poles, retrieving connectedness, self-expanding. And in the midst of these openings, a couple of direct looks at the Greeks!

There are big changes happening "throughout the land." And I don't mean the changes brought on by computer chips, techno-logical innovation, or the internet; biogenetics or nanotechnology; Elon Musk of Tesla Motors and his vision of artificial intelligence that will overtake human thinking; what Al Gore calls "the rein-vention of life and death" in cloning; genomes, bioweapons, and bioplastics. No, the changes that I mean here are the changes in how we see the world and the way things are and in how we envi-sion ourselves and our place in the universe.

In the fullest way imaginable, human beings want *to think and to be* in the fullest way possible. But we have inherited a think-ing that is bipolar. The more philosophical terms for this condition are duality-dualism and dichotomy. This means that we think and act from one of the "poles" more than from the other. Up to now I have given "indications" of what the names are for these two poles. Here I want to offer an overview of how to understand this, without getting involved in precise definitions. Rather, what fol-lows is a gathering of word-images that can help us get a feel for what is at stake here: **Learning to move – in thinking and experi-encing – from the either-or (dualism) to the both-and (non-dual at-oneness)**.

Both poles are essential; and they need to be connected, intertwined, or gathered – in the "one-ing both-and" non-dual dynamic of radiant emptiness. In thinking and in lived expe-rience, how are they "together" in "the way things are" and in mind's understanding of this way? Because the one pole is dominant in our culture and paradigm, this book emphasizes the other pole, the one that has become hidden and that has withdrawn from our everyday discourse. But it does not bury the dominant pole.

Of course, there are many voices today hinting at the "hidden" pole. But there are also many voices that cannot hear from the other side and that "swear" the legitimacy of the dominant over against the "illegitimacy" of the hidden.

Above all it is not easy to know the two poles as an at-oneness within the non-dual dynamic of their inseparability.

A. Gifts from the Greeks. Before going directly to the two "poles," I present a list of things that Western thinking and culture has inherited from the Greeks. It is not comprehensive. It is not directly about duality-non-duality. It is not saying that only the Greeks brought it. It is not saying anything about the contributions to thinking and to life that we have from non-Western sources. It is simply offered as a possible opening onto the way things are as we focus on retrieving Greek thinking.

For thinking mind and the way things are
space
time
energy
motion or movement
emergence vs. substance
evolving dynamic
dynamic evolving
harmonic resonance
"mythic" hiddenness
truth

The elements:
water fire air earth
AND
aether-void-space

Experience-interpretation-language of the both-and
experience and interpretation, language and saying
mythos and logos language distinguishable but not separable
(versus seeing mythic and logical language as an either-or)

B. The two orders of Dionysian and Apollonian. We have already
seen how Nietzsche makes a big deal of these two orders. Dionysos
is the Greek god of dance, orgy, the intuitive, the less ordered.
Apollo is the Greek god of order, of less chaos, of light. Dionysos
is the Greek god of music, of tragedy, of the aesthetic. This list is a
kind of overviewing gathering.

Apollonian	*Dionysian*
sun god	god of grape and wine
daylight	night
light/radiance	sublime, the dark Hades
order	intoxication, frenzy/orgy/wild
order, moderation	spontaneity, fragmentation of order
submission to rule	sensual/earthy/natural
law and order	chaos
youth and beauty, Greek order	frenzy, orgy, wild
unity-imitation	ambi-valence, both-and
principle of individuation	ecstasy – being-outside-oneself, self-less orgy
measure and limit	no-boundary
sculpture	music, melody
surface images	depth
static	overflowing, dynamic

Nietzsche emphasizes the dramatic interplay of these two forces:

And as that happens, the Apollonian illusion reveals itself for what it
is, as the veil which, so long as the tragedy is going on, has covered the
essentially Dionysian effect. But this Dionysian effect is nonetheless so
powerful that at the end it drives the Apollonian drama itself into a
sphere where it begins to speak with Dionysian wisdom and where it

denies itself and its Apollonian visibility. So we could truly symbolize the complex relationship between the Apollonian and the Dionysian in tragedy with the fraternal bond between both divinities: Dionysos speaks the language of Apollo, but Apollo finally speaks the language of Dionysos, and with that the highest goal of tragedy and art in general is attained.[25]

C. How the words themselves reveal the two ways.

Words saying the static	*Words saying the dynamic*
substance metaphysics	relational world
static, changeless, invariant	fluid
rigid, stationary, fixed	pulsating process, diversifying, ambiguous
discontinuous, linear	cyclical, rhythmic movement
independent	interdependent, dynamic equilibrium
mechanical, inorganic	organic, relational, vital, kinetic
inert, inanimate or "dead"	alive, active, moving, breathing
isolated	free-flowing
passive	active with pregnant possibility
monads	interdependent confluences
Newtonian physics	quantum physics, relativity, complexity entanglement, oscillating/rhythmic movements, space as alive, spac-ing

Here the word-images say-show movement *from* a dualistic-rational science and metaphysics *to* a fresh opening:

- from atomism (problems are distinct and separate) **to seeing parts as enmeshed with one another (non-dual dynamic),**
- from mechanism (system viewed as mechanistic, like a machine – with precise adjustment and predictability, with perfect part-for-part replacement) **to seeing organic dynamic process,**
- from universalism (where one universal answer works for everything and is manageable from a centre of power) **to knowing awareness that is context- and place-specific, within conditions,**

- from static monism (one coherent explanation of reality, unified theory of everything) **to incomparable dimensions or interdependent conditions, even incoherent and unpredictable; gathered-connected but now as a dynamic oneness,**
- from objectivism (knowing with certainty, separate from values; we are apart from the reality we observe) **to the fact that what is is what it is with our participation, the observer is not separable from the observed.**

Dwelling in this movement, we can hear and become aware of the transformation that is calling us to the "beyond" from within it.

D. Two ways for human beings to live or to experience being alive.

* the way of connectedness and expansion, in which we experience ourselves and the world as non-separate relatedness or connectedness as such, dynamic, expansive, and expanding; in which we experience an inner spaciousness that expands beyond our skin and our "selves" and includes a deep experience of being one with all life, and
* the way of disconnectedness and contraction, in which we experience our "selves" and the world as separate, separated out, isolated, and in isolation, in which we experience an inner contracting, a self-contracting.

In this book I focus on early Greek thinking in order to retrieve connectedness, relatedness as such, and self-expanding – the non-dual dynamic of radiant emptiness, beyng-Ereignis – not because the other way is not useful or not part of the way things are, but in order to get a sense of how this refreshing, retrieving way feels more whole and how it might benefit us, our fellow humans, and earth.

E. Greek philosophy mirroring quantum physics and Buddhism. If I glean from all of the above word-images the words that crisply say what is at issue here – both in the traditional-inherited thinking (TI) and in the possibilities for thinking and learning to experience a non-dual dynamic (RR) that are in Greek philosophy's own words – I come up with something like the following schema:

Greek philosophy mirrors quantum physics and Buddhism as thinking moves

from the old TI "way things are"	*to a "new" RR "way things are"*
atoms = entities	relations, conditions
separate/discrete, independent	interdependent emergence, dynamic relational energy fields
static, objective substance	process-dynamic
external, structured reality of separate things	emptiness/space swollen with possibility, empty of form or structure

from the inherited TI knowing	*to a refreshing RR knowing*
objectification of "objective" by a positing ego-subjectivity or "objectifying subjectivity"	clarity of seeing using the hidden abilities of mind non-dualistic knowing awareness
conceptual, rational	non-conceptual experience/ awareness, full mindful participation, non-conceptually

j. Transition: An Invitation

At the end of my class in Greek philosophy at the University of Guelph in the fall of 2011, I put together the following thoughts, for my students to digest and eventually for them to be challenged, provoked, and stimulated by. I share them here as a kind of gathering of our journey of this book, as we start the refreshing, rethinking retrieval of the core words of the early Greek thinkers:

Dear Students,

As you move on from our work together, for the future and for your own development, I invite you to the following:

- Refrain from simply accepting the traditional and inherited interpretations.
- Pay attention to the Greek words, to your own non-conceptual experience and to critical thinking.
- Be aware that this is one interpretation, one that I feel strongly to be a beneficial way to do philosophy. At the same time check it out, don't simply believe it because your professor said so.
- Be aware that you may be confronted with alternative ways of engaging with Greek philosophy. Take on this responsibility.
- Bring respect to the subject matter and to your professors who might teach these matters in a different way.
- There is a natural and exciting tension in the two poles and the call for integrity as one grapples with living in both. Note that all humans have to deal with this tension.
- Think the possibility that our overall, inherited Western thinking is based on acceptance of static and independent things as "reality" – whereas today the cutting edge of thinking sees more the process and the not-simply-material way of the world. We see this in quantum physics (taking into account what is "beyond the physical"); in the very recently emerging research in neuroscience, having to do with a non-physiological dimension in the mind; in the Buddhist and Daoist ways of thinking-doing (saying and experiencing the space-like quality of mind as a dynamic of emptiness, i.e., no form, colour, texture); in the phenomena of chaos and uncertainty on all levels of today's world, from society to science to metaphysics. All becoming more and more part of the dialogue today.
- Education is an engagement:
    1. Attend to the text.
    2. See the open-endedness of the matter at hand.
    3. After a careful and critical thinking, draw your own conclusions, tested by your experience, open-mindedness, and critical appraisal.
- Be aware that traditional education normally does not quite know how to deal with this opening – pedagogical issues included. The how of teaching and learning is at stake here.

- Genuine learning will continue to do battle with institutional education – it is the nature of things, not good not bad.

My intention is to "quit" before you are ready for it. I leave things open-ended, on purpose. That is the way things are! Chew on it yourself. Note the difference between this and the fact that you need a grade for your transcript.

I am committed to creating an experience for you – whether or not I succeeded is for you to ponder.

Rather than seeking your assent, I want active participants in the dialogue, the question.

Above all enjoy the excitement, curiosity, and rich possibilities. The questions, not the answers!

Part Two

Enacting the Retrieval from "Here" to "There"

Part 2 goes deeper into the issue, using a language that is more philosophical. It situates my book within the overall project of Heidegger's thinking. As an entry into this project, it includes an extensive reading of David Bohm. Bohm is a physicist who broke out of the strictly scientific mode (or box) in a way that is useful for portraying the core issues. Bohm's language is helpful in going into the same realm of thinking that Heidegger's work does, while using a language that is more accessible to intelligent and fresh minds. Then part 2 delves into Heidegger's own thinking and way of saying it. Finally, it focuses on Daoism as an opening and measure for our work.

We are "here," some 2,500 years after the early Greek thinkers. So how do we get "there"? Our trajectory is not one that goes like an arrow, directly "there." The way is more like a circle, a circling around and back and forth. Thus, we will find ourselves moving "back" to where we were "before." Rather than a "tautology," this way belongs to the going itself – thus more than just "before." The going-back is the retrieval that is in front of us.

This work is an attempt to gather up, work through, and open up Heidegger's work on reading, hearing, and saying what early Greek thinking has to offer – traditionally called "pre-Socratic philosophy."[1] I do not use the term *pre-Socratic* to imply that, for example, Anaximander, Parmenides, and Heraclitus are significant only as their thinking comes "before" Socrates and is measured by Socrates and later Greek thinking. This idea is simply impossible and totally inappropriate, even as it has become unthinkingly common. Although impossible, it is put forth majestically as "reality" in no less a figure in the history of Western thought than Hegel, who calls Heraclitean *logos* a primitive and incomplete version of reason.

It is important that we not be tempted, following Hegel, to say that Anaximander, Parmenides, and Heraclitus are (simply?) part of a development that is somehow headed for "later Greek thinking" and beyond – that it needs later Western thinking for its completion, its own full enactment. This implies a chronological importance – namely, "under- or un-developed" thinking at that time versus a later time with more development. It implies that the work of the early Greek thinkers took place in the chronological unfolding of Western philosophy that we all too easily – and inappropriately – call a "progression."

It is possible if not likely that the "early Greek thinkers" are given less status because we only have fragments. Because they are only fragments, their importance is diminished. For example, when we look at the fragments of Heraclitus, we see a richness beyond measure. What if we had a few "books" by Heraclitus – as we have Socrates's dialogues by Plato and Aristotle's many books? Is it possible that we would give Heraclitus a status equal to Socrates, Plato, and Aristotle? I say that he deserves this status *without* any extant books.

We want to know, following Heidegger, how to refresh and rethink what the Greeks thought and said. Inspired by Heidegger's words and thinking on the Greek words, we come to know (a) the poverty of the traditional translations and interpretations and (b) the rich possibility that emerges when we see things anew and in a fresh way. This is retrieval.

Throughout his work Heidegger grapples again and again with the question of beyng/Ereignis as "itself" not a being, not a thing, even as it sustains and lets things/beings emerge. And throughout his life Heidegger grapples with the question of how to think the pivotal Greek words for saying-showing this no-thing, no-form dynamic in the richest way possible – and then how to retranslate those words.

Can we really ever go back like this, to recover and retrieve what the Greeks thought and said about the way things are? The answer to this question is in going the way. It cannot be handled in any other manner. Why? We have no tools to prejudge what is possible here. It cannot be done rationally or logically. When we read and hear what the Greek words say, it is precisely that which is not logical that emerges for our thinking. We keep our eyes, ears, and heart open to this possibility and necessity, as we traverse the terrain of this book.

In the foreword to *Vorträge und Aufsätze* (GA 7:1) Heidegger writes:

> ... a realm must be prepared for what, from time immemorial, is thinkable or to be thought but is still unthought. From within this free play of space what is unthought lays claim on thinking.*[2]
>
> Whereas the current and familiar representational thinking, technical in the broadest sense, still wants to advance [to make progress] and takes everything by storm, now and then guiding ways free up a view to an incomparable massif [*ein einziges Ge-birg*].[3]

We cannot just move on, leaving "it" behind. When opening up to Greek thinking, we do not concoct or order the world. We do not control it. Such would *not* be a new and refreshing retrieval. Rather, we are engaged in a reading, hearing, and thinking that *lets emerge*, where what the Greeks heard and thought and said emerges from what remains hidden in Greek thinking, naturally and perhaps necessarily.

Part of this "unthought" belongs to our age, in which we focus on things and concepts or what can be seen and measured. We have a hard time finding and then opening up any region that is precisely not a thing, is not something, is no-thing. In order to enter such a site, we need to "return" to an "other beginning," one that is not represented in what we have inherited, which Heidegger calls the "first beginning."

---

* Ἀλήθεια

Seen from our vantage point, the first beginning of what Western philosophy became is a dualistic metaphysics. (In a few pages I will explain what this means.) So the move to the "other beginning" is not just measured from our vantage point but is also and powerfully part of the "unthought as such," namely the hidden-withdrawing from the certainty of conceptualizing thinking. This opens and lets emerge what we are going for, the no-form non-dual dynamic at the heart of the "other beginning."

This other beginning is not behind us but in front of us. We might say that it is "timeless" in the sense that it is outside time as we usually think it. Why is this "other beginning" – which is at work beyond and other than what we know – so hard for us to approach? And to hear? Because we are "entangled" within what we have inherited,

> insofar as, through what followed it [the beginning], we continue to be roofed over and covered up [locked in]. For this reason our view remains constrained and spellbound in the bounds of the traditional question: What is a being? (GA 65:185–6),

so that we are not able to see, let alone leap into, the region of the non-dual dynamic of no-thing radiant emptiness, what Heidegger's question of beyng calls for. (See the Interlude at the front of this book.) We must learn how to make this leap.

A glimpse ahead, setting the stage: ἀλήθεια/*aletheia*. As mentioned earlier, this word has been mistranslated for a long time now as "truth" or as correctness. I will go into much more detail in part 3. But, as a first nudge, what does the word *say?* For now I want to focus on the dynamic tension within the word ἀ-λήθεια – the non-dual togetherness of the *alpha-privativum* and the hidden (λήθη). Remembering our first glimpse of the Greek word, I want to hone in on the dynamic tension within the word as it says-shows **emerging (ἀ-) from out of the hidden (λήθη)**, where the key dynamic is ongoing unfolding, emerging, unhiding – *as such!* In this dynamic there is no "resolution" or "end result" of the movement of unfolding, unconcealing. No resting in *a being* or a concept. We must heed this dynamic. What "language" do we need for this?

First, we have to **situate our work here within the overall project of Heidegger's thinking,** what he called the "meaning of being" and then the "question of being" and then the "truth of being" – and in *Beiträge* "being as beyng as Ereignis." Second, we have to **understand why Heidegger turns to the Greeks.**

During his long pursuit of the question of being, Heidegger used a number of names to say "being" that is formless, no-thing, and non-dual. His insight was that we have inherited a thinking that deals only with beings, things, entities, substances – and not with that within which things manifest themselves, that which is no-thing, even as it is at work and as we can experience it. Along the way Heidegger realized that access to this region or dynamic of no-thing is not possible with concepts or conceptual logic/language. Whatever being "does," whatever the dynamic of being "is," whatever these other words for "being" say, it is always saying what is no-thing, even as it is at work and does something. We are called to open up, in knowing awareness, to this no-thing and no-form non-dual dynamic of radiant emptiness.

It "is" not, but it works and is in play. There is unfolding or emerging, even as there is no thing (no-thing) and "it" does not exist in time or place. It "is" nowhere and in no time. Dynamic unfolding, emergent emergence-withdrawal, granting-refusal, unconcealing-sheltering concealing, along with *Seyn* and *Ereignis* – all say a kind of radiant emptiness that is a dynamic of no-thing in its freeing and opening, a no-thing boundless potential, or: a non-dual dynamic of radiant emptiness.

How can we learn to hear and to say this dynamic of no-thing radiant emptiness, which is beyond our conceptual thought process? The self-revealing and self-sheltering as one? Always hiding within revealing and revealing within hiding? How can we find a way of saying what is no-thing and beyond concepts?

Let me repeat: Heidegger's many words for the question of being all intend to say what is no-thing whatsoever but lets emerge, what is no-thing whatsoever even as it is at work, what is no-thing whatsoever even as we can experience it. The dynamic that is named with these words is non-dual, radiates out, and can be said as "emptiness."

The dynamic of emptiness is a key to Heidegger's central and life-long question – and to why he turned to the Greeks, to find there the dynamic (movement) of coming together (non-dual), which radiates out from emptiness (no-thing, no form) and which we can learn to experience. Rich, freeing, and opening emptiness is the key to this work of thinking and the thread that guides and holds it together. There is no-thing "in" emptiness (being or beyng or Ereignis – all mirrored as emptiness). All phenomena unfold within the dynamic emptiness, which is primordially no-thing, does not exist as any "thing." It names a *dynamic*, not a thing or a concept.

We are not conditioned for seeing-saying-thinking this dynamic of no-thing, no-where, and no-time emptiness. But it is where Heidegger's thinking takes us.

Emptiness here is not negative or nihilistic. On the contrary, when we move within non-conceptual language and showing, we come to the richness of possibility that is said in this word. Emptiness or the empty is freeing, opening, full, and rich in possibility.

Using the word *emptiness* and *the empty* to say the meaning of being is at the crux of the section "Time-space as Ab-ground" ("*Der Zeit-Raum als der Ab-grund*"), which I call the crux of Heidegger's major work, *Beiträge zur Philosophie (Vom Ereignis)*. Here Heidegger shows what the dynamic of no-thing emptiness and "the empty" reveals in the search for the "meaning of being." He writes:

> *Ereignis*, [the word that Heidegger uses here to address the question of "being" aka beyng] attunes and sets the pace for the deep swaying of truth. The open of the clearing or lighting-up of self-sheltering is thus originarily not a mere emptiness of being unoccupied but is the attuned and attuning empty of the ab-ground [no-thing and no-form, but rich in possibility].
>
> The "empty" is also not merely the dissatisfaction or annoyance when an expecting and a wishing is not fulfilled. It [the empty] *is* only as Da-*sein*, i.e., as [the dynamic of] being reserved [restraint, *Verhalten-heit*], the holding back in the face of the staying away or self-withholding [*Sichversagung*], by which time-space grounds itself as the flashpoint [Dasein as *Augenblickstätte*] of decision.

The "empty" is likewise and actually the fullness of what is not yet decided and remains to be decided, [namely] what has the character of ab-ground [staying-away of ground], pointing to [dynamic, *weisend*] the ground, the truth of being.

The "empty" is the suffused distress [*die Not*] of the abandonment of being, but this [as] already shifted into the open and, with that, related to the uniqueness of beyng and its inexhaustibility.

The "empty," not as what comes with a lack and its distress, but rather the distress of being-reserved, which in itself is the throwing open that is a breaking open and starting of something – the grounding-attuning of the originary belonging-together. (GA 65:381–2)

- *Here we note the no-thing dynamic aspect of emptiness: the dynamic deep swaying; not a "mere emptiness of being unoccupied, but the attuned and attuning empty," that is, a dynamic attuning; "the fullness of what is not yet decided and remains to be decided," an active dynamic "pointing to [***weisend***] the ground, the truth of being"; the "empty" as "shifted into the open," with its inexhaustibility – opening as freeing dynamic; a distress that "as such is the throwing open that is a breaking open and starting of something" – the empty as no-thing dynamic that "starts."* **These words mirror and open up what David Bohm calls the "quantum potential" in quantum physics.**
- *What is at stake for Heidegger is mirrored in this long quotation: not an either-or but a both-and. Neither logic nor concepts can grasp this. At one and the same moment the dynamic here is:*
  - *the abandonment of being in metaphysics and*
  - *the distress in the no-way-out of this abandonment,*
  - *the unsettledness in what is not yet decided ...*
  - *all of which is **already shifted** – as **emptiness** – into the open or opening to the uniqueness of beyng as inexhaustible.*

We can distinguish these aspects of the dynamic, but they are intrinsically inseparable. It is as if we stand in the middle of the distress and the resolving of the distress at the same time. Love can be so powerful that it is painful. Or as Juliet says to Romeo: Parting is such sweet sorrow.

The many words for "being" that Heidegger used on his life-time quest – the question of being, the meaning of being, the truth of being, beyng, Ereignis, beyng as Ereignis, then ἀλήθεια, ἄπειρον, φύσις, λόγος, ἐόν ἔμμεναι, among other Greek words – are all attempts to say what is no-thing whatsoever but lets emerge, what is no-thing whatsoever even as it is at work, what is no-thing whatsoever even as we can experience it.

Now we turn to the second question: **What made Heidegger turn to the Greeks?** His ongoing search for the no-thing dynamic of "being" as a dynamic that is at work in the way things are, a dynamic that is no-thing whatsoever, took him to Greek thinking, including Aristotle but especially early Greek thinking and the possibility that therein was a lighting up of what his lifelong search wanted to find. This possibility was hidden from Western philosophy as it moved away from these early Greek thinkers, leaving behind and abandoning this organic, dynamic wholeness, forgetting the non-dual dynamic of radiant emptiness – aka the question of no-thing and no-form beyng-Ereignis. Thus, the call for retrieving what had been said there.

Heidegger turned to Greek thinking very early in his quest. The motivation for this turn was to retrieve Greek words and thinking, that is, to hear what the Greek words say, behind and beyond our inherited and "traditional" ways of thinking Greek philosophy. And he discovered that these key Greek words (a) had been mis-translated into Western languages and (b) had been camouflaged via the filters of Christianity and of Western rationalism.

Recall that as early as the 1920s Heidegger knew that the exist-ing words in Western philosophy were unable to say what he was pursuing by the question of being. He found the inherited Western language too limited, both in syntax and in grammar. Thus, even as he turned – quite early and then often – to the Greeks, he was mindful of what the Asian philosophers who came to Freiburg to study with him – the Chinese Daoists and the Japanese Bud-dhists – could offer in this pursuit. Above all, Heidegger used their understanding of Buddhism and Daoism as ways to **find a language** to say what he was after. Specifically, the Chinese phi-losophers brought an understanding of Daoist words and ways, while the Japanese philosophers brought the understanding of Buddhist words and ways.

a. Markers to Help along the Way

Here is an initial, pithy overview of what is at stake, using words that can perhaps "say" it:

1. Traditional, inherited (TI) words that reveal the way things are, what we know so well in our world:
   - dualistic,
   - conceptual, outside direct experience,
   - static substance, static beings, things
   - everything is a being.
2. Refreshing, retrieving (RR) words that reveal the way things are, what invites us to a new and richer possibility for living and knowing the world:
   - non-dual,
   - non-conceptual, in direct experience,
   - dynamic and changing, "things" as conditions
   - revealing no-thing emptiness.

Keep these words in mind as we move *from* "here" where we are (1) *to* what calls to us in our refreshing retrieving of Greek thinking (2). *From* dualistic, conceptual, static substance, static beings ... where everything is a being. *To* the non-dual, non-conceptual, dynamic and changing ... revealing no-thing emptiness that goes beyond things and lets things/phenomena be revealed within the withdrawal that is at its core. These two ways are distinguishable in language but inseparable in their own oneness or one-ing dynamic.

b. Using David Bohm to Retell the Story of This Book: The Road from Here to There and from There to Here

Imagine that you, the reader, are sitting with me on a bench in a grove of large, old trees in a park in Vienna, Austria. A place of respite, the energy of a silent forest, away from crowds, virtually alone. Sitting on this bench, I will try to describe again the story behind this book. (This retelling is less autobiographical than the first telling, in the Preamble.)

"Here" means where we find ourselves, at this point on the road from the Greeks, with today's version of how we see the world. What we have inherited and has become traditional. "There" means the beginning in its two senses: the historical beginning with the early Greeks *and* the timeless beginning in its dynamic sense of "starting," getting things started. Heidegger calls this "here" the first beginning. Retrieving *from "there"* means discovering what got lost on the way that moved *away from* the "starting" of Western philosophy. At one point along the road "from" the Greeks, the road taken abandoned another road, a road not taken. Heidegger calls this the other beginning. Once we have found and unfolded this other beginning "there," we are automatically "here" again. Finding that this step is already "here," since this other beginning – the road not taken, abandoned, hidden, and lost – is nowhere and in no time, in no specific place or time, also known as timeless and non-localizable.

The way in which I will retell the story of this book here is to present four pathways along which to catch a glimpse of (a) the traditional, inherited (TI) ways (here) and (b) the refreshing, retrieving (RR) ways (there). The latter is what we in this work seek to discover in Greek thinking – lost and hidden, waiting to be unfolded. (In this section I will use a different language, a different set of word-images.)

Starting from the "here" of traditional, dominant ways of framing the issue – and seeing

1. **the world as fragmentary and**
2. **the world as mechanistic –**
   we move "there," to the way
3. **beyond the world as static and independent substances and**
4. **thinking beyond metaphysics.**

As part of a different language, I will use words from the physicist David Bohm to mirror both the "here" from where we are and the "there" that we want to retrieve. As far as I can tell, more than any other physicist-scientist, Bohm is exploring, in his own way, the same region as Heidegger the philosopher. Bohm is true to the thinking that he experienced, in the same way that Heidegger is true to the thinking that he experienced. I choose this mirror (Bohm's words from quantum physics) to provide a different and maybe useful way to get to the same dynamic that we find in Daoist and Buddhist views and that Heidegger found in early Greek thinkers. I deem it useful to hear Bohm's words, which are different from Heidegger's, as a helpful way to point to the non-dual dynamic of radiant emptiness.

It is possible that David Bohm's work is as original and astounding as Albert Einstein's.[4] But he is much less known, because of several controversies:

1. He had brief ties with suspected communists and was called before Joseph McCarthy's House Un-American Activities Committee in 1950, where he refused to speak against his colleagues, including his former teacher, J. Robert Oppenheimer. Although acquitted in 1951, his colleagues did not support him, encouraging him to leave the country. He went first to Brazil and then to Israel, ending up in England. This journey resulted in a kind of obscurity.
2. His colleagues marginalized him for challenging the standard interpretation of quantum theory. I believe that the "threat" he posed to the dominant view of quantum physics played a role in his expatriation.
3. His interest in the phenomenology of consciousness – which was important for him to understand the "wholeness" that he saw at the core of things – put off many of his colleagues, who viewed it as not scientific enough.
4. All in all, his "penchant for questioning scientific and social orthodoxy was the natural expression of a rare and maverick intelligence."[5] Perhaps too rare and too maverick for some important people in the field? His subsequent marginalization contributed to his not becoming more widely known.

Bohm describes the way things are in the world view that dominates in Western philosophy and science as static, fragmentary, "inherently divided, disconnected, and 'broken up' into yet smaller constituent parts,"[6] mechanistic, "a set of separately existent, indivisible and unchangeable 'elementary particles.'"[7] Bohm sees this world view as *secondary*. The world view that is primary and fundamental is "a process of movement, continuous unfolding and enfolding from a seamless whole."[8] Bohm describes it as unending-flowing movement, undivided-unbroken wholeness.

We have seen this refreshing way in Eastern thinking. Bohm sees it there as well, noting that in the East this way of thinking never fell out of sight. We have seen it in contemporary physics, especially in quantum physics. Bohm also sees it there, noting that the principal figures in the unfolding of this "new physics" were unable to take their thinking as far as he knew it needed to go. Finally, Bohm also sees how the Greeks had some grasp of the undivided dynamic wholeness, although he did not go into this matter in detail.

First foray. Viewing the world as fragmentary. "Here" everything – things as we know them, concepts, beings, soul-mind, self-ego, transcendent being – is experienced dualistically as fragmentary. Whatever things are, they are taken as separate parts, either as they are in the world or as abstracted into concepts. Things are substances, often understood as material or measurable in the way that matter is measurable. And they are understood as static.

Things are seen as independent and static. The word *substance* comes from the Latin *sub-tare*: to stand firm. As things stand firm in their independence, the world is dualistic. And this dualism gets hardened into concepts. Standing-firm or static, things lose the dynamic that is at the core of their make-up.

We have concepts for things, and we are confident that the concepts tell everything that there is to know. We think that by measuring and conceptualizing things we have grasped them fully. But we have experiences that are not conceptualizable. Experiences that do not lend themselves to a full transparency of concepts. Love, grief, ecstasy, friendship, dying. These are non-dual and always dynamic. They are deeper than any conceivable description. We are aware of these, even as they are not conceivable or determinable. In lived experience they are one dynamic whole. In our concepts they become fragmentary.

We think and experience things as fragmentary and static rather than as a non-dual dynamic of wholeness. We experience the world as separate organisms or items. We have fragmented families, fragmented cities, fragmented states of matter. And fragmentary thought.

And our history of seeing the world is mirrored in how we have read and interpreted Greek philosophy, in what Heidegger calls the first beginning. (What I have just written in the above paragraphs describes this beginning.)

Is it possible that there is another thinking happening in the texts of Greek philosophy? Heidegger says Yes, and we are trying to discover and understand this new, rich possibility in early Greek thinking. Is it possible that the world that is measurable and measured, determinable and intellectually conceivable, is only one part of the whole of thinking and experience? And that the Greek thinkers were wise enough to see and know that this part is encompassed and sustained within a dynamic that is deeper and holistic and non-dual? And immeasurable? Let us pursue this possibility.

On the way "there" we ordinarily start by observing that, although the Greeks may have "said" this non-dual dynamic, it was hidden from them and unknown to them. And we usually mean by this that the Greeks did not experience this – thus it was "unknown" in this way. But, given that the very dynamic we are wanting to discover is itself hidden and non-conceptual, I want to explore the possibility that the Greeks indeed "knew" this dimension (this other beginning) as well, the one that we "here" usually and traditionally do not know and experience. That, within the non-dual dynamic of the other beginning, the Greeks experienced both beginnings in a one dynamic whole, an organic wholeness.

Heidegger's search for beyng/Ereignis as not beings/things/entities and not sayable in conceptual language – what I call the non-dual dynamic of radiant emptiness – led him "back" to the Greeks, to discover this other beginning, that is, what got lost in the first beginning. And to show that the Greeks had words for this non-dual dynamic of no-thing whatsoever, as it is at work and as we can experience it, this is the **retrieval** we are making.

Can we read Heidegger to reveal that this no-thing dynamic (which works and which we can experience) is inherently part of Greek thinking and saying? And can we retrieve this from Greek thinking? This unthought in Greek philosophy? Known and experienced and said, but hidden and unthought? Not merely hidden to and unthought by them, but – knowing and experiencing the very non-dual no-thing dynamic as itself immeasurable, indeterminable – hidden and withdrawn in its core aspect? This is where we are going.

Now, to quote Bohm:

> One might in fact go so far as to say that in the present state of society, and in the present general mode of teaching science, which is a manifestation of this state of society, a kind of prejudice in favour of a **fragmentary self-world view** [bold print by me] is fostered and transmitted (to some extent explicitly and consciously but mainly in an implicit and unconscious manner).[9]

- *The fragmentary world view (named by Heidegger the "first beginning") dominates today and is "prejudiced" consciously, but mainly implicitly and unconsciously.*

> Some might say: "Fragmentation of cities, religions, political systems, conflict in the form of wars, general violence, fratricide, etc., are the reality. Wholeness is only an ideal, toward which we should perhaps strive." But this is not what is being said here. Rather, what should be said is that wholeness is what is real, and that fragmentation is the response of this whole to human action, guided by illusory perception, which is shaped by fragmentary thought.[10]

- *Dynamic wholeness is at the core of the way things are.*
- *Fragmentation is guided by an illusory perception or concept, itself shaped by fragmentary thought.*
- *The wholeness that is said in "the non-dual dynamic of radiant emptiness" is "real" and not the other way around, as if what is fragmented, dualistic, and measurable is "reality."*

The notion of a separate organism is clearly an abstraction, as is also its boundary. Underlying all this is unbroken wholeness, even though our civilization has developed in such a way as to strongly emphasize the separation into parts.[11]

- *Organism as separate is an abstraction.*
- *Underlying everything is unbroken wholeness.*

However, it has been found that even the "elementary particles" can be created, annihilated, and transformed, and this indicates that not even these can be ultimate substances but, rather, that they too are relatively constant forms, [which are] abstracted from some deeper level of movement.[12]

- *Even elementary particles are not "ultimate substances," for they can be "created, annihilated, and transformed."*
- *They are "relatively" constant forms … **abstracted** from a deeper movement, which is without form and itself not a thing.*

Second foray. Viewing the world as mechanistic. Let's start with Descartes's famous "machine metaphor." It is usually called a metaphor, but in its outreach it is taken literally. It is also called a postulate or a fact. Regardless of which of the three descriptors you use in describing Descartes's "machine," the outcome is the same:

1. For Descartes there are three substances: God, thinking beings (*res cogitans*) – also called immaterial mind – and extended matter (*res extensa*). Things extended in space are measurable, physical, and quantifiable things.
2. Extended or measurable things are made up of parts, like a machine.
3. Importantly, these things include the human body, which then gets taken as a machine.

Here are two quotations from Descartes. Please notice how the human body is taken to be an organism and a machine.

I should like you to consider that these functions [e.g., passion, memory, and imagination, from the text preceding this sentence] follow from the mere arrangement of the *machine's organs* [italics mine] every bit as naturally as the movements of a clock or other automaton follow from the arrangement of its counter-weights and wheels.[13]

Now a very large number of the motions occurring inside us do not depend in any way on the mind. These include heartbeat, digestion, nutrition, respiration when we are asleep, and also such waking actions as walking, singing, and the like, when these occur without the mind attending to them. When people take a fall, and stick out their hands so as to protect their head, it is not reason that instructs them to do this; it is simply that the sight of the impending fall reaches the brain and sends the animal spirits into the nerves in the manner necessary to produce this movement even without any mental volition, *just as it would be produced in a machine* [italics mine].[14]

Over the subsequent two centuries, with the rise of and dominance by empirical science – which studies measurable things/ beings – this "machine metaphor" became a "reality" and central and essential for the conception of everything physical, that is, all organisms, including the human organism. If the machine is a bunch of parts that work together to "do something," and if all things physical, including the human organism, are viewed as machines, then the mechanistic world view reduces everything in the world to what is quantifiable, that is, measurable.

When we say that the world we live in is a *mechanistic world,* what does this mean? That the enormous diversity of things found in the world – in experience and in science – gets reduced completely and absolutely and unconditionally to simply the effects of a defined and limited set of laws ... a fixed and limited mathematical scheme ... with exhaustive formulations ... quantitative changes ... and a certain predictability. Things as or in these machines can be fully understood through the application of systematic, "objective" research methods.

I call this "the mechanistic assumption." We can notice the first move away from this assumption when we note how at one point in everyday discourse the word *mechanistic* took on a negative meaning. "If you describe a view or explanation of something as **mechanistic**, you are criticizing it because it describes a natural or social process as if it were a machine ... a mechanistic view of things that ignores the emotional realities in people's lives."[15]

The wrongness of the mechanistic world view is obvious when we focus on the living organism. Organisms are by definition very different from complex machines. The living world is about processes and interdependent dynamics. So, when biology reduces the organism to a machine and when it understands the living cell as an intricate part of a machine, then the living cell is reduced to the quantifiable. How often did or does molecular biology eliminate the dynamic and self-organizing, the fluid and non-quantifiable process of a living organism? The phenomenon of life itself is not thus reducible.

What is left out? Qualitative changes as well as living processes are not possible within the mechanistic paradigm. An unlimited number of possible qualities exist interdependently in the organism. An organic dynamic wholeness holds a richness that cannot be exhausted within the mechanistic framework. When it comes to the human being and his or her body as a machine, the whole of *experience* is left out.

Now, to quote Bohm:

The theory of relativity was the first significant indication in physics of the need to question the mechanistic order ... [when] it implied that no coherent concept of an independently existent particle is possible, neither one in which the particle would be an extended body, nor one in which it would be a dimensionless point. Thus, a basic assumption underlying the generally accepted form of mechanism in physics has been shown to be untenable.[16]

[T]he non-local, non-causal nature of the [interdependent] relationships of elements distant from one another evidently violates the requirements of separateness and independence of fundamental constituents that is basic to any mechanistic approach.[17]

To begin with undivided wholeness means, however, that we must drop the mechanistic order.[18]

- *from dualism to the non-dual: the particle is not an extended body but is interdependent, within the "non-local, non-causal nature of the relationships of elements,"*
- *from abstract, conceptual to the non-conceptual in experience: "no coherent concept of an independently existent particle possible,"*
- *from static to dynamic: not a dimensionless point but an array of dynamic interdependent conditions,*
- *from metaphysical beings to the no-thing, no-form emptiness: the "non-local ... nature of the relationships," the dynamic of "undivided wholeness."*

Third foray. Viewing the world beyond static and independent substances. Here I turn to **the way things are as a dynamic of interdependent conditions**, rather than starting with the dominant paradigm of static and independent substances.

Naturalist and mountaineer John Muir writes:

when we try to pick out anything by itself, we find it hitched to everything else in the universe.[19]

Biologist Lynn Margulis writes:

The fact that we are connected through space and time shows that life is a unitary phenomenon, no matter how we express that fact. We are not one living organism, but we constitute a single ecosystem with many differentiated parts. I don't see this as a contradiction, because parts and wholes are nested in one another.[20]

Physicist David Bohm writes:

Throughout this book the central underlying theme has been the unbroken wholeness of the totality of existence as an undivided flowing movement without borders.[21]

What the words of these three writers say about a non-dual, dynamic, organic whole – boundless, without borders – were and still are on the margins of our inherited, dominant world view. Awareness of this dynamic is growing and may one day be on the front pages. Perhaps our work in retrieving this kind of thinking in Greek texts will aid this development …

Let us offer some examples of moving beyond static and independent substances to interdependence and wholeness.

1. Let's say, I have high blood pressure and take medication for it. But it causes headaches, so I take medication for it. And that disturbs my sleep, so I take a sleeping pill. I am living in a world of duality. The three pills are "defined" independently of one another. It is like throwing three different and independent things together, even though no one studied the possible results of their being taken together. Each pill is for a separate condition, independent of the other two. But my physical condition is interdependent. Thus, the three pills show a dualism thrown at a non-dual, interdependent system, my body, "denying" interdependent conditions.

2. When I was ten years old, my mother was recovering from surgery, so I did most of the cooking for the family. From her rocking chair she would guide me as I made dinner after dinner. One day I asked her if I could bake an angel food cake. She said, Yes, of course! So I went about mixing the batter. The recipe called for a half-teaspoon of cream of tartar (for those readers who do not know, cream of tartar is the agent that keeps the egg whites from collapsing). Alas, I could not find cream of tartar in the cupboard. Since my mother was dozing, I decided that such a small amount could not make a difference, so I went ahead without it.

   When the cake came out of the oven, it was flat, totally flat – and black! My mother looked at it and asked what happened. I told her everything, including that I had not put any cream of tartar in. (She just laughed and laughed!) As John Muir says, when we try to pick out anything by itself, we find it hitched to everything else. The cake was a bunch of interconnections, not a group of independent and isolated items.

3. In 1850 the Mississippi River flowed without obstruction. Before that year, there had been no changes to the river that were

made by humans. But from 1881 to 1912 the US Army Corps of Engineers built a series of six dams, to improve transportation on the river as well as to limit or prevent flooding. These were called the Headwaters Dams, since they were built from the headwaters of the Mississippi River to the Twin Cities. The next major development was in the 1930s, when the Nine Foot Channel project was completed. This involved a series of locks and dams south of the Twin Cities to Iowa. Besides controlling or mitigating floods, this marked the start of creating a nine-foot deep channel for barges on the river, which is maintained to this day.

We can begin by saying that the river has been significantly engineered for going on 150 years. We can also list several "benefits":[22] improved navigation, flood control and mitigation, hydroelectric power, recreation, and stabilization of the river channel itself. But let us look more closely. In order to take possession of the land that would become reservoirs, the government had to displace the Ojibwe people. This went against legally binding treaties. The Ojibwe eventually settled and accepted money for moving to the White Earth Reservation in northwestern Minnesota – far from the banks of the Mississippi, which had been their home for generations, if not centuries. Without saying whether that change was good or bad, let us just say that in historical terms it was part of a bigger interconnected system, one that went beyond the "benefits" listed above. It is also a first indication that there is no such thing as one independent and separable dimension to this whole project. Nothing! Every aspect of the river is intertwined, both before being humanly engineered and after.

What all happened to the Mississippi when we ignored its natural interdependency as well as the interdependent conditions?

- It brought an end to the freely changing river channels, straightening those channels and thereby reducing the river's free-flowing dynamic.
- It changed the way the sediment in the river was handled.

- It transformed the river's water quality and ecology.
- It disconnected the river channel from the floodplain, thus "engineering" it away from its natural dynamic.
- It altered the floodplain. Before the river was engineered, the floodplain received natural fertilizer from the flood waters. Afterwards, in the engineered system, the nutrient-rich sedimentation no longer provided the floodplain with that fertilizer. This led to the use of chemical, synthetic fertilizers and an increased nitrogen load, which drained from the floodplain and entered the river, which then flowed down to the Gulf of Mexico, creating a "dead zone"[23] in the gulf, which by 2017 had reached a record extent of almost 9,000 square miles. The dams changed the biotic and abiotic processes in the river. And the fishing industry suffered from the dead zone.

And then there is cotton. As long as the river flowed naturally – before 1881 – regular flooding made much of the floodplain of the lower Mississippi watershed unusable for growing cotton. After the levees were built, these lands were available and quite suitable for growing cotton. Levees reduce the natural flow. But this increases the use of the floodplain – or what *was* the floodplain – for cotton. Expanded cotton growing led to boll weevil infestation, which led to increased use of insecticides. And the residue from the insecticides flowed into ...

... the Mississippi River, which had once been a natural, complex, interdependent organic and physical ecosystem. Now it is a complex, humanly engineered system. Either way – before or after engineering – the life of the river involves myriad conditions coming together. And they are inseparably interconnected (non-dual) and ever-moving and changing (dynamic). (How many of the people involved, then and now, are aware of the interdependent and intertwining complexity of this?)

When the conditions that make up a thing are interrupted (the German word for "conditions" is Be-*ding*-*ungen*, i.e., the conditions that make up a *Ding*), does the thing still exist? Is the

Mississippi River still a river? This is part of what Heidegger is saying when he tells us to let the technical object be, while being open to the deeper conditions that make a thing a thing.

4. In the opening scene of William Faulkner's *As I Lay Dying*, Addie Brunden's oldest son, Cash, a good carpenter, is building her coffin – "under the window" where Addie lies dying. She is "watching Cash yonder" as he works. A coffin handcrafted specifically for the dying person, by someone in deep connection with her, with wood from the family's own forest. A bevvy of interdependent conditions.

   Compare this to what usually happens today. The funeral home picks up the corpse from the hospital, less often from the home, and prepares it for viewing. A day or so later – and today sometimes longer – the family is invited for a "viewing." This coffin is commercially made, perhaps in China.

   Note the intricate and intimate interconnectedness in Faulkner's story. Note all the distancing from the body and the coffin and the survivors in the funeral home story. Interdependent conditions dynamically intertwined versus many ways of distancing.

5. David Orr, a well-known professor of environmental studies, told me about a hand-carved wooden letter opener he had received from a friend as a gift. And he named the interdependent conditions: natural wood, hand-carved by a friend, meant to last. Again, a whole set of interdependent conditions versus a factory-made letter opener, made in China and bought at Walmart – with built-in obsolescence – and nary a nod to interdependent conditions and a holistic dynamic.

All five of these examples show the difference between a dualistic and distant situation in which there are many isolated parts, and **a dynamic of interdependent conditions**. My intention here is to emphasize – over against this distance and separation – everything "hitched to everything else in the universe," "connected through space and time," "a single ecosystem with many differentiated parts." Quoting Bohm from earlier: their "central underlying theme": "the unbroken wholeness of the totality of existence as an undivided flowing movement without borders."

Fourth foray. Thinking beyond metaphysics. The words that philosophy uses to say the "here" of the now are: metaphysics of substance, metaphysics of presence, or just "metaphysics."[24] That is the word Heidegger uses to name the dominant paradigm in today's world. And it is what makes up the first beginning. Inherent in this naming and describing are the words "dualistic, conceptual, static, substance-beings ... where everything is a being." And there is no inclusion of the no-thing dynamic of the immeasurable emptiness.

The metaphysics of substance is all about static and independent things/beings. It does not account for what we experience that is not a thing-being. It does not account for the question of being – what Heidegger along the way calls the meaning or truth of being, eventually using other words for this dynamic, for example, beyng, Ereignis, *physis, logos, aletheia*. The latter three mirror, of course, his turning to Greek thinking for inspiration in opening up the "question of being" beyond what dominates in Western metaphysics.

The metaphysics of presence involves reducing things/beings, "reality," including the highest being, to what is present (presence) and to what has an identity. It holds the notion that there is a total correspondence of thought to what is in the world, including what we experience. Total identity and nothing not transparent, such that what is non-transparent is taken as non-existent. To wit: the ideal is seen as something that thought can reach and define-measure ... because it is conceived as ... transparent!

Metaphysics (of substance, of presence, or just "metaphysics") seeks "static, independent beings" – no becoming and no change. It finds this in the intelligible world, in which something like unchanging being is discovered. This yields a kind of transparent world, a world of presence only. An absolute presence, if you will.

Following along with this traditional definition of metaphysics, Western philosophy got trapped in the dualistic enterprise. It is *this* understanding of Greek philosophy that got carried over into Christianity with its dualism of body versus soul-mind and into modern philosophy, which, for the most part, stresses the *cogito* and subjectivity, along with or over against the world and "objects." Seen from the history of philosophy and our standpoint, it is this part of Greek philosophy that is the "first beginning," as Heidegger calls it.

Moving into possibility. Along with and following after Heidegger and inspired by his thinking, we turn to early Greek thinking, in order to uncover and retrieve the "other beginning," the one that thinks and says what is not visible or objectifiable and that is immeasurable. Without form, no-form, no-thing, it provides a fresh opening, even as it is carried along with and sustains what is form and are beings-things. This goes beyond what we can know conceptually and beyond where we normally think metaphysics can go.

No-form is empty of form, or: emptiness. Dynamic with interwoven conditions, it is non-dual. As non-dual no-form, radiant emptiness shows itself as free, open, full of possibility.

Using the language of quantum physics – a language less ensconced in the tradition of Western philosophy – we can say that this immeasurable no-form dynamic is a dimension that is *not* determinable, not exhausted in "things" like atoms and quarks. Structures do appear as "things" and are seemingly conceptualizable (made into abstract concepts) … but only in a limited way, given how they depend on context and conditions, which always *change*. This is where the quantum **potential** comes in.

When we look for the substance of the "boson particle," we find this to be true only relatively, because it is always in a context that is essentially unlimited. In other words, as physicist Sean Carroll says, we did not find the boson particle, but rather "the particle that it decayed into."[25] The Higgs boson particle turns out to be a field or a force, which in turn is something more than physical. Can we say that the field-force is without form, even as it participates in the "forming" of some thing?

Now, to quote Bohm:

[The holomovement] may lie outside of time as we ordinarily know it. If the universe began with the Big Bang and there are black holes, then we must eventually reach places where the notion of time and space breaks down. Anything could happen … Within the singularity none of the laws as we know them apply. There are no particles; they are all disintegrated. There is no space and no time. Whatever is, is beyond any concept we have at present. The present physics implies that the total conceptual basis of physics must be regarded as completely inadequate. The grand unification [of the four forces of the universe] could be nothing but an abstraction in the face of some further unknown.[26]

- *The holomovement, also known as unbroken wholeness, lies (Bohm: **may** **lie**) outside of time as we know it.*
- *No particles, no space, and no time.*
- *"It" is beyond any concept had at the time.*

How does one imagine or come to know or be aware of a no-form and no-thing dynamic … and then how is one to say it?
Bohm:

I propose something like this: Imagine an infinite sea of energy filling empty space, with waves moving around in there, occasionally coming together and producing an intense pulse. Let's say one particular pulse comes together and expands, creating our universe of space-time and matter. But there could well be other such pulses. To us, that pulse looks like a big bang; In a greater context, it's a little ripple. Everything emerges by unfoldment from the holomovement, then enfolds back into the implicate order. I call the enfolding process "implicating," and the unfolding "explicating." The implicate and explicate together are a flowing, undivided wholeness. Every part of the universe is related to every other part but in different degrees.[27]

- *Bohm's attempt at this is: "**Imagine an infinite sea of energy filling empty space** " … space as empty? space as no-form and not physical in any way?*

- *"The implicate and explicate together are a flowing, undivided wholeness. Every part of the universe is related to every other part but in different degrees." This interrelatedness is what he calls "a flowing, undivided wholeness."*
- *Was Bohm close to what Heidegger calls the no-thing of beyng, beyond things/beings? Is the "flowing, undivided wholeness" a name for the non-dual dynamic of radiant emptiness?*

It would be **the holomovement, you see, the flowing movement**. But it goes beyond that. We could say that even at this level there is a way of looking at it in which **emptiness is the plenum**, right? ... This is a well-known idea even in physics. If you take a crystal that is at absolute zero, it does not scatter electrons. They go through it as if it were empty and as soon as you raise the temperature and [produce] inhomogeneities, they scatter. Now, if you used those electrons to observe the crystal ... all you would see would be these little inhomogeneities and you would say they are what exists and the crystal is what does not exist. Right?[28]

- *Is the emptiness as plenum that physics knew well "empty" of form or things/beings? That would be in line with what Heidegger calls open, freeing, full "emptiness."*
- *Could one then say that emptiness equals plenum? Heidegger says that one aspect of emptiness is "full." If emptiness is "full," what is it full of? Potential. The no-form dynamic of radiant emptiness is "full of" potential. Or, as Bohm names it: **quantum potential**, which is dynamic in the holomovement, which is immeasurable/boundless, that is, not physical. Remember: For Heidegger emptiness is opening, freeing, rich or enriching and: full!*

What we perceive through the senses as empty space is actually the plenum, which is the ground for the existence of everything, including ourselves. The things that appear to our senses are derivative forms, and their true meaning can be seen only when we consider the plenum, in which they are generated and sustained and into which they must ultimately vanish. This plenum is, however, no longer to be conceived through the idea of a simple material medium, such as an ether, which would be regarded as existing and moving only in a three-dimensional space. Rather, one is to begin with the holo-movement, in which there is the immense "sea" of energy described earlier.[29]

- *"What we perceive through the senses* **as empty space is actually the plenum,** *which is the ground for the existence of everything."*
- *The true meaning is achieved "only when we* **consider the plenum, in which they are generated and sustained and into which they must ultimately vanish."**
- *"This plenum is, however, no longer to be conceived through the idea of a simple material medium."*
- *Rather* **the holomovement, the unbroken wholeness, the immense "sea" of energy underlies everything.**
- *Do these words say no-form, no-thing? Is the* **plenum** *of the* **holomovement** *the non-physical and no-form* **dynamic of radiant emptiness?**

Does Bohm realize that he has come to the point where empty space as a plenum – that is, full – no longer describes the "material medium," as his words imply? And is his plenum an emptiness with no-form and no-thing and no beings/things at all? I think that Bohm is at the same flashpoint as Heidegger is – mirrored in the words "non-dual dynamic of radiant emptiness." If we read this last quotation carefully, he seems to say it, although subtly.

[However] this process, in which exist infinitely varied types of natural laws, **is just the process of becoming, first described by Heraclitus several thousand years ago** (although, of course, by now we have a much more precise and accurate idea of the nature of this process than the ancient Greeks could have had).[30]

Now that Bohm has turned our gaze to the Greeks, I present two quotations by Bohm:

One may speculate that perhaps in ancient times, the men who were wise enough to see that the immeasurable is the primary reality were also wise enough to see that measure is insight into a secondary and dependent but nonetheless necessary aspect of reality.[31]

- *immeasurable ... as not calculable or conceptualizable ... emptiness without form.*

The ancient Greeks had the idea of an increasing perfection [unbroken wholeness] ... Modern physics contains the idea of successive positions of bodies of matter and the constraints of forces that act on these bodies. The order of perfection investigated by the ancient Greeks is now considered irrelevant.[32]

Taking these two quotations together, I suggest the following reading: The early Greek thinkers knew about the immeasurable organic wholeness ("the increasing perfection") – a no-form dynamic that cannot be grasped in concept, thus aka radiant emptiness – but this thinking got lost and covered over as time went by and as this power of Greek thinking slipped away. I also suggest that Bohm either got to this point in his language or, given the limitations in language, *almost* got there. I would say that his *thinking* got there and that his *language* came oh so close!

Let us close this section with a rather simple statement by Bohm: "The electron itself can never be separated from the whole of space, which is its ground ['empty space' or no-thing, no-form radiant emptiness or beyng as Ereignis]."[33]

c. From Bohm to Heidegger: How to Go beyond Dualism, Conceptualism, Stasis – into the Dynamic of the Immeasurable Radiant Emptiness

This is unfamiliar territory. It is about direct, unmediated knowing. Not conceptual, not dualistic or abstract. This kind of knowing is somehow familiar to us on a more concrete, "everyday" level. Examples of this are: I know that this coffee is excellent. I know that this chocolate is very good. Grandma knows that you love her. I knew that you were coming. I just know when it is time to leave. We call this "intuition" or "direct unmediated knowing." We can also call it "awareness" purely and simply.

But the knowing we are after on this level of dynamic-radiant emptiness – knowing on this level of the way things are – is "philosophically" rather unfamiliar to us. So how do we come to know it – and to say it in a manner that is fitting to this knowing? As we look directly at "how to do this," two intertwined aspects of the question emerge. One, what about this no-thing no-form emptiness, which is non-dual and dynamic? Two, how to say it? Especially since our usual and hardened grammar and syntax do not readily yield to what is called for here, which is, a language that is not abstract and conceptual, but rather is a "showing" – what I call poi-etic saying.

I will now present some of Bohm's meanderings on how to come to this kind of knowing. After the quotation I will give a "reading" of the quotation – an interpretation, if you will. Then I will try to answer the above two questions: How does this work here: *Knowing beyond dualism, conceptualism, stasis – within the dynamic of the immeasurable radiant emptiness*? And how can we come to understand the unusual language that is called for?

First, let us hear Bohm on this matter:

> The first step would be to stop doing anything and to let the dust [being stirred up entirely by our concepts] settle. Then I would look without trouble. Similarly, if the brain can refrain from "trying" to resolve its conflicts, these will vanish of their own accord, spontaneously and naturally, leaving the "emptiness" in which clear perception takes place … We must be intensely aware of how the mind is working, without attempting to do anything about it. This awareness is enough. Real awareness already is action, without the need for a "choice" by the "self" to do something … No choices, decisions, or efforts are needed … To really see deeply the nature of this illusion [of the dust of concepts that hide what is] is action enough. For in the light of this perception, it has to collapse.[34]

Here is my reading of it: The cloud of dust hides what is going on. The dust is our inherited set of concepts, which are illusions. So we let the dust settle. We are aware as we wait. When we refrain from "trying" to resolve the conflicts between our conceptual understanding and are open to what will appear when we stop trying, the conflicts "will vanish of their own accord." This happening will be spontaneous and natural. And it will leave us with the "emptiness" in which clear awareness takes place. Becoming aware of how the mind works, we attempt nothing. "This awareness is enough." This awareness is already action. No need to "choose" or to do anything. To see deeply these illusions – the dust of our concepts – is the only action needed. In the power of this awareness (Bohm: "in the light of this perception") the illusion collapses.

Ask yourself this question: Is it the brain or the mind that refrains from "trying" to resolve its conflicts?

This is our guide. *How* we then make it happen … this takes practice!

Again, Bohm:

> While man's scientific instruments do constitute, as we have seen, an effective extension of his body and his sense organs, there are no comparable external structures that substitute for the inward side of the perceptive process (in which the invariant features of what has been experienced are presented in the "inner show") … So there is always finally a stage where an essentially perceptual process is needed in scientific research – a process taking place within the scientist himself.[35]

As I read and interpret Bohm here, he talks about an "inner side of the perceptive process" and "an essentially perceptual process within the scientist himself." This may appear a little problematic for our purposes. For two reasons: One, an inner side of perception implies an external side as well – a dualism that does not fit on the path we are following. Two, it is not clear what the words *perception* and *perceptual process* in these two quotations actually say here.

When we understand perception here to mean the awareness that the first quotation names, then it becomes clearer. With the awareness that the first quotation talks about, the inside versus outside as well as the implied body-aspect of perception lose their dualistic feel. For awareness is at the core of the non-dual dynamic that we seek to know here. Would it make more sense to stay with the word *mind*?

My sense is that Bohm is carefully, modestly, and honestly pursuing the same flashpoint that this book is working with. But the language that is available to him as a scientist lacks the non-conceptual and non-dual saying that is called for here and that we want to learn. Check it out for yourself. Namely, the place at which Bohm wants to arrive is similar to ours in this book, but the language available to him is lacking. I have found this more often in scientists' work. With total honesty in their thinking, they are trying to come to this place, but they do not have the language to say it. For example, they talk about "particles" that have no form, or the Higgs boson "particle," but what happens when that field or a force is an immeasurable no-thing? And although Bohm uses the word *mind* above, he also uses the word *perception* in a somewhat ill-defined manner. Hmm.

> If, after reasonable efforts, a proper accommodation of this kind [of the old, inherited paradigm with the new way of organic wholeness] is not achieved, then what is needed is a fresh perception of the whole fact. This now includes not only the results of experiments but also the failure of certain lines of theory to fit the experimental results in a "common measure." Then, as has been indicated earlier, one has to be very sensitively aware of all the relevant differences which underly the main orders in the old theory, to see whether there is room for a change of overall order.[36]

Here I propose a rewording, using the language he did not have at his disposal: If, after reasonable efforts, a proper accommodation (of the old, inherited paradigm with the new way of organic wholeness) is not achieved, then what is needed is a fresh, phenomenological look at what is at stake here. This now includes not only the results of experiments but also one's *experience* of the matter at stake as well as the failure of certain lines of theory or abstract concepts to fit the experiential results in a "common measure." Then, as has been indicated earlier, one has to be sensitively aware of all the relevant differences that underlie the main orders in the old theory, to see whether there is room for a change of overall order, that is, of the old order paradigm. This change, then, requires the awareness described in the earlier quotation – awareness that is already an action, no effort needed. I quote: "We must be intensely aware of how the mind is working, without attempting to do anything about it. This awareness is enough."

It is my sense that *this* is what Bohm is going after.

> The notion that the one who thinks (the Ego) is at least in principle completely separate from and independent of the reality that he thinks about is of course firmly embedded in our entire tradition ... But this confronts us with a very difficult challenge: How are we to think coherently of a single, unbroken, flowing actuality of existence as a whole, containing both thought (consciousness) and external reality as we experience it?[37]

Here, in Bohm's own words, is his "correction" of the dualistic outer-inner and of the limitations of the word *perception* above.

If we read these words carefully and with an open mind, open to possibilities of thinking, then we might get a glimpse of how to do this. At the very least we come to an awareness that the usual thinking mode is not sufficient to reach this domain of no-form dynamic emptiness.

Now let me turn to Heidegger.

The Memorial Address. In part 1 I looked at this. Here I want to focus on *conceptualism and stasis – and then move into the dynamic of immeasurable radiant emptiness.*

Heidegger distinguishes between calculating thinking (*das rechnende Denken*) and mindful or minding thinking (*das besinnliche Denken*). In part 1 I quoted Heidegger to say that calculating thinking is trapped in the "jaws of planning and computation, of organization and automatic operations" (GA 16:522).*

And "the world now appears as an object that calculating thinking attacks, which nothing should be able to resist any longer" (523). Calculating thinking is planning, investigating, researching,

---

* Unless otherwise noted, all numbers in parentheses in this section are from this text.

setting up a business or industry. Calculating thinking rushes from one opportunity to the next. It never stays still, never comes to mindfulness.

But there is another way to think. First, minding thinking is a hinting thinking, because what it involves is less transparent, perhaps even non-transparent. Let us listen to Heidegger, now with the focus on *how to go beyond dualism, conceptualism, stasis – into the dynamic of the immeasurable radiant emptiness.*

> Minding thinking. When we come to know what is own to us as humans, namely that we are thinking beings, we become minding beings. We are oriented to think. Minding thinking is careful, minding thinking [*nachdenken*] of the sense of things, which is at work in everything that is. (520)

> This minding thinking [*das besinnliche Denken*] requires a greater effort … a longer preparation … a more subtle care/diligence … And it must also be able to wait, just as the farmer [has to wait] to see whether the seed sprouts and grows to maturity [becomes ripe]. (520)

The words that come up to say minding thinking are:

- *careful minding of the sense of things*
- *more subtle*
- *learning to wait.*

What belongs to this "deep" way to what is, to the way things are? It "demands from us that we do not remain one-sidedly stuck in an idea-conception and that we do not keep rushing on a single track in a conceptual direction" (526). Letting calculating thinking – the mindset of technicity – simply *be*, can minding thinking open out onto "thing" as inseparable phenomenon within the no-thing, non-dual dynamic of radiant emptiness? Here is Heidegger's response to the question:

> We can use technical objects as they were meant to be used. But we can simultaneously let these [technical] objects just be and not intrude on us in

our inner and ownmost being. We can say "yes" to the unavoidable usage of technical objects, and at the same time we can say "no," insofar as we bar them from claiming us totally and thus bending out of shape, confusing-unhinging, and finally demolishing what is ownmost to us. (527)

As we try to learn how to do this, we hear these words:

- *let technical things be and not "intrude on us in our inner and ownmost being,"*
- *acknowledge "unavoidable usage of technical objects," while we*
- *keep them "from claiming us totally" and*
- *keep them from destroying "what is ownmost to us," namely, minding thinking.*

These words announce what we have to watch out for and a kind of invitation to "start" thinking in the way required here. They are more like warnings than methods. However, if we begin to hear these words, we are already on the way to the How. (See p. 121.)

Heidegger calls for two ways: One, releasement to the things (*die Gelassenheit zu den Dingen*). This lets us see things as more than technical. Not denouncing or wanting to destroy what is technical in things, but to see the "more than," to experience things in the richness of their flourishing, as what is own to things – as phenomena inseparable from something that is vaster, while hidden. Heidegger will name this: beyng as Ereignis. I name it the nondual dynamic of radiant emptiness. These two ways of saying this dynamic are "saying the same."

Two, openness for the mystery (*die Offenheit für das Geheimnis*). When we become aware that in the technical world (the world of technicity) there still dwells a hidden sense, this lets both of these strategies show the connection to the hidden, to what comes forth to us, in things. What shows itself, emerges ... and simultaneously withdraws.

About these two ways:

Releasement to the things and openness to the mystery belong together. They preserve for us the possibility to stay in the world in a totally other way. They promise us a new ground and soil on which we can stand within the world of technicity and, unthreatened by it, can endure. (528)

I highlight these word-images:

- *opening to the mystery as a way of awareness*
- *a new way of staying in the world: just awareness*
- *seeing the "more than" the technical and conceptual aspects*
- *experiencing things in the richness of their flourishing*
- *inseparable from something that is vaster*
- *emerging and withdrawing.*

Gathering the saying within these words, we see some of the aspects that go beyond our understanding of the chronological "beginning" with the Greeks – from the "here" of the first beginning, as we have come to understand it – to the other beginning, aka the "starting," as what gets things started for our thinking. This way is less conceptual-intellectual, less dualistic, and not static. And we have a first inkling of how the non-dual, inseparable dynamic of radiant emptiness gets thought in Heidegger: Nothing is thrown out or removed. The question becomes: How can we think the "starting" of another beginning, as it introduces an *other*, transforming way of thinking and as it opens our seeing and hearing to things beyond their being technical objects? Beyond to what the words beyng, *dao*, buddha mind, the immeasurable quantum potential and field of energy in quantum physics – and the non-dual dynamic of radiant emptiness – want to say.

The grounding-attuning of thinking in the other beginning. (The German reads: *Die Grundstimmung des Denkens im anderen Anfang.*) The aims here include (a) overcoming the duality of metaphysics – overcoming the limits of the first beginning – and (b) learning to dwell within the non-dual dynamic of the crossing. Here Heidegger says: "*What grounds and attunes thinking in the other beginning* resonates in attunings that can only be named faintly" (GA 65:14).

The German word for "faintly" is *entfernt*. The word is a bit difficult to translate here:

at a distance,
in a wandering way,
indirectly,
windingly,
vaguely
Latin *vagus*: wandering.

These words mirror that what Heidegger is doing – and what we are trying to show and do – is not familiar territory. This in two ways: One, the pathway of this book is not familiar to us in the West, particularly at this time. Two, the distancing – wandering, windingly and faintly – belongs to the way itself, to the region of emptiness that we are wandering around in, the way to which we are called in this endeavour.

Heidegger says that we are in the crossing … from becoming aware of what the first beginning entails to an opening to the other beginning, which emerges in its richness and possibility. Using words as a mirror, it is the move *from* traditional, inherited (TI) words that reveal the way things are as we know so well in our world: dualistic, conceptual, outside direct experience, static, substance-beings … everything is a being … *to* refreshing, retrieving (RR) words that reveal the way things are in a new and richer possibility for living and knowing the world: non-dual, non-conceptual, in direct experience, dynamic and changing … revealing no-thing emptiness.

Here is Heidegger's schema for this grounding-attuning of thinking in the other beginning. I will work with it on a simplified level in order to show how these four dynamics function within our project here, retrieving Greek philosophy.

das Erschrecken : *startled dismay*
die Verhaltenheit : *reservedness*   } *die Ahnung* : *intimating*
die Scheu : *awe*

Startled dismay is the aspect – of the crossing from first to other beginning – that is moving *from* metaphysics as we know it in the first beginning – for example, in epistemological certainty or objectifying subjectivity or the straightforwardness of the being of metaphysics – *to* the echo of self-hiding sheltering in the "other" beginning. This is what we want to retrieve from Greek thinking. In this opening, what has seemed familiar (the first beginning) becomes strange and confining. What is unfamiliar and unknown is the abandonment of and by being. The startled dismay arises when we become aware and *experience* something missing. "Being" that is no-form and no-thing and *not* beings … turns out to be nothing like what we have thought it was, namely the being of metaphysics. This is startling or shocking. "Startled dismay is *returning from* the ease of comportment in what is familiar … *back to* the openness of the rush of the self-sheltering" (GA 65:15). Note that the words we use for the other beginning intimate this "hidden" aspect: non-conceptual, opening, freeing, and full dynamic of radiant emptiness. These words point the way when we turn to the Greeks and "retrieve" what got covered over. Heidegger's words in *Beiträge* for this dynamic are: *beyng, beyng as Ereignis*. (The words *beyng/Seyn* and *Ereignis* say and show Heidegger's attempt to think this "nothing like.")

We are startled and dismayed at how this no-form beyng has been abandoned in metaphysics (the first beginning) and how there is a "hint" of the turn within beyng. **Awe** opens up this hint as it attunes thinking to the nearing of what is the most distant in the starting (the other beginning), that is, that which "gathers in itself all relations of beyng" (GA 16:520). Far from shyness (the usual meaning of *Scheu*), this awe sees the power of beyng and Ereignis, *including* its reservedness. One could say: A kind of haunting awe in the face of the initially faint awareness of the no-thing no-form non-dual dynamic of radiant emptiness.

Thus **reservedness** is the midpoint holding together the **startled dismay** of standing in the first beginning – being aware of what is missing, what has been abandoned – and **awe** in the face of the rich possibility held within beyng as Ereignis or as radiant emptiness – we might say: held non-dually.

Reservedness names the holding-back of the deep swaying of beyng. Here belong the words: hiddenness, not-granting, immeasurability, reticence, sheltering-concealing. All of these words say: We do not yet know how to travel in the other beginning. And when we *do* travel there, the self-withholding named in these words will not go away! For this withdrawal or hiding-sheltering belongs inseparably to the beyng-Ereignis of the crossing.

Intimating opens up the breadth of what is hidden in abandonment of and by beyng and what is not-granted – the sheltering-concealing as well as the reticence. Heidegger says:

> Intimating in itself holds open the attuning power and grounds it back into itself. Towering far above all uncertainty of mere opinion [common sense], intimating is the hesitating *sheltering* of the unconcealing of the hidden as such, of the refusal. (GA 65:22)

Now we can say: **Intimating** is the move *from within* our forgetfulness of being and from the abandonment of and by being (**startled dismay**), and, heeding this, moving through **awe** in the face of the possibility in the other beginning, *to* the **shelteredness** that is central to this **dynamic**.

Words to hearken to:

- *the **startled dismay** that arises when we become aware of and experience something missing in fragmentation, dualism, and the abstractness of metaphysics*
- *the **awe** that attunes thinking to the nearing of what is the most distant in the starting (the other beginning), that is, Heidegger's beyng that is no being or thing … or what I am calling the non-dual, one-ing dynamic of radiant emptiness*
- *the **reservedness** as the midpoint holding together (a) what is missing and abandoned in the first beginning of metaphysics and (b) the rich possibility held within beyng as Ereignis or as radiant emptiness in the other beginning*
- ***reservedness** as the holding-back, hiddenness, not-granting, immeasurability, reticence, sheltering-concealing*

- *intimating as the move from within our forgetfulness of being (**startled dismay**), through **awe** in the face of the possibility in the other beginning, to dynamic **reservedness** or **shelteredness**.*

All of these word-images, taken together, determine the style of thinking that gets started in the other beginning (the starting). What grounds and attunes the other beginning "can hardly ever be known merely by one name, especially in the crossing to that beginning" (GA 65:21).

Heidegger reminds us of something crucial about words to think-say the other beginning:

> Every naming of the grounding-attunement with a single word is based on a false notion. Every word is taken from tradition. The fact that grounding-attunement of another beginning has to have many names does not argue against its at-oneness [its non-dual, inseparable character] but rather confirms its richness and strangeness. (GA 65:22)

It is, all of it, an at-oneness – rich and strange.

Given that conceptual language dominates today, we thinkers, in the crossing from the first to the other beginning, need to go a stretch of the way with the language of concepts, because only by our dismay and intimation and awe – along with the reservedness or reticence of beyng – can thinking and language overflow this container (conceptual language) and emerge to say beyng in the other beginning.

Try this: Abide actively within the duality (of subject/object, subject/predicate, body/mind, I/world). Go deep – all the way – into the thoughts and duality. Truly inhabit that place. Then in awareness, let it go without judging or evaluating. Dwell there awarely in this letting-go. Without trying to eliminate the power and clinging of duality, let it just be. Then – maybe! – there arises only awareness without form or duality. And maybe the sprouting of radiant emptiness will show itself of its own accord. Within the full flourishing of the dual/conceptual is the emerging non-dual and non-conceptual. Heed the full blossoming of the non-dual dynamic of radiant emptiness.

Here I repeat the words of Bohm:

> We must be intensely aware of how the mind is working, without attempting to do anything about it. This awareness is enough. Real awareness already is action, without the need for a "choice" by the "self" to do something.

The refreshing retrieval of what got lost in Greek philosophy, covered over in the "here" of Western philosophy today, is our joy-filled task. We are asked to go "there" – behind and beyond the traditional, inherited (TI) words that reveal the way things are and that we know so well: dualistic, conceptual, outside experience, static, substance/beings ... everything is a being ... And from within "there" to discover and come to know and experience the refreshing, retrieving (RR) words that reveal the way things are in a new and richer possibility for living and knowing the world: non-dual, non-conceptual, in experience, dynamic and changing ... revealing no-thing emptiness.

d. Poi-etic Language: Saying as Showing

Honestly, the distance from "here" to "there" is both very long and quite near. The "there" is very far away from what we usually experience, know, and think – and very far away from knowing how to say "it." It takes courage, and it takes time. This is true above all for how we use language, how we say things. The big question is: How to say "it." And the "there" is quite near, if we only open up to it.

Here is a description of the "here" that we want to move out from. Hermann Hesse once wrote:

> The mind favours the definite, the solid shape. It wants to be able to depend on its symbols [markers, signifiers, distinguishing characteristics, words]. It loves what is, not what is becoming, what is real and not what is possible.[38]

We are accustomed to wanting words to denote the definite, solid, and "real." Hesse is describing the mind that our culture gives more credibility to as well as what the words show: what is solid, what is measurable, what is definite or definable. And this mind wants its words to say this aspect of the way things are. This language is propositional and definitional – and dualistic and conceptual. It defines by distinguishing – that is, by creating – duality. And this mind does not trust the non-dual dynamic of what is in process, becoming, within possibility; nor does it have any idea how to say the no-form no-thing dynamic.

Where we are going requires a more open-ended language. A language that says and shows dynamic and becoming rather than static and interdependent conditions rather than solid things. A language that says and shows the wholeness or *non-dual* dynamic of radiant emptiness, aka beyng, Ereignis, quantum potential, *dao*, buddha mind, plus all those key Greek words that part 3 works with. And above all a saying language, one that goes beyond things/beings and that says/shows the immeasurable radiant emptiness, the **empty** of space beyond concepts, beyond to the no-thing beyng that holds beings, radiant emptiness that contains what emerges within this dynamic – no-form no-thing within which form and thing manifest. We need a way of saying that is poi-etic.

The language needed here is one that is not fragmentary. Quoting David Bohm:

What, then, will be our question, as we engage in this inquiry into our language (and thought)? We begin with the fact of general fragmentation. We can ask in a preliminary way whether there are any features of the commonly used language which tends to sustain and propagate this fragmentation, as well as, perhaps, to reflect it. A cursory examination shows that a very important feature of this kind is the subject-verb-object structure of sentences, which is common to the grammar and syntax of modern languages. This structure implies that all action arises in a separate entity, the subject, and that, in cases described by a transitive verb, this action crosses over the space between them to another separate entity, the object.[39]

Bohm says that we are "often able to overcome this tendency toward fragmentation by using language in a freer, more informal, and 'poetic' way"[40] "by saying that *all* is an unbroken and undivided whole movement, and that each 'thing' is abstracted only as a relatively invariant side or aspect of this movement."[41]

I call this poi-etic language. Let me repeat what I wrote in "Suggestions, Guidelines" at the very beginning of this book:

> The word comes from the Greek ποίησις, which in turn stems from the verb ποιέω. Ποίησις does indeed mean the art of poetry, for example, "that is poetic language." But ποιέω also says: I do, make, gather, create, celebrate, produce or bring about. So ποίησις has two meanings: One, poetry, poem. Two, creation [creat**ing**], a making, bringing forth, letting emerge. The hyphen (a) keeps fresh our understanding that what is going on here is more than simply "poetic" and (b) gives our thinking-saying a space for staying open to when the word also says dynamic open-ended potential aka full emptiness!

On a practical level, how can we do this? It is virtually impossible to avoid the usual subject-verb-object structure, but we can allow our saying to break free of this structure in small ways. Sometimes we write poetry. Sometimes we write *as if* it is poetry. What we can do as often as possible is use verb forms, for example, participles and gerunds that end in -*ing*. Flourishing, gathering, unfolding, recovering, thinking, retrieving, and so on. Less static and closed, more dynamic and opening.

The most important way to move into poi-etic saying is to constantly remind ourselves that our saying is dynamic, in line with the dynamic of the no-form no-thing beyng or the non-dual dynamic of radiant emptiness, as well as the phenomena or things seen as interdependent conditions. For example, we can learn to "hear" the dynamic quality in such words, that is, from attention to attending, from implication to implying, from awareness to being-aware, from emergence to emerging, from manifestation to manifesting, from experience to experiencing, and so on. We can learn to "hear" and to say words that show continuing conditions or modes of activity.

In a deep sense, poi-etic language draws thinking out of a text and back into its saying power. Language shimmers in that tension, revealing or making-manifest and nourishing the back-and-forth movement, within the never-ending revealing and the "never" of sheer withdrawing. The movement of this language hovers in *the word and its saying* of the way things are. The word bears up and places (or holds in place) that hovering, that moving back and forth, the circling in and out – the non-dual revealing/hiding, disclosing/sheltering, never-ending dynamic of a showing that is non-dually both the transparent and the non-transparent, that is, what does not show itself.

Language, then, is a poi-etic saying, rather than logical-propositional. Connotation rather than denotation. Dynamic rather than static. Inexhaustible rather than definite. Open-ended rather than defining. And saying is a showing. What provides, catapults, enables and quickens in the showing that saying is is its coming into its ownmost or flourishing for what it is as owning. Quoting Heidegger: "The quickening in showing of saying is owning [*Das Regende im Zeigen der Sage ist das Eignen*]" (GA 12:246).

Part of what poi-etic, imaging thinking in philosophy does is to reawaken the senses and nuances that are hidden and traced in language and coax these poi-etic words back into that dynamic where the originary sense of what is at stake in the Greek words dwells.

e. *Dao* as Measure and Opening for Our Work, in Its Saying Power

I will now spend some time looking at *dao* (also known as *tao*), both as a *word* that "says" and as *way*-dynamic. If we come to understand and experience what Daoism offers, we can use it as an opening. We can let the non-dual no-thing and no-form dynamic of *dao* inform and afford to us a richer, refreshingly new feel for the words that mirror our concern in this work of thinking – as we contemplate this move from the substance feel of nouns to the dynamic-flowing feel of verbs and verbal nouns (gerunds), to hearing the non-dual beyond subject-predicate, to experiencing the non-dual intertwining of saying the word and what is said in the word.

Here I will be using two translations of the *Tao Te Ching*, aka the *Daodejing*. Each one has a rich commentary.

- *Daodejing: "Making This Life Significant": A Philosophical Transla-tion*,[42] translated with commentary by Roger T. Ames and David L. Hall.*
- *Tao: A New Way of Thinking*,[43] translated with introduction and commentaries by Chang Chung-yuan.**

Note that I will use the spelling *dao* when I am writing. But I will keep the spelling *tao* when it appears in a quotation

The *dao*. *Dao* as word. *Dao* as way. *Dao* as rich and full empti-ness. The intertwining of *dao* as word and *dao* as way. Usually in the West the word *dao* – or *tao* – has been translated as "way": road or path. The first thing we can say is that the word *dao* says dynamic movement. The English word *way* carries this move-ment with it: pathway, byway, entryway, wayfarer, being on the way, wayward. Most of the senses of the word *way* **say** something ongoing, changing, dynamic. Second, as way it is itself no-thing, thus a useful "way" to say no-form emptiness, beyng, or Bohm's immense and infinite "sea" of energy.

Heidegger describes *both* the movement-change of being-under-way in thinking *and* what is experienced in the way gone, namely, the open expanse that is being, as "way":

> But whoever knows what it means to be underway in a deep, necessary sense knows how the view of the way-to-go that opens out in front of him is constantly changing, just as is the view of the way just gone – especially when this being-underway is not meant personally or bio-graphically but is experienced in the historical unfolding of Dasein.[44]

---

* Numbers in parentheses in this section refer to this text.
** References to this book will appear in parentheses as Tao plus page number.

Heidegger calls his *Gesamtausgabe* "ways, not works" (*Wege, nicht Werke*). We are on the way. And the very point of beyng/ Ereignis is the way itself. All is way. Beyng is way-making. This thinking and saying is "underway."

Dao is Way. Yes, we are on the way. But more than that. *Dao* is the "principle" of all that is. *Dao* "as such" is no-thing, as everything arises through or within *dao*. *Dao* is "way" and "way-making." It *is* as dynamic unfolding. It is formless, as it is that which gives rise to all form. It is "itself" dark/obscure/withdrawing, even as it manifests light – as part and parcel of the one dynamic of no-thing radiant emptiness. *Dao* is that within which things arise as well as that which holds things when they "return." This dynamic shows *dao* for what it is.

Before we get to the intertwining of *dao* the word and *dao* the way, let us turn briefly to the description of the word *dao* in the introduction to the translation of the *Daodejing* by Roger T. Ames and David L. Hall.

There the authors tell us that *dao* is "primarily gerundive, pro-cessional, and dynamic: 'a leading forth'" (57). Following this state-ment, they say they "can identify three overlapping and mutually entailing semantic dimensions" to the word *dao*:

1. **momentum**: "sense of *dao* as unfolding disposition" as in "'life' or 'history' that resists resolution into familiar dualisms such as 'subject-object,' 'form-function' or 'agency-action' and so on." (58)
2. **way-making**: "Making way includes making productive adjustments in the direction of the lived experience by manipulating the more fluid and indeterminate opportunities that come with the unfolding of experience." (58)
3. **decidedly verbal**: "The swinging gateway – opening and then closing – is where/when *dao* spontaneously 'opens out' to provide creativity a space through which to make its 'entrance,' qualifying the processive nature of *dao* with the immediacy and specificity of the creative act." Here the image of non-dual movement of all that is named in *dao* shines in its ongoing waying, way-making movement, with

words like "the swinging gateway" that "spontaneously 'opens out'" or "the pervasive 'birthing' sense of an emerging world." (59)

This way-making – the hidden *dao* – is open and dynamic. Heidegger says that our task in thinking beyng is to have an experience of this:

> To experience something means: to gain access to something while underway or on the way. (GA 12:167)

> As *preparing* the way and way as *letting-come-forth*, waying and making-way (*Wëgen und Be-wëgen*) belong in the same realm of wellspring and stream as the verbs: *swaying* and *venturing* and *surging* (*wiegen und wagen und wogen*). Apparently the word *way* is an ur-word of language that speaks to minding humans. The guiding word in the poi-etic thinking of Laotse is *tao* and "basically" signifies way. But because we are prone to conceive of the way only superficially, as a section of road between two places, we have too rashly judged our word *way* to be unsuitable for naming what *tao* says ... Perhaps, hidden in the words *tao* and *way* is the secret of all secrets of a thinking saying, provided that we let these names return to their unsaid and are capable of this letting. Moreover, perhaps the enigmatic force [*Gewalt*] of the modern-day dominance of method actually arises from the fact that these methods, notwithstanding their efficiency, are only the wastewater of a vast and hidden stream, that of the way that makes-way for everything and that carries everything along. All is way. (GA 12:187)

We immediately notice two very important issues that are reinforced by Ames and Hall as well as by Heidegger:

1. Even as we are in the process of digging more deeply into the word *dao*, it is clear that the word says the non-dual, nonconceptual experience, dynamic and always ongoing unfolding, and the no-thing, formless radiant emptiness.

2. Already here, even before we turn to the crux of *dao*, we have strong hints that, whatever *dao* is and does, the saying aspect of *dao* is inherently intertwined. Heidegger says that

- *"the word **way** is an ur-word."*
- *"because we are prone to conceive of the way only superficially,"* we see the word **way** as *"unsuitable for naming what dao says."* Thus if *"we let these names return to their unsaid and are capable of this letting, then dao as word "shelters the secret of all secrets of a thinking saying" and is always a saying, a saying that shows.*

We will now look carefully at the two texts mentioned above, by Ames and Hall and by Chang Chung-yuan. First, we can get an overall view of what is at stake by reading their Introductions. Then we will focus on certain verses from the *Daodejing*, viz., the *Tao Te Ching* text itself.

In line with the role that Heidegger's thinking plays in *Tao: A New Way of Thinking*, Chang Chung-yuan points out that

Heidegger has developed a new way of thinking and the language to reveal it, which are not novel to Taoist philosophy. Heidegger is the only Western philosopher who not only intellectually understands *Tao* but has intuitively experienced the essence of it as well. (Tao, viii)

- *This is in line with and supports what we have been saying about the need for an intuitive, non-conceptual experience of thinking.*
- *Rather than taking this comment for granted, it is up to us as thinkers to check out in our own experience and critical thinking, whether this is true.*
- *For doing this, we have both Heidegger's and the Daoist words at our disposal.*

Heidegger maintains that metaphysical thinking has reached its completion. Completion in this sense means end. [This marks] the beginning of a new task of thinking. This new task requires thinking that is different from rational, scientific analysis. (Tao, x)

- *Again, this statement affirms the need for a new kind of thinking. We need to consider what this different thinking is, as well as the language that is called for to say it.*

This reminds me of how Heidegger's lecture *"Zeit und Sein"* calls for a "more originary" understanding. This "more originary" has the character of a return [*den Charakter eines Rückgangs*]. This is the step-back [*der Schritt zurück*]. It is necessary to discuss the whither and the how in this talk of [going] "back" (GA 14:35).

- *The enigma of the step-back mirrors the retrieval that this book is all about.*
- *Is it a step-back in time – to the Greeks, to dis-cover what got lost in what they thought and said?*
- *Or is it a step-back into the early Greek* **experience** *that is* **timeless***, that is, into the hidden formless dynamic, the thought and the unthought, the saying-showing of the no-form no-thing beyng-Ereignis – aka the non-dual dynamic of radiant emptiness?*
- *One can say that reading and hearing* **dao** *mirrors the same going-back.*

Returning to Chang's Introduction, he says:

The reality of *Tao* … is formless and can only be experienced directly and spontaneously through *ming*, or primordial intuition. Discursive reasoning cannot grasp the nondifferentiated reality of things. (Tao, xii)

As Chuang Tzu says: "Since we are all One, how can we express the One?" Thus, for Taoism, non-being is inexpressible and unthinkable, not because there is nothing to express or to think about, but because non-being is the higher unity of Being and thinking. (Tao, xii)

- *Whatever dao is, it is non-dual.*
- *The "unthinkable" says* **not** *dualistic, discursive, or* **conceptual** *thinking. This thinking cannot say the non-dual, because the no-thing dynamic of* **dao** *is itself beyond this kind of thinking.*
- *Dao as well as the emptiness that we are aiming to find in Greek thinking are both word-images for the no-form, no-thing opening, freeing dynamic of the empty.*

Now, whatever it is that we are seeking – in *dao* or beyng as Ereignis or radiant emptiness – it is beyond beings or things. Thus it is beyond "ontology" – a *word* that says both things/beings as well as the *study* of such beings. We have to understand *dao* as not-ontological or preontological, in both senses of the word:

> In the traditional Chinese interpretation, *Tao* is the highest attainment of primordial intuition. *Tao* is preontological experience, which is gained through the interfusion and identification of the subjectivity of man and the objectivity of things. This preontological, inner experience is the spontaneous reflection of one's being, which simultaneously transcends both time and space. This inner experience is nameless and formless, yet it is the fountain of potentiality from which all things emerge. (Tao, xv)

- *Preontological is more like "beyond" simply ontological. That is, dao is not prior to ontology but "beyond" it, including things/beings in the non-dual no-form dynamic that we experience without being able to conceptualize it.*
- *"One's being" here points to a dynamic that is beyond how we know ourselves, even as this dynamic includes us, non-dually, within the radiant emptiness.*
- *Reflection here is more like reflection in the mirror or in water, than like the reflection in thought.*

Heidegger says that the no-form and no-thing dynamic that he names beyng-Ereignis – and that is mirrored in the radiant emptiness of *dao* – is an awakening and nothing provable: "The awakening of Ereignis [here I add: *dao* as well] must be experienced. It cannot be proven" (GA 14:63). Our aim here is to make use of *dao* as it does what it does, as it is experienced, and as it **says** and **shows**. And as it provides an opening to our work here, namely rediscovering and retrieving what the early Greeks experienced, thought, and said before it got lost in the unfolding of Western metaphysics.

Earlier I quoted Heidegger: "Perhaps, hidden in the words *tao* and *way* is the secret of all secrets of a thinking saying, provided that we let these names return to their unsaid and are capable of this letting" (GA 12:187). If this "secret of all secrets" is the non-dual dynamic of radiant emptiness, then *dao* mirrors (a) the no-form, no-thing emptiness as well as (b) the myriad things and concepts that manifest. This shows the possibility that what is unmanifest reveals the manifest within it (the unmanifest). How can we think this logical conundrum?

After quoting Heidegger on the secret of all secrets, Chang uses an image from Buddhism to try to *say* this unconceivable "secret":

> "The mystery of mysteries" [Heidegger: "the secret of all secrets"] might be seen through the eye of Buddhism:[45] that is, the Dharma Eye, which sees differentiation; the Wisdom Eye, which sees non-differentiation; and the Buddha Eye, which sees both differentiation and non-differen-tiation.[46] Through the Dharma Eye one sees the manifestations of *Tao* in ten thousand things. Through the Wisdom Eye one sees the wonder of *Tao*. Through the Buddha Eye one sees the identity of the manifestations and the wonder of *Tao*. Thus, the three eyes lead one through the gate of all the wonders of *Tao* … [W]hen one sees nothing, one does not sim-ply see nothing. One sees that within nothing, ten thousand things are simultaneously concealed and unconcealed. When one sees being, one is not limited to the form of being. One sees that being is simultaneously the formlessness of being and the wonder of non-being. Therefore, Lao Tzu says:
>
> > Its wonder and its manifestations are one and the same …
> > Their identity is called the mystery [secret]. (Tao, 2–3)

- *Note how, in seeing being, one is not limited to being as a form. "One sees that being is simultaneously the formlessness of being," that is, being and non-being are inextricably non-dually bound within the "one" – or in its more dynamic rendering: one-ing.*
- *Nothing is no-thing, but still dynamic. Not simply nothing.*
- *Within no-thing, things/forms are "simultaneously concealed and unconcealed." Within the radiant emptiness of beyng/Ereignis/dao, there is manifestation: phenomena appear, things/forms are there … simultaneously and **within** the no-thing formless dao.*

What is seen in this chapter cannot be conceptualized ... one is freed from conceptualization and released to the total identity of the seer and the seen, which is the highest stage of the mystery of *dao*. Without this experience of identity, everything that has been said here would merely be the "rubbish" of conceptualization. It would be the manifestation and not the wonder of *dao*. One must simultaneously be free from both the wonder of *dao* as an object of study and from the idea of the mystery as subjective feeling. Then one will achieve what Taoists call *"wu o chü wang"* or "both things and myself are forgotten." Once one is free from both subjectivity and objectivity, one can enter the gate of *Tao*. (Tao, 2–4)

- *The undifferentiated here is Heidegger's beyng (named in the myriad ways that he does) as well as radiant emptiness, while the differentiated is the name for manifestations as things/beings-phenomena, which exist in the outer world.*
- *the non-dual dynamic of the "identity of the manifestations and the wonder of Tao" is at stake here, in two ways: one, this identity names everything about dao; two, the other two ways of seeing dao (the wonder of Tao as an object of study and the mystery as subjective feeling) are* **distinguishable** *"aspects" of dao, but there is no dynamic in which they are* **separable.**
- *Freed from the duality of both sides, one has achieved "what Taoists call 'wu o chü wang' or 'both things and myself are forgotten.'"*
- *Forgetting the duality of objects in the world and the subject, we achieve the site of the rich and enriching site of dao.*

I as well as Heidegger find the language used here – describing a non-Western view or understanding of *dao* – to be useful to us in the West, as it mirrors the non-dual dynamic of radiant emptiness. The language here is accessible to us in the West and fits well within the retrieval of the what the Greeks thought and said about these matters.

Let me now turn to the Ames and Hall Introduction. This introduction is quite different from that of Chang. It uses a different vocabulary and is more broad-ranging, including a focus on aspects of the *Daodejing* that are not so central to this project. Here I will tap into their Introduction to find the words that fit into the thinking of this book. I will use the following list of contrasts:[47]

Daoist way, fitting our primary focus	_More traditional Western way_
process, dynamic, flexible	static, end result, objects
direct experience	abstract, logical
intuitive knowing	rational knowledge
feeling (more than just emotional)	
non-coercive spontaneity	
non-conceptual knowing	
synthesis, gathering, whole	analysis, distinguishing, parts
creativity, wonder, emptiness	myriad things
field	focus on things

In what follows here, I simply line up quotations from their Introduction, to fit into each of the above items in the list.

Process, dynamic, flexible.

"… things are always transforming … ceaseless transformation … particular 'things' are in fact processual." (15)

"But there is also a fluid continuity that is captured in expressions such as 'passing' and 'returning.'" (36)

"… integrity in a processual worldview is not _being one_, but _becoming one_." (38)

"The world is a complex set of transformative processes, never at rest." (42)

"… world made up of objects … unchangeable things … independent of us … [versus world as] constantly transforming flow of events or processes" (43)

Direct experience.

"_Daodejing_ is to prescribe a regimen of self-cultivation that will enable one to optimize one's experience in the world. These same wisdom passages are an integral element in this process that … result in … personal transformation." (9)

"making this life significant"[48] (11)

"... a balanced complexity of experience involves recourse to distinctly nonlogical criteria." (32)

"Actions uncompromised by stored knowledge or ingrained habits are ... unmediated ... and spontaneous." (39)

"Spontaneity in the Daoist tradition entails a contingency that attend[s] to the ever-continuing process of experience." (69)

Intuitive knowing.

Our usual mistake: "In order to function effectively in negotiating our environment, we need to rely upon our ability to make distinctions. These distinctions in themselves are certainly functional and enabling, but can distort the way in which we understand our world ... We can easily overdetermine the continuity within the life process as some underlying and unchanging foundation. Such linguistic habits can institutionalize and enforce an overly static vision of the world, and in so doing, deprive both language and life of their creative possibilities." (45)

On the other hand: "for the Daoist, there is an intoxicating bottomlessness to any particular event in our experience" (18) – thus the need for intuitive knowing.

"The interfusion of the variables leading to a balanced complexity of experience involves recourse to distinctly nonlogical criteria." (32)

"Way-making (*dao*) really does things noncoercively." (23)

The place of intuitive knowing-awareness becomes quite clear in chapter 14 of the *Daodejing* (Ames and Hall, 9–6):

1. Looking and yet not seeing it
   We thus call it "elusive."
   Listening and yet not hearing it

We call it "inaudible."
Groping and yet not getting it
We thus call it "intangible."
Because in sight, sound, and touch it is beyond determination
We construe it as inseparably one.

Ever so tangled, it defies discrimination
And reverts again to indeterminacy.
This is what is called the form of the formless
And the image of indeterminacy.
This is what is called the vague and the indefinite.

Non-coercive spontaneity.

"[N]oncoercive action, unprincipled knowing, and objectless desire have the following in common: To the extent that a disposition defined in these terms is efficacious, it enriches the world by allowing the process to unfold spontaneously on its own terms, while at the same time participating fully in it." (44)

Synthesis, gathering, the whole.

"becoming whole in one's relationship" (16)

"[E]ach particular element in our experience is holographic in the sense that it has implicated within it the entire field of experience." (18)

Real creativity "entails the spontaneous production of novelty, irreducible through causal analysis." (17)

In "the living ecological system ... all participants are organically interdependent." (18)

"continuity is prior to individuality" (21), "spontaneity involves recognizing the continuity between oneself and the other." (24)

"[T]he mutual entailing of opposites means that whatever 'goes out' and becomes consummately distinct, also returns." (27)

[From chapter 40 of the *Daodejing*] "The events of the world arise from the determinate [myriad things], and the determinate arises from the indeterminate [creativity, wonder, emptiness]." (28)

"[T]he endless alternation between rising and falling, emerging and collapsing, moving and attaining equilibrium that is occasioned by its own internal energy of transformation." (28)

"Naming as knowing must have the provisionality to accommodate engaged relationships as in their 'doing and undergoing' they deepen and become increasingly robust. Such knowing is dependent upon an awareness of the indeterminate aspects of things." (46)

Creativity, wonder, emptiness.

"[R]eal creativity is a condition of this continuing transforming process." (16)

"spontaneous emergence" (17)

"Creativity is contextual, transactional, and multidimensional." (17)

"For the Daoist, there is an intoxicationg bottomlessness to any particular event in our experience." (18)

"The vague order displays an undifferentiated commonality of character." (30)

"[T]here is only the vital energizing field and its focal manifestations." (63)

Comparing focus and field.

"[T]he most productive relationship between the vagueness of the continuous field [creativity, emptiness] and the narrowness of insistent particulars [focus on myriad things]." (31)

Field: open-endedness or creativity.
Focus: the insistent particulars.

With that:

"the balance between focus and field" (31)

"[T]wo mutually reinforcing levels of awareness advocated in the *Daodejing*: what we might call focal awareness and field awareness." (33)

"[I]nsight governing field awareness ... foregrounds the relational character of the elements [particulars] within the matrix of events ... [and] discourages any proclivity one might have to isolate things." (34)

I now turn to the **how of language**.
From the Ames and Hall Introduction:

There is one general point that we would make in our interpretation of this classical Chinese language. Above all we have argued for a *processual* understanding of classical Daoist cosmology. If this account is persuasive, it means that the vocabulary that expresses the worldview and the common sense in which the *Daodejing* is to be located is first and foremost *gerundive*. Because "things" in the *Daodejing* are in fact active "processes" and ongoing "events," nouns that would "objectify" this world are derived from and revert to a verbal sensibility. The ontological language of substance and essence that is sedimented into the English language tends to defy this linguistic priority, insisting upon the primacy of "the world" rather than the process of the world "*worlding*" and the myriad things "*happening*." (57, italics in this paragraph are mine)

The Chinese character for the word *dao* "is primarily gerundive, processional, and dynamic: a 'leading forth'" (57).
And finally:

It is the need to reach beyond our current language that requires the use of *dao* as a style name that suggests its *bottomless possibilities* rather than as a proper name that captures its present character. *Dao* is a name that evokes the power of the *imagination* and its capacity to *inspire activity* that *goes beyond* the horizons of our present world. (70, italics mine)

I now turn to **the words of the *Daodejing*.** There are many teachings in the *Daodejing*. Among them are:

- balance and harmony with nature
- balance and harmony among humans
- non-coercive action[49]
- warfare and military strategies
- rulership and leadership[50]
- community and the body politic
- greed and humility
- immortality or longevity
- wisdom and moderation

The chapters I have chosen to present here focus mainly on those lines that, in *their wording* of *dao*, reveal and mirror to us the word-images that can help us think and to say Heidegger's beyng/Ereignis; the unbroken wholeness of Bohm's holomovement or his non-physical emptiness as plenum; the unconditioned, no-form mind as space in Buddhism – all of which fits within the rubric "non-dual dynamic of radiant emptiness." And it can help us retrieve that core dimension of early Greek thinking that got covered over in the dominant and traditional Western philosophy. In the language of the *Daodejing*, the focus here is on the myriad things and no-form, no-thing *dao*/way – or the determinate and the indeterminate.

Let us start with the first two lines of the text, which are most enigmatic starting words:

The *Tao* that can be spoken of is not the *Tao* itself.
The name that can be given is not the name itself. (Chang)

> Way-making [*dao*] that can be put into words is not really way-making.
> And naming [*ming*] that can assign fixed reference to things is not
>   really naming. (Ames and Hall)

Chang's commentary quotes the Buddhist *Te-ching* (1546–1623):

> The *Tao* that is explained here is the genuine, real *Tao* ... which is free
> from form, free from names, and cannot be expressed in words. What
> can be explained or named is not the genuine, real *Tao*. Even the word
> *Tao* itself is not a real name. (Tao, 2)

How to unravel these words? Since I do not know Chinese, I have
to rely on reliable translations – in this case Ames and Hall. The
word *ming* or *wuming*, they say, is "naming without fixed reference." So *dao* is not really "nameless," and that word in Chinese
means "nameless as not assigning fixed reference to things." We
need to make distinctions in order to function on the lived level.
But we are in danger of reifying and making a thing out of what
we distinguish:

> We can easily and at real expense *overdetermine* the continuity within
> the life process as some underlying and *unchanging foundation*. Such lin-
> guistic habits can institutionalize and *enforce an overly static vision of the
> world*, and in so doing *deprive both language and life of their creative pos-
> sibilities*. (45, italics mine)

These first lines of the *Daodejing* as way-making say the continuity and ongoing dynamic of no-form emptiness. Ames and Hall
go on to say another kind of naming: one that "understands the
name as a shared ground of growing intimacy" (45). They call this
"naming as knowing" and say: "Such knowing is dependent upon
an awareness of the indeterminate aspects of things" (46). This
"naming" is one that is an ongoing shaping but does not define,
a responding but not capturing in concepts, a saying-doing. Not a
fixed reference that masters and delimits something, but rather a
saying that opens, a saying that highlights the ongoing, indeterminate openness of *dao*.

First of all, I would "name" this more fluid and more showing than defining activity as "saying" and then "saying as showing." This saying is more open-ended and can "say" what is less determinable or even indeterminate. This saying is gerundive, that is, verbal, saying movement and not stasis, world as process rather than world as substance. **It is part and parcel of poi-etic language.**

This way of saying is about an open-ended dynamic, about "bottomless possibilities" (70) without form and boundless, without boundaries. It cannot in any way be dualistic, because there is nothing in the dynamic that can be separated out into duality.

With these things in mind, we look again at the two translations of the first two lines of the *Daodejing*, as "saying" the same thing:

> The *Tao* that can be spoken of is not the *Tao* itself.
> The name that can be given is not the name itself. (Chang)

> Way-making (*dao*) that can be put into words is not really way-making.
> And naming (*ming*) that can assign fixed reference to things is not
>   really naming. (Ames and Hall)

Dao cannot be put into words in the way of concepts or intellectual comprehension. *Dao* is not measurable. *Dao* says without defining or giving names as we usually understand names. *Dao* shows in saying. Thus the saying of *dao* and our responsive saying is far from what we usually mean by naming!

Another way to say this quandary for our minding thinking is that this way of language cannot name anything fixed or abstract or determinate, thus in this sense is "nameless." And nameless here does not mean is not "sayable." This is the way of poi-etic language and saying, as we showed earlier.

We must go beyond the way we normally use language today – beyond to poi-etic saying. We must go beyond language as defining and limiting – beyond to the saying of unlimited possibilities. Beyond to a saying that calls forth opening, freeing, dynamic of radiant emptiness, that is, another word for what *dao* says. Within this no-form dynamic of *dao*, myriad things manifest themselves as non-dually participating in the wonder of *dao*.

Dao is verbal, "leading forth," thus dynamically way as way-making. Not a thing but a dynamic.

I now turn to **the text of the *Daodejing*.** We will look in some detail at those chapters of the *Daodejing* that address our primary concern in this book: how *dao* mirrors the non-dual dynamic of radiant emptiness, which in turn mirrors Heidegger's beyng/Ereignis and the discoveries of quantum physics and the Buddhist understanding of no-form mind as space – and the same dimension hidden within early Greek thinking.

This is how I will organize this part: First, I will quote the lines from three translations, numbering them as follows:

1. Chang, *Tao: A New Way of Thinking*
2. Ames and Hall, *Daodejing "Making This Life Significant"*
3. Lau, *Tao Te Ching*[51]

Then I will weave together the sayings in a way that makes them available to our project here: retrieving Greek thinking to find a similar deep thread there. In other words: While hearing the various words and ways of saying the same, we can get a glimpse or have an experience of what is at stake. In that context, we will try to meld the saying of *dao* with the saying of Heidegger ... by letting the words that emerge in the *Daodejing* mirror and show the poi-etic words in our language, in order to return to the Greeks and retrieve in *their words* the dynamic we are pursuing and that is "pursuing" us. Here goes!

Some Guidelines for Reading and Processing Some of the Chapters of the *Daodejing*:

a. Using three translations is an attempt to get closer to the original, which most of us cannot read. Since we do not have access to the original, having several ways of translating the words offers a richer understanding. And above all, multiple translations hold us back from thinking that we can nail down the meanings.

b. Using my words "non-dual dynamic of radiant emptiness" as a guiding star to say-show what Heidegger says with beyng/ Ereignis, words that appear in the following chapters from the *Daodejing* that *say* this dynamic include *dao*, way, way-making, wonder, mystery, mother, nothing-nothingness, void, space, empty-emptiness, life-force, mysterious-dark female, non-being, the hub of non-being, the formless, immaterial, "elusive," indeterminacy, beyond determination, indefinite, evanescent, primordial beginning, destiny of being, original non-differentiation, all-pervading, origin, fetal beginnings. Note how many words are given for this one no-form dynamic of radiant emptiness, mirroring Heidegger's beyng/Ereignis!

c. Words saying the "things" that manifest and emerge from this *dao*-emptiness include forms, objects, substances, events, myriad things-creatures, manifestations, everything that is happening, clay pots or lamps of clay (all things), all things together in action, progeny (of *dao*, the mother).

d. Words that name the non-dual at-oneness of (b) and (c) include identity as mystery, obscure, forms within the ineffable and indistinct, images-events within the indefinite and vague, substance within the shadowy and indistinct.

e. Words to say the *dynamic* in this one-ing of empty no-being and "all that is" or whatever emerges within that dynamic include entry of all wonders, swinging gateway of the manifold mysteries-secrets, function of a thing arising from non-being-nothingness, adapting the nothing to kneading clay pots, the drawstring of way-making, the thread running through the way (*dao*), things unceasingly moving proceeding back to the origin, returning to equilibrium, returning to roots, *dao* nurturing all things, all things offering allegiance to an easy-flowing stream.

f. Remembering that this search to *say* the no-thing of beyng/ Ereignis or the dynamic of radiant emptiness calls for many "names," hear what Heidegger says about the work at hand:

Every naming … with a single word is based on a false notion. Every word is taken from tradition. The fact that the grounding-attunement of another beginning has to have many names does not argue against its at-oneness [its non-dual, inseparable character] but rather confirms its richness and strangeness. (GA 65:22)

Keeping in mind what we said a few pages ago as we read the first two lines of the book, we now look closely at several chapters of the *Daodejing* or the *Tao Te Ching*. Note that the numbers 1 to 3 refer to the three translations listed above: 1 = Chang, 2 = Ames and Hall, and 3 = Lau.

Chapter 1

1. Oftentimes without intention I see the wonder of *Tao*.
   Oftentimes with intention I see its manifestations.
   Its wonder and its manifestations are one and the same.
   Since their emergence, they have been called by different names.
   Their identity is called the mystery.
   From mystery to further mystery:
   The entry of all wonders!

2. The nameless is the fetal beginnings of everything that is happening,
   While that which is named is their mother.
   Thus, to be really objectless in one's desires is how one observes the
      mysteries of all things,
   While really having desires is how one observes their boundaries.
   These two – the nameless and what is named – emerge from the
      same source yet are referred to differently.
   Together they are called obscure,
   They are the swinging gateway of the manifold mysteries.

3. The nameless was the beginning of heaven and earth;
   The named was the mother of the myriad creatures.
   Hence always rid yourself of desires in order to observe its secrets;
   But always allow yourself to have desires in order to observe its
      manifestations.
   These two are the same
   But diverge in name as they issue forth.

Being the same they are called mysteries,
Mystery upon mystery –
The gateway of the manifold secrets.

- *The wonder of dao, the fetal beginnings, the nameless (as in having no fixed determination) is without form and no thing – without, free of, empty of every-thing.*
- *The named is the mother of myriad creatures, manifestations … also known as "things" or "beings."*
- *These two are a one and can be called the non-dual dynamic.*
- *Their sameness is called mystery, obscure, mystery upon mystery.*
- *The active, unfolding dynamic is the swinging gateway of the entire manifold of mysteries, secrets, wonders.*
- *We can know this if we are without desire or intention – "objectless in one's desires" – free of concepts, constructs.*

Chapter 4

1. *Tao* functions through its nothingness.
   And cannot be conceived of as full of things.
   Profound indeed, it is the model of all things.

2. Way-making being empty,
   You make use of it
   But do not fill it up.
   So abysmally deep –
   It seems the predecessor of everything that is happening.

3. The way is empty, yet use will not drain it.
   Deep, it is like the ancestors of the myriad things.

- *This chapter focuses on emptiness or the indeterminate dao – we can say: inexhaustible and immeasurable – even as myriad things emerge within the dao.*
- *Dao or way-making is at work in its nothingness or the empty.*
- *Dao cannot be drained or filled up.*
- *Dao is "abysally deep," without ground.*

Chapter 6

1. The spiritual reality of the void never ceases to exist.
   We call it the mystery of passivity.
   The entry to the mystery of passivity is the origin of the universe.
   Unceasing, it always remains.
   Drawn upon, it is never exhausted.

2. The life-force of the valley never dies –
   This is called the dark female.
   The gateway of the dark female –
   This is called the root of the world.
   Wispy and delicate, it only seems to be there,
   Yet its productivity is bottomless.

3. The spirit of the valley never dies.
   This is called the mysterious female.
   The gateway of the mysterious female
   Is called the root of heaven and earth.
   Dimly visible, it seems as if it were there,
   Yet use will never drain it.

- *This chapter continues the primary focus on the dao as indeterminate and no-thing with no-form.*
- *Dao as the life-force is timelessly there, emerging.*
- *It is the mystery of the dark, the void, female as the fecundity of radiant emptiness, the site of giving-life, site within which things emerge, without dominating, that is, the dynamic potential within which **things** become manifest.*
- *The word **passivity** here mirrors the **dynamis** in Aristotle – both words misrepresenting what is at stake. Not the **materia prima** or **unformed matter** of the traditional (TI) translations, mirroring something passive and waiting to be acted upon. Just as with Aristotle, the retrieving translation is more like "dynamic potential," as it mirrors a dynamic equilibrium, a dynamic stillness, ongoing and ever alive pregnant possibility. The process of creativity that has no beginning and no end, that is, is timeless.*

- *Here and in chapter 10 dao is called the mysterious female as the "indeterminate source spontaneously and inexhaustibly gives rise to the provisionally determinate phenomena that we experience around us" (85). Dark female as the "fecundity of emptiness" (86) that is at work in giving-life and letting-emerge, "without the presence of some controlling hand" (90).*
- *This no-form and no-thing dao can be called the state of non-differentiation or indeterminate, even as the determinate emerges within it as things-manifestations. C.G. Jung says about this: "The beginning, in which everything is still one, and which therefore appears as the highest goal, lies at the bottom of the sea in the darkness of the unconscious."[52] Since here we are saying-showing the dynamic that is beyond subjectivity, I would read the word **unconscious** to say: the darkness of inexhaustibility, of dynamic emptiness. Darkness of the dynamic fecundity of emptiness. This takes us away from the subjectiveness of the unconscious in/of the individual.*

Chapter 14

1. Gaze at it; there is nothing to see.
   It is called the formless.
   Heed it; there is nothing to hear.
   It is called the soundless.
   Grasp it; there is nothing to *hold* on to.
   It is called the immaterial.
   We cannot inquire into these three,
   Hence, they interfuse into one.

   Invisible, it cannot be called by any name.
   It returns again to nothingness.
   Thus, we call it the form of the formless
   The image of the imageless.
   It is the evasive.

   This will enable you to understand the primordial beginning.
   This is the essential *Tao*.

2. Looking and yet not seeing it
  We thus call it "elusive."
  Listening and yet not hearing it
  We call it "inaudible."
  Groping and yet not getting it
  We thus call it "intangible."
  Because in sight, sound, and touch it is beyond determination
  We construe it as inseparably one.

  Ever so tangled, it defies discrimination
  And reverts again to indeterminacy.
  This is what is called the form of the formless
  And the image of indeterminacy.
  This is what is called the vague and the indefinite.

  This is what is called the drawstring of way-making.

3. What cannot be seen is called evanescent;
  What cannot be heard is called rarefied;
  What cannot be touched is called minute.
  These three cannot be fathomed
  And so are confused and looked upon as one.

  Dimly visible, it cannot be named
  And returns to that which is without substance.
  This is called the shape that has no shape,
  The image that is without substance.
  This is called indistinct and shadowy.

  The ability to know the beginning of antiquity
  Is called the thread running through the way [dao].

- *The translations of key words here are quite different.*
- *The invisible dao is called in line 1–2: the formless; in line 2–2: elusive; in line 3–2: rarified. Given the focus of this book, I would use **formless**: the non-dual and no-form dynamic of radiant emptiness. Later the invisible dao is called immaterial (1), intangible (2), and without substance (3).*

Chapter 16

1. All things are together in action,
    But I look into their non-action.
    Things are unceasingly moving and restless,
    Yet each one is proceeding back to the origin.
    Proceeding back to the origin is quiescence.
    To be in quiescence is to return to the destiny of being.

2. In the process of all things, emerging together,
    We can witness their reversion.
    Things proliferate,
    And each again returns to its root.
    Returning to the root is called equilibrium.
    Now as for equilibrium – this is called returning to the propensity
        of things.

3. I do my utmost to attain emptiness;
    I hold firmly to stillness.
    The myriad creatures all rise together
    And I watch their return.
    The teeming creatures
    All return to their separate roots.
    Returning to one's roots is known as stillness.
    This is what is meant by returning to one's destiny.

- *Differentiation in the* **manifestations** *of dao, together in action, emerging together, the myriad creatures all rising together, and*
- *non-differentiation in the* **wonder** *of dao, attaining emptiness, seeing non-action of manifestations (as in non-coercive non-forcing action, like water that flows without force) or as "the absence of any course of action that interferes" with how things unfold, actions "uncompromised by stored knowledge or ingrained habits … unmediated … spontaneous" (39).*
- *The return from the* **manifestations** *of dao to the* **wonder** *of dao – here called origin or root – is the dynamic one-ing of the manifestations and the wonder of dao in their non-dual at-oneness. This is the non-dual dynamic of radiant emptiness.*

- *This **return to the non-dual oneness** of the dao is named here as origin-roots.*
- *This return to origin-roots is called no-form non-dual dynamic **equilibrium**, dynamically active **stillness**, or the "ringing of stillness" (Heidegger) as powerful movement, or*
- ***quiescence** in the way that "muddy water, when stilled, slowly becomes clear" (98) or the sounding word's return to soundlessness or manifestations of dao returning to the wonder of dao.*
- *This is dao's **destiny/propensity**, its natural inclination, its aptness, its way.*

Chapter 21

1. That which is inherent in the great attainment (void) is the echo of *Tao*.
   That which is *Tao* is indistinct and ineffable.
   Ineffable and indistinct, yet therein are forms.
   Indistinct and ineffable, yet therein are objects.

2. Those of magnificent character [*de*]
   Are committed to way-making [*dao*] alone. As for the process of
      way-making,
   It is ever so indefinite and vague.
   Though vague and indefinite,
   There are images within it.
   Though indefinite and vague,
   There are events within it.

3. In his every movement a man of great virtue
   Follows the way and the way only.
   As a thing, that way is shadowy [and] indistinct.
   Indistinct and shadowy, yet within it is an image;
   Shadowy and indistinct, yet within it is a substance.

- *Here I want simply to emphasize the words that say (a) what formless dao is while (b) yet therein is form.*
- *Ineffable and indistinct, indefinite and vague, shadowy and indistinct … while therein are forms-objects, images-events, images-substances.*

- *Gathering this: The process of dao or way-making is both ineffable-indefinite-shadowy **and** carries within it form-object-substance. Non-dual dynamic of radiant emptiness.*

Chapter 32

1. *Tao* is real, yet unnameable.
   It is original non-differentiation and invisible.
   Nevertheless, nothing in the universe can dominate it.

2. Way-making [*dao*] is really nameless.
   Although in this unworked state it is of little consequence [subtle],
   No one would dare to condescend to it.

3. The way is forever nameless.
   Though the uncarved block is small
   No one in the world dare claim its allegiance.

- *The only thing I want to say here is what Ames and Hall say about what "nameless" means, namely that dao is not really "nameless" but that the word in Chinese means "nameless" in the sense that it is "a kind of naming that does not assign fixed reference to things" (45). Nameless = undefined. Undefinable. But perhaps sayable poi-etically?*

Chapter 34

1. The magnificent *Tao* is all-pervading.
   It may penetrate to either this side or that side.
   It nurtures all things, but does not rule them.

2. Way-making [*dao*] is an easy-flowing stream
   Which can run in any direction.
   … all things offer it allegiance
   And yet it does not act as master.

3. The way is broad, reaching left as well as right.
   The myriad creatures depend on it for life yet it
   claims no authority.

- *Dao nurtures without dominating. The dynamic that is hardly known,*
  that is, hidden in its dynamism.

Chapter 52

1. When one is aware of the origin,
   One knows its manifestations.
   When one is aware of its manifestations,
   Yet abides with its origin,
   One never falls short in all of one's life.

2. You have to have gotten to this mother,
   Before you can understand her progeny.
   And once you have understood her progeny,
   If you go back and safeguard the mother,
   You will live to the end of your days without danger.

3. The world had a beginning
   And this beginning could be the mother of the world.
   When you know the mother
   Go on to know the child.
   After you have known the child
   Go back to holding fast to the mother,
   And to the end of your days you will not meet with danger.

***

On the next page – at the end of part 2 and anticipating part 3 (the Greek words themselves!) – I present a kind of collage ... a poe-tic saying ... "painting the picture," as it were.

These words:

Dao, way-making, the indeterminate, beyond all conditions (Daoism); mind, mind like space, no-thing and no-form, emptiness, clarity and emptiness of mind, mind as non-dually non-existent and not non-existent, timeless awareness, awareness beyond form, beyond all conditions (Buddhism); quantum mind, quantum field of energy exchange, the uncertainty principle, the incompleteness theorem, chaos theory, entanglement, the basic oneness of the universe, from not-real elementary particles to a world of potentiality, quantum web of connection, field = force flowing through the universe, vibrating and indeterminate packets of energy, quantum sea of light, zero point field, empty space of seething energies (quantum physics); energy fields, unbroken wholeness, non-local, non-causal relationships of elements, dynamic of empty plenum, undivided flowing movement without borders, holomovement, implicate order, infinite sea of energy in empty space (Bohm)

say, and in saying show and mirror to us

the no-form, no-thing and non-dual dynamic, not findable,
not graspable in concepts, but knowable in experience, the non-dual
    dynamic of radiant emptiness,

which is

beyond any frame of reference
the basis for everything
the radiant emptiness from where all things arise
that within which all things/beings arise and disappear

what Heidegger calls

beyng (German **Seyn**, over against **Sein**-being) … non-concealment-
Unverborgenheit … enowning-**Ereignis** … timing-spacing …
    emergent emerging (**anwesendes Anwesen**).[53]

**and what we, after and along with Heidegger,
will find in the Greek words**

apeiron, aletheia, physis, eon, logos, psyche, noos-nous.

Now to the Greeks!

Retrieving, by Refreshing, What the Greek Words Say and in Saying Show, Shaped by Heidegger

Part 3 goes directly to the main focus of the book, namely how that non-dual dynamic of radiant emptiness – aka dao, buddha mind, the field of energy in quantum physics, beyng/Ereignis – is a thread that runs through all of Greek philosophy, especially early Greek thinking. It is a careful and exciting turn to the originary meanings/sayings of seven key words (ἄπειρον, ἀλήθεια, φύσις, ἐόν, λόγος, ψυχή, νοῦς) and three Greek words that easily accompany the main thrust (ἀπορία, χώρα, ἕν), showing the work of refreshing and rethinking retrieving that is at the core of this writing project.

As we begin part 3, let me compare again the "traditional and inherited" and the "refreshing and retrieving" words, a pithy way of seeing the difference. The traditional and inherited (TI) – conceptual – words say the way things are as dualistic, static, substance beings … where everything is a being. The refreshing and retrieving (RR) – non-conceptual – words that say the way things are as non-dual, dynamic and changing, revealing emptiness – and especially words that say the *no-thing and no-form dynamic.*

Repeating what I presented earlier in the book, let me put these differences in a kind of chart, for easy reference:

a. Words that reveal the way things are in TI:
    the traditional and inherited way as
    • dualistic,
    • conceptual,

- static, substance or beings ...
- everything is a being.

b. Words that reveal the way things are in RR:
the refreshing and retrieving way as
- non-dual,
- non-conceptual,
- dynamic and changing ...
- revealing no-thing dynamic emptiness.[1]

Undoing our amnesia. What is the way there – to the early Greeks – given how far away our traditional and inherited way is from the refreshing and retrieving way?

From within the TI ways of thinking (the first beginning) it is not so easy to move to the RR ways of thinking (the other beginning). The way there is hardly travelled and barely known. Heidegger makes his way on this road with the awareness that thinking is not "there" yet – and, above all, that the "there" that thinking moves toward is different from the "here" where our normal, traditional, inherited paradigm has its footing. He is keenly aware of this when he says, in the dialogue with a Japanese:

> I was moved to attempt to walk a path without knowing where it would lead me. I knew only the first steps, because they were unrelenting in their beckoning, even as the extent of their reach shifted and blurred. (GA 12:87)

And it takes courage:

> It seems to me that, in the field in which we are walking, we will come to what is originarily intimated [*das Vertraute*], if we do not shy away from the passage through what is estranging. (GA 12:120)

Both-and, not either-or. In our usual way of thinking in Western philosophy we think dualistically. Since we do not know the RR ways so well, we do not give them the respect they deserve. But the RR ways of thinking – in thinking beyng as emptiness, dynamic, and no-thing – go beyond either-or. Radiant emptiness is a non-dual dynamic. Here I want to explore the possibility that the Greeks "knew" both ways and that, within the non-dual dynamic of the other beginning (RR), they experienced both as one.

***

Excursus: Note that the Daoist texts we just looked at stress this both as one, or both-and. Merging several ways of wording lines from Chapter 1 of the *Daodejing*, I offer this:

> The formless no-thing *dao* is called its wonder, which is the nameless.
> The emerging things-phenomena are called its manifestations, which are the named.
> Its wonder [the formless no-thing *dao*] and its manifestations [what emerges within the wonder of *dao* as phenomena-beings] are one and the same.
> Their sameness – or non-dual one-ing – is called the mystery.

Commenting on this chapter, Chang says:

> ... when one sees nothing, one does not simply see nothing. One sees that, within nothing, ten thousand things are simultaneously concealed and unconcealed. When one sees being, one is not limited to the form of being.[2]

Within no-thing, things/forms are "simultaneously concealed and unconcealed." Within the radiant emptiness of beyng/Ereignis/*dao*, there is manifestation: phenomena appear, things/forms are there ... simultaneously and **within** the no-thing formless *dao*. We could say that the first beginning sees only the manifestations of *dao* and not the wonder of formless *dao*.

Another set of word-images from the section on Daoism is that of field and focus. From the "Philosophical Introduction" in *Daodejing*:

> [T]the most productive relationship between the vagueness of the continuous field [creativity, emptiness] and the narrowness of insistent particulars [focus on myriad things].[3]

[T]he balance between focus and field.[4]

[T]wo mutually reinforcing levels of awareness advocated in the *Daode-jing*: what we might call focal awareness and field awareness."[5]

Field: open-endedness or creativity or radiant emptiness.
Focus: the insistent particulars, phenomena, beings.

End of excursus.

***

We in the West read Greek philosophy mostly to fit into the dominant Western paradigm, that is, dealing with what is dualistic and conceptual, with static, substances-beings, where everything is a being (TI: the traditional and inherited way). **The first beginning**. Here we want to let emerge **the other beginning**, where the key dynamic is beyng as dynamic emptiness, non-dual, non-conceptual, dynamic and changing … revealing no-thing emptiness (RR: refreshing and retrieving).

Do we see Greek thinking as only the first beginning, perhaps with intimating hints from the other beginning of which they were not aware? Or do we see Greek thinking as taking place within the non-dual dynamic of radiant emptiness (my way of saying Heidegger's one question, that of the truthing of beyng), in which both ways were non-dually one – the "mystery" of their "sameness"? That things/beings emerge, inseparable in the non-dual no-thing dynamic? Both ways/beginnings always already there, in a harmonious one? In any case, to "return to the Greeks" is to find what we have lost.

The richness of the both-and is significant, in that (a) the first beginning and the other beginning are not one after the other, since (b) the other beginning is timeless (it never started at any time and never comes at any time). We within the traditional Western paradigm feel as if the other beginning is unavailable and therefore does not exist. But what really happened is that it got covered over so completely in the unfolding of the history of Western philosophy that we are barely aware of it, if at all.

So how can we make the leap to the non-dual dynamic of radiant emptiness that is at the heart of this timeless starting, what Heidegger calls the "other beginning"? Well, we cannot start anywhere else except within the first beginning (TI). That's where we are! But when we are attentively aware and open, we realize that (a) something is missing and then come to (b) the non-conceptual experience of this other beginning (RR). In a sense we might say that if we stay actively within the first beginning and heed what emerges therein, our experience can move beyond reflection, to the site of the opening to this other beginning, which is what we aim to retrieve. In a sense, we might say that we learn to dwell within the duality until the moment that our experience opens up to the non-dual dynamic of radiant emptiness of its own accord. This is knowable beyond conceptualization and is sayable only in non-conceptual, poi-etic language. Perhaps these words sound strange, but try to stay open to and free for this possibility. I am confident that dwelling in this moment allows for the flashpoint of awareness of that emptiness (what Heidegger pursued all his life as the meaning or question of being).

(Note: For Heidegger's telling insight into this process – from things/beings to the formless dynamic of radiant emptiness, and so on – see the discussion of startled dismay, reservedness, awe, and intimating in part 2-c.)

Can we read Heidegger to say that this no-thing dynamic (which is at work and which we can experience) is inherently part of Greek thinking and saying? Yes! Can we read Heidegger – in his persevering pursuit of the meaning of being as no-thing, not a being, but within which all things/beings emerge – as prodding us to retrieve what the Greeks knew and said, so that we can retrieve beyng as no-thing radiant emptiness ... for our time and the transformation of thinking and language? Yes! As we read in a more Greek way than we have inherited, our refreshing retrieval will open us to the non-dual dynamic of radiant emptiness, aka beyng.

Everything is contained in this both-and, no-thing dynamic. This is not available to us in **concepts** or conceptual logic. The rich and full "empty" is freeing and opening to our **experience**. This is our challenge.

a. ἀπορία / aporia

Seeing things from where we are in the history of philosophy and thinking, we can benefit by starting from the opening that is provided in understanding what in Greek is called
aporia. This presenting of *aporia* will demonstrate how this last
part will work. First, I will present in schematic form how the
Greek word – here *aporia* – is thought in each of the two ways:
TI = traditional-inherited and RR = refreshing-retrieving. Then
I will work with texts from Heidegger that will point the way in
hearing these two ways. Finally, I will lay out how Heidegger's
words, joining with my own, open out onto what is possible for
us today, *as we, in reading and hearing, refresh what the Greek words*
say *for thinking*.

ἀπορία	TI	difficulty, question, problem
aporia		state of conflicting arguments
		cognitive state of no-way-out
		a logical-conceptual puzzle
	RR	no-way-out, undecidability, as *experience*
		condition of being perplexed
		"things about which we need to be puzzled"
		(Aristotle, *Metaphysics*, 995a24)
		a "living" puzzle

The first important thing to remember is that, here where we
are (TI), *aporia* usually or mostly refers to a mental-intellectual
problem: a logical impasse-enigma-conundrum. An internal contradiction of a logical disjunction. A paradox in thought and in
statements. It is an epistemological *aporia*. Or – as in deconstruction – *aporia* names the contradictory moment in a *text*: the text
undermines its own rhetoric. Seen conceptually, *aporia* says enigmatic, inexplicable, bewildering, strange, puzzling – being at a
loss, no-way-out, an impasse – but only *logically, in statements and
in texts*.

Well, *aporia* says something that goes way beyond the limiting
epistemological issue, beyond to the no-way-out or impasse in

direct experience. A perplexing difficulty or estranging puzzlement as *lived*, non-conceptually. It is on this sense of *aporia* that Heidegger focuses when he rethinks *aporia*. And it is this second sense of the word that fits within the journey of this book. Incomprehensible or no-way-out for *minding thinking* rather than whatever it is for calculating and conceptualizing thought.

First, we hear how Heidegger says the *aporia* that confronts us. He says it with the words *beings* and *being* (what Heidegger will later name: *Seyn/beyng*. Beings are phenomena in the world, things, what gets manifest. Beyng is the formless, no-thing dynamic of emptiness. Heidegger portrays the unresolvable tension – *aporia* – thus:

> We stand between two equally unsurpassable limits: On the one hand, as we think and say "being 'is,'" we immediately make being into a being and thereby deny the proper work [*energeia*] of being [later called beyng]. *Being gets disavowed by us.* But, on the other hand, as long as we experience beings, we can never deny the "being" and the "is." (GA 51:80)*

> On the one hand being cannot be gotten around; on the other hand, when entered into, being gets immediately made over into "*a* being." (81)

> In every attempt to think being, being always gets turned the wrong way and changed into *a* being and is thus destroyed in what it is in its core. And yet: Being in its otherness from beings [being that is other than beings, eventually called beyng] cannot be denied. (82)

> The word *being* is undefined-indefinite [*unbestimmt*] in its meaning, and still we understand it as defined [*bestimmt*]. "Being" turns out to be (shows itself as) something highly defined [but remains] totally undefined [*höchst bestimmt völlig unbestimmt*]. (GA 40:83)

---

* Unless otherwise noted, all quotations in this section are from this text.

Heidegger's and our search is for the no-thing no-form beyng, even as it almost inevitably gets taken as *a being*. If we overlay Heidegger's words *beyng* and *beings* upon the words we have been working with, then *beyng* says the no-form no-thing dynamic of radiant emptiness, *dao,* the indeterminate, buddha mind, quantum field, sea of energy in "empty space" or the immeasurable – and *beings* says phenomena, things, forms, manifestations, substances, myriad creatures.

In our usual comportment to no-form beyng, we find the *aporia* too much and quickly revert to beings. This reversion – abandonment of beyng – is done so decisively that we call this "loss" a gain! We focus on what is manageable and gives us more security.

> One is satisfied with beings and abandons being [*Sein;* one can hear this as "beyng"] so decisively that one does not see this abandonment at all for what it is [a loss], but rather takes it as a win [gain, *Gewinn*], as the benefit of not being continually disturbed in the pursuit of [engagement with] beings. From where does this remarkable contentment originate? (40)

We are presented here with an *aporia*, a place that is difficult or, from the TI perspective, logically impossible to pass through. What Heidegger proposes and evokes is different: not thinking as thinking *about*, but thinking as expanding into, having a genuine connection to this *aporia*, the **experience** of "no way out." Although this thinking is not easy, I find it exciting, moving as it does into and within the core of what makes us fully and richly human.

Gathering up: the place of the opening of the question is the *aporia* (no way out) of being's always getting turned into *a* being, and at the same time is incomprehensible in its "isness." Rather than thinking *about* this *aporia*, we are called to expand into the domain of being in its aporetic and unresolvable character – and to *experience* that.

Speaking about difference or dichotomy in the *aporia*, juxtaposing, as it were, is only logical or conceptual. When we open up to our experience in the *aporia* or no-way-out, then it is an *opening*! Expanding. This gets heard in the *energeia* or experience of opening. What is called for is a language that says this domain in its folding and unfolding, in the movement that it carries *in itself*. This calls for seeing and experiencing the aspects and shapes of the tension in the imaging of weaving and nuance rather than in any kind of epistemological juxtaposition or opposition.

How to enter the question or domain of being? Given that the place of opening is aporetic, how does thinking expand into this *aporia*? The German word for experience is *erfahren*, which means literally: to move or pass through, to go all the way into and through. Experiencing ourselves in the no-way-out of the *aporia* (namely, wanting to think beyng and finding ourselves capable only of returning to beings – wanting to come to know the **no-form** *dao* and finding ourselves limited to the **manifestations** of *dao*) – we need to go all the way into the no-way-out. To stay in the dynamic of the no-way-out, even as it presses upon us as we dwell within it. Note that logic cannot help, even as it tries to get out by jumping the fence!

In presenting the unresolvability (*aporia*) of this question, Heidegger opens up a pathway with several clues or steps as to how we in our thinking might enter into this space of unresolvability:

- **Opening our eyes.** In our insecurity, do we close our eyes and ears to the *aporia*? Or try to eliminate it by dismissing the question of beyng? Heidegger says there is a third option: that we move into and stay with the no-way-out, that, "as a starting and for the time being, we look around [browse] in this no-way-out situation and abandon the rush to get out of it" (82).
- **Staying in and with the no-way-out.** Finding that, as humans thinking, we are left in a region that simply has or is this utter openness, dynamically in tension. In this context Heidegger says:

In a strange sort of way being has burst open what is own to us as *human*. We belong to being and yet do not belong to it. We dwell in the region of being and yet are not able to be in it directly. We are as if homeless in what is most truly home. (89)

- *Being (**Sein**) here could well be said as beyng (**Seyn**).*
   This kind of dwelling is not possible via logic or concepts. For both are by definition dualistic and are far from experience. It is possible only in non-dual and non-conceptual dwelling in a no-way-out that is *experientially* non-dual and non-conceptual.
- **Staying within this domain of unresolvability.**

[T]he recollecting of being [gathering oneself unto being or beyng] is remembering [becoming wakeful to] the first beginning of Western thinking. This remembering [or being wakeful to] the first origin is a preparatory thinking [*Vordenken*] into the more originary starting [what gets things started]. (92)

This preparatory thinking needs to be *unbeeilt*: unrushed, needing its own time (not the hasty moving from one thing to another) (93). It also needs to be *ungerahmt*: unframed, not defined, needing its own opening and expanding (not the limitation of the space of positions or niches, as in "this niche" and then "that niche"). Here, to "remember" is to be transported into beyng itself, which unfolds in that timeless starting – still unfolds, even after the beginning of metaphysics and continuing into today's thinking, which normally focuses on beings alone. Being in its originary character as beyng is always close to us, as close as can be. Therefore, what seems like being transported into that domain is really only remembering and being awake to our being always already there.
- **Being aware and awake.** First we become aware that "this extreme no-way-out [*Auswegslosigkeit*] might come from being [beyng?] itself" (81). That is, it is where we find ourselves, even as we know that there is something more. The no-way-out reveals to us that something is confining and something is missing. Experience gives us a hint of an opening, that there is a rich possibility held within beyng as Ereignis or as radiant emptiness.
   Being within or expanding into the domain of the no-way-out, we become awake to the gathering of and opening to beyng. Very simply and in each case, this opening-gathering is a transformation (*Wandlung*) in our way of being. This transformation

needs a preparedness. This preparedness needs an attentiveness (*Aufmerken*). Finally, this attentiveness needs a first remembering of being (*erste Erinnerung in das Sein*) (cf. GA 51:93). All of this remains anticipatory. We simply cannot jump too quickly.

- **Trying another way of thinking.** In the unresolvability/*aporia* of the being-question, in the thinking that is called to respond to the *aporia*, and in going all the way through and into unresolvability, another way of thinking is called for. What is called for is a thinking that thinks the movement or *energeia* in the *aporia* of beyng, but not as an oppositional movement. What is called for is a thinking that does not go back and forth between differences, but one that expands into the clearing of the onefold of being-beyng in its own unique movement.

b. The Greek Words That Say Beyng as "Radiant Emptiness"

The primary Greek words that we will focus on are words that say this radiant emptiness that belongs to the question of being. The non-dual, no-form dynamic of movement, becoming, change – within beyng as radiant emptiness.

These key Greek words say beyng as radiant emptiness – what is no-thing whatsoever but emerges, what is no-thing whatsoever even as it is at work, what is no-thing whatsoever even as we can experience it:

ἄπειρον, ἀλήθεια, ἐόν, φύσις, λόγος, ψυχή, νόος/νοῦς.

We will look at each one of these Greek words, following the three steps outlined above: the TI–RR schematic, Heidegger's reading, my own gathering. We will show how Heidegger's reading of these Greek words, in their originary saying and showing, takes us from the traditional and inherited ways of thinking and saying to the refreshing and retrieving possibilities in the words and their saying. Then we see what we can learn and open up to after – following along with – Heidegger.

Before we turn to how Heidegger works with these Greek words, let me address how the TI and the RR words "fit together."

Up to now and for the most part, I have tried to let the RR words emerge "as if" this way of saying is more important than the TI word-images and sayings. We have to be careful here. A certain primary focus on the RR words is called for, in order to get a better feel for what is missing in philosophy and in experience – namely, the lack of focus and understanding – and above all *awareness* – of what the RR word-images open up for us. It is important to understand that the TI words belong essentially to the way things are *within* the dynamic named in the RR images and sayings. Methodologically, we might call the RR thinking of radiant emptiness an "add-on," always at the edges of what we already know and how we already think. But when we open up to what the RR images tell us, we realize that – far from being an "add-on" at the "edges" – these word-images take us to an experience of the core dynamic of emptiness that contains it all. **This** is the "true" of the way things are.

This means that both sets of words are fitting ways of reading, thinking, and saying what is at issue. Now, rather than the either-or of TI *or* RR, it is a matter of the both-and. That is, both ways of thinking and saying are there for the Greeks. These questions now are: One, how the Greeks thought and said the RR; and two, how to take into account that **both the TI and the RR ways** belong to the non-dual dynamic of radiant emptiness, which is the no-thing and no-form dynamic that holds and mirrors the "whole shebang."

Note that this challenge is very difficult to incorporate into our usual ways of thinking. This challenge hovers over what happens in part 3, for the simple reason that (a) our usual thinking is mostly regarding the TI words, and (b) we cannot just discard this way as we open up to the RR word-images. Therefore, anything this book says about this challenge is preparatory. My own thinking is on the way. We need time to digest what this means for experiencing, thinking, and saying the way things are.

Hear Chapter 1 of Chang's *Tao de Ching* on this one-ing of the two. I paraphrase:

> The wonder of the no-form no-thing "emptiness" of *dao*
> And its manifestations (things, phenomena)
> Even though they have different names

They are a one-ing (an "identity," obscure, a mystery).
[Chang's translation of last line of chapter 1:
"The entry of all wonders!"]

Once we are in step with the RR ways, experiencing, thinking and saying the non-dual dynamic of radiant emptiness, the *question* of "how the two?" – of the wonder of *dao* and its manifestations – falls away in the mystery of the one-ing. The "answer" has emerged indirectly in our experience. And we cay say it poi-etically. Once there, we will no longer yearn for logic!

i. ἄπειρον / apeiron, along with χώρα / chora

Anyone familiar with Heidegger's work with the Greeks might assume that I would start with ἀλήθεια / *aletheia*. That would make sense, but I choose to begin with ἄπειρον / *apeiron*, for the simple reason that here the waywardness of the TI interpretation is so obvious. And the saying that shows the RR is so rich, as it points very directly to the question at hand, that is, the central thrust of this book. Simply put: The pathway of refreshing, rethinking retrieving the other beginning in Greek thinking, where everything "starts" – still with us today, though hidden – is quite easy to follow with ἄπειρον / *apeiron*.

ἄπειρον	TI	infinite supply of basic, originative substance
apeiron		unformed mass of material
		material principle, spatially infinite
		unbounded primal matter (*prima materia*)
	RR	the no-thing dynamic protected from any boundary
		the **boundless** without form, that is, no-thing
		dynamic emptiness within which phenomena emerge
		the boundless that provides and sustains beings/things
		revealing and saying emptiness
		infinite as in "without boundary" in every sense of the word: non-dual, no-form, no-substance, no-thing … and dynamic, freeing, opening radiant emptiness

If we go beyond the traditional translation and interpretation of this Greek word – basic substance, unformed mass of material, spatially infinite primal matter (*prima materia*) – then we move into the possibility of thinking "anew" what is held in the Greek words as "starting" thinking, that is, the "other beginning."

First we look at the traditional reading of Anaximander, which has dominated Western philosophy's reading and interpretation of Anaximander for centuries. Specifically, we look at how Anaximander's key word ἄπειρον in the fragment ἀρχὴ ... τῶν ὄντων τὸ ἄπειρον is translated in the TI mode, as presented in Kirk and Raven's *The Presocratic Philosophers*.[6] They present three versions of Theophrastus's account of what Anaximander meant by ἄπειρον, which they call "originative substance." Note that the words used for translating ἄπειρον are entirely TI words. (What is in bold in these quotations is from me.)

Anaximander:

ἀρχή ... τῶν ὄντων τὸ ἄπειρον.

Apeiron is the beginning of everything.

Simplicius and Hippolytus:

Anaximander ... said that the principle [ἀρχή] ... of existing things was ἄπειρον, being the first to introduce [use] this name of the **material principle**.

Further interpretations of Anaximander's fragment, as presented by Kirk and Raven:
Burnet on Theophrastus:

... the **material principle** [ἀρχή] [is named] ἄπειρον ... [Anaximander] is the "first to name the substratum of the opposites as the **material cause**."

Kirk and Raven:

Aristotle ... took ἄπειρον ... to mean "spatially infinite."

… Theophrastus seems to have felt that Anaximander had given his **primary substance** a name which described its spatial property.

Gathering all of this together: ἄπειρον is primal matter, *materia*, spatially infinite substance, the "material cause." It is primal, "unformed" substance. According to the tradition, we could say that Anaximander understood ἄπειρον to be an infinite material source, such that the genesis of everything in the world would never suffer from a lack of *materia*. In this inherited way with words, ἄπειρον is both primal matter or material as well as unbounded, inconceivable, indeterminate – even divine. When we put both of those descriptions together – something material but also boundless – these wordings make it difficult to comprehend what ἄπειρον "really is"! How does the word ἄπειρον say anything at all about being an "unformed" material principle? Unformed and material do not go together.

The word ἄ-πειρον is made up of two parts: boundary, limit, end (πεῖρἄ or πέρας) and the *alpha-primativum*, meaning "not": bound*less*, limit*less*, end*less*. So ἄπειρον says "that which has no boundaries." Simply put, the word ἄπειρον says nothing at all of substance, let alone matter. "Unformed matter" is an oxymoron. Matter is by definition formed.

Rather, what is named ἄπειρον is no form and nothing physical or measurable. It is inexhaustible, has no origin, is timeless. It is a no-thing, no-form dynamic of "something" but is itself no-thing, thus empty. Empty of form. The dynamic of ἄπειρον is … simply boundless! A dynamic that is formless and no-thing. Thus it is a rich and enriching way of saying Heidegger's beyng or Ereignis – what I call the non-dual dynamic of radiant emptiness.

Let us now turn to Heidegger's reading of this Anaximander fragment ἀρχή … τῶν ὄντων τὸ ἄπειρον (the second part of Heidegger's 1941 lecture course, *Grundbegriffe*, GA 51:107–13).*

---

* Numbers in parentheses in this section refer to these pages.

Heidegger shows how the word ἀρχή means "that from which something proceeds." Here it does not say the beginning that, once it has been left, is no longer, that is, nothing is left behind. (This would be one way to say what Heidegger means by the first beginning.) Rather, ἀρχή says the "timeless" starting, originary as starting something.

Note that the traditional approach, including Kranz,[7] is to give two meanings to the word ἀρχή: the beginning and the principle. Principle can be heard as an opening to this dynamic of "starting."

Here Heidegger reads the word ἀρχή to say: that from which something proceeds, but

> in the proceeding out and its emergence it holds-retains precisely the determination of the going … The ἀρχή is the priming of the manner and region of the emerging. The priming goes ahead but still remains as the start and keeps to and with itself. (108)

Ἀρχή is not the beginning that is left behind in the movement forward. The ἀρχή releases the **movement** forward (gets it going, the start) as well as **what** moves forward "but in such a way that what is released remains held in the ἀρχή as setting-things-out [*Verfügung*]" (108). This names the "other beginning," the start, what gets it going, what starts it – timelessly.

Heidegger then turns to the word ἄπειρον, for that which has form (things, beings) is held within the formless or boundless, that is, ἄπειρον. He uses the same German word to say this: *Verfügung*: Setting-things-out. *Verfügen*: dispose, release, issue forth, set things properly, bestow. As things emerge (that which emerges), emerging or "setting-things-out is what it is in terms of the emerging and the how of that emerging … [ἄπειρον] names the emerging and that from which and back to which this emerging sways" (110).

It is not about some generic "material." Rather, with setting-things-out (*Verfügung*) it is a question of beyng as Ereignis as radiant emptiness. That is, ἄπειρον "is" not – is no-thing – but it sways or holds sway "deeply." Heidegger: "Τὸ ἄπειρον is the ἀρχή of being. Τὸ ἄπειρον is the refusing of boundary and refers only to being [beyng: no-form, no-thing]; and in Greek that means emerging [not beings or things, but precisely beyng, which is no-thing but is at-work]" (110). The German word for "emerging" is *die Anwesung* – note the dynamic that is named with the *-ung* suffix.

For what emerges, setting-things-out is that which protects from any boundary. [*Die Verfügung ist dem Anwesenden das der Grenze Wehrende.*] (112)

- *The non-dual dynamic that sets things out **also and in one** protects the emerging from any boundary.*

The difference and distance between Heidegger's reading of Anaximander and the traditional interpretations could not be more stark. And the question becomes: If one *really hears* the to-be-thought in the Greek words, how would a reading that mirrors the Greek word and its saying "look"? Most importantly, it would not let either ἀρχή or ἄπειρον be defined as something physical – for example, substance, which is unmoving – without any dynamic.

In the 1946 essay "Der Spruch des Anaximander," Heidegger writes: "The real core of emerging, and with that the difference [*Unter-schied*] between emerging and *what* emerges, got forgotten" (*Holzwege*, GA 5:364). A marginal note here says: "The difference meant here is infinitely other than all being that remains being *of* beings. Thus it is no longer appropriate (no longer in accordance) to name the difference with the word *being/Sein*" (GA 5:364).

Most importantly, the turn in Heidegger's saying here takes us directly to ἄπειρον and its richness and possibility. This is what Heidegger is pointing to when he talks about the "return" to the Greeks – what I call "retrieval." How are we called to think/say this return? How is this re-turn (turning back) to the early Greeks possible? And what can it yield for us today?

The retrieval takes place within an echo. First, it is not about returning-to (*zurückzukehren zu*) but rather a turning-to (*zu zukeh-ren*). Heidegger explains:

The return happens as an *echo*. It takes place as that hearing that opens itself to the word [*das Wort*, saying] of Parmenides as seen from our present era, the epoch of affording of being as regime of disposability [*der Epoche der Schickung des Seins als Ge-stell*]." (GA 15:394)

An echo is a reverberating, resounding – a mirroring – in which the play in the original word resounds. This is a far cry from replaying what we think of as what the original Greeks said or thought. Within that resounding from there to here – and within our thinking's response – lies evocative possibility. In the retrieving, in echo-thinking, the Greek saying-showing opens up the possibility of entering that place of opening named in the originary word.

This move from the TI wording to the RR saying opens up the dynamic of no-form and no-thing ἄπειρον. It is in this sense of "opening" that I quote from "*Das Ende der Philosophie und die Aufgabe des Denkens*":

> The phenomenon itself ... presents us with the task of sounding it out and learning from within it, i.e., of letting something speak to us [*uns sagen*]. Accordingly, the day may come when thinking will not recoil from [i.e., will be able to hear] the question of whether the clearing [*die Lichtung*], the free open [the opening as such, the place of opening as the place of beyng] is not that wherein pristine space and ecstatic time – and everything emerging and falling away from presence in them – truly occupy the site that gathers and shelters everything. (GA 14:81)

This site is beyng and is the same site shown and said in Anaximander's ἄπειρον. The clearing or freeing opening is no-thing and no-form – and itself boundless. In order to make this dynamic more clear and explicit, I turn to "The Saying of Anaximander" and to Heidegger's reading of it. This will also make clear how this dynamic of the no-form and no-thing beyng, Ereignis, ἄπειρον, or the non-dual dynamic of radiant emptiness, fits into the focus of this book.

The fragment reads:

ἐξ ὧν δὲ ἡ γένεσίς ἐστι τοῖς οὖσι, καὶ τὴν φθορὰν εἰς ταῦτα γίνεσθαι κατὰ τὸ χρεών· διδόναι γὰρ αὐτὰ δίκην καὶ τίσιν ἀλλήλοις τῆς ἀδικίας κατὰ τὴν τοῦ χρόνου τάξιν.

Heidegger's rendering into German reads:

> Von woheraus aber der Hervorgang ist dem jeweilig Anwesenden auch
> die Entgängnis in dieses (als in das Selbe) ... geht hervor entlang dem
> Brauch; gehören nämlich lassen sie Fug somit auch Ruch eines dem
> anderen (im Verwinden) des Unfugs ... entsprechend der Zuweisung
> des Zeitigen durch die Zeit.[8]

My translation of Heidegger's translation reads:

> The "from-out-of-which" emergence comes is, for everything that
> emerges, also the withdrawing into this (as into the same) ... [and] pro-
> ceeds in accordance with exigence (brook); for they let enjoining and
> thereby also reck belong to each other (in the getting over) of disjoining
> ... responding to the directive of time's coming into its own.

Note: At first I translated *"von woheraus"* as "that from out of
which" and then "the site from out of which." But there is no noun
here, thus I want to avoid any suggestion of substantiation – given
that Heidegger's German lacks any such "thing" or "place." Thus
my translation becomes more poi-etic. A good example of the need
for another way of saying, other than as a subject "from out of
which" and an object "into which."

Heidegger takes the first step into this saying with the words
γένεσίς and φθορὰ: emerging and disappearing, coming forth into
presence and withdrawing. Traditionally these words were taken
to be about things, beings: the coming forth of beings and their
going away. To think in a Greek way, we must think the "forth"
and the "away" "as such." When we do that, however, we see
that emerging and disappearing do not refer primarily to beings
but to the movement itself, that is, the words are to be taken *in
themselves* as describing *being* (the non-dual dynamic of radiant
emptiness, also known as beyng as Ereignis) and therefore they
say the emerging as such, rather than emerging and disappearing
things/beings.

This takes place κατὰ τὸ χρεών: in accordance with χρεών. The
usual translation is "necessity": what must inescapably be. But if

thinking expands into this word in its Greek-ness, the word suggests χράω, χράομαι – and χείρ, the hand. Χράω: I reach for, extend my hand – and then I hand over, let something belong. "Thus τὸ χρεών is the handing over of emergence; this handing over hands out (furnishes) emergence *to* what emerges and thus holds (in its "hand") and preserves what emerges as precisely what it is, holds it in its hand, i.e., in emergence itself" (GA 5:366).

Thus I translate κατὰ τὸ χρεών as "in accordance with exigence (brook)." *Exigence* is from the Latin *exigere*: to drive (as in the "drive shaft"), propel, empower (potent as making possible, thus the handing-over in Heidegger's words above). *Brook* is from the Old German *bruk*: to allow, let be, sustain, bear, hold, abide.

Tò χρεών – as handing over or furnishing – Heidegger ventures to call in German *der Brauch* (use-usage, making use of, service, serving oneself with something, the reach over); *brauchen* (to reach over, require); *sich gebrauchen* (lend oneself to).

> *Brauchen* thus says: to *let emerge* [*anwesen lassen,* italics mine] something that emerges as the emergent ... to hand out (furnish) something unto its *own deep sway* [*seinem eigenen Wesen,* italics mine] and to hold it as thus emerged in its preserving hand. (GA 5:367)

Anaximander's ἄπειρον is one of the key Greek words that say Heidegger's beyng: empty of form, no-thing, a non-dual dynamic. Beyng or the non-dual dynamic of radiant emptiness knows emptiness is

- dynamic above all
- opening
- freeing
- full as in fullness of the undecided-indeterminate of emptiness
- being indeterminate all the way, rich in possibility
- the hesitating holding-back that is "behind" what shows itself and is experienced as things/beings.

To say this requires hinting words rather than propositional words.

This letting and this handing-out and letting-emerge – as well as the preserving – is the no-thing and no-form non-dual dynamic of beyng, Ereignis, radiant emptiness that is said and shown in Anaximander's ἄπειρον.

***

Excursus: In a less philosophical language, what is going on here? To what is the opening we are searching for? And what is the opening to that open? And why is it so strange? In part, because of the almost exclusionary dominance of the power and "legitimacy" of rationalistic science and metaphysics, whose work and focus is limited to the natural world as physical – and measurable.

But we are after something that goes beyond this. To the immeasurable, formless dynamic. This is what our retrieval is all about. How can we – how dare we not – get back to and say this experience that goes beyond?

The history of Western thinking has focused on the manifesting of matter, and over time this got interpreted as more dense and more limited. But in the refreshing and retrieving way, things/beings are "less dense" than we imagine. We need another language – what I call a poi-etic language. Mirroring our experience, this language is non-conceptual. And from within it we can get in touch (become aware of) this "less dense" and go beyond to the field of no-density. Utter density has become the barrier to this dynamic. If we are aware of and think and say "that within which" in a dynamic rich in possibility, we learn to retrieve an awareness of a kind of limitless seeing and become potentially capable of knowing "all" of this.

The focus on Heidegger's no-thing and no-form beyng or Ereignis – and the retrieving of just this dynamic in Greek philosophy, for example, ἄπειρον – requires a non-conceptual experience. In turn, to think and say this experience calls for a poi-etic and non-conceptual saying. The quandary, then, lies in the fact that this view and experience is "beyond the physical," even as it is non-dually bound with our body, which is constituted by matter. And "beyond the conceptual," even as the conceptual is held within this no-thing no-form dynamic.

So how do we come to know and to say that which is no-thing and no-form while being necessarily in a body, a "thing" with form? It is not an either-or (such as the Cartesian *cogito ergo sum* in a body seen as a machine) but a both-and. This dilemma or *aporia* takes some effort to experience and think and say. But for sure it is an astonishing dilemma that no science or scientific instrument can resolve.

We will now focus on Plato's search for the dynamic "empty of all form," which he calls *chora*. End of excursus.

***

aa. Guidelines for Reading, Thinking, and Saying χώρα / chora

There are two reasons I include χώρα / *chora* within the section on ἄπειρον / *apeiron*:

1. The words ἄπειρον and χώρα are equivalents on one deep level of Greek thinking. And in his book *Greek Philosophical Terms: A Historical Lexicon*, Peters agrees with me.[9]
2. Socrates's conversation in the *Timaeus* that deals with χώρα opens up and reveals many aspects of ἄπειρον that Anaximander did not deal with, or that we have no access to.

Before we go directly to the section of the *Timaeus* that deals with χώρα, I want to share several ideas. Using a mantra from Heidegger, let me call these: What calls for thinking here?

I see a parallel here between Heidegger and Plato in how their thinking unfolded and "grew" over their lifetimes. Throughout his life Heidegger was after one question. First he called it the "meaning of being." Then, over time, the question of being, the truth of being, being or beyng as Ereignis, fouring of the fourfold, plus our Greek words – all names for a dynamic that is no-thing and no form and non-dual. Simply put, this pathway was very long.

During all this time, (a) in conversation with Daoist philosophers from China and Buddhist philosophers from Japan, he listened to their words and ways of thinking, looking for a new and *fresh wording* that could reveal what he was looking for, namely a way of thinking and saying the no-form no-thing dynamic of beyng; and (b) he tried to "retrieve" in the Greek texts a thinking and saying that would open up a dynamic *in the Greek words* that could help him in this lifelong search. These are the key words we are working with. It took Heidegger many steps over time to get there, as he worked through the myriad ways of philosophy, poetry, and even science.

At the end of the Introduction to *Sein und Zeit*, Heidegger says that the "vocabulary" available at the time was "awkward" and "ill-suited" for pressing on with the central question. And then he tells us why:

> [I]t is one thing to report on *beings* by explaining what they are; it is another thing to grasp beings in their *being* [later named beyng]. [This applies as well to experiencing and saying what the word χώρα / *chora* shows, i.e., the limits of traditional and inherited language.] For this latter task, not only are most of the words missing, but most notably the grammar ... and where the area of being to be disclosed is ontologically far more difficult than what was afforded the Greeks to think, the intricateness [enigma, indecipherability, *Umständlichkeit*] of developing the notion and the precision of expression increases. (GA 2:52)

As Heidegger continued, unwaveringly, on that one path, he got closer and closer to this central no-thing and no-form non-dual dynamic – the playing field of Ereignis aka *Eignis, physis, aletheia, apeiron*, and so on. And the words that were lacking and the grammar that was missing became somehow less and less. As exciting as it was, it was still seemingly impossible to cross the terrain to that playing field.

I propose that the same thing happened for Plato. Over the many years of his life of thinking, his questions went deeper, more subtle and often hidden. And towards the end of his teaching and writing career he got closer and closer to uncovering this same rich and enriching dynamic. I submit that the discussion on χώρα / *chora* in the *Timaeus* is the culmination. That is why the section of the *Timaeus* on the playing field of *chora* is so exciting and at the same time almost impossible to unravel. Indeed, whoever tries this discovers that the traditional and inherited ways of thought, language, dualistic metaphysics – including logic and merely distinguishing words – do not work. As some try to make the words of the *Timaeus* fit into some pre-established forms, we discover that the very terrain calls for something other than this. I now address several significant issues in this regard. As you read these next pages, keep in mind that these words fit for Heidegger *and* Plato!

Translation and interpretation. Above all, the question of translation and interpretation – joined at the hip – is central to reading, thinking and saying χώρα / *chora* as it emerges in Plato's *Timaeus*. In a genuine sense, there is no English word for χώρα. Thus the discussion of translation/interpretation at this point in the book.

Let's take another look at two key words in Heidegger's "kit of language tools": *Dasein* (often written as *Dasein*) and *Ereignis*. In the strict sense, *Dasein* can be translated as "being-there": da sein. But from the beginning of English translations of Heidegger (around 1960), *Dasein* was left untranslated. And still is, to this day. It has become an English word: Dasein (no italics! as noted in the discussion of Dasein in the Interlude towards the front of the book).

A similar – although not the same – thing happens with the word *Ereignis*. The word in normal German means "event or happening." Some have translated Heidegger's *Ereignis* in this way. Some have translated the word as "event of appropriation," taking into account the *eignen* part of the word: to fit, to be proper for, to be own to. When translating *Beiträge*, Professor Parvis Emad and I translated the word *Ereignis* as *enowning* – in part because of the many cognates of the word *eignen*.

Let us hear what Heidegger says about translating *Ereignis*:

> Thought from within what is indicated here, the word *Ereignis* is now to be spoken as the key word in service to thinking. Thought in this way, the key word is just as impossible to translate as the key Greek λόγος

and the Chinese *dao*. Here the word no longer means what we usually call any happening, an event [*irgendein Geschehnis, ein Vorkommnis*]. (GA 11:45)

I repeat here a quotation by Heidegger from towards the end of his life, one that underscores the intricateness of the word:

> "*Ereignis*" – the word that I used earlier
> – is too easily misunderstood,
> as if it only means "happening-event" [*Geschehnis*].
> "*Eignen*" [*Eignis*] – gazingly letting-belong
> in the clearing of the fourfold
> – owning-crossing-over [owning-over-to, *übereignen*],
> – full owning [owning-all-the-way, *vereignen*].

In this project I choose to leave word *Ereignis* untranslated and to see it as an English word. Thus, most of the time I write Ereignis, without the italics that belong to foreign words.

Translating the Greek word *chora* presents us with the same dilemma. Heeding Heidegger's comment about the German *Ereignis*, the Greek λόγος, and the Chinese *dao*, I do not translate the word χώρα/*chora*. This question of not translating χώρα will become paramount in a few pages, when we work through Plato's discussion of *chora*.

Now we look at the question of translation itself, to prepare ourselves for reading Plato on χώρα. I bring this up at this point in my project because, as I see it, Plato's working/playing with χώρα goes to the very heart of the matter in Greek philosophy.

Heidegger tells how every translation is always an interpretation:

Every translation that is taken by itself alone, made without the interpretation [laying out, *Auslegung*] that belongs to it, is open to all kinds of misinterpretations. For every translation is in itself always an interpretation. Implicitly [unexpressed, *unausgesprochen*], it carries within itself all approaches, views, levels of interpretation from which it comes.

Further, interpretation itself is simply the implementation of the translation that is still silent and has not yet entered the word that would accomplish this. Interpretation and translation are in their ownmost core the same. Therefore, since the words and writings in the native language often need interpretation, translating within the own language is also constantly necessary. Every saying, talking and answering is a translating. Thus, the fact that most of the time two different languages come into play is not what is ownmost to translating ...

For only the originary thinking hides in itself that treasure that can never be thought through completely – and can each time be understood "better," that is, other than what the instantaneously meant wording says. In the run-of-the-mill situation there is only what is understandable, and nothing of the kind that constantly requires more originary understanding and interpreting and that might itself call forth [evoke, call for, *hervorrufen*] the times that are necessary to recognize again what was supposedly known long ago – and to translate it ...

Only what is truly thought has the good fortune again and once again to be understood "better" than it understood itself [*"besser" verstanden zu werden, als es sich selbst verstand*]. And this understanding-better is never the contribution of the interpreter, but the gift of what is interpreted. (GA 55:63–4)

Here Heidegger is saying several things, all of which apply to working with the key word χώρα in the *Timaeus*:

1. You cannot translate without interpreting.
2. Any genuine thinking carries within it a possibility that goes beyond what the thinker said or could say. This "beyond" is the gift provided by *what* is being translated-interpreted.
3. This is not about what the original thinker said, but rather about understanding something "better" than it understood itself. That is, any great thinking "constantly requires more originary understanding and interpreting," something that the honest original thinker welcomes. "For only the originary thinking hides in itself that treasure that can never be thought through completely – and can each time be understood 'better,' i.e., other than what the instantaneously meant wording says."

This applies to Plato's words in the *Timaeus,* as he – like any seeking thinker – works through the dynamic that is named χώρα/*chora*. In line with his pursuit, he may be barely aware of the implications and possibilities held within his words on paper. I want to draw out these implications and possibilities that are *in deed* in the words. This work involves a reverence for "the translation that is still silent and has not yet entered the word that would accomplish this," that is, for the "gift of what is interpreted."

The many words. Just as Heidegger needs several words as he pursues his lifelong quest to experience and to think and then to say beyng – what I call the non-dual dynamic of radiant emptiness – so too does Plato find himself using several names to get to what he will in the end call χώρα/*chora*. This will become clear as we read and think and say in English the three words: ὑποδοχή/*hypodoche*, then ἐκμαγεῖον/*ekmageion*, and then χώρα/*chora*. These word-images, taken together, determine the style of thinking that "starts" our translating, interpreting, or laying out and then says what Plato wants to say. What grounds and attunes the matter being said "can hardly ever be known merely by one name, especially in the crossing to that beginning" (GA 65:21).

Here Heidegger says something crucial about words to think-say the other beginning – words that apply to our task here:

> Every naming of the grounding-attunement with a single word is based on a false notion. Every word is taken from tradition. The fact that grounding-attunement of another beginning has to have many names does not argue against its at-oneness [its non-dual, inseparable character, *die Einfachheit*] but rather confirms its richness and strangeness. (GA 65:22)

The fact that Plato uses three words in his seeking does not argue against the oneness that is being said, but rather confirms its richness and strangeness. The very unfolding of his thinking is mirrored in the three words that he uses – the first two words eventually culminating in the third word: χώρα. (I remember Derrida once saying that he never found a core concept that could be contained or defined in one word.) Within this idea, for sure *chora* is a word that proves his point. *Chora* is not intelligible or sensible and is not contained within philosophy's usual logic and grammar. *Chora* is a word outside dictionaries or the world of "references." The dynamic that is experienced, said, and shown in *chora* is "beyond"!

Openings, not theories. As my thinking struggles with this core dynamic in the *Timaeus*, it is driven by the seeking, the openings, the possibilities – and not by theories. As I read and see it, at this point in the *Timaeus* Plato attempts to go beyond "theories" or concepts. Thus, I would say that for Plato here it is not about metaphor – too linguistically defined and bound – but a thinking beyond metaphor. This beyond is ours to experience, once we – who dwell in the limits of concept, metaphor, and the "reality" of things – move beyond these limits. This move is natural, it belongs to who we are as thinking beings. It is just that we are not aware of this, so we see it as unnatural.

Dwelling in this enigma, we realize that it requires another path in thinking, one that is open to and responding to a certain call/ claim – one that we find in Heraclitus, Fragment B50: Listening, not to me but to *logos*, it is wise to grant that all is one. *Logos* here understood as gathering. (We will look into this fragment later, when we focus on λόγος as a key Greek word.) And the only dynamic where the one or one-ing happens is the no-form no-thing dynamic that is often named as the "space" of *chora*.

What drives us in our thinking here are the same words in Greek philosophy, but over time they were thematized into traditional, inherited (TI) ways. The dynamic we are after lies hidden "beyond" what we have been given up to now. Above all, these words go beyond concepts – beyond, to what shows itself to or in experience as no-thing no-form dynamic. To follow these movements in thinking this dynamic, it is important to be open to how thinking "starts." For now I would ask it this way: What claims us in the starting that comes from *chora*-as-space-empty-of-form? And how does our thinking respond in knowing awareness to that claim? First, dwelling in the no-way-out of the limits of metaphysics and rationalism. Second, opening to the dynamic radiant emptiness of *chora*. Third, taking this experience into account as we learn to hear, think, and say *chora* – something akin to *dao*, buddha mind, beyng as Ereignis, the immeasurable quantum potential ... what I call the non-dual dynamic of radiant emptiness.

bb. Reading, Thinking, and Saying χώρα / chora

We will now read and translate-interpret the pertinent passages in the *Timaeus*. The discussion of χώρα / *chora* is in the early part of the second of three main sections of the *Timaeus*. First, I will walk us through the most pertinent passages leading to and dealing with χώρα / *chora*. While doing this, I will try to provide a perspective by which (a) moving with and following Heidegger makes sense, (b) the very dynamic named in χώρα / *chora* will reveal itself, and (c) the opening here takes us to an *experience* of this no-form and no-thing χώρα / *chora*.

The translations from the *Timaeus* are my own, with the help of these translations:

1. Plato. *Timaeus*, vol. 9 of *Plato in Twelve Volumes*, W.R.M. Lamb, transl. Harvard University Press, 1925.
2. Plato. *Timaeus*, in *Timaeus and Critias*, D. Lee, transl., revised by T.K. Johansen. Penguin Classics, 2008.
3. Plato, *Timaeus*, vol. 3 of *The Dialogues of Plato*, B. Jowett, transl. Oxford University Press, 1892.

48b

We must therefore retrace our steps, to find another fitting start [ἀρχὴ] [and begin again, a new starting], just as we did with the previous matters. We must, that is, consider the "how" of the unfolding [φύσις] of fire, water, earth, and air for or in behalf of [πρὸ] the coming into being [γένεσις] of the world and what happens to it [γένεσις]. For no one has yet disclosed their generation [coming to be].

ὧδε οὖν πάλιν ἀναχωρητέον, καὶ λαβοῦσιν αὐτῶν τούτων προσήκουσαν ἑτέραν ἀρχὴν αὖθις αὖ, καθάπερ περὶ τῶν τότε νῦν οὕτω περὶ τούτων πάλιν ἀρκτέον ἀπ' ἀρχῆς. τὴν δὴ πρὸ τῆς οὐρανοῦ γενέσεως πυρὸς ὕδατός τε καὶ ἀέρος καὶ γῆς φύσιν θεατέον αὐτὴν καὶ τὰ πρὸ τούτου πάθη· νῦν γὰρ οὐδείς πω γένεσιν αὐτῶν μεμήνυκεν …

- *The task at this joining is to open up the "starting," that is, a fresh way to come to know and be aware of the "starting," in experiencing just what this starting is. It is not a beginning in chronological time, but rather the timeless and ongoing dynamic of the active "starting." The question of this starting is the unfolding and its "how." Plato has Socrates saying that no one has ever revealed this how. What drives Plato's* **chora** *is the question of how to recognize, experience, think, and then say this dynamic.*
- *Gathering the sense of this passage: Focusing on the four elements does not really get at the deeper issue. Rather, the issue is the "how" of the unfolding, this understood outside time, that is, not temporal as in "before the elements" in time. The word* **πρὸ** *here points to what is itself timeless. We could say "that within which things emerge," the formless dynamic, here named* **γένεσις.**
- *Plato's Socrates then goes on (48c-d) to say how this present matter at issue in the discussion is difficult, that the task is of great magnitude. And that he will do his best to give an account (**logos**), calling upon the divine, who will protect, deliver, and lead us through this novel logos. (The divine mirrors the non-transparent and hidden* **mythos***).*
- *With this calling-upon, Plato's Socrates shows in experience (**ergon**) that the very issue here is unavailable to thinking within the usual linguistic/conceptual apparatus. We must go beyond this. This is the flashpoint that we, with and following Heidegger, come to know in the experience of awareness – as the no-thing and no-form and non-dual dynamic of Heidegger's* **Ereignis** *(later named* **Eignis***) and of the key Greek words that we are taking up in this part of the book – a dynamic that I call the non-dual dynamic of radiant emptiness. For Plato here, the difficult but exciting journey – makeable only if we shed some of our limited ways of language and conceptualization – is named first* **ὑποδοχή,** *then* **ἐκμαγεῖον,** *and then* **χώρα.**

48e–49a

Let's have a new starting point. [Up until now] we distinguished two kinds [εἴδη] – we must now point out a third [γένος]. Two were enough at an earlier stage, one kind for the intelligible and unchanging [νοητὸν καὶ ἀεὶ] model and a second kind for the imitation of the model, namely what comes into being and is visible [γένεσιν ἔχον καὶ ὁρατόν], believing that two would be enough. But now the conversation [our gathering of thoughts, λόγος] seems to compel us to try to reveal in words a third kind [εἶδος] that is difficult-baffling and obscure. What must we suppose its dynamic potential and its unfolding [δύναμις καὶ φύσις] to be? Something like this: It is [dynamic] receiving [ὑποδοχή] and, as it were, the nurse of all becoming [πάσης εἶναι γενέσεως ὑποδοχὴν αὐτὴν οἷον τιθήνην].

Ἡ δ᾽ οὖν αὐθιςἀρχῆπερὶ τοῦ παντὸς ἔστω μειζόνως τῆς πρόσθεν διῃρημένη· τότε μὲν γὰρ δύο εἴδη διειλόμεθα, νῦν δὲ τρίτον ἄλλο γένος ἡμῖν δηλωτέον. τὰ μὲν γὰρ δύο ἱκανὰ ἦν ἐπὶ τοῖς ἔμπροσθεν λεχθεῖσιν, ἓν μὲν ὡς παραδείγματος εἶδος ὑποτεθέν, νοητὸν καὶ ἀεὶ κατὰ ταὐτὰ ὄν, μίμημα δὲ παραδείγματος δεύτερον, γένεσιν ἔχον καὶ ὁρατόν. τρίτον δὲ τότε μὲν οὐ διειλόμεθα, νομίσαντες τὰ δύο ἕξειν ἱκανῶς· νῦν δὲ ὁ λόγος ἔοικεν εἰσαναγκάζειν χαλεπὸν καὶ ἀμυδρὸν εἶδος ἐπιχειρεῖν λόγοις ἐμφανίσαι. τίν᾽ οὖν ἔχον δύναμιν καὶ φύσιν αὐτὸ ὑποληπτέον; τοιάνδε μάλιστα· πάσης εἶναι γενέσεως ὑποδοχὴν αὐτὴν οἷον τιθήνην.

- *The word* **νοητὸν** *is an adjective from* **νόος/νοῦς**, *which among other things says* **awareness**. *With this in mind, we have to be careful not to limit* **νοητὸν** *to "intelligible" as we know it and might subsume it under conceptual. For it can also be understood as "minding-awareness." Thus* **νοητὸν** *says "experience of being aware" that is other than activity of the intellect.*

The word ὑποδοχή is the first name Plato gives to the "third kind," that is, the no-thing no-form dynamic that he is on the way to. The second name on the way is ἐκμαγεῖον. The third name he uses on the way is χώρα, "itself" or "as such." Starting with the word ὑποδοχή, Plato's thinking and saying moves beyond, to the fuller and richer – and more fitting – word χώρα. I would say that both ὑποδοχή and ἐκμαγεῖον are "on the way" to χώρα. We can watch the development "on the way" as we read and think through the following passages from this section of the *Timaeus*.

Often ὑποδοχή is translated as "receptacle." But the Greek word says the "*dynamic* receiving" rather than a static receptacle – or any receptacle at all. Following on what is more dynamic-moving in the word, ὑποδοχή says the formless dynamic activity of "receiving," leaving behind the static nature of the word *receptacle*. Whatever ὑποδοχή is or does, it is not a substance, not passive-inert, and not mechanical. It is not a thing, thus the English word *receptacle* is somewhere between misleading and simply wrong. It is not mass on which something is stamped. It has no qualities of its own. What I translate as "dynamic receiving" says a welcoming, harbouring, supporting, stewarding, and holding-sustaining. This is other and way more than "receptacle"!

(Note: Much of what I say here applies to the other two names for the dynamic being disclosed in the conversation, namely ἐκμαγεῖον and χώρα. Some say ὑποδοχή = χώρα and translate both words as "receptacle," thus conflating the two entirely and hiding the dynamic no-thing dimension of the words. This is my response: They are not exactly the same and should not be translated with the same English word. However, since all three words are part of Plato's thinking, which is "on the way" (*unterwegs*) and a seeking thinking, they do mirror one another in the ongoing, difficult but exciting development of the thinking.)

Most importantly, we are called to read and hear Plato's words here (48e–49a) as going beyond our normal ways, for example, these Greek words do not name an entity, distinct and with form. Nor a metaphysics of beings. Nor do they exemplify forms.

After highlighting the crucial word ὑποδοχή, I will now point out ways in which to hear several other words in this passage and then say what is being thought and said:

- *Plato makes us aware of how tough this task is … because of the very obscure dynamic we are seeking to uncover and to say.*

- Here the word **νοητὸν** refers to one of the two kinds mentioned here. Later we will see the same word referring to **νοητὸν** as saying the minding-nous that is "beyond" humans. (Much more on **νοητὸν** and **νοῦς** later in part 3.)
- Addressing the question of what this third kind entails, Plato asks: What must we suppose its **δύναμις** and **φύσις** to be? I translate these two words as "dynamic potential" and "unfolding." Dynamic says something in movement and changing. Unfolding says birthing, emerging, coming to be, mirroring how Heidegger retrieves the meaning of **φύσις** that got lost, up to our time. (Much more on **φύσις** later in part 3.)
- Lee translates these two words as "its powers and nature"; Lamb, as "its essential property." Jowett, on the other hand, translates these words a bit more freely as the "nature" of "this new kind of being." All three translations hide the dynamic aspect of this third kind, as well as its being a no-form and no-thing dynamic.
- Plato's answer to his own question goes like this: The dynamic and unfolding of this third kind is the **ὑποδοχή** (dynamic receiving) and **τιθήνη** of all becoming.
- The word **τιθήνη** says "nurse," **but also** : one who bestows-gives-grants, endures, lets come into being, makes happen and nurtures. **τιθηνέω** : I tend, I hold as in take care of, I foster. These words enrich the Greek word's saying, giving more weight to the dynamic action character of what the "dynamic potential and unfolding" is here. Taking all of this into account, I might say "the dynamic and unfolding of this third kind is receiving-holding and nurse-nurturing of all becoming" – in the non-dual dynamic of the radiant emptiness of no-thing, no-form beyng or radiant, opening-freeing emptiness in its indeterminateness as such.

50c

The same account [λόγος] applies to the unfolding-receiving of all bodies [τῆς τὰ πάντα δεχομένης σώματα φύσεως]. That must always be the same; for, while it is always receiving all things, it never departs at all from what is own to its dynamic [δύναμις] and never in any way, or at any time, takes on a form [μορφή], like that of any of the things which enter into it. In its unfolding [φύσει] it [ἐκμαγεῖον] is the

receiving of all impressions [or on which impressions are made] and is stirred and informed by them ...

ὁ αὐτὸς δὴ λόγος καὶ περὶ τῆς τὰ πάντα δεχομένης σώματα φύσεως. ταὐτὸν αὐτὴν ἀεὶ προσρητέον· ἐκ γὰρ τῆς ἑαυτῆς τὸ παράπαν οὐκ ἐξίσταται δυνάμεως – δέχεταί τε γὰρ ἀεὶ τὰ πάντα, καὶ μορφὴν οὐδεμίαν ποτὲ οὐδενὶ τῶν εἰσιόντωνόμοίαν εἴληφεν οὐδαμῇ οὐδαμῶς· ἐκμαγεῖον γὰρ φύσει παντὶ κεῖται, κινούμενόν τε καὶ διασχηματιζόμενον ὑπὸ τῶν εἰσιόντων.

- *The first line tells of the no-form and no-thing dynamic that we are exploring. At this moment in the text Plato does not give this dynamic the name ὑποδοχή . Is he thinking of ὑποδοχή ? Or is this "nameless" as Plato is on his way to the second of the three words? Or is his seeking mind awareness moving away from any name at this point? Certain is that the words are saying the receiving movement – or dynamic receiving.*
- *And that by virtue of what is own to its dynamic (δύναμις), which it never departs from – is always formless – unlike any of the things that enter it.*
- **Here Plato introduces the second name for the dynamic that one is seeking to experience, to know, and to say: ἐκμαγεῖον:** *what receives and "holds" impressions as it is itself no impression. It "holds" as in "wipes away" the forms/impressions within its no-form no-thing dynamic. The verb ἐκμάσσω says here: I wipe away all forms-impressions, I take them back into the formless no-thing dynamic of* **chora.** *To wipe "dry" of forms. It wipes away, as it were, all the shapes of things/impressions as they are received back into the no-form and no-thing energy field or dynamic.*
- *Normally the word ἐκμαγεῖον means the wax or mass before an image is impressed upon it. But Plato says quite clearly here that the dynamic receiving never takes on form. It is open to receive impressions while it itself is unshapeable, no-form, and no-thing, with no limits, no boundaries.*
- *This is the difficulty and dilemma: How to come to experience what holds impressions and so on, but is itself no-form and thus no appearance? Something at the core of what we are now thinking is ... well, illogical! The dynamic receives all things but never takes on the form of the things*

that are received and enter it. We need a fresh way of language-saying. Clearly Plato is going way beyond what the word means in normal usage.

- *Having offered that "illogical" wording, we affirm that logic cannot go here. The dynamic of receiving is a keeping of forms in its holding, while never becoming a form. So, the things which enter into it either (a) let go of their own forms as they are received or (b) keep their forms within the no-form receiving and holding. (This enigmatic statement mirrors the core dilemma of the non-dual and no-form dynamic of radiant emptiness, beyng/Ereignis, dao, buddha mind, and the field of energy in quantum physics – here in Plato named χώρα.*

- *Conceptual thinking and logic cannot handle this. It either goes crazy or simply denies that what is being considered here is at all possible. On the other hand, what if we use non-conceptual experience and thinking and poi-etic language? Is it possible, then, that the logical dilemma resolves into a one-ing of the experience and awareness? What if we simply say both-and? Here and not here simultaneously? No-form and form in a one-ing that logic cannot access? A provocative possibility, one that Plato's Socrates certainly does not cancel out, yet! (Is this the same enigma (no-way-out) when we say that the non-dual dynamic of emptiness – beyng, buddha mind, dao – "holds within it" the duality of things and phenomena?) I leave both questions open for now. Let's go on!*

- *Given the non-dual at-oneness of ὑποδοχή and ἐκμαγεῖον, we open up to the possibility of the no-form and no-thing dynamic holding what has form and what is a thing, as it returns to "there" from where it emerged. Holding form while it "as such" is formless, non-dual dynamic. This calls for a fresh way of saying. Saying poi-etically, we show how – within the non-dual oneness of the no-form no-thing dynamic emptiness – the no-form holding dynamic "holds" the things "returning." It is a both-and: they are both at once and in oneness.*

- *Note: Lamb translates ἐκμαγεῖον as "molding-stuff" – implying some "thing"! I assume that Lamb let the wax in an earlier passage inform his translation of ἐκμαγεῖον as thing-like. Clearly Plato has moved beyond this limitation of the wax-image used earlier. And Lamb did not notice. Yes, ἐκμαγεῖον is still "waiting for an impression to be stamped on it," but that dynamic which is waiting is no-thing and no-form and invisible.*

- *Is this perhaps Plato opening up to the dynamic that he can "barely" experience or say? A hinting of χώρα ? It calls for us to find a fresh way of saying. And it portends the discussion on dream-like and dreamy that comes at 52a–b.*

50d–e

that in which the coming to be (of what comes to be born) ... this wherein it [the appearance] is set and stamped, could not possibly be suited to its purpose unless it is formless and itself free [devoid] of all those forms [πλὴν ἄμορφον] that it is to receive from elsewhere. For, if it [that in which] were like any of the forms that enter it, then whenever any opposite or entirely different nature was received, it would receive them badly or not matching, by inserting a visible shape of its own. Wherefore, that which is to receive all elements [γένη] is to be void of all forms [εἰδῶν].

τὸ δ᾽ ἐν ᾧ γίγνεται (τὸ γιγνόμενον) ... τοῦτ᾽ αὐτὸ ἐν ᾧ ἐκτυπούμενον ἐνίσταται γένοιτ᾽ ἂν παρεσκευασμένον εὖ, πλὴν ἄμορφον ὂν ἐκείνων ἁπασῶν τῶν ἰδεῶν ὅσας μέλλοι δέχεσθαί ποθεν. ὅμοιον γὰρ ὂν τῶν ἐπεισιόντων τινὶ τὰ τῆς ἐναντίας τά τε τῆς τὸ παράπαν ἄλλης φύσεως ὁπότ᾽ ἔλθοι δεχόμενον κακῶς ἂν ἀφομοιοῖ, τὴν αὑτοῦ παρεμφαῖνον ὄψιν. διὸ καὶ πάντων ἐκτὸς εἰδῶν εἶναι χρεὼν τὸ τὰ πάντα ἐκδεξόμενον ἐν αὑτῷ γένη.

- *No form. Boundless. That in which the coming to be takes place, wherein the appearances are received, is formless, that is, free of all forms that it receives from elsewhere.*
- *Note how here Plato says what is at issue in the dynamic without using a noun to describe it. Rather he simply says "that in which" – leaving matters less defined and less designated. Should we assume that Plato means ὑποδοχή or ἐκμαγεῖον? Or is Plato's thinking-saying here going beyond the words that sound as if they are saying "things" – beyond and less specific but more revealing of the no-thing and no-form dynamic? Dare we – or dare we not! – go there?*
- *Where the Greek says "that in which" without a designation of what the "that" is, two of the translations simply add the word **substance**, even though there is **no word** in the Greek text that points to substance.*

51a–b

In the same way, that which is to be fitted to receive, frequently over its whole extent, the copies of all things intelligible and eternal must itself, in the unfolding, be devoid of all forms [εἴδη]. Thus the mother and the active receiving [ὑποδοχή] of all created and visible and in any way sensible things, is not to be termed earth, or air, or fire, or water, or any of their compounds or any of the elements from which these are derived. Rather, it is a kind [εἶδός] invisible and formless, all-receiving and in some most perplexing [mysterious, puzzling] and most baffling [incomprehensible, extremely hard to grasp] way partaking of mind [νοητόν]. In saying this we shall not be wrong.

ταὐτὸν οὖν καὶ τῷ τὰ τῶν πάντων ἀεί τε ὄντων κατὰ πᾶν ἑαυτοῦ πολλάκις ἀφομοιώματα καλῶς μέλλοντι δέχεσθαι πάντων ἐκτὸς αὐτῷ προσήκει πεφυκέναι τῶν εἰδῶν. διὸ δὴ τὴν τοῦ γεγονότος ὁρατοῦ καὶ πάντως αἰσθητοῦ μητέρα καὶ ὑποδοχὴν μήτε γῆν μήτε ἀέρα μήτε πῦρ μήτε ὕδωρ λέγωμεν, μήτε ὅσα ἐκ τούτων μήτε ἐξ ὧν ταῦτα γέγονεν· [51b] ἀλλ᾽ ἀνόρατον εἶδός τι καὶ ἄμορφον, πανδεχές, μεταλαμβάνον δὲ ἀπορώτατά πη τοῦ νοητοῦ καὶ δυσαλωτότατον αὐτὸ λέγοντες οὐ ψευσόμεθα.

- *This dynamic of "mother and active receiving" is in itself without form or shape or characteristics. It never changes in the manner of aspects. It cannot change, for it is formless and boundless. There is nothing to change. It holds all things but itself never and in no wise assumes shape-form (μορφή).*
- *That which appears (the phenomenon or appearance or manifestation) has visible form, whereas that in which it appears is "devoid of all forms" (εἴδη). Its kind is invisible and formless: ἀνόρατον εἶδός τι καὶ ἄμορφον.*
- *Regardless of the changes or forms that take place in the things-objects that become – and however that happens – the formless "space" that contains-holds, that is, the dynamic of receiving, does not change. Since it is formless, there is nothing "there" that could change.*

Here is my reading, in the form of a sketch, of the final sentence of the above text:

ἀνόρατον	ἄμορφον	πανδεχές
invisible	no-form	all-receiving

εἶδός
the kind, what is own to it.

μεταλαμβάνον
partaking in, thrown together non-dually

νοητοῦ (of *nous*)
mind, here the *nous* that is beyond form and beyond human *nous*

δυσαλωτότατον
hard to attain, unremitting (not just comprehend intellectually or even in *logos*) = experience

ἀπορώτατά
perplexing, cannot see-get through

And with that we come to the "killer"! This is the passage where the word χώρα is introduced:

52a–b

... a third kind [γένος], that of χώρα [formless "space"], eternal, indestructible, providing room for everything that comes to be [manifests],

τρίτον δὲ αὖ γένος ὂν τὸ τῆς χώρας ἀεί, φθορὰν οὐ προσδεχόμενον, [52b] ἕδραν δὲ παρέχον ὅσα ἔχει γένεσιν πᾶσιν,

- *This is the first mention of χώρα. Given how the dynamic has been said up to now, including with the names ὑποδοχή and ἐκμαγεῖον, I have put the word **space** in quotation marks, lest we automatically conclude that we know what the word is saying here. If I could, I would "translate" the word as "space-empty-of-all-form-and-no-thing."*

having nothing to do with the senses, it is caught hold of in an illegitimate or bastard kind of λόγος that is hard to see as trustable [creditable] ...

αὐτὸ δὲ μετ᾽ ἀναισθησίας ἁπτὸν λογισμῷ τινι νόθῳ, μόγις πιστόν,

- Read: *having nothing to do with senses, anything composite, all phenomena.*
- Read: *The* λόγος *named here is a kind of* λόγος *that we are not familiar with, that is, does not "count" in our usual discourse. This "new and fresh," unfamiliar* λόγος *is hardly or scarcely trustable – trustable only with difficulty ("toil and pain"). Note that Jowett's translation "hardly real" for* μόγις πιστόν *is an example of a typical translation, one that "knows too much" in adding the word* **real**, *which is not there in the Greek text. The temptation to draw conclusions is strong, because one is uncomfortable with the openendedness of the Greek itself.*

in the face of this χώρα [i.e., the third kind as "space"] and seeing dream-like [as if dreaming], we say that somehow and by necessity everything is somewhere in some place and [but] dwells in [withdraws into] a "space," whatever it be [χώρα τις], i.e., that which is nowhere in heaven or earth [and] is no-thing.

πρὸς ὃ δὴ καὶ ὀνειροπολοῦμεν βλέποντες καί φαμεν ἀναγκαῖον εἶναί που τὸ ὂν ἅπαν ἔν τινι τόπῳ καὶ κατέχον χώραν τινά, τὸ δὲ μήτ᾽ ἐν γῇ μήτε που κατ᾽ οὐρανὸν οὐδὲν εἶναι.

- Let us take the three major word-images in the order that they appear in this passage. First, ὀνειροπολοῦμεν: *dream-like, as if in dreaming – owing to our dreamy condition. Here Plato is not talking about an actual* **dream**. *Rather dream-like, pointing here to the power of the non-transparent, which we must somehow learn to hear and to say. Taking Plato's word* **mythos** *into account, we can say that the dynamic we are after is itself and as such not available to intellectual or conceptual comprehension. It is a kind of saying that is poi-etic, that is, can only be reached in a language other than that of concepts and definitions. The Greek here says: dreamy, dream-like: a fleeting, shadowy image, lacking certainty as in a kind of hunch – non-transparent as in a mythos:* ὀνειροπολέω = *I am haunted by dreams.* ὀνείρωξις = *dreamlike.*

- *Second, ἔν τινι τόπῳ: we grant that everything that is, every being, every manifestation-phenomenon, has to be somewhere – "in some place, whatever that may be" – whereas the "space" we are seeking to come to know is no-thing and no-where. When the indefinite adjective τις modifies the noun τόπος, we hear something like: τόπος whatever it be, some kind of τόπος, τόπος in some fashion or measure, a certain τόπος. In any case it is " that which is nowhere in heaven or earth [and] is no-thing."*

- *Third, κατέχον χώραν τινά: "space," whatever it may be (χώρα τις), is elusive, non-transparent. We know that this χώρα τις is no-thing and formless. The same is true here as for τόπος. Again, when the indefinite adjective τις modifies the noun χώρα, we hear something like: χώρα whatever it be, some kind of χώρα, χώρα in some fashion or measure, a certain χώρα. Barely if at all knowable. Or: knowable, not in a cognitive knowing but in knowing awareness, that is, non-conceptually.*

- *Remember: χώρα whatever it may be ... is nowhere in heaven or earth [and] is no-thing! Again, it is "space-empty-of-all-form-and-no-thing."*

Gathering the key dimensions of the dynamic at issue in these passages and in accord with the reading I have presented, let me highlight them:

1. Plato's thinking and saying of the dynamic is "on the way" (*unterwegs*). The thinking is in movement, because the formless dynamic that he was and we are seeking here is so strange to our way of thinking – and clearly to Plato's ears as well – and is itself not static and cannot be forced into some place, as might be possible for things and forms.

   Given the obscure at the core of the dynamic, we need a language and saying that is less conceptual and less definitional. We need a non-conceptual and indirect way of saying, a language that above all opens *us* to "that in which," almost without a name. The λόγος is bastard-spurious, perplexing, and is dream-like (non-transparent as in μῦθος).

2. This is highlighted in the Greek words χώρα τις. In its being devoid of forms, formless, invisible, non-transparent, it is not possible to grasp it by reason: That in which – named χώρα – is not available to cognitive knowing. It is only available to knowing awareness. It is only poi-etically thinkable. And it is sayable only in poi-etic language.
3. This no-thing and no-form dynamic is … always dynamic, in movement, unfolding, coming into being or becoming. The Greek word φύσις becomes a marker for saying the always ongoing no-form no-thing dynamic of emerging-unfolding.
4. Most significantly, *all three words* that Plato uses to circle around what is at issue – named first ὑποδοχή, then ἐκμαγεῖον, and then χώρα – point to and say how "that in which" is formless, no-thing, boundless, invisible, devoid of all forms. When Plato's Socrates says this dynamic as "that in which," thus leaving out any noun, any implying of thing or substance disappears. **Note that this seemingly simple fact undoes all attempts to name χώρα as something, as substance, as moulding stuff, as receptacle, and so on.**

In a kind of gathering of this momentous flashpoint – as we hear and think and say the no-form and no-thing non-dual dynamic of beyng-Ereignis, of χώρα as "space-empty-of-all-form-and-no-thing-being," and of radiant emptiness – I now turn to Heidegger's words "from" χώρα.

First, I present a quotation from Heidegger on χώρα; then, a quotation from Heidegger mirroring his own wording on the question and language of beyng.

> That in which something becomes [τὸ ἐν ᾧ γίγνεται] means what we call "space." The Greeks do not have a word for "space." This is not a coincidence; for they do not experience the spatial from *extensio*, but rather from the place (τόπος) as χώρα, which means neither place nor space, but what is taken up and occupied by what is standing there. Place belongs to the thing itself. The various things each have their place. What is becoming [emerging, *das Werdende*] is brought into and out of

this "local" [whatever it may be] "space" [whatever it may be]. For this to be possible, however, the "space" must be devoid of all the modes of appearance that it is meant to be able to absorb from somewhere or other. For if it were similar to any of the forms of appearance that enter it, then, when taking in forms – some of them opposite, some of them entirely different – it would allow a poor realisation of the model, in that it would at the same time bring its own appearance to light. [That is:] that in which the things that are coming-to-be [emerging] are placed ["received"] must not present an own aspect and an own appearance.[10]

The reference to the passage in the *Timaeus* [50e] is meant not only to illustrate how the παρεμφαῖνον and the ὄν – appearance and being as lastingness [ever and always] – belong together. It is also at the same time to suggest that, in the interpretation of being as idea in Platonic philosophy, the reshaping of the barely grasped essence of place (τόπος) and χώρα into a "space" ["Raum"] determined by extension is prepared for. But couldn't χώρα stand for: that which separates itself from every particular [instance, form, thing], that which withdraws-from [all forms, things, appearances], in such a way that it precisely allows for the other and makes "place" for it? [*Das Sichabsondernde von jedem Besonderen, das Ausweichende, das auf solche Weise gerade anderes zuläßt und ihm „Platz" macht?*]. (GA 40:70–1)[11]

• *This ὄν – being as lastingness – is a word saying what Heidegger calls beyng, that is, no-thing, formless, the non-dual dynamic of radiant emptiness.*

When a few pages later Heidegger focuses on the word *Sein*, we see the mutual mirroring of the dynamic at issue in Plato's χώρα and Heidegger's *beyng/Seyn*. We can then let these two sections mirror the thinking-saying of the non-dual dynamic of radiant emptiness – in its no-form and no-thing and invisible but functioning – named as χώρα or *beyng-Ereignis*.

The word "being" [beyng?] is thus indeterminate in its meaning, and yet we understand it as determinate. "Being" turns out to be something highly determinate [but] completely indeterminate. According to the usual logic: there is an obvious contradiction here; something that con-tradicts itself cannot be; there is no such thing as a square circle. And yet there is that contradiction: being as something determinate [but] com-pletely indeterminate. If we don't fool ourselves and take a moment in the midst of our everyday affairs and distractions, we find ourselves in the thick of this contradiction. This condition of ours is more real than almost anything else we call "real," more real than dogs and cats, auto-mobiles and newspapers.

The fact that for us "being" is an empty word suddenly takes on a completely different complexion. In the end we become suspicious of the alleged emptiness of the word. If we look more closely at the word, then it turns out in the end that, despite all the blurring and confusion and generality of its meaning, we mean something specific. This deter-minate is determinate like that and unique in its own way that we even have to say:

Being, which belongs to any and every being and is scattered in the most common, is the most unique ever.

... Being cannot be compared with anything else. The other to it is simply the "nothing." And *there*, there is nothing to compare. If being thus represents what is most unique and most definite, then the word *being* cannot remain empty either. In truth, it is never empty. We can easily see this for ourselves by making a comparison. When we perceive the word "to be," in hearing it as a sound or see-ing it in writing, then there is something immediately different from the sound and letter sequence "abracadabra." It is true that this is also a sequence of sounds, but, as we say here directly, it is mean-ingless, even if it has its meaning as a magic formula. On the other hand, "being" is not meaningless in this way ... There is no empty word at all, only a used up [exploited, *vernutzt*] one, which remains a filled-up one. The name "being" retains its power of naming. That directive "away from this empty word *being* and towards particular beings!" is not only a rushed directive but also a highly questionable one. (GA 40:83–4)

(Let us pause here and tend to the words *Sein* and *Seyn*. This lecture is from 1935. Heidegger puts the word *Sein* in quotation marks: "*Sein*," putting the reader on notice that with the quotation marks "being" is moving beyond the being that is named in the ontological difference: being over against beings (*Sein* over against *Seiendes*). Soon – in *Beiträge zur Philosophie (Vom Ereignis)* from 1936–8 – he will show this difference by introducing for the first time the spelling *Seyn*. In hindsight it becomes clear that the *Sein*-being he addresses in the above quotation could well have been written as *Seyn*/beyng. I refer you, the reader, to the "Interlude" toward the beginning of this book.)

These two quotations from Heidegger show how χώρα in Plato and beyng in Heidegger "say" the same. In both quotations Heidegger is warning us thinkers not to rush so quickly away from the open-ended χώρα or beyng, in order to find the seeming security of things, appearances or particular beings. Whether it is "the reshaping of the barely grasped essence of place (τόπος) and χώρα into a "space" determined by extension" or the "rushed directive … away from this empty word *being* and towards particular beings!" – in either case Heidegger's warning is to not jump to security and certainty. Rather, we are called to dwell in the enigma or no-way-out of the no-form no-thing dynamic of χώρα or beyng/Ereignis or radiant emptiness.

***

Clarifying the view. Since my reading of *chora* in the *Timaeus* stems from how I see things at this point in my life of thinking – and differs from most other readings – it behoves me to explain the "clearing" in which I do this reading. Thus, I will now offer some comments and ruminations – including some repetition – on what I have just worked through.

In other words. That is, calling to mind the salient aspects of the discussion in Plato's *Timaeus* – in the voice of Socrates – let me simply put into my own words what is going on.

How to say the "what" here? This "third kind" is that of space-empty-of-all-form, which is timeless, indestructible, actively receiving-holding-releasing – or releasing-receiving-holding – and is the dynamic "space" for everything that comes to be. Remaining itself "as such," it encompasses/holds what manifests (as phenomena, etc.) non-dually within *chora*. The "what" of emergent phenomena has form and co-heres along with and within the no-form no-thing *chora*.

How to experience and to know "it"? Let go of the traditional language of subject-object and the metaphysics of subject-predicate – subject and then something predicated of it. Leap beyond to a non-reflective, non-conceptual awareness ... to a poi-etic saying. With open awareness, let the obscure/withholding and hidden dynamic show itself in the leap. This leap beyond propositional, conceptual language to poi-etic thinking-saying shows the obscure and hidden no-thing dynamic emerging in this leap. To move in this way is not a weakness but a strength – and takes courage.

It is hard to resist the urge to give *chora* form and concept, whereas *chora* is "as is" (or: does what it does) totally outside all determination. Repeating the quotation from above, where Heidegger addresses how the Greeks had no word for "space":

> That in which something becomes [τὸ ἐν ᾧ γίγνεται] means what we call "space." The Greeks do not have a word for "space." This is not a coincidence; for they do not experience the spatial from *extensio*, but rather from the place (τόπος) as χώρα, which means neither place nor space, but [says] what is taken up and occupied by what is standing there. Place belongs to the thing itself. The various things each have their place. What is becoming [emerging, *das Werdende*] is brought into and out of this "local" [whatever it be] "space" [whatever it be]. For this to be possible, however, the "space" must be devoid of all the modes of appearance that it is meant to be able to absorb from somewhere or other. For if it were similar to any of the forms of appearance that enter it, then, when taking in forms – some of them opposite, some of them entirely different – it would allow a poor realisation of the model, in that it would at the same time bring its own appearance to light. (GA 40:70)

Beyond our usual way of thinking and saying. Beyond rational intellect or calculative ordering, this section of the *Timaeus* calls for another way of thinking and saying-showing. Here Plato is not reaching for conceptual structures or theories. This is not Plato's height of *intellectual* prowess. Rather, it is the farthest point of his seeking – **from within** his experience. Hidden within his poi-etic words is this opening.

If the *meaning* of *chora* has to rely on the language of concepts and traditional logic, then we are lost. However, if the "meaning" comes from "outside of" reflection, then we are in the realm of experience, that is, knowing awareness that does not rely on subject-predicate or on propositional statements. Are we capable of making this move within our experience of awareness and thinking … including critical thinking? This is a knowing that is not bound within the intelligible.

And from this angle the invisibleness of *chora* is not a problem. For *chora* as no-form no-thing *is indeed* invisible, but that does not say that it is not at work or that we cannot experience "it." Herein lies the challenge for thinking: How can something that is no-thing be at work and a dynamic that we can experience?

It is *noesis* – not as intellectual knowing but as knowing awareness – that opens the way to the non-dual thinking of *chora*.

A kind of a "kind beyond kind" is, then, the opening beyond dualistic thinking, to a no-form dynamic. *Chora* partakes of *noesis* as knowing awareness rather than as intellectual knowing in concepts.

Here is the problem we must overcome: Our inherited thinking tells us that "to say" equals "to give some determination" either as thing or as concept. But this limits language to dualistic and propositional language, when what we need is a poi-etic language or saying that shows rather than defines.

Chora and its cognates.

χώρα   space in which a thing is, cavity, field,
            one's proper place, vacancy,
            as it was, undisturbed,
            empty field that enables-affords

χωρέω	withdraw, be in motion, have room for, hold-contain, have power or potential,
χῶρος	a place that is cleared (nothing in it), space, room, space "in which"
χώρημα	cavity, space, vacancy, emptiness
χώρητικός	capable of, able to contain
χωρέειν	to withdraw, to be in hiding, to be in motion, to have room for, to hold-contain, … giving way, withdrawing, receiving and being in movement, dynamic

Adding to what Socrates describes as aspects of *chora* and in all the word images and what they "say," we hear how *chora* is invisible, all-receiving, having no form. The dynamic of space-empty-of-form gets richer.

***Chora* and *mythos*.** In its core aspect as *mythos*, *chora* either strangles us – when we approach it with our usual concepts and definitions – or is the opening to all possibility, when we let go and say "it" poi-etically. Boundless like ἄπειρον. Let me explain.

In the remarkable opening to his reading of Platonic dialogues, John Sallis offers the insight of the mirror-play of *logos*, *mythos*, and *ergon* as the key to reading what I will call the Socratic dialogues of Plato:

> *logos: speech, speech gathering thought*
> *mythos: the opaque, darkness, nontransparent*
> *ergon: deed, action*

Sallis writes: "*The totality of this mirror-play constitutes the dramatic character of a dialogue.*"[12] *Mythos* names "a bond to something intrinsically opaque, a bond to an element of darkness."[13] Referring to Heidegger, Sallis indicates that *mythos* and *logos* are of the same. It is not as if *logos* destroys *mythos* ("the prejudice of modern rationalism thinks that *mythos* is destroyed by *logos*"). Referring specifically to the *Apology*, Sallis writes: "the *logos* unfolds into a *mythos* the very telling of which exemplifies in *ergon* – and is, in effect, *said* to exemplify in *ergon* – just that practice the organisation of which is being related."[14]

Here Sallis explains the subtle but core interplay of *mythos* and *logos*. The "darkness of *mythos*" is in contrast to the "light of *logos*." But since *mythos* is also spoken, the contrast is "within *logos* itself." Then he warns us: "*mythos* is not to be taken, in advance, as merely an inferior kind of *logos*."[15] *Chora* names the darkness or invisibility of *mythos*, even as it contains non-dually the gathering and saying of *logos*.

When applied to the task at hand – namely how to experience and think and say *chora* – the invisible, indeterminate withdrawal that is *chora* is the *mythos* within which *logos* unfolds, as we open to the no-form dynamic of *chora*.

In the *Timaeus* Plato has Socrates showing this inherent opaqueness in *chora*. It is extremely difficult to put into words. In a sense *chora* is a "kind" that is beyond what kinds can be. It is hard to make the turn to the clearing in the deepest forest. We think it is somehow easy to work in *logos*, but we discover the virtual impossibility of saying *chora* in *logos* ... for its *mythos* aspect.

We are a bit dismayed when, getting to the end of the dialogue, we realize that Socrates does not return to the discussion of *chora*, as if he abandons it. And we regret the lack of resolution. But what is own to *chora* and what it calls for does not require but rather eschews any kind of "resolution." Given that *chora* has shown itself as an invisible and indeterminate no-form dynamic, the expected "resolution of the plot" is superfluous. More than that, it is impossible, so long as we know the sway of the no-thing dynamic. Indeed, we have been carrying *chora* and this opaque unfolding-holding-receiving dynamic along all the way.

This *not returning* to *chora* at the end of the dialogue mirrors *mythos*. Also, at the center of *chora* is an invisible and indeterminate no-form dynamic, which holds and lets manifest from its living potential, then the driving "force" is sheer openendedness – in which there are no boxes. Seeking a resolution is putting *chora* back into a box. This does not fit its boundlessness and living potential.

Just as for Heidegger Ereignis takes us beyond concepts and the definitional language that is traditionally used in philosophical discourse, so too for Plato *chora* takes us beyond the usual linguis-tic-conceptual framework. Beyond to poi-etic language, which says-shows the no-form no-thing indeterminate dynamic of *chora*. This opening is a markedly "new" start for thinking.

Heidegger pushes the envelope of language and conceptual thinking, in order to come to non-conceptual, poi-etic awareness and to say-show the no-form and no-thing non-dual dynamic of beyng as Ereignis. So, too, Plato's Socrates pushes the envelope of arguments and a *logos* disconnected from *mythos*, in order to say-show the same no-form and no-thing non-dual dynamic, here named *chora*. We could say that Socrates pushes *beyond* arguments and a *logos* disconnected from *mythos*.

Perhaps one can say that Sallis, prophetically, as it were, gives wit-ness – already in 1975, when he first wrote this book – to the return of thinking to the timeless "start" when he writes: "the *mythos* thus serves as a way of openly granting a concealment, hence, as a way of knowingly bearing testimony to human ignorance – to the involvement of a concealment and an ignorance at least in the beginning of philosophy if not in its fulfillment."[16]

Sallis's reference to ignorance could stem from his mentor, Edward Ballard, and Ballard's book *Socratic Ignorance*.[17] But the "ignorance" meant here is not what we usually mean by ignorance: inexperience, stupidity, unenlightenment, dopiness, uninformed, naivety.

I maintain that the "ignorance" that Ballard and Sallis are refer-ring to is more like not-knowing *conceptually*, in the sense of the hidden of the non-resolvable, the non-definable, the non-concep-tual. This "ignorance" is a not-knowing or is awareness of the hid-den non-dual dynamic of radiant emptiness and its power to let emerge. Also named beyng/Ereignis. Also named buddha mind and *dao*. Also named the no-thing quantum potential in the field of energy in quantum physics. And present in Greek thinking, as exemplified beautifully in Plato's Socrates and his pursuit of the no-thing no-form (and no "kind" at all!) as said with the word χώρα. Χώρα as the timeless no-form no-thing dynamic of beyng, Ereignis, ἄπειρον – or the non-dual dynamic of radiant emptiness.

As timeless, this dynamic is the ever-renewing starting, outside of time as we know it, in "space" that is no place: *chora* as the space-empty-of-form.

As he stayed the course, Plato's Socrates was digging deeper, tending constantly to the accompanying remitting withdrawal that gets "said" with the word χώρα. Socrates the philosopher becomes Socrates the seeker-questioner, who with non-conceptual awareness moves to that which cannot be known conceptually or said conceptually. Beyond textual analysis, it is knowable only poi-etically.

The how of going. Do not let denomination and our usual discourse define the way, that is, intellectual grasping for definition. Rather, leap into experience of the sheltering holding refreshing dynamic, which is also emergence. The dynamic *as such*! One could ask: In imaging what is own to *chora*, what is there to bind us? It does not bind but rather frees us. It calls to us to think and say it outside the parameters of Western metaphysics and the usual way of language (traditional discourse, dualistic predication, etc.).

Retreat from the language of rational discourse but not from all ways of saying. Conceptual and dualistic languages cannot go there. These languages must retreat. And poi-etic language and saying take on the task of saying-showing that which traditional discourse cannot handle.

Maxims for going the way of *chora*. Try these:

- Don't let the words limit.
- Be open to what comes in saying that opens.
- Let go of the sea of words that we have.
- Let this unlimiting drive become the "new" way.
- When you catch it, then you abide there.
- Two opposites in union. The both-and.
- Draw on the experience of two opposites in their non-dual at-oneness.
- Let the words in their poi-etic saying be transforming.

- Know awarely non-dual emptiness, hidden but shining, sheltered but radiant.
- Take your time. The way there takes time, because it is a bit strange. Strange does not mean not true.
- Experience opening until you know it in awareness and non-conceptually. Then realize that it was always there.

Ponder these:

- Dynamic fullness emerges within the opening of emptiness.
- Dynamic emptiness thrives.
- Expectations and concepts get in the way.
- There are no boxes.
- Repeating is useful.
- The way is the starting, not itself any thing.
- What lets emerge and is itself no-thing is always fresh. Without form or definition.

Maybe, just maybe, the word χώρα comes very close to saying the nondual dynamic of radiant emptiness. Rich, full, freeing, opening emptiness.

***

I'm often asked if there is something I think writers *ought* to do,
and recently in an interview I heard myself say:
"Several things. Love words, agonize over sentences.
And pay attention to the world."
– Susan Sonntag

Quantum theory provides us with a striking illustration
of the fact that we can fully understand a connection
though we can only speak of it in images and parables.

Behind this outward display of criticism and skepticism
lies concealed a deep philosophical interest
even in those dark areas of reality of the human mind,
which elude the grasp of reason.

Whenever we proceed from the known into the unknown,
we may hope to understand; but we may have to learn
at the same time a new meaning of the word *understanding*.

– Werner Heisenberg

At the still point of the turning world.
Neither flesh nor fleshless;
Neither from nor towards; at the still point, there the dance is,
But neither arrest nor movement.
And do not call it fixity,
Where past and future are gathered.
Neither movement from nor towards,
Neither ascent nor decline.
Except for the point, the still point,
There would be no dance, and there is only the dance.
I can only say, there we have been: but I cannot say where.
And I cannot say how long, for that is to place it in time.
Words strain,
Crack and sometimes break, under the burden,
Under the tension, slip, slide, perish,
Decay with imprecision, will not stay in place,
Will not stay still.

Trying to use words, and every attempt
Is a wholly new start, and a different kind of failure
Because one has only learnt to get the better of words
For the thing one no longer has to say, or the way in which
One is no longer disposed to say it.
And so each venture
Is a new beginning, a raid on the inarticulate.

– T.S. Eliot, from *The Four Quartets*

ii. ἀλήθεια / aletheia

In the retrieval that we are trying to make here, ἄπειρον/*apeiron* is perhaps the clearest and shiniest word-image to exemplify our task. And χώρα/*chora* pushes things to the very edges of what is at stake: the no-thing and no-form dynamic that we want to experience, think, and say. As χώρα mirrors Heidegger's "other beginning" – as beyng/Ereignis, Bohm's holomovement that is not physical, buddha mind and *dao* – what χώρα offers is "it."

Having said that, ἀλήθεια/*aletheia* is the broadest and deepest word-image in early Greek thinking. It is by far the primary Greek word-image that Heidegger uses in his own quest. At the very end of his lecture course on Parmenides in the winter semester of 1942–3 (GA 54), Heidegger says that the dynamic of ἀλήθεια is pretty much "it" when we look for the core of the starting of Greek thinking:

> As the deep sway [*Wesen*] of the rising-emerging [*Aufgang*] (φύσις), ἀλήθεια is itself [as such] the starting [*der Anfang*]. The journey to the house of the goddess [Ἀλήθεια] is the thinking towards the starting. The thinker thinks the starting by thinking Ἀλήθεια. Such commemorating [*Andenken*] [i.e., ἀλήθεια] is the sole concern of thinking [*Denken*]. As the dictum of the thinker, this concern counts as *the* word of Western saying [*Sage*]. (GA 54:242)

The Greek word for "truth" is ἀλήθεια/*aletheia*. But the dominant and now traditional (TI) meaning of truth has its roots in the human intellect, connected with *doxa* and *episteme*. The opposite of this "truth" is falsity. It says that truth is not in things (Aristotle, *Metaphysics* 1027b–1028) but in the faculty of judgment, namely how human judgment connects in concepts that which corresponds to what is out there, in the things.

But the word *ἀ-λήθεια* has a very different meaning, stemming from what the word itself says. Literally, the word says nothing of the truth as just explained. The Greek word λήθη says forgetfulness, oblivion, concealing, hiding, the unseen hidden. (λήθη is connected with the verb λανθάνω, I escape notice, I am unseen by others.) With the *alpha primativum*, ἀ-λήθεια says the not-hidden, not-concealing, *and* the emerging from within λήθη. Thus ἀ-λήθεια says "un-forgetting" or "un-concealing" or *disclosing* as the non-dual dynamic of λήθη and the ἀ-. We can say, of course, that this dynamic is more about things than about the human mind that "thinks" and creates concepts. But then, it goes beyond things, beyond to the no-thing and no-form dynamic as such, which allows for and sustains all coming-to-be of things. Notice that going-beyond does not mean leaving-behind. The dynamic that we are aiming for – to become aware of and to say-show – includes both (a) τὰ φαινόμενα and (b) the hidden dimension within which τὰ φαινόμενα emerge, that is, the no-thing and no-form non-dual dynamic of the hiding-sheltering and the emerging "as such." This dynamic cannot be measured or conceived by the intellect. But it still has – above all else has! – the dynamic of opening, freeing, enriching as phenomena get revealed. Thus the non-dual dynamic of radiant emptiness, the no-form and no-thing dynamic – Heidegger's beyng/Ereignis – is the being-at-work (*energeia*) itself and not the *what* of the things. And we can experience "it"!

The word ἀλήθεια appears in the fragments of Heraclitus and Parmenides. Our task here is to retrieve the *issue* hidden in the word ἀλήθεια and to try to think its deepest saying, which got covered over in the development of Western *philosophy as metaphysics, in the Christian paradigm, in the rationalism of the Enlightenment, as well as in misleading translations of the Greek texts.*

For Parmenides, ἀλήθεια means the uncovering or disclosing, that which is behind what is disclosed (the manifestation of things/beings) in a kind of self-sheltering that makes all showing possible. For early Greek thinking this says emerging of what is always remained essentially tied to λήθη, to what is not present, that is, to a dynamic hidden or withdrawing. Disclosure was understood as emergence (the coming to be of what is) from out of withdrawing λήθη. It is precisely this dynamic that is at the crux of Heidegger's beyng and is what I call the non-dual dynamic of radiant emptiness. Ἀ-λήθεια – as λήθη and the ἀ- in their one-ing or at-oneness – says-shows the no-thing no-form dynamic that lets be manifest all that is. It is the coming-out-of-hiding and the hiding-withdrawing, experienced, thought, and said as a non-dual one dynamic. Retrieving this "word" recovers its freshness – a freshness that we want to retrieve in a refreshing rethinking of this Greek word.

The traditional-inherited (TI) and the refreshing-retrieving (RR) ways:

ἀλήθεια TI   correctness, truth over against falsehood
aletheia   *veritas, die Wahrheit* – as in "not a lie"
               propositional truth, in judgment, not in things
               truth as correspondence
          RR   emerging, coming forth
               coming out of the hidden, not-concealing
               disclosing
               emerging from within the hidden or withdrawing
ἀληθές TI   correct, true – as in "not false"
alethes
          RR   phenomena as they appear, as they emerge from
               unconcealment

Ἀληθές is *das Wahre*: the true. Without thinking, we all understand "the true." We know in what the true consists. A good example of this is: What you say is true, that is, corresponds to the facts or to reality. Normal translations of the early Greeks – Heraclitus and Parmenides – take this meaning of ἀληθές for granted and suggest that for Heraclitus the issue is merely putting that into practice. This is the traditional-inherited (TI) way of truth. Heidegger says that this reading of Heraclitus is simply a matter of

> expressing correctly what is correct [the traditional meaning of "true" as corresponding to things] and translating it correctly into action. (GA 55:360)*

---

* Unless otherwise noted, all references in this section are from this text.

That is,

> Saying and doing becomes true and is true when it is ordered "according to the essence of things," that means: is in "correspondence" with the things. (GA 55:360)

This is how truth became correspondence in various forms – as seen in Aristotle–Aquinas–Kant, and so on.

Heidegger gives us a first glimpse of what is missing in this understanding of ἀλήθεια-truth and ἀληθές-true when he invites thinking to go beyond this inherited and traditional meaning of the word. This TI translation "lets it all appear in the most 'lovely' harmony and smoothness" (360). But it cannot be what Heraclitus and Parmenides meant, because this traditional meaning of ἀλήθεια-/ and ἀληθές/true "first appeared in the formation of metaphysics with Plato and Aristotle" (361) without taking into account the deeper saying of the word in Parmenides and Heraclitus. This later view also "ignores the grandeur [dignity, noble bearing, die Würde] of originary thinking in favour of the commonplace [platitude, banality, der Gemeinplatz]" (361).

Heidegger then turns our attention to the task at hand, namely, to retrieve the originary saying by going beyond the limitations of the traditional translation/reading. To wit: ἀλήθεια is a word-image that mirrors the non-dual dynamic of radiant emptiness, that is, the no-thing and no-form dynamic of holding and sustaining and letting-emerge. Itself no thing and in that sense non-extant, even as it is the basis for all emerging and all that emerges, that is, phenomena.

Heidegger then describes this entire conundrum as well as possibility for thinking:

> The word in the Heraclitus fragment [B112] that one translates with "the true," ἀληθέα, is to be taken word-for-word [wörtlich, true to the original] and means, in what is own to it [im Wesen]: "the disclosed [das Unverborgene, the unconcealed, the unhidden, the revealed]." Ἀλήθεια – unconcealing [Unverborgenheit] is a fundamental word of originary Greek thinking. Even as the translation as "truth" is so common and

even as the essential determination of truth as the correspondence of the statement with the thing is still so familiar to us, we must be mindful that the saying was spoken in the time of pre-metaphysical thinking, at a time when the words and especially the fundamental words unfolded [*entfalteten*] their originary power of naming. (361)

For the Greeks their experience of beings is so rich and so concrete and *impacts* [concerns, applies to, strikes, *betrifft*] the Greek person so much that there are significant synonyms (Aristotle, *Metaphysics A*): τὰ φαινόμενα, τὰ ἀληθέα. Thus it makes no sense to translate τὰ ὄντα literally as *beings*. With that, one does not open up to what beings are for the Greeks. Beings are actually τὰ ἀληθέα, what gets revealed-disclosed in [the dynamic of] disclosing [*die Unverborgenheit*], that to which hiddenness [*Verborgenheit*, withdrawal, concealment] is denied for a time; it is τὰ φαινόμενα, that which shows itself from itself [self-showing]. (GA 15:327)

Before we delve fully into our task here, let me pose a few questions: Do we know whether, when Homer wrote that the "saying" was ἀληθές, he meant to say that what was said was "true" as in correct, that is, a statement that was propositionally true? Or did he want to say ἀληθές, the "true," as in revealing what is – a saying that was not logically meant or testable, but rather a saying that matches what is, that reveals in a way that is "true" to the world and what it "said"? I suggest that the answer to these questions is not clear in Homer.

What would it mean to say that there might be a dual character in Plato when he talks about ἀλήθεια as correctness *and* as unconcealing-revealing-coming-forth? Is it possible that he was aware of both meanings? Is it possible that he knew the difference and did not clarify which meaning was meant, simply because the Greeks always knew from the context which sense was meant? And that they saw both of them in a onefold, that is, distinguishable but not separable, that is, ἀλήθεια as correctness is non-dually embedded in ἀλήθεια as unconcealing-coming-forth out of the hidden? And that we have to work hard to decipher what Plato meant?

Given that the dynamic of ἀλήθεια is pretty much "it" when we look for the core of the starting of Greek thinking, the following words of Heidegger apply to ἀλήθεια: "*that which, un-unfolded, in its greatness thrusts forward into the future,* so that the *return into the beginning* could thus be a leap forward into the future – of course only on the one condition that we *really start with the starting* [*wirklich mit dem Anfang anfangen*]" (GA 45:110). This "beginning" names *der Anfang* as the "timeless" start, what gets thinking going (the other beginning).

Heidegger asks whether, in grounding truth as correctness of statements in disclosure of what is (ἀλήθεια), the Greeks have sufficiently asked about "ἀλήθεια in what is *its* own [ἀλήθεια *in ihrem Wesen*)" (GA 45:111).

Parmenides and ἀλήθεια. We look first at Parmenides, who named *the* issue for thinking: ἀλήθεια. Here we go deeper into Parmenides's sayings. Later we will go deeper into Heraclitus's sayings.

Parmenides:

Fragment 2, 3–4

How there is coming to be (at all) and how not coming to be cannot be. This is the reliable way of going (for it goes the way of ἀλήθεια).

ἡ μὲν ὅπως ἔστιν τε καὶ ὡς οὐκ ἔστι μὴ εἶναι,
πειθοῦς ἐστι κέλευθος – Ἀληθείῃ γὰρ ὀπηδεῖ -,

Fragment 1, 28–30

... but it is fitting that you come to know everything: the unwavering heart of well-rounded ἀλήθεια, as well as the holding of opinions by mortals, in which there is no reliability in terms of ἀλήθεια.

Χρεὼ δέ σε πάντα πυθέσθαι
ἡμέν Ἀληθείης εὐκυκλέος ἀτρεμὲς ἦτορ
ἠδὲ βροτῶν δόξας, ταῖς οὐκ ἔνι πίστις ἀληθής.

And why does the thinker need to know "the holding of opinions by mortals"? To attain a distance from convention, in order to be open to "the unwavering heart of well-rounded ἀλήθεια." This is why Parmenides says:

Fragment 1, 26–8

It is not ill fate that has sent you on this pathway but rather the powers of what is fitting and in accord – for it lies off the beaten track of humans – but rather [it is] empowering and fitting.[18]

ἐπεὶ οὔτι σε μοῖρα κακὴ προὔπεμπε νέεσθαι
τήνδ᾽ ὁδόν – ἦ γὰρ ἀπ᾽ ἀνθρώπων ἐκτὸς πάτου ἐστίν-,
ἀλλὰ θέμις τε δίκη τε.

"Fitting and in accord" with – or "empowering and befitting" – *what*? What has brought the thinker onto this pathway – unlike the usual pathway of humans – is fitting to and in accord with ... ἀλήθεια. And thinking has to take "another" path, not the path of convention that humans usually tread.

This recommendation made by the goddess Ἀλήθεια is fitting to the quest of the thinking-saying of Parmenides *and above all* to the thinking quest of the work of thinking presented here.

Heidegger writes: "As the deep sway [*Wesen*] of the rising-emerging [*Aufgang*] (φύσις), ἀλήθεια is itself [as such] the starting [*der Anfang*]" (GA 54:242). It is that in terms of which thinking gains insight into coming to be "as such," that is, the no-thing dynamic that is hidden in the "what" of coming to be, τὰ φαινόμενα, τὰ ἀληθέα. Regardless of how we name this "what" – what emerges, things/beings – there is this powerful and formless dynamic within which whatever appears appears. This is the field or force or no-thing dynamic, the non-dual dynamic of radiant emptiness, that this book is focused on and working with. That is, there is always already – "timelessly" – a coming-forth, an emerging that is itself not a thing, has no form, is thus fittingly named emptiness – a rich, full, freeing, opening emptiness. Ἀλήθεια, non-concealing/emerging, is that which guides thinking when it thinks the question of εἶναι: coming to be. Ἀλήθεια is the momentum that bestows to *what is* its bearing; it holds what comes to presence in its proper place within the dynamic of ἀλήθεια-non-concealing/emerging.

> Disclosure [*Unverborgenheit-ἀλήθεια*, coming-out-of-hiding, non-concealing, emerging] is, as it were, the element in which there is in the first place something like being as well as thinking and their belonging-together. (GA 14:85)

In Heidegger's Zähringen seminar of 1973, he read a short text in which he focused on the words Ἀληθείης εὐκυκλέος ἀτρεμὲς ἦτορ. The traditional German translation that Heidegger gives (without naming his source): "*der Wahrheit, der wohlgerundeten, unerschütterliches Herz*": "The unshakeable heart of well-rounded truth" (GA 15:403).

We know that the word ἀλήθεια – or ἀ-λήθεια – says *Un-verborgenheit*: dis-closure, non-concealing. We know that this is not truth understood as validity of statements of propositions. But what does *Unverborgenheit*-unconcealment say? Heidegger:

> In order to better understand the revealing that reigns in the unconcealment, we focus on the epithet εὐκυκλέος. Well-rounded is something that we take as property of things. But disclosing [*Entbergen*], non-concealing [*Unverborgenheit*], is not a thing. We get closer to its bearing [*Walten*] if we translate εὐκυκλέος as "affordingly encircling [*schicklich umkreisend*]." (GA 15:404)

Again, focusing on the word εὐκυκλέος, Heidegger writes:

> Εὐκυκλέος is usually understood as "well-rounded" and then is meant as property of things.

> But since here the word indicates ἀλήθεια and since disclosing [*Entbergen*] is nothing thing-like, it cannot be translated in this way. It must be understood differently. Therefore, we think εὐκυκλέος as "the well-enfolding, affordingly encircling [*das Wohlumfangende, schicklich umkreisend*]." (GA 15:396)

These words reveal ἀ-λήθεια as a no-thing dynamic, the radiant emptiness that bears and sustains and lets emerge all things, phenomena as disclosed, τὰ φαινόμενα as τὰ ἀληθέα. It is the same dynamic named in "radiant emptiness," as well as indirectly in Anaximander's ἄπειρον and directly in Plato's χώρα.

Heraclitus and the λήθη in ἀλήθεια. The best way to "start" our thinking here is to ask the question: What happens to our understanding of things/beings when we rethink and retrieve this Greek dynamic of ἀλήθεια/λήθη?

What do we usually mean or say when we are thinking about beings/things? Things/beings are thought as separate static substances,

- mere entities, something that exists "out there," over against the *anima* or *intellectus* of Scholastic philosophy,
- things that are other in the outer world, over against the inner world of Cartesian *cogito*,
- things as objects of Kantian objectifying subjectivity.

But if we take seriously Heidegger's lifelong pursuit of the question of beyng as the no-thing and no-form dynamic within which all things emerge and to which all things return, then "emerging things" are something other than independent, static substance things. We have already pointed to the need to go beyond this limited view by quoting Heidegger. I now repeat that quotation:

> For the Greeks their experience of beings is so rich and so concrete and *impacts* [concerns, applies to, strikes, *betrifft*] the Greek person so much that [these] are significant synonyms (Aristotle, *Metaphysics A*): τὰ φαινόμενα, τὰ ἀληθέα. Thus it makes no sense to translate τὰ ὄντα literally as *beings*. With that, one does not open up to what beings are for the Greeks. Beings are actually τὰ ἀληθέα, what gets revealed-disclosed in [the dynamic of] disclosing [*die Unverborgenheit*, ἀλήθεια], that to which hiddenness [*Verborgenheit*, withdrawal, concealment] is denied for a time; it is το φαινόμενον that shows itself from within and out of itself. (GA 15:327)

With this in mind, I focus on Fragment B112 of Heraclitus and offer (a) a translation of the fragment and (b) Heidegger's expanded translation of the fragment.

> **Minding thinking is the highest excellence, and wisdom [is] gathering the unconcealed [disclosed, ἀληθέα] and acting in accord with φύσις [as active unfolding], hearkening to [heeding] it.**

> τὸ φρονεῖν ἀρετὴ μεγίστη, καὶ σοφίη ἀληθέα λέγειν καὶ ποιεῖν κατὰ φύσιν ἐπαΐοντας.

Heidegger adds τοῦ Λόγου at the end of the fragment:

> τὸ φρονεῖν ἀρετὴ μεγίστη, καὶ σοφίη ἀληθέα λέγειν καὶ ποιεῖν κατὰ φύσιν παΐοντας (τοῦ Λόγου).

He says that this fragment "resonates in the unspoken addition, but for us an addition that has to be expressed" (GA 55:373). With this addition Heidegger then offers an expanded translation of the fragment:

> Das sinnende Denken ist der höchste Edelmut und dies, weil das Wissen ist: das Unverborgene (aus der Verbergung für diese) zu sammeln im Hervor-bringen seiner gemäß dem Aufgehen – (all dies doch) im Hinhorchen auf die ursprüngliche Versammlung. (373f.)

Here is my translation of Heidegger's *expanded* translation:

> **Minding thinking is the highest excellence [nobility] and [it is] this because knowing awareness is: gathering the unconcealed (from within the concealing and in accord with itself), in bringing it forth in accord with the emerging [*Aufgehen*, φύσις] – (all of this however) in hearkening to the originary gathering.**

Ἀληθέα λέγειν: **gathering the unconcealed.** We heed Heidegger's warning that τὰ ὄντα cannot simply be translated as beings/things, but rather as the disclosed, aka phenomenon (what shows itself). That is, τὰ ὄντα must be taken together with τὰ φαινόμενα and τὰ ἀληθέα. And all three are held within ἀλήθεια – or: ἀ-λήθεια. One can write this word-image as ἀλήθεια-λήθη or λήθη-ἀλήθεια or ἀ-λήθεια.

***

Excursus: At this point I take a break – stop at the side of the road, as it were – and go deeper into the question of which English words best translate-*say* what the word ἀ-λήθεια or *Unverborgenheit* says. I start with some of the German words that Heidegger uses to say ἀ-λήθεια. Note that these are creative renderings and not "just" translations. At the end I simply list various possibilities in English.

a. *Not about beings (das Seiende) but the leap into beyng, leaving behind the ontological difference*

From *Beiträge* (GA 65)

definitively released from all beings or everything that is
Endgültig abgelöst von allem Seienden (329)

vibrating of [non-dual no-form no-thing] beyng as such
Schwingung des Seyns selbst (372)

the trembling of the vibrating of beyng as such
Das Erzittern der Schwingung des Seyns selbst (372)

b. *the dynamic of opening-rising-emerging, opening as such*

From *Grundbegriffe* (GA 51:112)

For what emerges, setting-out is that which protects from any boundary.
Die Verfügung ist dem Anwesenden das der Grenze Wehrende.

From *Seminare* (GA 15:405)

emerging: emerging as such; coming-forth, coming-forth as such
anwesend: anwesen selbst

c. *the non-dual dynamic of coming-forth and withdrawing as an active*
   (ergon) one-ing

   From *Heraklit* (GA 55:171–81)

   disclosure, unconcealing, revealing of self-hiding, withdrawal
   Unverborgenheit des Sichverbergens

   The rising-emerging into disclosing-non-concealing
   Die Entbergung in die Unverborgenheit

   The rising-emerging holds sway as unconcealing.
   Das Aufgehen west als Sichentbergen. (GA 7:278)

   From *Beiträge* (GA 65)

   hiding self-sheltering and disclosing
   Verbergung und Entbergung (330)

   lighting-up, clearing, opening of withholding or self-sheltering
   Lichtung des Sichverbergens (329)

d. *highlighting the dynamic and potential of the hidden, withdrawing*

   lighting-up, opening for the withholding
   Lichtung für das Sichverbergen (241)

   self-sheltering as withholding of the ground
   Sichverbergen als Versagung des Grundes (379)

   the hesitating-halting, wavering-quivering withholding-withdrawing
   die zögernde Versagung (383)

   the "distance" of undecidability
   Die "Ferne" der Untentscheidbarkeit (382)

In this last entry (d) undecidability takes on a key role:

> The "empty" is also and intrinsically the fullness of not-yet-decided, to be decided. (382)

> But withholding [*Versagung*] is not nothing, but rather an excellent, originary mode of letting-unfulfilled, letting-empty; with that, an excellent mode of en-opening. (379)

> The self-opening for the sheltering-hiding [*Verbergung*] is originarily the "distance" of undecidability" (382)

This means that the no-thing and no-form hidden-withdrawing is **sheer possibility**. Free of being ordered or put into "boxes," it is the "foremost" dynamic within which everything is possible:

> ... *withholding [**die Verweigerung**] is the foremost and utmost gifting of beyng, indeed its originary deep sway as such* [**Wesen**]. It takes place as the withdrawal [**der Entzug**], which draws into the stillness in which truth – according to what is own to it – comes anew to the decision on whether it can be founded as the clearing for self-sheltering [***als die Lichtung für das Sichverbergen***]. This self-sheltering is the revealing of the withholding [***das Entbergen der Verweigerung***], is letting-belong to the strangeness of another beginning. (241)

Hearing this in its rich possibility, we see how Heidegger finds the "foremost" key to this non-dual dynamic within the unhiding hiding, the rising within the hidden sheltering. That is, the fullness of disclosing, revealing-opening-emerging – the fullness of *Unverborgenheit* – abides in the potential of the undecidable "rising" hidden-sheltering.

Reminding ourselves of the Greek words and translations (λήθη: oblivion, forgetfulness, concealment; λανθάνω: be-remain hidden or covered, escape notice, something not being noticed, forget ...

be latent, be dormant; ἀ-λήθεια: λήθη and emerging out of λήθη – the active one-ing dynamic), here is an array of English words for ἀλήθεια-λήθη or λήθη-ἀλήθεια or ἀ-λήθεια:

> concealing-non-concealing
> covering-uncovering, disclosing
> hiding-revealing
> veiling-unveiling
> withdrawal-manifesting
> furling-unfurling
> enfolding-unfolding (Bohm)
> self-sheltering-emerging

End of excursus.

***

I return to the λήθη in ἀλήθεια. The issue of ἀλήθεια points initially to what comes to appearance, and it seems easy to think ἀλήθεια as what has left λήθη behind. But the non-dual dynamic of "coming out of hiddenness" does not leave λήθη. The emerging of ἀ-λήθεια, as well as *what* emerges (things, phenomena), stay within the λήθη. For in the end, this dynamic is the astonishing issue that transposes us into wonder. How are we capable of this λήθη?

Heidegger begins his interpretation of Heraclitus *and* his own pathway of thinking with Fragment B16 of Heraclitus thus:

How could anyone hide from that
which never goes under?

τὸ μὴ δῦνόν ποτε πῶς ἄν τις λάθοι;

For Heidegger, this fragment belongs at the very outset of any reading-interpretation of the fragments of Heraclitus. It is the fragment that starts our thinking, then and now and always:

withdrawing-emerging, dis-closure, hiding-revealing: "Perhaps [Fragment B16] should be for us the *first*, in terms of its core [intrinsic, *innere*] ranking and its leading importance" (GA 7:267).

The fragment is in the form of a question and begins with the last word of the saying: λάθοι, from λανθάνω: I am/remain hidden or covered, I escape notice, forget … am latent-dormant. How could anyone (τις) remain hidden from that which never goes under (τὸ μὴ δῦνόν ποτε)? In a series of carefully thought out responses to the possible meaning of that phrase, Heidegger works towards an originary way of thinking that *one* realm of disclosing-unconcealing-unveiling-unfolding: the no-thing and no-form non-dual dynamic of beyng/Ereignis, aka radiant emptiness.

Literally and at first glance τὸ μὴ δῦνόν ποτε means: what does not go under. How could anyone remain hidden in the presence of that which does not set? Then Heidegger thinks what δῦειν meant for the Greeks: to go into something, to go under (e.g., the setting sun going into the sea), to go under or behind the clouds. "As the Greeks thought it, going under takes place as a going into hiding" (GA 7:274). Thus what does not go under is that which does not go into hiding or disappear.

What does not go into hiddenness or hiding is something that is always in the movement of emerging (*Aufgehen*). It is the continual coming out of, the continual uncovering or disclosing. But what about the hiding within which the emerging happens? This hiding-concealing λήθη is not some static realm devoid of movement – as if a hidden and somehow passive basis of what comes to be. Rather, the hidden character of disclosure (λήθη) is a no-thing and no-form *dynamic*. And this non-dual *dynamic* is at work in the very disclosing-unconcealing-emerging that cannot "escape" from the movement of λήθη. We are confronted with both λήθη and ἀ-λήθεια within the non-dual dynamic of λήθη and the emerging from within and out of λήθη.

Does this not remind us of the enigmatic dynamic of Plato's *chora* – here emphasizing the dynamic of the holding-withdrawing and the manifestings as all-in-one?

In order to let this dynamic unfold, we must enter into the part of the non-dual dynamic that is foreign to us, namely the non-dual dynamic of the enfolding and unfolding in its one-ing. How to do that?

It is not about some*thing* that moves into or out of hiding/ λήθη – the enfolding – but is rather about the entire non-dual dynamic, what Bohm calls the holomovement. When Heraclitus names the hiding/λήθη in terms of never setting, he provides an impetus for thinking "it," but "it" cannot be taken by itself. In one word Heraclitus names both the not-going into hiding and the ever-pervading emerging: the never going into λήθη and the ever-pervasive emerging from out of the dynamic that it is. The onefold one-ing moment of the essential interplay "into" and "out of" is the non-dual dynamic of disclosing-unfolding. Thus Fragment B16 says: How could anyone remain hidden from this interplay of δῦνόν and μὴ δῦνόν ποτε, this movement into and out of λήθη? This interplay within the non-dual dynamic is the central issue for thinking-saying. (This dynamic is the one named in all of the seven key words of early Greek thinking that we are focusing on here.)

This non-dual dynamic of radiant emptiness – beyng/Ereignis – is what Heidegger is retrieving in the words of the early Greek thinkers. And this retrieval calls for a thinking and a saying that is beyond logic and conceptualization. This is why Heidegger calls it the unthought, that is, the conceptually unthinkable. In its character as hidden, it is thus "unthought."

Only that which ἀλήθεια as clearing [*Lichtung*] grants is experienced and thought, not what it "is" as such.

This remains hidden. Does that happen by accident? Does it happen only because of a negligence of human thinking? Or does it happen because the self-hiding [*Sichverbergen*], the hiddenness, the λήθη, belongs to ἀλήθεια – not as a mere addition, as a shadow belongs to light but as the heart of ἀλήθεια? And does there reign in this self-hiding of the clearing of emerging yet another hiding and preserving, from within which disclosing-unfolding [*Unverborgenheit*] can first of all be granted and in this way what emerges can appear in its emergence?

If that be the case, then the clearing is not only the clearing of emergence [Anwesenheit], but rather clearing of the hiding self-sheltering emergence, clearing of the self-sheltering hiding. (GA 14:88)

The coming together of λήθη and ἀλήθεια is not a static unity. It is not a hollow oneness. Rather, it is a dynamic movement, a belonging-together in the non-dual dynamic. This is the crux that thinking must penetrate, holding it open as the no-thing and no-form dynamic that it is. It is the dynamic of beyng/emptiness that lays claim to thinking and within which what emerges in emerging out of hiding must continually be held.

Thinking responds to the movement of disclosing so that thinking itself can move and go the way of disclosing, whereby this thinking is readied in the response as the flashpoint for disclosing/ἀλήθεια. Then Dasein as flashpoint can refresh and retrieve what is its issue, can regain a bearing to the non-conceivable non-dual dynamic of radiant emptiness.

The interplay between ἀλήθεια and λήθη is from within a holding, self-sheltering. Thus, there is an interplay within the non-dual onefold dynamic that it is: the dynamic at-oneness of the interplay emphasizes both emerging and withholding. This is its essential character. For if there were only emerging, coming to be, that would destroy the interplay (that is what the reduction of the unthought to the thought does). On the other hand, if there were only withholding, withdrawing, then the dynamic would lose its enabling power. (The loss of this enabling power is precisely what took place in the turn into metaphysics, which forgot the issue of disclosing as such and dealt only with *what* emerges – the manifest, phenomena, things/beings – understanding the enabling only in terms of beings or what becomes manifest, resulting in losing sight of radiant emptiness. Or in Heidegger's words: losing sight of the no-form no-thing beyng as Ereignis.

The non-dual dynamic is always at work and thus always remains involved in the emerging of whatever is. The "being" of anything is never separate from the dynamic of disclosing-non-concealing.

We have inherited a way of thinking by which we think everything that is as something in itself, separate from the ἐνέργεια-dynamic of the disclosing/ἀλήθεια. In traditional thinking (TI) we give a meta-physical import – a kind of preference – to what is present, what has come to be. Consequently, we think that what does *not* show itself as something ... *is not*. The issue that Heidegger thinks in thinking λήθη-ἀλήθεια is nothing that is. It is without form and substance. It is no-thing, yet it is at work and we can experience "it." It is this awareness that calls for naming "it" with a saying that is not about things and is not dualistic. Thus, Heidegger calls beyng/Ereignis the enriching, freeing-opening of emptiness.

To call the issue ἀλήθεια is to let *that* dimension or dynamic be seen that lets beings and phenomena unfold into what they are to be within enriching emptiness – and that enables all thinking and awareness of it. Ἀλήθεια names the issue in a new way: it focuses on that no-thing no-form dynamic of radiant emptiness within which things/beings emerge. The focus is on the **movement** or **dynamic** of coming to presence, on disclosing as such.

iii. *φύσις / physis*

The traditional-inherited (TI) and the refreshing-retrieving (RR) ways:

φύσις	TI	nature, physical nature, natural order,
physis		physics, natural science
	RR	an emerging-abiding prevailing
		rising-emerging, emerging rising
		the dynamic emptiness, no-thing
		"birthing" or emerging dynamic
		the growing process and principle of movement and
		life but itself no-thing opening-revealing emptiness

The Greek word *φύσις* usually gets translated as "nature" (Latin *natura*). And today's concept of physics stems from this Greek word. The traditional, inherited meaning of this Greek word is: physical nature or material. Going back to the early

Greek thinkers, tradition calls them *"physiologoi"* and maintains that Greek philosophy (all the way from Thales to Aristotle) focuses on the physical/material elements, referring to objects of nature or atoms as physical. The tradition says that some early Greek thinkers focus on the four material elements – fire, water, air, earth – which got reduced to the physical, then or in the later periods.

Above all, it is important to recognize how this limiting view was carried over in the translations from the Greek. When Anaximander holds that all these elements originally arise from the ἄπειρον, the "boundless" or "the infinite," this is taken to be something like a primal mass – and is traditionally and usually still considered physical. And we tend to interpret all of this as a very primitive philosophical speculation, as if the Greeks were not able to think beyond these "simple" concepts.

Thinking *beyond* this limitation means going beyond the traditional "reducing to the physical" and retrieving another saying and another translation of what these elemental words of Greek thinking "say." If φύσις names a dynamic that is not reduced to the physical, then it points to the no-form and no-thing of the deep swaying of beyng – or to the non-dual dynamic of radiant emptiness.

When I check dictionaries for the meaning of the Greek word φύσις, I get, first of all, "nature," then "natural order." Over time the knowledge of "nature" or φύσις changed into a natural science about matter and its motion in or through physical space and time. Even Einstein, who discovered the curvature of space, thus space as dynamic – and then space as the fourth dimension of "space-time" – never abandoned the idea that this space was still physical. As we have inherited it, the discipline of physics is about the basic principles of the physical world in which we live.

For sure Aristotle thought beyond this simplistic world view of φύσις. For example, for Aristotle the word φύσις says "the growth process or *genesis*" (Aristotle, *Physics* 189b and 193a).[19] Or: φύσις as "the principle [ἀρχή] and cause [αἴτιον] of motion and rest for the things in which it is immediately present" (*Physics*, 192b).[20]

Ἀρχή and αἴτιον do not limit φύσις to physical *materia*. But the dominant paradigm that came after Aristotle carries this reduction, in such a way that it still dominates our understanding of "nature" as something physical.

(My observation is that some of today's quantum physicists understand that this limitation leaves much out of the picture and that these physicists in their honesty begin to think how the way things are in the universe involves something that is not limited to physical substances. With this move within quantum physics, the cutting-edge thinking by some physicists moves outside the limiting realm of Greek φύσις as "merely" nature or physical nature. But, even as they move beyond the limitation of a dualistic physical world, they are often hampered by the language that they as physicists have at their disposal when thinking-saying this "beyond." (David Bohm is a possible exception, with his notions of holomovement and enfolding and "the immeasurable.") Is it possible that we philosophers can help the physicists name the physics that goes beyond the merely physical? That we can help them see how already in Greek thinking there is this opening, which today's physicists are seeing for the first time? That we can help them in *their* retrieval?)

But what if the Greeks in general, including Aristotle, were on to something "beyond" the physical and more like the no-thing dynamic of emptiness – or Heidegger's beyng? What if theirs was a thinking that was not limited to or defined by what is static/ inert or dualistic (over against mind or ψυχή) – and what if philosophers and scholars who came after the Greek thinkers "read into" the Greek words, thereby reducing them so that they referred to merely physical things? To say it another way, what if, while saying that everything is water or fire or air, we can retrieve the possibility that these word-images in early Greek thinking come from a thinking that is not limited to the physical and the dualistic?

Let us return to the dictionaries. As I said, φύσις is "nature," "natural order," "outward form." But φύσις is also: growth, originating power, origin, force, birth. These meanings go way beyond φύσις as physical nature and thus way beyond what φύσις has become as "physics."

This second set of meanings for φύσις takes us to the verb φύω, from which φύσις comes. And φύειν says: bringing forth, begetting, birthing, arising, springing up, engendering, growing, becoming, swelling up (as in seeds as they sprout); φύσις as originating power (thus not a thing); springing up, growing. These words say-show a dynamic movement and not things. *This* φύσις says-shows the no-thing and no-form dynamic.

In *Heraklit* (GA 55)* Heidegger shows how to move beyond φύσις as things in nature, physical nature, and "natural order": φύσις is not "the name for nature over against history" (300). Nor is it the name for "nature in the sense of the lawfulness of what appears and what unifies the appearances in their objectivity" (299). Rather:

> The core feature of φύσις ... is the rising [*Aufgehen*] that rises from within itself, which is at the same moment the withdrawing [*verschliessend* going-back-into-itself*]. (298)

It is that which unfolds of itself and stays hidden as it unfolds.

> Φύσις names the rising that at the same time sways deeply [*west*] as going back into itself. In the originary onefold [*Einheit*] of both there sways deeply that for which φύσις is the originary Greek name: what we call being [*Sein*, later *Seyn*-beyng]. In what belongs to rising as its own, however, there lies the letting-come-forth, namely into the open: unconcealing, Greek ἀλήθεια. (365)

In *Einführung in die Metaphysik* Heidegger says that φύσις

> has nothing at all to do with a naturalistic interpretation. Beings as such in the whole [another way that Heidegger uses earlier to say "beyng"] is φύσις – i.e., has as own to it the character of an emerging-abiding

---

* Unless otherwise noted, numbers in parentheses in this section are from this volume.

prevailing [*aufgehend-verweilende Walten*]. This is then experienced first and foremost as that which in a sense emerges [*sich aufdrängt*] in the most immediate fashion and which later signifies φύσις in a narrower sense. (GA 40:19)

Φύσις is not simply something like nature as substance or thing or being, but it is a dynamic emerging-abiding prevailing or holding sway as such, that is, no-form and no-thing dynamic. It is *Wesung*, that deep swaying that is dynamic emptiness, no-thing whatsoever, which contains and sustains all appearances or phenomena. That means: all things in the way that they are, namely phenomena, are bound non-dually to the non-dual, no-thing dynamic of radiant emptiness. Φύσις is one of the names in early Greek thinking that says-shows this dynamic of radiant emptiness – what Heidegger calls being, then beyng, then Ereignis. And he finds this non-dual no-thing dynamic of radiant emptiness – beyng/Ereignis – mirrored in these words from early Greek thinkers.

Let us try this out with Heraclitus, Fragment B123: φύσις κρύπτεσθαι φιλεῖ. This is almost always translated as: Nature loves to hide. But if we apply what we have now learned about φύσις, it becomes way more exciting. The no-thing dynamic of originating power, birthing, engendering includes within itself the hiding, withdrawing from presence, self-sheltering. Or as Heidegger translates this fragment: "The emerging [*Aufgehen*] grants favour to the self-hiding" (110).

This is how Heidegger translates Fragment B123 in his 1944 lecture course "*Logik. Heraclits Lehre vom Logos*" (GA 55). But in his essay "Aletheia (*Heraklit*, Fragment B16)" from 1954 (GA 7), he goes deeper into this fragment and expands the scope of his thinking. In the long quotation that follows, carefully tend to his thinking along these lines.

This quotation is presented without interruption. Since it may be hard to follow at first, let me offer a few pointers, to guide and help as we read:

1. Among other things this segment from "Aletheia (*Heraklit*, Fragment B16)" from 1954 (GA 7) is a shining example of Heidegger's

thinking-saying at its best. It moves slowly, circling back again and
again, each time going deeper into the question at hand.

2. Without explicitly using the words we have been using,
   Heidegger is precisely in that field in which we have been moving
   in this book: beyng/Ereignis as no-form and no-thing dynamic.
   Empty of form, this dynamic is as much filled with possibility
   as it is empty of things/beings. It radiates with the enriching
   possibility for the thinking that this realm or dynamic calls for.
   This emptiness is about no-thing and is "empty of content." And
   with that it is about the radiating open-opening, freeing, and
   the fullness of how the indeterminate of radiant emptiness – aka
   beyng-Ereignis – flourishes. Keep this in mind as the thinking-
   saying here circles and circles again.

3. One dimension of going-deeper is how Heidegger speaks of
   the non-dual dynamic of the hiding-concealing and the rising-
   emerging that is the core issue. See how his thinking moves here
   regarding the dynamic intertwining of these two sides of the
   same coin. In the beginning he tells how they are very near to
   each other, in the closest proximity. Along the way he moves with
   subtlety until he says that the two "sides" not only are non-dually
   connected, but are the same! He finally comes to a thinking-
   saying of the "one."

4. Heidegger says: because the dynamic we are moving within is so
   complex and difficult to say, the "many names" that are needed
   are a sign of its richness and difficulty in comprehending. Keep
   in mind the list of Heidegger's words to describe the *lethe/aletheia*
   dynamic in the previous section on *a-letheia*. Use whatever clues
   or strategies you have to get into this complex – what he calls at
   the end of the quotation a "richness of its simplicity"!

5. Remember how we got to this point in the unfolding of the core
   issue along with the ins and outs of experiencing, thinking, and
   saying "it." The non-dual dynamic of radiant emptiness is one
   way to say that which is no-thing and has no-form, even as it is
   at work and as we can experience it. This dynamic is also called
   buddha mind, *dao*, field of energy in quantum physics, and
   beyng/Ereignis. Going this way calls for a thinking that is not
   conceptual and a language that is poi-etic.

6. All of this says the richness of the no-thing and no-form dynamic we are *retrieving* in early Greek thinking!

Now to the long quotation from the essay "Aletheia (*Heraklit*, Fragment 16)":

> We must pay attention to [this]: φύσις and κρύπτεσθαι, rising (revealing as such) [*Aufgehen (Sichentbergen)*] and concealing [*Verbergung*], are named in the nearest proximity possible. At first glance, this may seem strange. For, if φύσις as rising [opening, *Aufgehen*] turns away from something or even turns against something, then it is κρύπτεσθαι, concealing as such [withdrawal, *Sichverbergen*]. But Heraclitus thinks both of them in their nearness to each other. Their proximity is even specifically mentioned. It is determined by φιλεῖ. Revealing loves the hiding itself [*das Sichverbergen*]. What does this mean? Does the rising [opening, emerging, *das Aufgehen*] seek concealment? Where should this be and how, in what sense of "being"? Or does φύσις have a certain, occasional, apparent preference for hiding instead of rising-emerging, just for a change? Does the fragment say that rising-emerging shifts into hiding-withdrawing, so that first one prevails and then the other? Not at all. This interpretation misses the meaning of φιλεῖ by which the relationship between φύσις and κρύπτεσθαι is named. Above all, this interpretation forgets what is decisive, what the saying offers to thinking: the way in which the rising-emerging [*Aufgehen*] sways deeply [*west*] as unconcealing [*Sichentbergen*]. If we already dare to speak of "swaying deeply [*wesen*]" with regard to φύσις, then what is own to it [*das Wesen*] is not ὅ τι, the what of things ... The fragment is not thinking of φύσις as the essence [*die Wesenheit*] of things, but the deep swaying (verbal) [*das Wesen*] of φύσις.
>
> As such, the rising-emerging always already tends to self-closing [*Sichverschließen*]. The one remains contained in the other. As itself hiding-withdrawal, the κρύπτεσθαι is not a closing up, but rather a hiding-sheltering [*ein Bergen*] in which *the core possibility of rising-emerging is preserved and to which the rising-emerging belongs* [italics mine]. The hiding-sheltering guarantees to unconcealing-revealing what is own to it [*sein Wesen*]. Conversely, in concealing or self-sheltering dwells the restraint of the inclination for unconcealing-revealing. What would a

hiding-sheltering be if it did not hold to itself in its turn [as it turns] towards rising-revealing?

So φύσις and κρύπτεσθαι are not separated from each other, but rather mutually inclined towards each other. They are the same. Only in such inclination does the one grant to the other what is own to each [*das eigene Wesen*]. This mutual favouring is what is ownmost to φιλεῖν and φιλία. The fullness of this "owning" resides in this inclination of rising-emerging and hiding-sheltering to bow to each other.

The translation of the fragment B123 φύσις κρύπτεσθαι φιλεῖ could therefore read: "The rising-emerging (from within the hiding-sheltering) grants favour to the hiding-sheltering."

We still think φύσις superficially when we think of it only as rising and letting-rise and *then still ascribe properties to it* [italics mine], thereby ignoring what is decisive, namely that the rising-emerging not only never eradicates the hiding-sheltering, but needs it, in order to sway as it sways [i.e., without properties!], as un-concealing [*Ent-bergen*, disclosing] ...

[There is a realm that] the floating intimacy of rising-emerging and hiding-concealing creates and pervades. This intimacy harbours the union and one-ness [one-ing, *die Ein-heit*] of the ἕν – the "one"* that the early thinkers presumably saw in the richness of its simplicity, a richness that remains closed to posterity. (GA 7:277–9)

After our focus on φύσις from Fragment B123, I return to Heidegger on Fragment B16: τὸ μὴ δῦνόν ποτε πῶς ἄν τις λάθοι; Usually translated as "How can one stay hidden in the face of that which never goes under? Or as Marcovich translates it: "How could anyone escape the notice of that which never sets?"[21]

Heidegger points out that, as we *experience* "that which never goes under," we are almost forced to turn the negatively expressed saying into the positive ... For here it becomes clear that "never going under" means "forever emerging": φύσις – ζωή. (GA 55:109)

---

* The "one" that Heidegger refers to here is central to Heraclitus' thinking-saying. I will focus on this "one" at the end of the section on *λόγος*.

Note that the self-hiding is what holds the emerging from ever coming to completion. And this mirrors what belongs to φύσις in its ownness as timeless and no-thing, non-dual dynamic.

Is this a leap of faith on Heidegger's part? The "never going under" says the "forever emerging"? And then identifying this with φύσις? We do not need a philologist or a classics scholar. Rather we are called to check it out in our own experience, in awareness and critical thinking.

We end this discussion about the word φύσις with a clue from Kranz's *Wortindex*, where Kranz introduces the word φύσις with the German word *Entstehung*: emergence, arising.[22]

Φύσις and ἀλήθεια together. Now that we have thought through and said φύσις and ἀλήθεια as no-thing no-form emptiness, whose indeterminateness mirrors futural possibility without limits, let us focus on how Heidegger unites the two, that is, thinks them in their non-dual one-ing.

As we go along, we remind ourselves that, when read in the refreshing and retrieving way, all seven key words open up to the same no-thing and no-form non-dual dynamic. All seven key words "say the same." Here we focus on how Heidegger brings φύσις and ἀλήθεια into a one-ing at-oneness.

A little before the long passage just quoted from the essay on ἀλήθεια – as he "retrieves" and rethinks ἀλήθεια – is where Heidegger first turns to φύσις. He explains it this way:

> Heraclitus thinks of the ever-lasting rising [*das Aufgehen*], not something that devolves on rising-emerging as a property and also not the universe that is affected by the rising-emerging. Rather, Heraclitus thinks rising and only this. In the thinking-saying word, the always and ever lasting rising is called φύσις. We would have to translate it in an unusual but appropriate way with the word "*Aufstehung* [emerging]," corresponding to the common word "*Entstehung* [e-merging]." (GA 7:277)

- *There is a slight difference between* **Aufstehung** *and* **Entstehung**. *The prefix* **ent-** *suggests emerging as "from or away from." Here the "away* *from" is the hiding-enfolding. The **auf-** suggests emerging as "rising or opening or coming-up" as such.*

- *Both hiding-sheltering and rising-emerging as such say the same non-dual dynamic, but with this nuance just explained.*

I turn now to *Heraklit* (GA 55), where Heidegger quite explicitly thinks and says the one-ing of φύσις and ἀλήθεια:

τὸ μὴ δῦνόν ποτε is φύσις; this is the reciprocal favour of rising and self-closing; this favour is the ἁρμονία ἀφανής, the hidden joining [*Fügung*] that imbues everything. (171)

Never perishing [τὸ μὴ δῦνόν ποτε] is quizzically seen as that which decides on the possibility and impossibility of being hidden, namely being hidden and not being able to be hidden. (172)

The not hiding is revealing, persisting in the non-concealing and disclosure; in Greek: ἀλήθεια ... Ἀλήθεια, the concealing into disclosure, is what is own to φύσις, the rising-emerging ... (173)

If we think the fragment more in the starting mode [*anfänglicher*] with regard to disclosure [*Unverborgenheit*] and coming-out-of-hiding [*Entbergung*], then it becomes clear that, in the deep swaying of φύσις and in the deep swaying of that which, in coming-out-of-hiding [*entbergend*], is in accord with it, ἀλήθεια reigns as originary unifying [one-ing] principle. (174)

I close this discussion of φύσις by turning back to Anaximander and his statement (from Simplicius) that from where all things emerge is neither water nor any of the elements, but rather "**τινὰ φύσιν ἄπειρον: a boundless unfolding-birthing, whatever that may be.**"[23]

***

Excursus: Now that we have looked at φύσις and then φύσις and ἀλήθεια together, I want to present a gathering of the many aspects of this non-dual dynamic, showing (a) how all aspects are dynamic and not static, (b) how in their one-ing there is nothing that is separated out from the non-dual dynamic, and (c) how those aspects that we perceive and think of as separate – either as things or substances or as concepts – are non-dually ensconced within the non-dual dynamic.

What I present on the next page looks like a regular chart, with its distinctions and seemingly separate items. I have annotated the chart to stress that there is only one dynamic, in which the several distinctions serve us in coming to know the various aspects of the *one* dynamic. We are able to distinguish these in our language and concepts, but they are inseparably one in what is own to the one-ing. When we are minding, then our mind sees them all as being in the non-dual dynamic of radiant emptiness.

Beyng or the Non-Dual Dynamic of Radiant Emptiness
Manifesting Things aka Phenomena
All as a One-ing Dynamic

The Both-And*

Disclosure, unconcealing, revealing of self-hiding, withdrawal
vibrating of non-dual no-form no-thing beyng
hiding self-sheltering and disclosing
trembling-vibrating of beyng as such.

Λήθη χώρα	φύσις** ἀ-λήθεια	ἀληθέα***
self-sheltering hiding	birthing revealing	the disclosed beings/ things
hesitating withholding	emerging: emerging as such	manifested, the emerged, the world
enfolding, harbouring	unfolding coming-forth	the unconcealed, unhidden
the hidden, hiddenness	disclosing, unhiding	phenomena, things
concealment	unconcealing	the unconcealed
withdrawal	manifesting	ἀληθέα

---

* The following set of word-images mirror the non-dual dynamic of concealing-revealing.

** I include φύσις here because it says the same as ἀ-λήθεια. Although the word emphasizes the **action itself**, it also shelters the no-form no-thing and dynamic withdrawing-concealing along with that which gets manifest or disclosed – all within the non-dual dynamic of radiant emptiness, aka beyng. There is no "third" aspect as such. Rather, by emphasizing this seemingly third aspect, we are emphasizing movement from and to. But since all is one, this too is not separated from the non-dual one.

*** These words say that which is manifest, for example, things and all that is. They name things with form and mirror the duality within this realm.

The Flashpoint (*Augenblickstätte*), Da-sein or Human Being Aware, Who Marks the One-ing Dynamic in and of Which It Nondually *Is*

For sure the "action" or movement (*kinesis*) is dynamic. The no-form no-thing concealment or withholding is always dynamic. And the manifested, things and phenomena, are dynamic by virtue of the non-dual no-form dynamic of beyng, *dao*, buddha mind, the no-form field of energy of quantum physics dynamic within which they emerge and which "receives" things/beings-forms. Even as the things or phenomena can be perceived or conceptualized as separate and even static, they are what they are by virtue of the no-form no-thing non-dual dynamic. As inhering within or emerging within this dynamic, they are more "conditions that make them up" rather than "things themselves."

And human Dasein in its awareness heeds and marks this one-ing dynamic while being *within* the one-ing of the non-dual dynamic of radiant emptiness, aka beyng as Ereignis.

iv. ἐόν / eon

The word ἐόν is the Ionian for ὄν, part. neut. of εἰμί. The plural ἐόντα means, virtually universally, "beings." Thus, ἐόν has been widely used for the singular of this word and has often been taken to mean thing, that is, *what* manifests. But there is good evidence that ἐόν cannot simply be reduced to things/beings – and rather has to name something like a no-form and no-thing boundlessness. As we will see in this section, ἐόν "names that which, as still un-spoken – unspoken [*ungesprochen*] in thinking – is ascribed [*zugesprochen*] to all thinking. The word names that which from then on lays claim to all Western thinking, whether expressed or not" (GA 5:351). We will follow this path.

The traditional-inherited (TI) and the refreshing-retrieving (RR) ways for saying ἐόν:

ἐόν	TI	what is, always *a being*
eon		things: the singular of ἐόντα
	RR	participial: *movement* of emerging rising-emerging, emerging rising unfolding from within enfolding emergent emerging

The clear evidence that ἐόν is not a thing and is without form, thus belonging with the same dynamic that we are always opening up to, comes from Parmenides, Fragment 8, lines 3–6:

> There is only one road to go, namely that [there is] isness [ὡς ἔστιν]. There are many markers for this: ἐόν is ungenerated and ἐόν is lasting, whole, unique and unwavering and without end. Not that "it" once was or that "it" will be, because "it" is now, together, all, one, indivisible.

Μόνος δ᾽ ἔτι μῦθος ὁδοῖο λείπεται ὡς ἔστιν· ταύτῃ δ᾽ ἐπὶ σήματ᾽ ἔασι πολλὰ μάλ᾽, ὡς ἀγένητον ἐὸν καὶ ἀνώλεθρόν ἐστιν, οὖλον μουνογενές τε καὶ ἀτρεμὲς ἠδ᾽ ἀτέλεστον· οὐδέ ποτ᾽ ἦν οὐδ᾽ ἔσται, ἐπεὶ νῦν ἔστιν ὁμοῦ πᾶν, ἕν, συνεχές·

- *What is this isness? The Greek word here is* **ἔστιν**: *normally "he-she-it" is. But there is no modifier and no subject. The word stands by and for itself. Given the attributes of this dynamic that are listed here, this "isness" must be boundless, thus no-thing and no-form.*
- *I have chosen to use "is" in quotation marks. My sense is that it is hard to find an English word to say just what the "is" is. And of course that is the problem and the challenge. How to say "is"? "Is" is no-thing, no-form, boundless, a dynamic one, ungenerated and therefore "timeless."*
- *I translate the line about no past and no future in a way that says that it is not as if it once was or will be. Rather, the "now" is somehow timeless, as it needs to be in order to be "it" – whose name is* **ἐόν**.
- *Here are the various ways that one might translate each of the words in the list of attributes for the word* **ἐόν**:

ἀγένητον	*uncreated, unoriginated*
ἀνώλεθρόν	*indestructible, lasting*
οὖλον	*whole, of one piece, indivisible (non-dual)*
μουνογενές	*unique, singular*
ἀτρεμὲς	*unwavering, unshakeable*
ἀτέλεστον	*endless, without end, lasting*
ὁμοῦ	*together, all at once*
πᾶν	*everything, all, entirety*
ἕν	*one, undivided*
συνεχές	*together, whole, uncountable, continuous, indivisible*

As we have just witnessed in the last section – on φύσις – Heidegger thinks the "one" of ἀλήθεια in its one-ing with φύσις. In *Der Spruch des Anaximander* Heidegger connects ἀλήθεια to ἐόν. He says that in Parmenides ἐόν (as the no-thing no-form dynamic within which emerges ... things, phenomena, *what* emerges) is thought from within the "hidden and unlaunched [staying hidden] fullness of unconcealing [*Unverborgenheit*, ἀ-λήθεια] of the ἐόντα, the *Unverborgenheit* with which the early Greek world [of thinking] was conversant" (GA 5: 352). That is, ἐόν and its dynamic is at work within ἀλήθεια, and the two are one in a non-dual one-ing.

It is this ἐόν as *Anwesen*-emergence to which Heidegger turns in the "Seminar in Zähringen 1973" (GA 15:395–407).* The seminar took place on 6–8 September 1973. At the very end of the three-day seminar Heidegger read a short text on Parmenides: ἀληθείης εὐκυκλέος ἀτρεμὲς ἦτορ: "The Unwavering Heart of Well-enfolding Ἀλήθεια." The text itself appears on pages 403–7. The protocol from Heidegger's oral reading is on pages 397–400. (The short text that Heidegger read is one of Heidegger's last pieces of writing. It opens up a new dimension or turn in the work of thinking that we call "Heidegger.")

The context in which Heidegger read this brief text on Parmenides was the question of entering into being, also named beyng. It is the same theme as the one named with the words *apeiron, aletheia, physis*, as well as the words we will come to next: *logos, psyche*, and *nous*. And it is the same dynamic or energy field that is named in "non-dual dynamic of radiant emptiness."

Heidegger brings ἀλήθεια and ἐόν together and shows that they say the same, namely the freeing and opening non-dual dynamic of radiant emptiness – aka beyng/Ereignis – that is at the heart of Heidegger's lifelong pursuit.

From the protocol:

Ἀλήθεια is not an empty openness, nor an unmoving chasm. One has to think it as the movement of unconcealing, which revolves around ἐόν

---

* Unless otherwise noted, all references in this section are from this volume.

in a way that is own to it ["as such"], that means emergent: emerging as such [ἐὸν ἔμμεναι, *Anwesend: Anwesen selbst,* coming-forth: coming-forth as such]. (398)

Thought in its Greek way, the word εἶναι says: emerging [coming forth, unfolding, *Anwesen*]. We cannot stress enough how much *more revealing* (how much more it shows) and thus how much more precise the Greek language is here. (397)

Heidegger says ἐόν as *Anwesend: Anwesen selbst:* Emerging: emergence itself; Unfolding: the unfolding itself. Heidegger wants to stress the *movement* of coming forth *as* coming-forth, the *movement* of emergence *as* emerging. Movement is a dynamic, not a thing or a being. It is "as such," with no form, and is no thing and has no properties.

> But a question arises: Where and how does emergence itself hold sway [*west*]?
> Answer: It sways in disclosing [*Unverborgenheit,* unconcealing, emerging out of hiddenness, i.e., ἀλήθεια]. (398)

From "Der Spruch des Anaximander":

> But ἐόν, "being [*seiend*]," is not only the singular of the participle ἐόντα, "beings [*Seiendes*]." Rather ἐόν names the singular as such, which in its singularity is solely the uniquely one-ing one [*einzig das einzig einende Eine*], prior to every number. (GA 5:345)

> Without exaggeration ... we could say that the fate [*Geschick,* affordance] of the West depends on how the word ἐόν gets translated, provided that the interlingual translation[*Übersetzung*] rests on the intralingual translation [*Übersetzung*] to the truth of what comes to language (gets said) in ἐόν. (GA 5:345)

The short text that Heidegger read to the participants in the Zähringen seminar begins by thinking ἐόν in Parmenides in terms of *Unverborgenheit*-disclosure: ἀ-λήθεια as the unconcealing of hidden, self-sheltering (*entbergendes Bergen* as the fullness of *Unver-borgenheit*). It then naturally unfolds to include ἔστι γὰρ εἶναι and ἐόν.

Referring to ἐόν – but including all of these words named here – the protocol reads: "The question now is whether we are capable of hearing this Greek word, which speaks of ἔστι and εἶναι" (397). Or as Heidegger said it in the reading itself: "we must ask ourselves if we think the Greek saying of the words ἔστι and εἶναι also in a Greek way; and even more, if, when we use the words 'is' and 'being,' we think precisely enough at all" (404–5). From Heidegger's text:

> Thought in the Greek way, the word εἶναι says: "emerging [*anwesen*]." This verb speaks more precisely. It brings us, in a greater revealing, closer to the matter [*Sache*] for thinking. In accordance with this we must render ἔστι γὰρ εἶναι as: "emerges, that is to say emerging [*anwest nämlich anwesen*]." (405)

> ἔστιν εἶναι: emerges emerging (as such) [*anwest anwesen (selbst)*]. The name for this issue for thinking in Parmenides is: τὸ ἐόν. This fundamental word for his thinking names neither "beings [*das Seiende*]" nor "being [*das Sein*]." We have to think τὸ ἐόν as a participle. Then the saying says: "emerging: emerging as such [*anwesend: anwesen selbst*]." (405)

What is being thought here is not being in its difference from beings, but rather emerging as such: beyng as emerging, or simply, emerging as such. The word of Parmenides that names this issue is ἐόν. Heidegger says ἐόν as the energy of emerging, the emerging as such, without any form and no-thing.

From Heidegger's text:

> The question is: Where and how does emerging emerge? Answer: "onwards" ... into disclosure. If this is the case, then ἐόν, the only matter for thinking, is "the heart" of disclosure." In verse 4 of Fragment 8 Parmenides explicitly names τὸ ἐόν – : ἀτρεμὲς, "never trembling." "Abiding in itself as such, τὸ ἐόν tunes and governs disclosing." (405)

Heidegger shows unwavering – "never trembling" – force of this abiding when he quotes Fragment 8, 29:

Persisting as same in the same, it abides in accord with itself.

Ταὐτόν τ' ἐν ταὐτῷ τε μένον καθ' ἑαυτό τε κεῖται.

One could say that it

- lasts, is lasting
- is unperturbable, in its no-thing no-form
- is intrepid
- is unwavering,
- simply abiding in its limitless dynamic.

Τὸ ἐόν allows thinking to think the one, the one-ing, in its ongoing work of emerging. As non-dual dynamic, no-thing and no-form, ἐόν is as such straightforwardly the one or one-ing, in its ongoing dynamic emerging. Thus, it is no-thing, neither in thinking nor in the dynamic itself; it never allows one or the other dimension to settle out and be "at the bottom" or "at the top." For there is no bottom or top, no centre or limit. The word *emerging-Anwesen-ἐόν* has no dichotomy, as it carries within it the highest energy and movement.

Having no parts and no extension, ἐόν is "simply" and as such: one-ing, at-oneness. I quote Fragment 8, 22–5, in this regard:

Nor is it divisible, since it is all the same,
and there is no more of it in one place than in another,
to hinder it from holding together, nor less of it, but everything is
    full of ἐόν.
Wherefore all holds together; for ἐόν comes together with ἐόν.

Οὐδὲ διαιρετόν ἐστιν, ἐπεὶ πᾶν ἐστιν ὁμοῖον·
οὐδέ τι τῇ μᾶλλον, τό κεν εἴργοι μιν συνέχεσθαι,
οὐδέ τι χειρότερον, πᾶν δ' ἔμπλεόν ἐστιν ἐόντος.
Τῷ ξυνεχὲς πᾶν ἐστιν· ἐὸν γὰρ ἐόντι πελάζει.

- *There is no boundary, no limit and no centre. No-thing and no-form. There is only at-oneness in one-ing. Dynamically.*

Thinking needs to be careful, lest the realm that is opened up here close up again because of our metaphysical grammar. The realm of ἐόν/*Anwesen*/emergence is thinkable but not provable. Thinking's access to ἐόν/ἀλήθεια is not through logic or the metaphysics of rational assertion. It is difficult to think the unprovable; but more than that, it is difficult to think ἐόν/ἀλήθεια that is movement/tension itself, with no fixed point or foothold, in a way that is "away from" the footholds that always already come with our language (subject–predicate; subject–object; philosophies of substance). We speak "awkwardly," because the *question* of ἀλήθεια cannot be held open in the logic of our traditional language.

Although thinking necessarily deals here in the realm of the unprovable, it is this realm that provides the only possible access to ἐόν/ἀλήθεια. Parmenides (Fragment 1, 28) says that we need to "come to know" everything in its core (search for the bottom of it). This is a nonordinary experience (on the byway), although most proper and natural. Reading Fragment 6, 1 – χρὴ τὸ λέγειν τε νοεῖν – we learn that the gathering-saying (λέγειν), which lets be shown, and understanding (νοεῖν), which goes along with λέγειν, are the ways of experience that are proper to the realm of the non-provable.

How do we gain access to what is said-shown in the word ἐόν? On hearing this word, we are called to foster an enriching contact with the possibility of ἐόν, to be open to what we read in our reading as it turns its gaze to us. Reading in this way, we "fall into round" – to use a potter's expression – and reading/thinking/saying takes its cue *from* that which gazes upon it. This is the ἐόν/emergence that we retrieve in early Greek thinking. In our reading/hearing, retrieval stems from attentiveness to precisely this domain and calls for a thinking that reads properly, rather than a thinking that runs roughshod over the written text, always already knowing what is to be found there. Think of this mode of thinking-reading as a handicraft. It works by handling the words, the reading. This is the place of ἐόν as such – ἐόν in its suchness, the suchness of ἐόν. Thus, ἐόν turns its gaze and touches us; it is the name for the opening cast to us by the unresolvability of beyng/Ereignis, radiant emptiness. It is thinkable poi-etically, not dialectically. It calls for a hinting-intimating thinking, rather than the direct hit of a calculating, resolving thinking. And it is said poi-etically.

What is the core that is necessary for this experience of thinking? It is ἐόν ἔμμεναι (from Fragment 6,1) – *Anwesend Anwesen:* the movement of emergence as it emerges.

> This, emergence-emerging itself permeates the encircling disclosure, which deftly [*shicklich*] discloses it. (399)

I close with a quotation from Heidegger, tying everything in a kind of one-ing dynamic. The first version is from the protocol; the second, from the text that Heidegger read.

> Ἀλήθεια is not an empty openness, nor an unmoving chasm. One has to think it as the movement of unconcealing, which revolves around ἐόν in a way proper to it [as such], that means emergent: emerging as such [*Anwesend: Anwesen selbst*, coming-forth: coming-forth as such]. (398)

> Accordingly, we cannot envision ἀλήθεια as vacant-stiff openness [*leere starre Offenheit*]. Rather, we have to see it as the [movement of] nonconcealing [coming-out-of-hiding, *Entbergung*] that affordingly encircles [*schicklich umkreisend*] το ἐόν, "emerging: emerging as such." (406)

- *ἀλήθεια* as "the encircling that unfolds of itself," *εὐκυκλέος* as "affordingly encircling [schicklich umkreisend]." Thus the "well-enfolding, affordingly encircling" is: *τò ἐόν itself!*
- *We have now seen that, along with* **φύσις**, *the dynamic of ἐόν is also a one-ing with* **ἀ-λήθεια**.

v. λόγος / logos, along with ἕν / hen

The traditional-inherited (TI) and the refreshing-retrieving (RR) ways for saying λόγος:

λόγος   TI   logic, word, reason, rational account
logos   definition, rational faculty
              discourse, word, language, name
        RR   a saying
              gathering, gathering-lay
              from λέγειν: saying and gathering
              saying-revealing
              saying gathering thought

In a written statement that stands as a "preface" to the lecture-course *Logik: Heraklits Lehre vom Logos*, Heidegger says:

> The intention of this lecture is simply to get to originary "logic." But "logic" is originary as the thinking of *the* λόγος [that happens] when originary λόγος gets thought and is in place in thinking for thinking. This transpired in Heraclitus' thinking. Thus the intention [here] is simply to follow thoughtfully what Heraclitus says of λόγος. What he says should become considerably more precise. (GA 55:185)*

The direction of Heidegger's thinking here is a step back from the logic of subjectivity and technological reason, toward originary and elemental λόγος as gathering.

For a long time now Western philosophy has translated this word of Heraclitus with words that centre on reason and the rational. This turn essentially took place with the Latin translation of λόγος into *ratio*. This translation – and therefore concomitant way of thinking – dominates today, even when interpreters of Heraclitus recognize some original force of the word and the fundamental ambiguity that resounds in Heraclitus's λόγος.

By not releasing λόγος from the encrustments of *ratio*, the metaphysical tradition has reduced the word to being merely past: *vergangenes*, gone in its own right and absorbed into the linguistic and conceptual structures of metaphysics:

> For logic, λόγος is λέγειν as propositions and judgments, is the activity of *ratio*, is operation of reason. "Logic" is the doctrine of reason. (234)

---

* Unless otherwise noted, numbers in parentheses in this section refer to this text.

When *logos* got translated into Latin as *ratio*, what *logos* was all about for Heraclitus got covered over, hidden and forgotten – ever since. But how do we come to an understanding of what the word λόγος says **in Heraclitus?**

For a fuller picture of the many meanings for the one Greek word λόγος, I looked through several Greek dictionaries. I found the following definitions for *λόγος*: the word by which the inner thought is expressed as well as the inner thought itself; a saying, speaking, that which is said or spoken; word, language, name; mere utterance (no action); sentence, statement; dialogue, conversation, discussion; talking about a person; a saying, report, narrative; prose writing; oratory; the right to speak (as in "giving someone the word"); and, of course, that which is laid out in reason or logic (proposition, principle; articulation). We see that this last meaning, which has dominated for a long time now, is only one of many "translations" of the word *λόγος*.

In offering an opening for us to think λόγος in its rich possibility, Heidegger (a) questions the traditional, inherited (TI) translation of the Greek λόγος and (b) offers an opening to what has become hidden in our inherited translations and interpretations of Greek philosophy. In doing this, he tackles the move from hearing the word *λόγος* in the first beginning of Greek philosophy (metaphysics) to hearing it within the "other beginning," namely there where the "starting" is still open to our thinking, being not just past and gone but in front of us, for vibrant and fresh considerations.

The words *λόγος-ratio-logic-reason* become a question when we go *beyond* the limitations of metaphysics – *to* the originary sense of λόγος and λέγειν: non-dual dynamic of gathering.

> For ἓν πάντα εἶναί contains this, that the one – as the one-ing [*vereinen*] of everything, the being of everything – makes up the being of beings as a whole [later *Seyn, beyng*]. Λόγος as such is the one one-ing everything [*das Alles vereinende Eins*]. (286)

This joining, uniting, one-ing is the no-thing and no-form dynamic of beyng/Ereignis and radiant emptiness, said with the word λόγος. Note that this "one-ing" is the always already ongoing dynamic of the "one." It is not about some action being taken "along the way." Rather this one-ing is part and parcel of the no-thing and no-form non-dual timeless dynamic as such. The word *unity* is misleading, for it implies something static, without movement, and too abstract.

The "one" (ἕν / hen) that is within λόγος. The joining of λόγος and the "one" (ἕν) permeates the entire discussion. This "one" (ἕν) is not "a being" and is dynamic, not static.

Contrary to the other key Greek terms in part 3, there is not a translation issue with the Greek word ἕν. Here it is about how to *hear* the Greek word, how thinking-saying moves into the "one" – which inheres in all the key words in part 3. I make this Greek word explicit here, under λόγος, because the two words are "joined at the hip," as it were. Hear Heraclitus (Fragment B50):

> **If you listen, not to me but [heeding] λόγος, it is wisdom to agree that all is one.**

> οὐκ ἐμοῦ, ἀλλὰ τοῦ λόγου ἀκούσαντας ὁμολογεῖν σοφόν ἐστιν ἓν πάντα εἶναί.

It becomes clear that the "problem of the one and the many" exists as a problem only because the traditional/inherited reading or interpretation of the early Greeks saw the "one" as itself a thing or a form. Once we retrieve what the early Greeks in fact experienced, thought, and said – once we experience the opening in early Greek thinking – this way of thinking gets thrown overboard!

The question of the "one" arose when philosophers tried to find something that "held everything." This urge seems to be natural. But the question became a problem when interpreters of the early Greeks took any "one" – that which could unify all things – as itself a thing/being, a substance or form. Looking for a unifying principle or something that everything had "in common," traditional readers came up with a highest form, qualities that all things shared, names that things/beings have, or the "essence" of things or of all things.

One could say that this search was "how to find a 'one'" in the midst of diversity. And some prioritized and honoured diversity, while others wished for and honoured the one. The tendency was to look for and find a supreme one that unifies. But these interpreters always landed on some form or some being: highest being (e.g., god) or highest form (e.g., the good).

But what happens when we learn to experience, to think, and to say the one as a no-thing no-form non-dual dynamic? Like the one and one-ing of beyng/Ereignis (Heidegger), of *dao* or emptiness of mind (Daoism and Buddhism), or the no-thing no-form quantum potential in the field of energy (quantum physics)? Or the no-thing and no-form that is experienced and thought and said by the early Greeks, in the seven key words?

The dynamic that is said with all these words mirrors and says how the early Greeks experienced the world and the way things are as ἄπειρον / *apeiron* ... χώρα / *chora* ... ἀλήθεια / *aletheia* ... ἐόν / *eon* ... λόγος / *logos* ... φύσις / *physis* ... ψυχή / *psyche* ... νόος, νοῦς / *noos, nous* ... Here we focus on λόγος.

In one fell swoop, as it were, Heraclitus stands outside – or beyond – the limitation that came after, which reduced the one to a thing or form. First, this pathway takes us far beyond the simplistic notion that λόγος is about reason or logic. Then it takes us to the dynamic of gathering and then – beyond a static "one" – to gathering into the one as a dynamic, a one-**ing**. And then to the no-form and no-thing non-dual dynamic that both λόγος and ἓν say-show in *their* joining-gathering, a *one-ing itself* of the two words for one-ing and gathering.

> Λόγος is the self-announcing one one-ing everything [*alles vereinende Eine*]. Λόγος is the one-ing [*das Vereinen*] of everything [a gathering]. Thus, what λόγος now means, namely the one-ing one, this meaning of Λόγος is fundamentally different from the meaning of λόγος that "logic" thinks when it thinks it as "statement" and "speaking," as "talk" and "word," as "judgment" and "reason." (286)

- *Λόγος as "one-ing" is the gathering-into a non-dual formless one; formless dynamic one in turn opens the way that mirrors how λόγος and ἓν are "one."*

In order to get to the core of λόγος, Heidegger goes into the connection of λόγος with λέγειν. Λόγος as this one-ing points precisely to what λέγειν says: "λόγος and λέγειν mean 'gathering' ['*lesen*,' '*sammeln*'], i.e., of course! one-ing and [joining into a one, *doch Einen und Vereinen*]." (286).

Having opened λόγος to the saying and then gathering aspects of what the word says in Greek, we find ourselves in unfamiliar territory. Here Heidegger says:

> The translation of λέγειν as letting-gathered-lying-there [*gesammelt-vorliegen-lassen*] and λόγος as gathering-laying [*lesende Lege*] may seem strange. But it is healthier for thinking to wander into the strange instead of installing what is familiar and known. Apparently, Heraclitus alienated his contemporaries in a wholly other way by interweaving the words λέγειν and λόγος – words that they were familiar with – into such a saying [λέγειν as letting-gathered-lying-there and λόγος as gathering-laying] and by making λόγος the leading word for his thinking. (GA 7:231)

- *Λέγειν means both to gather and to say. Gathering, including gathering in words.*
- **Λόγος** *means* **lesende Lege.** **Lesen** *is to gather, as in to harvest.* **Lege** *is an unusual word. Of the many German dictionaries that I use, I find it only in* **Grimms Wörterbuch.** *There it says that* **Lege** *means both the action and the place of laying. For this reason I translate these two words as gathering-laying, rather than the most common English translation: gathering-lay. As I see it, the less dynamic "lay" is not dynamic and is somehow very difficult to hear, in the sense of comprehend.*

Here Heidegger shows not only how estranging this may be for us today but also how estranging it may have been for Heraclitus's contemporaries. In any case it calls for a renewed and fresh look at how to translate the Greek word into our language and then how to think and say it.

Now I return to Fragment B50. First, the translation as given above:

If you listen, not to me but [heeding] λόγος, it is wisdom to agree that all is one.

Here is what Heidegger calls a "clarifying" – an annotating, illuminating, amplifying, *erläuternd* – translation of Fragment B50:

> Do not listen to me, the mortal speaker; but pay attention to the gathering laying [*lesende Lege*]. First belong to [*gehört*] this [laying, *Lege*], then truly hear it [*hört*]. There *is* such a hearing, provided that a letting-emerge-together takes place to which the whole – the gathering-letting-lie, the gathering laying – has arrived. When a letting-lie of the letting-emerge takes place, something is afforded [*Geschickliches*]. For what is truly afforded, affordance as such, is: the unique-one unifying everything [holding everything as one, one-ing everything, *das Einzig-Eine einend Alles*]. (GA 7:230)

- *Belong to the gathering laying, make it your own, "own" it as in "it is essential to being joined to it as such."*
- *Hear it, get to know it, be open and pay attention, be mindful in a non-conceptual experience.*
- *What is afforded to us in this awareness is the very one-ing that the gathering is. Gathering and one-ing mirror each other is their at-oneness.*
- ***das Einzig-Eine einend Alles**: the unique-one one-ing all that is. **Einend** comes from the verb **einen**: to one, to bring into one, to let the one emerge as that from within which all manifesting takes place.*

Given that λέγειν means say, speak, recount, tell, *and* pick up or gather – and given that the saying-speaking dimension of the Greek word is more familiar to us (even as the tradition has reduced that part of the word) – in this essay on Fragment B50 Heidegger wants to open up the "true" saying of the word in its meaning of gathering, gathering-laying. Still and always, the two ways of saying afforded in the words λόγος and λέγειν belong within a one-ing (holding as one, non-dual dynamic). How do we learn to hear-say both aspects of λόγος and λέγειν in their one-ing? If we get this, then we also get what this whole project is about.

However we understand this retrieval of what the word λόγος says, it is indubitable that it names the "one" that is formless and no-thing and dynamic:

[In Fragment 50] Heraclitus names Λόγος in a way that makes it clear that λόγος announces itself and how it [λόγος] thereby lets what is properly own to it be heard: ἓν πάντα εἶναί – all things are one. This is what λόγος discloses. It can only disclose this if it *is itself* the opening. For λόγος cannot be something still-yet "alongside" the one and "alongside" all things, if it itself "is." ... For ἓν πάντα εἶναί contains this, that the one [*das Eins*] – as the one-ing [*vereinen*] of everything, the being of everything – makes up the being in the whole. Λόγος as such is the one one-ing everything [*das Alles vereinende Eins*]. (285–6)

The one is no-thing and no-form. It is the name for a non-dual dynamic within which all things flourish and within which everything emerges and is manifest – and to which all things return. The "space-that-has-no-form" is the "ensoncer," and the way that things are is as ensconced within this "space." Sheltered, held, protected.

After all of this, we refresh our thinking by repeating what I quoted earlier:

λόγος and λέγειν means "gathering" ["*lesen*," "*sammeln*"], i.e., **of course!** one-ing and uniting [*doch Einen und Vereinen*]. (286)

I close this section on λόγος / *logos*, along with ἓν / *hen*, by presenting several additional Heraclitean fragments, ones that shed light on λόγος and ἓν.

B31

The sea fans out and fills up its measure in accord with the same λόγος [gathering] that was there before it became earth.

θάλασσα διαχέεται καὶ μετρέεται εἰς τὸν αὐτὸν λόγον, ὁκοῖος πρόσθεν ἦν ἢ γενέσθαι γῆ.

- *The λόγος that "fills up its measure" is always and everywhere the same, the "one" or "one-ing" gathering. This gathering λόγος is the non-dual, no-thing dynamic that is own to itself and that "owns" all things, including human beings. This λόγος is timeless and no-thing and no-form ... radiant emptiness or beyng-Ereignis.*

B33

And it is the affordance, too, that we obey the counsel of one.

νόμος καὶ βουλῇ πείθεσθαι ἑνός

- *The **νόμος** that is said here is almost always translated as "law." But its sense is that of affordance, as it says affordance from within the one one-ing itself or as such.*
- *The word **νόμος** stems from the verb **νέμω**: dispense, afford, or bestow unto; inhabit, dwell in, abide in; hold sway.*
- *Thus **νόμος** is something that the wisdom of the whole has reached in a kind of dispensation or affordance.*

B10

Joinings: wholes and not wholes; brought together, pulled apart; in unison, discordant; and from all things one and from the one all things.

συνάψιες ὅλα καὶ οὐχ ὅλα, συμφερόμενον διαφερόμενον, συνᾷδον διᾷδον, καὶ ἐκ πάντων ἓν καὶ ἐξ ἑνὸς πάντα.

B54

The hidden harmony [concordant sounding-joining] is better than the open-manifest.

ἁρμονίη ἀφανὴς φανερῆς κρείττων.

B112

Thinking is the highest excellence, and wisdom is: saying-gathering what is revealed [disclosed] and acting in accord with φύσις, while tending to it [φύσις].

τὸ φρονεῖν ἀρετὴ μεγίστη, καὶ σοφίη ἀληθέα λέγειν καὶ ποιεῖν κατὰ φύσιν ἐπαΐοντας.

B1

Although λόγος is timeless, humans have no understanding, either before they have heard or after. For, although all things happen in accordance with λόγος, men seem as if they had no experience of it [are ignorant], each time they undertake words and deeds – whereas I for my part set forth [relate], distinguishing each thing according to φύσις and explaining how it truly is. As for other humans, what they do when awake escapes them, just as they forget what they do when asleep.

τοῦ δὲ λόγου τοῦδ ἐόντος ἀεὶ ἀξύνετοι γίνονται ἄνθρωποι καὶ πρόσθεν ἢ ἀκοῦσαι καὶ ἀκούσαντες τὸ πρῶτον· γινομένων γὰρ πάντων κατὰ τὸν λόγον τόνδε ἀπείροισιν ἐοίκασι πειρώμενοι καὶ ἐπέων καὶ ἔργων τοιούτων ὁκοίων ἐγὼ διηγεῦμαι κατὰ φύσιν διαιρέων ἕκαστον καὶ φράζων ὅκως ἔχει· τοὺς δὲ ἄλλους ἀνθρώπους λανθάνει ὁκόσα ἐγερθέντες ποιοῦσιν ὅκωσπερ ὁκόσα εὕδοντες ἐπιλανθάνονται.

- *As timeless, **λόγος** cannot arise or disappear, as it is always timelessly "there." It can have no parts and is no-thing. A no-form dynamic. This is that by which it belongs to our list of seven.*
- *Heraclitus tells us that humans are not aware of this **λόγος** dynamic.*
- *All things are in accordance with the no-thing and no-form **λόγος** as a **one-ing**, and that means distinguishing all things according to **φύσις**.*
- *What **λόγος** and **φύσις** in their no-form dynamic do got covered over in Western thinking. Our pathway here is to refresh and rethink and retrieve the non-dual dynamic of **λόγος**.*

vi. *ψυχή / psyche*

Here are the words that translate the Greek word *ψυχή* in both the TI and the RR ways:

ψυχή psyche (human)	TI	soul, mind, reason, spirit, conscious self, vital spirit Latin: *anima, res cogitans* German: *Seele, Geist*
	RR	breath of life, life-energy animating force
(beyond human)	TI	world soul Latin: *anima mundi* German: *die Weltseele*
	RR	all-pervading life-energy formless awareness

(Note: Greek ψῦχή: literally "breath," derivative of ψῦχειν "to breathe, blow.")

I offer a trajectory of what has happened to the Greek word ψυχή in the history of Western thinking:

– *Psyche* went from this rich human and beyond-human activity said with the Greek word ψυχή …
– … to being reduced to *anima* or soul, including that soul's being created by a divine power, with soul quite distinct from the body and mostly thought as static,
– … to being reduced to the *res cogitans* as quite distinct from the body, which now is a machine (Descartes),
– … to being reduced to the seat of objectifying subjectivity (Kant),
– … to being reduced to absolute reason (Hegel),
– … to being reduced to something that computers can do as well as humans (AI) or that emerges from the physiological brain (traditional neuroscience).

How do we recover from this extreme reduction of the word psyche, i.e., the limiting and covering over of the word and its saying in early Greek thinking?

The roadbed from λόγος to ψυχή is made smooth with two Heraclitus fragments, both of which are as rich and exciting as they are difficult. Let me start with these:

B45

You can never discern the boundaries of ψυχή, even if you traverse every pathway, so deep [profound, immense] is its λόγος.

ψυχῇ πείρατα ἰὼν οὐκ ἂν ἐξεύροιο, πᾶσαν ἐπιπορευόμενος ὁδόν· οὕτω βαθὺν λόγον ἔχει.

- *It is extremely hard to decipher what **ψυχή** really says in early Greek thinking. For sure this fragment calls on us to pause ... especially since for a long time now people have assumed that they know what **ψυχή** means.*
- *Core to this question and its difficulty is what this fragment says: What **ψυχή** says-shows in Heraclitus is well-nigh impossible, **because its λόγος – as gathering –** is simply unfathomable. Once again it calls for extreme reticence in the face of this depth in the gathering-**λόγος** that holds **psyche's** deep sway. That is, the boundaries of **ψυχή** are as unknown to us as they are in themselves hidden and reserved.*

B115

To the ψυχή belongs [unique to the ψυχή is] self-increasing λόγος.

ψυχῆς ἐστι λόγος ἑαυτὸν αὔξων.

- *The **ψυχή** is what it is, whatever that is, because what is own to **ψυχή** depends on **self-increasing λόγος**. We now know that **λόγος** is a no-thing and no-form dynamic as movement of beyng-Ereignis or as the non-dual dynamic of radiant emptiness. The early Greek thinkers experienced the power and energy of this "no-thing beyond-beings" dynamic. And they said it in their writings.*
- *How can we understand the "self-increasing" that Heraclitus says here? For sure it is nothing static! For sure it says-shows the inherent power of this dynamic. It is about growing, increasing, expanding.*

Beginning this section in this way is meant simply to bring our awareness to the fact that we in our traditional-inherited way of thinking have no idea what ψυχή says for the early Greeks. We also have no idea how to bring the opening that belongs to refreshing, rethinking retrieval to bear on the question. Above all, it is a warning for us to step back, take a breath, and move cautiously. Cautiously here means: Not to assume that we already know.

Let us proceed, then, with this caution and this warning.

Using the Latin *anima* and the English *soul* and the German *Seele* to translate ψυχή is so commonplace that virtually no one even asks whether these words are true to what the Greeks said with the word ψυχή. With the usual translations, we have inherited a limitation or reduction of what this word originarily says in Greek thinking – including and especially as the *individual* human *psyche*. It is almost the same as with the word χώρα, namely, it is barely possible to say in English – or German – what the Greek word says.

When the Greek word ψυχή got translated into Latin as *anima* and in English as soul-mind-reason, it was like a lightning bolt of missing what the Greeks were saying. Translating Heraclitean ψυχή as "anima" and then "soul" does not fit. Nor do the German words *Seele* and *Geist*.

Aristotle, for example, says that ψυχή is the principle of life of any living being and that the human ψυχή is the principle of human life. And a number of aspects belong to this ψυχή: *nous*-awareness, *sophia*-wisdom, *episteme*-knowledge of things that cannot change, *theorein*-insight, *logos* as speech-gathering-thinking. This shows how the word ψυχή points to an immense complexity.

As a kind of introduction to the two indivisible vectors of ψυχή – the human and the beyond-human aspects – let us start with Peters's *Greek Philosophical Terms*. He says that *psyche* means: breath of life, ghost, vital principle, soul, anima. He writes:

> For Homer *psyche* is the "breath of life" (and also, in what may be a completely different stratum of belief, an individualized "ghost" that lives on in an attenuated fashion after death) that escapes, normally, from the mouth of the dying hero ...[24]

- *Liddell-Scott questions the idea of "breath" as found in Homer.*[25] *There they translate the word, in one of its meanings, as "ghost, departed spirit." They also call* ψυχή *in Plato* **"the immaterial principle of life."**
- *In any case this way of reading* ψυχή *renders it as individual and as an entity. Just as do the words* **anima, Seele, Geist,** *and* **soul.**

When Peters offers the idea that Anaximenes extends "the soul-principle to the universe at large,"[26] this opens the door to read *psyche* as the name for some dynamic force/energy that encompasses a meaning of the word that goes beyond humans and beyond any entity. In the *Timaeus* Plato refers to the "soul of everything" – ψυχή τοῦ παντός (*psyche tou pantos*) – which Peters calls the "world soul." Here we stop to ask: Does "world soul" really say what the Greek wants to say? In a moment we will take up the question of *psyche* as beyond the individual-personal.

Gathering: Peters opens the door to the human and beyond-human *psyche* without going into the ramifications of this astounding truth, namely that the human and beyond-human *psyche* are two inseparable aspects of the dynamic oneness of *psyche*.

Let us now look at the word itself and at the various translations in the various dictionaries, in order to open up the many possibilities for hearing the word *psyche*.

Often the first English word for *psyche* involves "life." An animating force, a principle of life, immaterial principle of movement, source of life-energy, the "lifeblood." Peters: the vital principle.

English usage says what the word *psyche* says in a number of ways: I put my heart and soul into this work. I sold my soul. (Which "soul" did I sell? My essence as an individual?) I didn't have the heart to kick him out.

With these examples of usage, as well as the several translations of the word, maybe the best way to say ψυχή is: the English word *psyche*. The problem is that the English word is used in so many places and ways that it is overused and even used up! *Psyche* the ancient Greek goddess; *Psyche* as in Designer Clothing; *Psyche* the magazine; *Psyche* the band. Notably, the word and discipline and practice of "psychology" easily hides this core meaning of "dynamic" life that belongs to the Greek saying. (Note: It is easier to get to the core meaning of *chora* than to the core meaning of *psyche*!)

No wonder that Heraclitus tells us:

B45

You will not find the boundaries of ψυχή, no matter how many paths you travel. So deep is its λόγος.

ψυχῆ πείρατα ἰὼν οὐκ ἂν ἐξεύροιο, πᾶσαν ἐπιπορευόμενος ὁδόν· οὕτω βαθὺν λόγον ἔχει.

- *Now that we know λόγος as gathering – a non-dual dynamic beyond things and beyond form – the λόγος-gathering that happens in ψυχή is primordial and not conceptualizable.*

B85

It is hard to fight with desire; for whatever it wishes [to get or have], it purchases at the cost of ψυχή.

θυμῷ μάχεσθαι χαλεπόν· ὅτι γὰρ ἂν θέλῃ, ψυχῆς ὠνεῖται.

B115

Φυχή has a λόγος that, from within and out of itself, becomes ever richer.

ψυχῆς ἐστι λόγος ἑαυτὸν αὔξων.

- *Here I translate ἑαυτὸν αὔξων as "becoming ever richer." A few pages ago I said "self-increasing."*
- *It is pretty obvious that ψυχή is not limited to the human ψυχή. It is also quite obvious that ψυχή says something that goes way beyond what we normally think of as soul.*

Given the extreme opacity – for what is "hiding" in these words – I now play with my two options for translating the "saying" of this fragment. These wordings are meant to open our thinking to the vastness of what is being said. Remember that (a) every translation is an interpretation that (b) hears the original with a kind of honing and (c) provides openings for our experience, thinking, and saying.

Φυχή has a λόγος that, from within and out of itself, becomes ever richer,

- *stressing the **dynamic quality**, the ongoing becoming of λόγος-gathering.*

To the ψυχή belongs [unique to the ψυχή is] self-increasing λόγος,

- *stressing the belonging, what the **ψυχή** "has," how **λόγος** inheres in ψυχή – and emphasizing the dynamic quality of ψυχή as well.*

And now the question: **Is the ψυχή that is named in these three fragments referring to the ψυχή within humans or to a ψυχή that points beyond? Perhaps it refers to both dimensions and to a non-dual dynamic. In any case it is still virtually impossible to find an English word. Whether within or beyond humans – or both –** we might use the English word *mind* as a way to render *psyche* into English. Even with this suggestion the problem is not solved, for the simple reason that the English word *mind* has itself so many meanings.

Now, what happens when the word **ψυχή points us beyond humans, beyond individual ψυχή, and beyond being an entity? And beyond concepts? What happens then? We turn to the** *Timaeus*:

30b

Thus, according to this gathering [λόγος], we must declare that this natural order [κόσμος] has disclosed itself as a living being endowed with a ψυχή – in truth [full disclosure, ἀληθείᾳ], owing to divine providence.

οὕτως οὖν δὴ κατὰ λόγον τὸν εἰκότα δεῖ λέγειν τόνδε τὸν κόσμον ζῷον ἔμψυχον
ἔννουν τε τῇ ἀληθείᾳ διὰ τὴν τοῦ θεοῦ γενέσθαι πρόνοιαν.

- *The whole of what is (**κόσμος**) is living within and out of the beyond-
  human **ψυχή**. In Greek thinking the divine can be read as the non-
  transparent-hidden beyond the human dynamic.*
- *What is this **ψυχή**? If it is intrinsic to the **κόσμος** – the natural order
  of the way things are – then this natural order includes the beyond
  human **ψυχή** and we are – pardon the pun – "way out there"! However,
  given that emptiness and the beyond-human **ψυχή** are without-form
  and timeless, there is no way out there. As no-thing and formless, this
  dynamic of radiant emptiness has no extension – that which is not and
  has no form, even as it is at work and even as we can experience it.*
- *Some people may want to say that this no-thing and no-form dynamic
  of "the whole of what is" or the natural order (**κόσμος**) is "some **thing** "
  and in some way true. However, we must be careful here!*
- *The phrase "cosmic consciousness" may be well-intentioned to
  mean this realm, but both words are imprisoned within concepts and
  abstractions.*

34b

He stretched the ψυχή into the middle, shining throughout the whole.

ψυχὴν δὲ εἰς τὸ μέσον αὐτοῦ [τοῦ κόσμου] θεὶς διὰ παντός τε ἔτεινεν.

- *The "spirit" of the universe? The **ψυχή** of the All?*
- *For sure this **ψυχή** goes way beyond an individual soul!*
- ***Πυχήτοῦ παντός.***

In usual parlance this is called the "world soul" – Greek: ψυχή τοῦ
κόσμου (*psyche tou kósmou*); Latin: *anima mundi*. The usual interpretations say-imply some kind of higher power, which is usually
taken to be an entity of some kind.

  The first big question is how to say ψυχή τοῦ παντός in English.
Given the road that we have just gone, one can for sure not simply
say "soul." And given the complexity and diversity of the word

mind, we have to hesitate with that word as well. But what can we *say* about the dynamic as such? For one thing, ψυχή in early Greek thinking goes beyond beings and forms.

The dynamic named with the words ψυχή τοῦ παντός is "before" and outside all form. (To call it "matterless form" begs the question.) In its as-suchness it is not any substantial thing at all. It is a non-dual no-thing no-form dynamic. It is all-pervasive, it pervades the world of forms and things and phenomena. One might say that it governs, organizes, and preserves the whole.

As we pointed out in the last section, on *logos* and the *one*, there is no solution to the problem of the one and the many if both are entities and have form. But if we come to know the dynamic of the one as itself no-form and no-thing, there *is* a way out. Remembering the dynamic no-form *chora*, we can apply the same thinking to *psyche*: As no-form and no-thing "one," this dynamic generates or governs the world while it "as such" is not diminished – as "it" is a no-form no-thing dynamic. And as we will see with *nous*, *psyche* also "spreads itself out" into things and phenomena without itself getting "caught" in forms. We could say that *psyche* illuminates things/beings-forms without losing its no-form and no-thing "status." In its as-suchness, *psyche* – along with **chora** and the non-dual dynamic that is experienced, thought, and said in all seven word-images – does not include forms or any material thing.

Here we ask: Does the ψυχή τοῦ παντός "exist" before the rest of the cosmos? Or was it always already? Timeless and boundless ψυχή? I would put the question to Plato's *Timaeus*.

vii.   *νόος, νοῦς / noos, nous*

I have put ψυχή / **psyche** and νοῦς, νόησῖς / **nous, noesis** last in the list of seven key words. Why? Because these two early Greek words show a focus both on "us" humans and on that dimension or dynamic that is beyond us. It says both us and beyond us in a non-dual dynamic – pointing to the dynamic of radiant emptiness, also known as beyng/Ereignis in Heidegger. These two key Greek words open us to this non-dual dynamic. A fresh look, a refreshing retrieval.

These last two words are a kind of culmination. The first five words opened us in our thinking primarily to the way things are, enclosing things as manifest (things, beings, phenomena) within the non-dual and formless dynamic of radiant emptiness, *dao*, beyng-Ereignis, and so on. The "human" was included within the non-dual no-thing dynamic of radiant emptiness (aka beyng, *dao*, and so on), but it was not made explicit. The last two – ψυχή and νοῦς-νόος – make explicit where humans fit, that is, within the one dynamic of being-human and being-beyond-human. And *nous* opens the door to awareness on both levels.

Here are the words that translate the Greek words νόος-νοῦς in both the TI and the RR way:

νόος, νοῦς	TI	intelligence, intellect, reason
noos, nous		intelligence, intellect
		reason, mind
		cognitive principle
	RR	mind
		mind, heart, soul, feeling
		heedful-attending knowing
		heart and soul
		wisdom
		awareness
		mind beyond the immanent
		indemonstrable principle
νοέω, νοεῖν	TI	think, apprehend by thought, reflect
noeo, noein		think out, devise, conceive
		think, suppose, contrive, devise
	RR	take notice, see, be aware of
		keenly note, become aware
		be minded, minding
		awaken and hold in awakeness

νόησις	TI	intelligence, mental perception
noesis		idea, concept, intellect
	RR	minding, processes of thought
		operation of *nous*, "*nous* at work"
		intuition (as opposed to reasoning)
		hidden work of awareness
		minding activity, within *kinesis*-dynamis

The first thing we need to know is that in Greek philosophy the word *nous* clearly refers to a *human and* a *beyond human* element. For example, in his glossary of Greek terms Kranz has two segments under the word *nous*: human *nous* and divine *nous*.[27]

The latter is usually named θεός-*god* and θειότατος-*divine*. How to read these two words depends on how the Greeks understood the gods and the divine.

We must be careful not to read into this matter from our point of view. What the Greeks thought and said with the word *nous* is far from our cultural and inherited way of thinking *nous*. And it is just as hard for us to decipher what early Greek thinking meant by "god" – as with all the key words of early Greek thinking. From where we are today, it seems to me that we must (a) make sure that we do *not* conceive of θεός/*god* in the traditional-inherited manner but rather (b) open our thinking to "god" as the name for the dynamic that is beyond humans and things and that is not transparent to reason.

Already in the fifth century BCE Metrodorus of Lampsacus (d. 464 BCE), stressed that the Greek deities "were to be understood as allegorical modes of representing physical powers and phenomena."[28] Simply put, we can read "allegory" to mean a broader and less literal message. Allegory says hidden meaning. It is an allusion, indirect and "playful" (from Latin *ludere*, to play). For example, the dimension of the "divine dynamic" alludes to the crucial dimension of humans as the flashpoint experiencing the dynamic of "beyond-human." There is something "more-than and not limited to" the human in the flesh – of which we are participant, non-dually, and which we know and can experience, even as it is no-thing and has no-form. When early Greek thinkers used the name θεός, they were referring to this dimension or dynamic.

There is no definitive answer to the question "What do the Greeks want to say by 'divine mind' – θειότατος νοῦς?" What to do? First, as I just said, it is abundantly clear that the Greeks did not have a concept of "god" like the one we have inherited. Second, they did not have the notion of "one god." And, as we have just read, already in the fifth century BCE Metrodorus stressed that the Greek divinities "were to be understood as allegorical modes of representing physical powers and phenomena."

With these comments as a background, I propose that – rather than worrying about *our* notions of god versus *theirs* – we can use a bunch of words to say what is hidden in their words θειότατος and θεός. We can be pretty sure that the words *god* and *divine* say what (a) goes beyond humans, (b) is hidden or indirect, and (c) carries a powerful dynamic that they heeded and tended to. And had something to do with a no-thing no-form boundless dynamic.

In this spirit I offer some words that can take us closer to the workings of this power that they name θειότατος and θεός. The story of the Delphic Oracle shows all of this:

- more than human, beyond ordinary knowing
- sacred, sublime, breathtaking
- hidden, inscrutable, cryptic, invisible
- unimaginable, inconceivable, non-conceptual
- stunning, awe-inspiring, amazing.

I will first look more closely at human *nous*. Then I will focus on *nous* that is beyond human. In making this distinction in thinking – for the sake of emphasizing the "beyond human" *nous* – it is imperative that we remember that the two are wedded – for purposes of my overall focus, *wedded non-dually*.

I quote Peters as a traditional witness to this weddedness:

The soul [ψυχή] is capable of two activities: when "turned upward" it gives itself over to *noesis* [the work *of* νοῦς] ...; when "downward," it connects with *aesthesis* (the physical, perception/sensation) ... *noesis* is immediate ... a vision of unity; our image of it ... deals with plurality, and the more one frees oneself from the composing and dividing ... the more one will be assimilating oneself to the true operation of *nous* ... [thus keeping] the human soul [ψυχή] perpetually linked, via the *nous*, to the *kosmos noetos*.[29]

- *Note how, in a very traditional way, Peters simply puts forth the notion that the human* **νοῦς** *is "perpetually linked" with the beyond-human* **νοῦς**, *without marking the deeper connotations of this linkage.*
- *The word* **ψυχή**. *Keep in mind that the words – the Latin* **anima** *or the German* **die Seele** *or the English* **soul** *– do not do justice to what the Greeks said with the word* **ψυχή**.
- *We could call the activity of* **νοῦς** *that is not enclosed within the human the "cosmic* **νοῦς**," *in line with this passage from Peters. The* **κόσμος νοητός** *is usually translated as "intelligible universe." Intelligible here belongs to the TI ways. And as we continue with* **νοῦς-νοεῖν-νόησις**, *we will come to know why "intelligible" and "cosmos" hold us back. These word-images need to be refreshed and rethought* **and retranslated**, *thus retrieving what the Greeks actually thought and said.*

The Greek word νόος/νοῦς. The usual rendition of this word in English is misleading and or simply wrong. When I google "nous,"[30] this is what comes up: *Nous* is:

a. "the basic understanding or awareness that allows human beings to think rationally."
b. "commonly translated as "mind" or "intellect."
c. "intelligence acuity."
d. "awareness that allows human beings to think rationally."

All of these renditions are TI. The word *awareness,* which belongs to RR, is reduced by the role that the rational plays. I use this example from Google in order to show how far the usual renditions are from the RR ways.

First I turn to Heidegger as he plays with the word *νοεῖν*. This is from his lectures titled *Was heißt Denken?* from 1951–2 (GA 8).* He

---

* Unless otherwise noted, numbers in parentheses in this section refer to this text.

is working with the first line from Fragment 6 of Parmenides's poem.

Χρὴ τὸ λέγειν τε νοεῖν τ᾽ ἐὸν ἔμμεναι·

The usual translation of this fragment goes like this:

It must needs be that what can be thought and spoken of is.[31]

Or:

That which can be spoken of and thought must needs be.[32]

This fragment carries three of our seven key words in early Greek thinking, words that say what Heidegger calls the question of beyng, that is, the non-dual dynamic of radiant emptiness. We have already studied λέγειν and ἐόν. Now we focus on νοεῖν. We pay attention to how Heidegger reads and hears the word.

If we translate νοεῖν as "hearing" or "taking in [*vernehmen*]," we move more prudently [more carefully, more cautiously] than if we straightaway say "thinking" – and with that assume that what is said [with this word] is obvious. (205)

With this step, Heidegger begins a rather careful, step-by-step digging into this word in Parmenides. He says that "as long as we do not get involved [i.e., in experience] with what is at stake in what is said with the word νοεῖν" (205), we don't gain anything when we say "taking-in" rather than "thinking." Taking it in (*vernehmen*) is the same as gathering it (*aufnehmen*). He says:

What is taken in [heard] in the word *νοεῖν* turns us on [gets us going], such that we really take it up [*vornehmen*] and start something [get engaged] with it. (206)

Νοεῖν is tending to [nurturing, taking care of, being mindful of] something.

The noun that belongs to νοεῖν – νόος, νοῦς – originarily and almost exactly means what we earlier described as the fundamental meaning of *Gedanc* [inmost mind, the heart, the heart's core, one's innermost essence], *An-dacht* [reverence], *Gedächtnis* [mind]. (206)

Here is Heidegger on the word *Gedanc*:

> *Gedanc* means: the mind, the heart, the bottom of the heart, that innermost part of the human being that reaches the furthest outward and into the outermost – and this so decidedly that, properly considered, it does not allow the idea of an inside and an outside to arise.[33] (150)

- *This "reaching" mirrors and says the human **νοῦς** within the beyond-human **νοῦς**. With this move we see the full picture of what is at stake in **νοῦς**. Namely, Heidegger is pointing us to the awareness that the Greek word family **νοεῖν-νόος-νοῦς** (a) does not belong to logic or intellect or anything cognitive and (b) opens thinking to mind, minding, awareness, tending. Awareness and tending involves **vernehmen**: taking it in, and **vornehmen**: taking it up, actively tending to it. Finally, "no inside and no outside" (c) points to the non-dual one-ing dynamic: human and beyond-human as one.*

I will now walk us through the last two paragraphs of this same lecture (210–11). Some of it is a repeating of what we just looked at. This walk-through, along with its repetitions, will help us deepen our understanding. So let us begin. Note that what follows is both quoting (what is in quotation marks) and paraphrasing Heidegger.

- In its origins in early Greek thinking, the word νοεῖν does not mean "thinking." More precisely, it does not mean thinking as we today generally conceive it, namely its being reduced to logic and intellectual "thinking."
- What prevails in the word νοεῖν is a hearing-gathering and taking-in [*vernehmen*], that is, is not simply a passive accepting. This is emphasized by Heidegger with the word *vornehmen*: take up actively. With awareness. Bohm: "Real awareness already is action."

- Already up front, νοεῖν hears and takes-in what is being said by actively taking it in [*in die Acht nehmen*], tending to it, and holding it there [*behalten*].
- Letting it come to our attention. Attention is an awakening and standing watch [*die Wacht*] over what is at issue, actively taking it into its truth [*in die Wahr **nehmen**, wahrnehmen*].
- This requires a holding or safe-keeping, which is accomplished in the gathering said in λέγειν.
- "Therefore νόος and νοῦς do not originarily mean what evolved as reason."
- Rather, originarily νόος means *das Sinnen*: bearing in mind, calling to mind, being mindful of, being attentive or awake; *Grimms*: musing, brewing over, abiding in (Latin: *pensare*, to ponder, to weigh carefully). Note that the German word *der Sinn* covers a lot of territory, including a felt sense of what is at stake. A far cry for simply "meaning" or "making sense" or the "five senses." This is not about emotion. Rather a feeling for what is true, which one then takes to heart. A felt sense. What the heart senses. Awareness.
- This is a being-mindful-of that holds something in mind and takes it to heart (*sich zu Herzen nehmen*).
- Therefore νοεῖν also means what we understand by the word *wittern*, normally used with animals: to scent something, as when we say "I smell a rat."
- "Human scenting here is to know intuitively." Heidegger hearkens back to the old word in German. "*Ahnen* stems from the impersonal '*es anet mir*' or even '*es anet mich*'": It comes to me, it comes over me, it gets handed over to me.
- In English we say: I suspect, intuit, have an inkling. Negatively: *keine Ahnung*, no inkling of it. I have no idea. For example, I had no idea of the answer on the exam.
- "The true inkling [intuiting, *Ahnen*] is the way in which what is at the core of things comes to us, what gives itself over to us in actively taking it in [*in die Acht nehmen*], so that we hold it therein."
- "This intuiting is not the preliminary step on the way to knowing. It is the hangar that hides, holds, and shelters everything that is knowable." One might say that intuiting belongs to knowing that is non-conceptual and poi-etic. Rather than being a preliminary step, this intuiting *is at the core* of νοεῖν.

- "We translate νοεῖν as: actively taking it in." And actively taking it up.
- What is actively taken in in νοεῖν is precisely what is gathered in the beyond-human non-dual dynamic that is named beyng, *dao*, buddha mind, and the nonphysical energy field of quantum physics.

The issue is not to know, but to be awake to. Heraclitus (B40) tells us:

Learning of many things does not teach wakefulness [νόος].

Πολυμαθίη νόον (ἔχειν) οὐ διδάσκει.

Νοεῖν is to be awake to, to be aware of, to take into one's care, to take up. Νόος is insight or wakefulness to. Humans with νόος are awake, alive to, have their attention directed intently towards, are intently open to. The openness of νόος is not a passive receptivity; it is a being prepared intently – νόος: to be awake, to be intently ready for taking carefully in.

> In νοεῖν what is taken in involves us, such that we take it up expressly and that we start something [get something going] with it. (206)

We could say that νοεῖν is a dynamic knowing awareness that is intrinsically active. That is the opposite of a passive conceptual knowing. In his essay "Aristotle, An Introduction," Jacob Klein writes:

> This state and manner of being is a state and manner of being in which we are not closed up but *open*. Wakefulness is openness – the very openness of a huge open door ... This state or manner of being is commonly called in Greek νοῦς or νοεῖν.[34]

What is ensconced in and brought along with in these last pages is a kind of transition to the "beyond human" that shows itself in νοῦς-νοεῖν-νόησις:

- the "divine dynamic"
- the "more than," not limited to humans

- "the true operation of *nous* … [keeping] the human soul [*psyche*] perpetually linked, via the *nous*, to the *kosmos noetos*" (Peters)

- "What is taken in [heard] in the word νοεῖν turns us on [gets us going], such that we really take it up [*vornehmen*] and start something [get engaged] with it" (206). We become engaged in what νοεῖν starts and gets going in us, namely the non-dual dynamic of no-thing no-form beyng or radiant emptiness.
- "The true inkling [intuiting, *Ahnen*] is the way in which what is at the core of things comes to us, what gives itself over to us in actively taking it in (*in die Acht*), so that we hold it therein" (206). What is at the core of things is the no-thing no-form dynamic of radiant emptiness, what Heidegger calls beyng/Ereignis.

We now turn directly to νόος, when and as it says that which is **not enclosed within humans. Beyond the physical and forms** – and human beings. (Peters: "In a number of places Aristotle compares human and divine noesis."[35]) Even though we make this distinction in looking at the word's various senses-sayings, what is at work is a non-dual oneness or one-ing. That is, the at-oneness of human νόος and beyond human νόος and all that is manifest therein.

Klein explains this step, that is, a direct transition to νόος that is "beyond" things and us – *and* is another name for the non-dual dynamic of radiant emptiness and being/Ereignis:

Νοῦς becomes *what it truly is* when it is *one* with what is understood, *one* with the νοητά [what is known or that of which one is aware], that is to say, when the εἴδη νοητά have done their work. Only then can the νοῦς be said to be wakefulness "at work," to be ἐνέργεια νοῦς [mind-at-work], only then is the νοῦς "at its own end, is it ἐντελέχεια νοῦς." But Aristotle's thought, anticipated to a degree by Anaxagoras and by Plato, goes one crucial step further: the very being of this accomplished νοῦς is nothing but ἐνέργεια, and conversely, being-at-work *is* νοῦς – impartible (ἀμερής), indivisible (ἀδιαίρετος), impassive (ἀπαθής), unchangeable (ἀναλλοίωτος), undying (ἀθάνατος), eternal (ἀΐδιος).

It is eternally "at work," and it itself, as being-at-work, is its own eternal life (ζωή) and its own eternal delight (ἡδονή). It is deity (ὁ θεός) [read: the non-transparent *mythos*]. [*Metaphysics* Λ 7, 1072b 26–1073a.] The entire heaven (ὁ οὐρανός) and Nature (ἡ φύσις) [unfolding, birthing, generating] hang upon (ἤρτεται) this kind of "capital beginning (ἀρχή) [principle, starting dynamic]." [*Metaphysics*, Λ 7, 1072b 13–14].[36]

- *"[A]nticipated to a degree by Anaxagoras and by Plato": We have already delved into Plato's* **chora**, *and in a few pages we will dig deep into Anaxagoras's* **voῦς**.
- *These words describing* **voῦς**, *which Klein draws from Aristotle's text, offer a rich opening to the aspect of* **voῦς** *that goes beyond human* **voῦς** *as well as beyond forms, things/beings, and concepts.*

ἀμερής	impartible, without parts (no form)
ἀδιαίρετος	indivisible (one)
ἀπαθής	unaffected, not liable to change
ἀναλλοίωτος	unchangeable, unalterable
ἀθάνατος	undying, everlasting
ἀΐδιος	eternal, ever living, everlasting

- *I stress: "***voῦς*** is nothing but* **ἐνέργεια** *" and "is its own eternal life (***ζωή***) and its own eternal delight (***ἡδονή***)."*

Among other things, Klein's words here point us to the voῦς that is a no-thing no-form dynamic at work within and beyond human voῦς. Since voῦς is no-thing and open and free – simple in the sense that it is "as such" *no-thing* – its non-dual dynamic cannot be captured with the intellect. Thus the need for a poi-etic language.

Two quotations from Peters:

> [re Empedocles] … *nous* is separate from [more than?] the mass upon which it works (fr. 12); but it is also curiously immanent; see *noesis*.[37]

- *Immanent and not immanent; an activity that is* **both-and**: *both immanent and transcending. Being a non-dual dynamic, I would say that* *the νοῦς that is "more than" is distinguishable from but not separate or separable from the activity of human νοῦς.*

[re Plato] On a number of occasions we are informed that *nous* must exist in a soul (see *Soph.* 249a, *Phil.* 30c, *Tim.* 30b), and there are no grounds for thinking that this refers only to human intellects [*nous*, better said: human *nous*].[38]

- *Note that Peters calls* **nous** *"the intellectual principle." As we have seen,* **νοῦς** *is often translated as "intellect" in the TI ways. This is certainly* **not** *a fitting word for RR thinking-saying.*
- *An immanent* **nous**-*mind and a* **nous**-*mind beyond the human* **in a non-dual dynamic.** *How can it be otherwise?*

Aristotle, *Metaphysics*, XII-9, 1074b 15ff.:

Concerning νοῦς, there are some aporias. First of all, it is the most divine [θείοτατον] of the things that are manifest to us ... Now, if it thinks/ minds [νοεῖν] nothing, then it is as someone sleeping. On the other hand if it *does* mind, but has some other power over it ... then it could not be the best independent thing, for it is minding's being-at-work [ἐνέργεια νοῦς] that gives it its place of honour as originary unfolding. Now, if it is not an activity of minding but a potency ... something else would then be more honourable than νοῦς, namely *what* it thinks ... then the activity of thinking would not be the best thing. Therefore what it minds is itself, [i.e., happens without anything else being the basis of it], if it is the most excellent thing and its minding is minding of minding.

- *Νοῦς as* **minding.** *Knowing awareness, thinking, minding. Or: the mind at work being aware. Hearing, taking-in, actively thinking as tending-to. How do we say all of that within a translation of a text, as is the case here? How to keep all of that in mind when we read "mind" and "minding" in this passage from Aristotle?*
- *As already mentioned, we do not quite know all of what the Greeks meant with the word* **divine.** *In any case the word* θείοτατον *says what is more than human or excellence to the highest degree. Knowing how the non-dual dynamic of radiant emptiness says that which is no-thing and no-form and not dual ... might help us to understand the "divine"* **νοῦς.**

- *Whatever else Aristotle is being wary of, the one thing that is clear is that he is thinking νοῦς in a manner that mirrors the **non-dual dynamic of no-form, no-thing emptiness**. That goes beyond humans.*
- *Gathering some of what Aristotle says here: "for it is minding's being-at-work [ἐνέργεια νοῦς] that gives it its place of honour as originary unfolding," and is minding as such, or as Aristotle says: "minding is minding of minding" – or: minding as such. That is, no-form and no-thing: boundless boundary as in "unlimited."*
- *Note how similar these words of Aristotle are to the words of Plato on χώρα. One can hear νοῦς as boundless, with no form and being no thing. And in its being boundless, it is non-dual.*

Peters on Aristotle:

> Now the *proton kinoun* is described as *nous* and its *energeia* as *noesis* (*Meta.* 1072b), but it is clear that this must somehow differ from the operations described in the *De Anima* [i.e., this *nous* is not limited to or the same as the *nous* immanent in human beings]. In the first instance, cosmic [i.e., "divine" as in more than human] *nous* is not activated by something else, since this would be to say that it is in potency to something else and thus not an unmoved mover [i.e., not a dynamic unto itself, as such, with nothing else being the basis of it]. The cosmic *nous*, then, does not *become* its object; it *is* its object [i.e., it is unto itself what it is, lasting-timeless, as no-form and no-thing dynamic]. (*Meta.* 1074b)[39]

- *Minding is minding of minding, **νόησις** is **νόησις** of **νόησις**, or: minding-**νοῦς** is simply the non-dual dynamic of what is no-form no-thing emptiness – now **aware** emptiness. (See part 4.)*
- *I would not say "cosmic **νοῦς** ... is its object." It is obvious that this **νοῦς** as said here has nothing to do with objects.*

In a kind of gathering: The more-than-human νοῦς, being simply mind-minding with nothing composite or measurable, is not encompassable with anything physical. Aristotle says how the immanent νοῦς is made to be-at-work (see *De Anima*, III, 5) and becomes knowable in our awareness by virtue of the working of νοῦς that is more than the *nous* that is immanent in humans and that is always already at-work, simply in and of itself at-work in its mind-minding (*Meta.* 1049b). This νοῦς is simply a dynamic, no-thing ἐνέργεια, not graspable or conceptually knowable, even as it is at-work and even as we can experience it.

Some people call this a transcendent νοῦς and a faculty of the "world soul." But these words tend to substantiate νοῦς, which is impossible because it is no-thing, has no form, and is unconceivable ... even as we experience it intuitively in awareness.

We need a language that goes beyond defining or keeping the image of substantiation – as in world soul, the one, divine, cosmic νοῦς. What is own to νοῦς is its being itself no-thing and no-form dynamic, as it holds and lets manifest things and forms and concepts. Can we let go of our tendency to see only immanent, human νοῦς and open our thinking to the more-than-human νοῦς – as a "beyond" that we are one with and can know experientially?

Anaxagoras

When one counts the lines from all the fragments of Anaxagoras, one finds that the theme of *nous* comprises roughly half of them. In spite of this, many "histories" of this early Greek period either do not mention Anaxagoras at all or do not mention this theme of νοῦς – at all! An example of this is Guthrie's *A History of Greek Philosophy*. Then, when dealing with Anaxagoras, many who do take up νοῦς take it to mean something physical or corporeal – for which, as far as I can see, there is no justification or evidence.

As we go along, I will try to show how Anaxagoras confronted the same challenge that Plato had with *chora* in the *Timaeus* and that Heidegger had with his burning question of being, later known as beyng/Ereignis. That is, the dynamic that each was pursuing was virtually impossible to put into words. We need to always keep this in mind. Why so difficult? Because the no-thing and no-form dynamic essentially withdraws from concepts and from things/beings, that is, withdraws from our TI ways of thought and language.

We have shown how Heidegger describes this extreme difficulty. We have shown how Plato's *chora* reveals the same dilemma. Now it is Anaxagoras, with his νοῦς, who comes up against this wall. The dynamic as such is the crux.

It is for this reason that (a) both Plato and Aristotle praise Anaxagoras for putting *nous* as the first principle, which is not about things/beings but rather an attempt to experience, think, and say this most profound and exciting no-thing dynamic, but then (b) express their disappointment, each in his own way.

Plato is at first delighted to hear how for Anaxagoras it is the being-at-work (*energeia*) of *nous* that lets emerge all that is, the whole of what manifests – called *kosmos*. Plato sees this to be "as good as possible" an explanation (*Timaeus* 30-a-b). At first this new way of thinking-saying turned Socrates on. But he was disappointed when he saw where it went ... or did not go:

[M]y extravagant expectations were all dashed to the ground when I went on and found that the man made no use of νοῦς at all. In the ordering of things he ascribed no causal power whatever to it, but rather to airs and aethers and waters, and a host of other strange things. (*Phaedo*, 97b8)

The same disappointment happened for Aristotle. First he praised Anaxagoras, who "stood out like a sober man from the random talkers that had preceded him" (*Metaph.*, A 3, 984b15–18). But then he says:

Anaxagoras sees νοῦς as a *deus ex machina* to account for the formation of the world; and whenever he is at a loss to explain why anything necessarily is, he drags it in. But in other cases he makes the cause to be anything [else] but νοῦς. (*Metaph.*, I-5, 985a 18–21)

Anaxagoras speaks less clearly about these things; for many times he rightly and truly says that νοῦς is the cause, while at other times he says it is ψυχή; for (he says) it is in all animals, both great and small, both honoured and dishonoured. But it is not apparent that what is intelligently called νοῦς is present in all animals alike, nor even in all men. (*De anima* I-2, 404 b 1)

Anaxagoras uses νοῦς as a device by which to construct the universe, and when he is at a loss for the cause why anything necessarily is, then he drags this in, but in other cases he assigns any other cause rather than νοῦς for what comes into being. (*Meta.* I-5, 985a 18)

But what if? What if Anaxagoras honoured the complexity of νοῦς in its vastness (read: human and beyond-human, non-dually) by *not* resolving the dilemma and staying in the no-way-out? What if Anaxagoras respects the seeming irresolvability (a) of things/ beings, (b) the νοῦς that we know as "human," and (c) the beyond-human νοῦς?

The same dilemma encounters Heidegger's lifelong pursuit, named the question of truth, the meaning of truth, beyng/*Seyn*, beyng as Ereignis; Plato's groundbreaking pursuit, named *chora*; quantum physics and its pursuit, named the immeasurable field of energy, unbroken wholeness, holomovement, enfolding-unfolding. It continues for us, given the dominant TI language that we have inherited. And it is *this* language that was used when later Western thinking turned to the earlier Greeks. We are stymied when we try to express a non-conceptual experience and thinking in a language that is meant to express what is sensuous, what is a thing, what is measurable. The conceptual language of metaphysics and things/beings is simply inadequate. So the turn to poi-etic language is called for ... and is not easy.

Behind Aristotle's hand-wringing is the extreme difficulty of *saying* this νοῦς *at all*! Might we say that what Aristotle calls a "contradiction" – and bemoans – is more a poi-etic saying of the "openendedness" that belongs to νοῦς? Might we, then, say that, rather than a contradiction, Anaxagoras's unresolved struggle is a sign of a thinker's greatness?

Now we focus directly on Anaxagoras's νοῦς. First I turn to Peters, who gives a somewhat "generic" understanding of Anaxagoras on νοῦς:

Indeed *nous* does not seem to be a cognitive principle at all but rather a cosmological one. It initiates motion ... and guides and rules all (fr. 12).

What Anaxagoras is obviously offering is the presence of some intelligent and hence purposeful principle in the universe.[40]

- *Removing any implication of universe or ordered cosmos, for cosmological, read: "all that is."*
- *Removing any implication of the cognitive-intellectual, for intelligent, read: "knowing-aware."*
- *Removing any implication of a moral principle, for purposeful, read: "directing-guiding."*

Klein keeps the word in Greek: νοῦς. Most translators and commentators, however, use the English word *mind*. For example:

According to Anaxagoras, the agent responsible for the rotation and separation of the primordial mixture is Mind or *nous*: "And when Mind began to cause motion, separating off proceeded to occur from all that was moved, and all that Mind moved was separated apart, and as things were being moved and separated apart, the rotation caused much more separating apart to occur" (fr. 13) ... But how is this explanation to be understood? ... But what exactly is Mind, according to Anaxagoras?[41]

Now we go directly to Anaxagoras:

B12

All other things have a share of everything, while νοῦς is boundless and self-ruling, and has been mixed with no thing, but it alone is as such [itself by itself]. For if it were not by itself, but were mixed with anything else, it would partake in *all* things if it were mixed with any; for there is a share of everything in everything, as I have said before. And the things mixed together with it would prevent it from having power over any thing in the same way that it does, being alone by itself [as such, of one piece, unto itself]. For it is the finest [as in most refined-delicate][42] of things and the purest, and it maintains full discernment concerning everything and has the greatest strength. And of the things that have life, both greater and smaller, νοῦς holds sway.

τὰ μὲν ἄλλα παντὸς μοῖραν μετέχει, νοῦς δέ ἐστιν ἄπειρον καὶ αὐτοκρατὲς καὶ
μέμεικται οὐδενὶ χρήματι, ἀλλὰ μόνος αὐτὸς ἐπ᾿ ἑαυτοῦ ἐστιν. εἰ μὴ γὰρ ἐφ᾿
ἑαυτοῦ ἦν, ἀλλά τεωι ἐμέμεικτο ἄλλωι, μετεῖχεν ἂν ἀπάντων χρημάτων, εἰ
ἐμέμεικτό τεωι· ἐν παντὶ γὰρ παντὸς μοῖρα ἔνεστιν, ὥσπερ ἐν τοῖς πρόσθεν μοι
λέλεκται· καὶ ἂν ἐκώλυεν αὐτὸν τὰ συμμεμειγμένα, ὥστε μηδενὸς χρήματος
κρατεῖν ὁμοίως ὡς καὶ μόνον ἐόντα ἐφ᾿ ἑαυτοῦ. ἔστι γὰρ λεπτότατόν τε πάντων
χρημάτων καὶ καθαρώτατον καὶ γνώμην γε περὶ παντὸς πᾶσαν ἴσχει καὶ ἰσχύει
μέγιστον· καὶ ὅσα γε ψυχὴν ἔχει καὶ τὰ μείζω καὶ τὰ ἐλάσσω, πάντων νοῦς
κρατεῖ.

This long quotation reminds us of Plato's *chora*. Remember
that Plato's Socrates talks of *chora* as "never taking on a form"
and "free of all form" and "without form." Even though Anaxagoras does not speak of formlessness, he uses words-images
that can only mean formlessness. Words like *boundless, spontaneous, unto-itself, timeless, unmixed* ring out, letting the non-dual
dynamic of radiant emptiness resonate. Since νοῦς is no-thing
and open and free – simple as in "mixed with no-thing" – its
non-dual dynamic points to a beyond-human *nous* and cannot
be captured with the intellect. Realizing that the word νοῦς is
hard to translate and that the English word *mind* makes sense
in a way, let me now address two questions: What *is* νοῦς? And
what does νοῦς *do*?
    What **νοῦς** "is":

ἄπειρον	boundless, infinite
αὐτοκρατὲς	self-powered, spontaneous
μέμεικται οὐδενὶ χρήματι	not mixed with anything, unmixed
μόνος αὐτὸς ἐφ᾿ ἑαυτοῦ	alone unto itself, as such
καθαρώτατον	purest, unsullied, freest, open space
λεπτότατόν	finest, most delicate, most refined

Mind/νοῦς is unconstrained, infinite, powerful and ever-there,
the purest of all dynamics, master of itself. Mind/νοῦς is unique,
unlimited, pure, and with itself as such. Mind/νοῦς is free, lasting,
dynamic emptiness. It has its dynamic within itself. Something like
the non-dual dynamic of radiant emptiness.

What **νοῦς** "does":

πάντα διεκόσμησε	regulates, musters, guides everything
τὰ πάντων κρατεῖ.	prevails, arranges, holds sway over all
ἤρξατο κινεῖν (fr. 13)	starts the movement, enables, takes the lead in movement
ἤρξατο περιχωρεῖν,	starts the rotating or gets it started

Gathering the key word-images from this fragment, we hear how νοῦς masters, prevails over, lets emerge, directs, holds, generates and holds, without getting mixed in things (*chora*) and thus formless.

***

Upon reflection, here at the end of part 3, it may seem as if, here and there, the evidence is scant and my reading a bit of a stretch. But more to the point: It is my hope that from now on, whenever we read the words of these Greek thinkers, we will never again simply accept that the translations are "telling the truth." If nothing else, we will see beyond the mistranslations. And we will be confident that these Greek thinkers are pointing us to a realm or dynamic that has been covered over by Christian "philosophy" by a dualistic metaphysics, by the dominance of reason and concepts – and by mistranslations.

There is so much more that one could delve into. I am confident that this writing will open the doors, open our eyes, and open our mind – to the next step.

Part Four

Bringing the Book to a Close

Part 4 brings the book to a close. First, it takes a bigger look at aware-ness, which came to the fore in the discussion of nous at the end of part 3. Second, it looks at how we can learn to experience and think and say this "it." Finally, it takes a brief look at the "next steps," that is, some aspects of the project that are not fully discussed in this book and are called for, several topics that call for more exploration.

a. From Saying Consciousness to Saying Awareness

For starters, I will repeat some of the words that appear in the Pre-amble regarding timeless wisdom and awareness. At that point these words focused on something more general and were meant to set a tone. That was *before* we worked through the seven key words from the Greek thinkers.

> Let me play with the words "timeless wisdom." **Wisdom** here means both understanding and experiencing. **Timeless** here says a dynamic and an **awareness** that is without centre or limit, boundless, lasting, imperishable, abiding-enduring, vast, and "biding" in the sense of trustworthy. This timeless wisdom is, then, not a thing or no-thing, not a concept or beyond concepts, non-dual and not encounterable in comparing. It is emptiness – what I call "the non-dual dynamic of radiant emptiness." It is undifferentiated, even as it manifests different states of the non-dual dynamic or interdependent conditions by which

things/beings-concepts emerge within a non-dual whole that is beyond parts.

This timeless wisdom is known indirectly and said poi-etically. It is more spacious. It shows vastness. Since it is no-thing and non-conceptual, we in our awareness might say "is as is" or "as such." This "is as is" or "as such" can be named the unmanifest field or dynamic of emptiness – or beyng.

We might say that buddha mind is unconditioned as in "beyond all conditions." That *dao* is unconditioned. That quantum physics pushes the envelope in this direction. That Bohm calls it "the immeasurable." And that we have found the same dynamic at work in Greek thinking.

Our **mind and awareness** mirrors this non-dually. We in our **knowing awareness** participate in the "as such." This enriches us. We find our bliss and deep meaning in realizing and living it.

This non-dual dynamic of the "as such" is at our core within the enveloping wholeness. It is like the ocean in its depth, not the waves. It goes beyond ourselves. Even though it is often named a supreme being, phenomenologically it is beyond even this limiting identity. Certainly it is beyond all dogmas and beliefs. We could call it boundless.

In response to the question *"How does this timeless awareness fit into your project in this book?,"* I wrote in the Preamble:

A very good question! First, let me say that I want to focus on this "timeless wisdom" – by way of "wandering" amid word-images that can open us up to what is going on in "just is" – as **a kind of awareness**.

Now to your question. With these poi-etic images in mind, let me focus on the project of this book ... These are specific markers for opening up the sayings of Greek philosophy that got covered over and hidden.

- the **non-dual**, which encompasses the either-or separation of dualism, but *holds and embeds it in* the non-dual dynamic – a oneness or a one-ing,

- the **non-conceptual**, which encompasses the rational-intellectual conceptualization as the dominant mode of thinking, but *holds and embeds it in* a thinking emerging from concrete lived experience,

- the **becoming**, which encompasses what is static, solid, hardened, independent, but *holds and embeds it in* the ever-changing *dynamic* within which phenomena emerge, the changing conditions that come together to shape what is,
- **emptiness**, which encompasses the quantitative, rational description of things in the world, but *holds and embeds it in* the immeasurable that is in everything but is itself not anything, no-thing – whose names are beyng-Ereignis (Heidegger), mind and emptiness (Buddhism), *dao* (Daoism), and the immeasurable field of energy (quantum physics).

Here (in part 4) we need to add **non-dual dynamic of radiant emptiness** *as awareness.*

Let me start with Leo Strauss:

This quest for the beginnings proceeds through sense perception, reasoning, and what they call *noesis*, which is literally translated by "understanding" or "intellect," and which we can perhaps translate a little bit more cautiously by "awareness," an awareness of the mind's eye as distinguished from sensible awareness.[1]

Then Jacob Klein:

Wakefulness is openness – the very openness of a huge open door ... This state or manner of being is commonly called in Greek νοῦς or νοεῖν.[2]

Wakefulness and awareness are synonyms. This awareness is openness. The dictionary says that *nous-noesis* is awareness, that is, the opposite of discursive thought. Given this dynamic, we have to decipher the various Greek words. Aristotle, for example, says that *psyche* is the principle of life of any living being and thus of the human *psyche*, which is the principle of *human* life. And a number of aspects belong to this *psyche*: *nous*-awareness, *sophia*-wisdom, *episteme*-knowledge of things that cannot change, *theorein*-insight, *logos* as speech-gathering-thinking.

If we start with νοέω, we find the following translations (among several other, more common ones): see, notice, perceive, perceive with the mind's eye, be aware, perceive with the mind, heed, be minded. Then, νοῦς is: awareness, alertness, aliveness, knowing awareness (among other more used translations).

With all of this in mind, I repeat the long quotation from Klein, one that I presented earlier in the section on νοῦς/*nous*. But now I will put the English translations of the Greek words in the text itself, with the Greek in brackets. Notice how the sense of awareness moves from human awareness to beyond-human awareness.

> Awareness [wakefulness, νοῦς] becomes *what it truly is* when it is *one* [i.e., non-dual] with what is understood, *one* with what is known or that of which one is aware [νοητά] ... Only then can the νοῦς be said to be wakefulness "at work," to be awareness-at-work [ἐνέργεια νοῦς], only then is the awareness "at its own end, is it being-at-work-in-its-intended aim [ἐντελέχεια νοῦς]." But Aristotle's thought, anticipated to a degree by Anaxagoras and by Plato, goes one crucial step further: the very being of this accomplished awareness [νοῦς] is nothing but being-at-work [ἐνέργεια], and conversely, being-at-work *is* awareness [νοῦς] – impartible (ἀμερής), indivisible (ἀδιαίρετος), impassive (ἀπαθής), unchangeable (ἀναλλοίωτος), undying (ἀθάνατος), eternal (ἀΐδιος).
>
> [Awareness] is eternally "at work," and it itself, as being-at-work, is its own eternal life (ζωή) and its own eternal delight (ἡδονή). It is deity (ὁ θεός) [read: the non-transparent *mythos*]. [Meta. XII-7, 1072b 26–1073a.] The entire heaven (ὁ οὐρανός) and unfolding, birthing, generating [φύσις] hang upon (ἤρτεται) this kind of "capital beginning (ἀρχή) [principle, starting dynamic]." [Meta. XII-7, 1072b 13–144][3]

- First, it is human **νοῦς** that is named *wakefulness ... a wakefulness at work – ἐνέργεια νοῦς – an openness and awareness "of a huge open door."*
- When active in this way, that is, "at work," then **νοῦς** is aware, fulfilling what is own to it as **νοῦς** – ἐντελέχεια νοῦς.
- Second, following Anaxagoras and Plato, Aristotle speaks of a **νοῦς** that is "nothing but ἐνέργεια." That is, a **νοῦς** beyond the human **νοῦς** whose "very being ... is nothing but ἐνέργεια." This **νοῦς**-at-work "is eternally

'at work,' and it itself, as being-at-work, is its own eternal life (ζωή) …
It is ὁ Θεός, that is, the non-transparent mythos."
- *This mirrors the no-form and no-thing non-dual dynamic that is at the*
  core of this book. Buddha mind, dao, the energy field of quantum physics,
  *and Heidegger's beyng-Ereignis – **the same dynamic that is at work***
  in Greek thinking.

A number of times throughout the writing of this book, I felt that the non-dual dynamic of radiant emptiness – beyng, Ereignis, mind, *dao*, the field dynamic of quantum physics – has to be "aware." And now we hear how the word νοῦς says **awareness.** How is this dynamic "aware"? This is what we are trying to experience, to think, and then to say: Timeless and limitless awareness.

And then I found several instances *outside* philosophy where the author uses words like awareness and consciousness – with reckless abandon! For example, *The Self-Aware Universe: How Consciousness Creates the Material World* by Amit Goswami. Or *The Self-Aware Emptiness of the Quantum Universe* by Graham Smetham.[4] And then I found this amazing quotation from Humberto Maturana and Francisco Varela: "Living systems are cognitive systems, and living as a process is a process of cognition. This statement is valid for all organisms, with or without a nervous system."[5] In my view, their use of the word *cognitive* does not take us all the way to "aware," but it is a big step. They could just as well have said "systems of awareness" and "living as a process of awareness."

So this idea of "beyond-human awareness" is already out there! What to do? I turned to Buddhism. Here is a quotation that explicitly talks of awareness (*Gewahrsein*) in our minds, but clearly opens the gate to something that we are non-dually a part of, that is, awareness as such:

Awareness is like a thread that runs through each of our experiences. Our thoughts and emotions are constantly changing. Our reactions and perceptions come and go. Yet despite these changes, our awareness is always present. It is wide open and accepting like the sky, immeasurably deep and wide like the ocean, and stable and lasting, like a massive mountain.[6]

Since awareness as such is not divided or divisible, has no form and no limit, our awareness is one with awareness as such. We *are* this awareness and we are *in this awareness* with no duality: only **one** awareness. Logic and concepts cannot attain this non-conceptualizable dynamic. But intuition and experience and poietic thinking and saying can.

Things manifest themselves in space but never become permanent-static-independent substances. "Substance" is just a concept. It is both "not-real" (not permanent and unchanging and independent substances) and impermanent emergent co-dependently arising conditions. Mind is aware of this emergence – knowing awareness – and participates in the manifestation of things in the everyday world of things and quantifyings – aware as in not daunted by the many obscurations built into the subject-object paradigm. Simply put, mindful or "minding" participation in the way things are overcomes the dualism of subject-object, by practising the way of knowing awareness in mindful participation.

We know how νοῦς is (among other more usual translations): awareness, wakefulness, aliveness, knowing awareness. This follows from how **νοέω is: notice, perceive, perceive with the mind's eye, be aware, perceive with the mind, heed, be minded**.

Awareness happens on the human level – **and** is at work as the no-thing, no-form non-dual dynamic of radiant emptiness, aka buddha mind, *dao*, beyng. One could say that in this dynamic human mind melds – is always melding – with the non-dual dynamic of radiant emptiness. And we humans serve as the flash-point for this timelessly non-dual melding. **All of this is there in Greek thinking**.

Enjoy these word-images. Let them take our mind to what we already experience and then to what is possible – also there for our experience. Check out the experiences of these awarenesses and intuitions, with critical thinking.

Why awareness instead of consciousness? It might seem that the two words *consciousness* and *awareness* say the same thing.

However, there are differences in their etymologies and differences in their usage.

Conscious is from the Latin *conscius* (*con+scire*): to know with others and in ourselves. **Conscious**: conscious mind, having mental faculties; conscious of one's self, self-conscious, self-cognition; individual awareness of one's unique thoughts, memories, feelings, sensations, and environments; possessing awareness or consciousness. **Consciousness** is a state of being aware of something within oneself: inner-subjective awareness vs. outer awareness; conscious vs. unconscious-sleeping; consciousness and loss of consciousness; consciousness vs. the physical body.

Of course, there are those scientists who believe that consciousness emerges from the physical brain. For example, that billions of neurons cause a conscious experience, that the cerebral cortex is or causes consciousness, that consciousness is in the brains of highly evolved organisms, or that some manner of electrochemical balance in the neural system makes up consciousness. There is nothing in experience that can prove this. Thus these are simply concepts without experiential basis.

Finally, there are two things that make these inherited concepts of "consciousness" not so useful in saying what is at stake in this work. One, given all the ways that the word *consciousness* has been used, the word has taken on a kind of specificity – albeit in varied iterations. And what we are seeking is a no-thing no-form nondual dynamic that is precisely beyond specificity.

Two, within these words and descriptions of consciousness given above are hidden words of duality that point to either-or matters – x versus y, conscious versus unconscious, consciousness over against the physical body.

I will try to show how the word *awareness* moves outside these either-or dualities. Note that, whereas the word *consciousness* has been in use for centuries, especially in the inherited works of philosophy and psychology, the word *awareness* is hardly ever used in these systems of thought. The lack of use of this word offers a freshness that the oft-used word *consciousness* does not. In addition, it is an Anglo-Saxon word. And Anglo-Saxon words in general have less baggage than Latinate words, for example, those in the Romance languages.

When we look for the etymology of the word *aware*, we learn the following: It stems from the Old English *gewær* (cognate with Old High German *gawar, giwar*, Middle High German *gewar*, modern German *gewahr*).[7] *Gewær-gewahr* as aware, watchful, vigilant.[8]

The German word *gewahr* says: *aufmerksam*: attentive, alert, mindful; *bemerkend*: aware. In Old High German *giwar* says: *achtsam*: mindful, attentive. In Middle High German *gewar* says: *beachtend*: minding, *aware, to become aware of*, as in *"gewahr warden"*).[9]

It is not hard to apply **awareness** on the level of humans. It is more difficult to understand awareness when it applies to the "beyond human" – to what Klein calls "the very being of this accomplished νοῦς" as "nothing but ἐνέργεια, and conversely, being-at-work *is* νοῦς [awareness]" – impartible, indivisible, impassive, unchangeable, undying, and eternal – "eternally 'at work,' and it itself, as being-at-work, is its own eternal life (ζωή) and its own eternal delight (ἡδονή)."

Awareness is nowhere, is without centre or boundary, is timeless and not contained "in" space. Awareness is "precisely" nonspecific! Awareness is also non-dual, because it has no form. Taking this road, νοῦς/mind names the non-dual dynamic of emptiness as awareness, for example, buddha mind, *dao*, the energy-field of quantum physics, as well as beyng/Ereignis in Heidegger. Not having the history that the word *consciousness* has, including self-consciousness, the word *awareness* is more opening and freeing, freer of concepts – "it itself" or awareness "as such." Timeless awareness, non-dual and no-thing and no-form.

The Indian guru of non-dualism, Nisargadatta Maharaj, helps us understand *awareness* in its difference from *consciousness*:

> Awareness is primordial; it is the original state, beginningless, endless, uncaused, unsupported, without parts, without change. Consciousness is on contact, a reflection against a surface, a state of duality. There can be no consciousness without awareness, but there can be awareness

without consciousness … Awareness is absolute [boundless, limit-less], consciousness is relative to its content; consciousness is always of something. Consciousness is partial and changeful, awareness is total, changeless [lasting], calm and silent. And it is the common matrix of every experience.[10]

- *Obviously this distinction is not absolute. On the poi-etic way of saying, the word-images used are meant to activate and point to a non-conceptual awareness.*
- *The words in the first sentence are words for the non-dual dynamic of radiant emptiness – as well as buddha mind, dao, beyng, and the no-form energy field of quantum physics.*
- *All that emerges is manifesting within the non-dual dynamic of emptiness as awareness. This awareness has no-form and is* **unmanifest**, *even as things/beings/phenomena manifest within awareness. Think Anaximander's* **apeiron**. *Think Plato's* **chora**. *Think Anaxagoras'* **nous**.

And:

There is nothing outside of awareness, because everything is awareness.
    There is no outside. Everything that seems outside is inside, and yet, there is no inside either. There is no outside or inside.
    We are all separated by our uniqueness, and yet we are all part of the whole. The whole is not separate from anything. Awareness is not broken off into pieces; it is universally whole and unbreakable, limitless in its infinite expansiveness.[11]

- *Everything is* **awareness**. *Thus we could say: Buddhism might say that everything is* **awareness as mind**. *Daoism might say that everything is* **awareness as dao**. *And Heidegger might say that everything is* **awareness as beyng**.

And:

Awareness is a multidimensional experience and this awareness is infi-nite in its horizons. The innate qualities of awareness are spaciousness or openness or emptiness. Another quality of awareness is luminous radiance and still another is awareness as energy. Awareness is alive and is both vast stillness and unceasing movement.[12]

- *These words are ways of saying the non-dual dynamic of radiant empti-ness as awareness.* **And we as Dasein are the flashpoint within which we are who we are and come to know this dynamic.**

Given how far our thinking is from this timeless awareness, it takes some doing to learn how to hear-say-do it. But for sure we can now say that the seeds were planted in Greek thinking. Indeed, the seeds were not only planted – they sprouted, emerged from the soil, and flourished. As νοῦς/awareness, as ἐνέργεια νοῦς (wakeful-ness being "at work"), as ἐντελέχεια νοῦς (νοῦς "at its own end"), as νοῦς/awareness that is nothing but ἐνέργεια, non-dual,impartible, indivisible, impassive, unchangeable, undying-lasting, eternal. It is eternally-lastingly "at work" "as such." And is its own eternal delight. The timeless awareness of beyng/Ereignis, buddha mind, *dao*, the non-physical energy field of quantum physics and the non-dual dynamic of radiant emptiness – all words saying the no-form no-thing that is at work in the non-dual dynamic … **awareness**. And in reading the Greeks, it is the word *nous* that carries us to this awareness.

We have come to the place where the no-form no-thing non-dual dynamic is … awareness! By extension Heidegger's beyng, *dao*, buddha mind, and the energy field of quantum potential in quantum physics all say awareness. Awareness "as such." Aristot-les' νοῦς as awareness that is "its own eternal delight."

Yet most of us have little experience of this. How is that pos-sible? We have barely any awareness of the no-form no-thing non-dual dynamic.

Clarifying the view. Since what I write here about awareness stems from how I see things at this point in my life of thinking – and is quite unusual for a "work of philosophy" – it behoves me to explain the "clearing" in which I do this reading. Thus I will now offer some comments and ruminations – including some repetition – on what I have just worked through. This highlights the key dimensions of the dynamic awareness.

1. Central to the awareness dynamic is how it shows the one-ing of human awareness and the all-pervading "beyond human" awareness.
2. This one-ing, no-thing and no-form dynamic of timeless awareness is also found and said in the field of energy or quantum potential in quantum physics, the *dao*, and buddha mind.
3. Awareness is non-dual and no-thing radiant openness.
4. Our human awareness **in time** is non-dually a part of – or inherently belonging to – the **timeless, formless awareness** of radiant emptiness **reaching beyond humans**, aka beyng or *dao* or buddha mind.
5. We who are in time can experience and think and say this timeless awareness. This simultaneous knowing awareness of the awareness of radiant emptiness is freeing, enriching, opening, full awareness-emptiness (cf. GA 65:221–4). It is the "dynamic unfilledness" as an "open expanse of possibility" (GA 7:170). To quote Heidegger:

> The "empty," not as what comes with a lack and its distress, but rather the distress of being-reserved, which in itself is the throwing open that is a breaking open and starting of something – the grounding-attuning of the originary belonging-together. (GA 65:381–2)

   This emptiness is above all awareness.
6. When we, the flashpoint, experience the field of awareness, we experience it as the expanding or going-beyond our human awareness. Of course, since there is no dualism in awareness, our own awareness is one with the non-dual dynamic of awareness-emptiness. Therefore, as flashpoint, we simply "see" or experience what is always there timelessly – beyng, *dao*, buddha mind, or the quantum realm. In order to do this, we let go of our usual dualizing mind – which can distinguish and conceptualize this dynamic – and let awareness show itself as the no-form and no-thing dynamic that it is.

7. As phenomena (things, beings) emerge within awareness,
   a. they do not leave aware emptiness, even as they are things in duality, and
   b. awareness never becomes dual or some *thing*, and
   c. all is held within the timeless awareness of radiant emptiness.

This is the dynamic that Heidegger wants to say with the word *ab-ground* (*Ab-grund*). If we think ab-ground as the "staying away of ground" and think it as aware, this is a useful mirror by which to experience, then to think, then to say the non-dual dynamic of radiant emptiness. And this non-dual, dynamic, radiantly aware emptiness – which we now know to be at work in *dao*, buddha mind, and the quantum realm or field of energy – **is also there in full force in Greek philosophy, especially in the early Greek thinkers.**

b. How to Think and Experience and Say "It": Meanderings

The "it" here is what Heidegger calls beyng/Ereignis, what Buddhism calls mind and emptiness "like the infinity of space," what Daoism calls *dao*, what quantum physics calls the quantum potential. It is also what Heidegger – and this book – seek to retrieve in the Greek words discussed in here in part 3: *ἄπειρον / apeiron … χώρα / chora … ἀλήθεια / aletheia … ἐόν / eon … λόγος / logos … φύσις / physis … ψυχή / psyche … νόος, νοῦς / noos, nous.* **This "it" is also what I am calling the non-dual dynamic of radiant emptiness.**

I call this section "Meanderings" for the simple reason that this "how" cannot happen through logic or conceptual thinking or propositional sentences. Meandering is above all indirect and follows a winding course. To meander says roving, hovering, roaming, wandering, winding ways. These ways can be said only with a non-conceptual thinking and saying, a way of saying that is poi-etic.

Let's start with Heraclitus, Fragment B18: **If you do not expect the unexpected, you will not find it; for it is undetectable and inacessible**. We must go beyond conventions. This means that we go – beyond the encrustation of concepts that obscures – to the unexpected. Parmenides (Fr. 1) tells us that "it lies off the beaten track." This requires an openness and active attending. Some kind of alertness for what shows itself in the opening.

The "it" cannot be grasped through our normal intellectual inquiring, but rather requires an intuitive, minding mind. Rather than remaining trapped within our usual perspective of "objectivity," we dwell in a fluid, indirect, and resonating language within non-conceptual awareness. Releasing our knowing awareness from the habitual ways of thought.

I return for a moment to Heraclitus, Fragment B50: **Listening, not to me but to *logos*, it is wise to grant that all is one**. This one or dynamic one-ing is at the heart of the "it" we are pursuing. "One" simply says that "it" is boundless, without duality, no-thing and no-form. But "it" is at work and we can experience it. Every one of those Greek words says this one or one-ing.

Perhaps simplistically, one could say that there is a natural ambiguity in the language of the early Greek thinkers. Indirect and poi-etic, resonating with what is being thought, experienced, and said there. This is what we are retrieving. This language penetrates beyond the language of substance, metaphysics, and concepts. It is a saying-showing that opens to the originary no-thing dynamic.

Heraclitus, Fragment B93, says: **The lord whose oracle is at Delphi neither speaks out nor hides, but gives hints**. Our dualistic sentence structure hides this dynamic. This hinting requires the poi-etic, non-logical thinking and non-propositional language, mirroring the ambiguity in what is said-shown in all these Greek words.

Fragment B54: **A hidden harmonic connection is stronger than [surpasses] an apparent one**.

Fragment B123: ***Physis* loves to hide**. That is the usual translation one finds. But in the section on *physis* in part 3 we heard Heidegger's expanded translations:

- The emerging [*Aufgehen*] grants favour to the self-hiding. (G55:110)
- The rising-emerging (from within the hiding-sheltering) grants favour to the hiding-sheltering. (GA7:279)

The utter indirectness of all four of these Heraclitus fragments says-shows the "it" that works but is non-manifest.

Own to this one-ing is something more than a mere lying hidden. Rather, it is hidden and hinted at as an *active* hiding. The hidden is neither accidental nor peripheral, because what is own to "it" is to be invisible – as are beyng/Ereignis, buddha mind, *dao*, quantum potential, and all the Greek words whose powerful saying we with Heidegger try to retrieve. One could say that for Heraclitus everything that exists participates in the dynamic one – not at a beginning at some point in time, but as always timelessly participating in the one fluctuating dynamic of the one.

How do we come to experience "it"? It is not graspable through our usual intellectual inquiry. It calls for non-conceptual awareness, an active attending to, a being alert. Being indirect, it calls for intuitive, mindful minding. We come to it with careful waiting and knowing awareness that we are part of it. Beyond arguments and definitions and propositions. Beyond duality and empirical measuring. We learn to dwell in the active "still point" of the dynamic of the non-dual intertwining of form and formlessness. Alive herein, we learn to wait.

To get there, we hear Heraclitus shock us out of the ordinary and the expected. We hear Parmenides tell us that we have to get off the beaten path of our habitual thinking. We need to get away from conventions in order to experience, think, and say how "it" is at work in the one-ing of the dynamic, which is in us even as "it" is a "more-than-human" that we participate in. "It" is timeless. To know it, we penetrate the veils – also known as the "expected" in our concepts – and open to beyng, *logos*, radiant emptiness. We are ourselves not "it" but in it. We and the world participate in "it." We can say that we humans are the **flashpoint** (*Augenblicksstätte*) for and in which "it" emerges – and we mark it with "our" awareness, non-dually one with awareness as such.

As we open to this experience, learning how to be present to it, here are some of "its" qualities by which to know it: Above all, it is a no-form dynamic that is non-dual, that is, a one-ing. There is no separation, anywhere. "It" is a non-dual dynamic, a **one**-ing. Then it is boundless, undefined, unlimited. Being boundless, it is time-less. It holds and embraces all possibility, even as "it" is no-thing. **And "it" is awareness.**

The physical world cannot exist without it and its empowering, even as we normally understand the physical world without being aware of the "it." And to the extent that we today deny this, we are imprisoned within our own systems and concepts.

Again, language. In order to do justice to the project of retrieving what the early Greeks thought and said, we accept the challenge of retranslating and rethinking these key Greek words. I talked earlier about the natural ambiguity in the Greek language of the early Greek thinkers. This stems from the inherent tension that the words carry with them – held within their cryptic style. This is mirrored in their attempt to think and to say what their *experience* of the cryptic "it" is. Going concretely there in an *indirect* and poi-etic language. Saying-showing but not defining, knowing the richness of this way. Knowing that while being open to the power of beyng, emptiness, and so on, the boundless in "it" wants the poi-etic. Stretching our thinking accordingly. Saying *must* go beyond ordinary language.

The "one" is own not to things and forms but rather to the no-form *active* non-dual dynamic. This no-form "one-ing" lets all that is emerge and yet itself remains as "it" is. What the no-form non-dual dynamic lets emerge does not alter the dynamic. Even as *what* manifests changes as the forms change, the "it" of the no-form non-dual dynamic of radiant emptiness is not diminished. It is this that we must learn to think and experience **and say**.

Moving towards Heidegger's Leap. Now a few words to gather where we have come, here (in part 4, after focusing on the Greek words (part 3): *ἄπειρον/apeiron* ... *χώρα/chora* ... *ἀλήθεια/aletheia* ... *ἐόν / eon* ... *λόγος / logos* ... *φύσις / physis* ... *ψυχή / psyche* ... *νόος,* νοῦς / *noos, nous.* The "it" here is also what I am calling the non-dual dynamic of radiant emptiness and what Heidegger calls beyng and Ereignis.

"It" is no-thing whatsoever, no form, a non-dual one-ing dynamic, which, while itself not available to our intellect, is the basis for all that is. One could call it the field as "holding" of all that is or as "dynamic receiving" from which all things manifest. It is an everlasting or "timeless," ever-active, creating dynamic. It is limit-less. It is radiant, in that this field of emptiness radiates out. As all manifestations (phenomena, things) appear, "it" is experienced as no-form no-thing non-dual dynamic. Not being anything physical and not having form, it is boundless.

One could say that we have to learn how to "enter" "it." The problem, though, is that we are always already in it, participating in what it does. So entering or stepping into it calls for changing our awareness of what it is and who and where we *already are.* Stepping into it is about our openness to awareness of what is non-dually already there – even as we carry veils that hide it. By going beyond those veils and by participating in it, we "change" it – as in quantum physics our observing changes what is. "It" can easily allow this, since all is there in "its" oneness or one-ing.

Given that the one-ing of the dynamic is always already there, what keeps us from it? Our habits of conceptualizing, the limita-tions of logic, substance metaphysics, the perceived need for epis-temological certainty. On the other hand, we know the "how" here by becoming aware of moments of openness and uplifting. The moment when, reading a captivating novel, we put the book down, look into space with an awareness of the "more than," in our awareness of the oneness of all things. Or a movie that grabs us in a similar way: When the movie is over, we continue to sit entranced, our mind's having been "lifted" to a space beyond. Beyond our usual awareness, beyond our thinking and feeling habits, "beyond the pale" as in beyond all boundaries.

Eventually we come back "to our senses," get up and meet our friends again … and chitchat about the weather and where the car is. And where we will go to have a drink. With that, the moment of being in the open-ended and rich condition of "stepping out of" or "entering into" "it" has passed. We have caught a glimpse of this moment of beyond – and have delighted in it – and then we return to our habitual self and the boundaries that it sets. Above all, we have learned to discount this moment of "ecstasy" as not natural and an aberration of who we really are.

If we could learn to take these ecstatic moments seriously, we could see them as essential to the "it" that holds and guides all things, while remaining itself no-thing at the core part of who we are. Timeless awareness leaps out – as things and the "it" and we within it, non-dually – as we learn to think and say this dynamic poi-etically. We join with the non-dual dynamic of radiant emptiness (aka beyng, *dao*, buddha mind), that is, we become aware of what we always already are. Heidegger says that Dasein is the flashpoint (*die Augenblicksstätte*) where the whole of the one-ing of "it" gets sighted, experientially known, and marked in poi-etic saying.

This same dynamic is mirrored in quantum entanglement: "An entangled system is defined to be one whose **quantum state** cannot be factored as a product of states of its local constituents; that is to say, they are not individual particles but are an inseparable whole. In entanglement, one constituent cannot be fully described without considering the other(s)."[13] In entanglement we experience ourselves as participating in "it." In a sense we become it – better said, we become aware of being one with it. The "it" of this participation is where these entangled particles are not physically connected, even as they instantaneously and timelessly share information with one another.

Subatomic entities exist within a dynamic of potentials, until they "come to be" by an act of observation and/or measurement. Our world is a "participatory phenomenon," requiring the act of observation – and thus consciousness itself.

This is a move to awareness. Human and beyond-human awareness, as a one-ing. It is the "leap" that will take us there. Awareness is that within which all things-phenomena appear.

In his article on consciousness and quantum physics, John Nwanegbo Ben writes the following:

We cannot really explain the nature of reality without consciousness. The concept of reality can only be understood by the conscious awareness of what we perceive as reality. This brings to mind the idea of Protagoras of Abdera who said that "Man is the measure of all things."[14]

- *Can one read this "conscious awareness" as both (a) our conscious awareness and (b) the beyond-humans and all-encompassing awareness that we are one with, that we perceive?*
- *If we can say that, then the quotation from Protagoras says that we humans are indeed the flashpoint for this awareness emerging. That is, as "measure" we humans ascertain and become aware of what is own to "it," being the flashpoint in which it appears and is known in experience.*

And:

Consciousness encapsulates mind and matter and expresses itself in various dimensions. Consciousness is energy and it vibrates in relation to the channel it is directed to.[15]

- *If consciousness is energy, then we can just as well say awareness is energy.*
- *If awareness is energy, then it is at the core of the non-dual dynamic of radiant emptiness or the core of beyng/Ereignis or what is at the heart of νοῦς, both human and beyond-human νοῦς – in a non-dual no-form and no-thing dynamic.*

The Leap. Given what is own to "it" – beyng/Ereignis, emptiness, along with the originary saying-showing in the key Greek words in retrieval – it becomes clear that we cannot gain access to "it" through logical arguments or conceptualization. Nor can we start from substance metaphysics. Rather, "it" calls for blasting through our traditional and inherited ways of thinking, to find ourselves dwelling in a dynamic that the veils make seemingly impossible to become aware of. It is as if we find ourselves jumping off the cliff of habits and inherited ways of seeing the world. It is this blasting through or jumping off that Heidegger calls "the leap (*der Sprung*)."

So, here at the end of the book, I turn to Heidegger's *Sprung*: The **Leap**. I will present a series of quotations from Heidegger's texts. Note three aspects that appear in these texts:

1. The whereunto: Unto where does the leap go?
2. The "wrong" way: What are the ways that do not work for the leap?
3. The way: What are the ways that do work for the leap?

Please keep these three aspects in mind, as "markers." First I simply I present some salient quotations. Then I will gather the various word-images in them that point to one or another of these three aspects.

I will start with quotations from *Beiträge* (GA 65):

> The leap, the most daring aspect of originary thinking, lets – and throws – everything familiar behind, expecting nothing directly from beings. Rather, before all else, [the leap] springs open [our] belonging to beyng in its full swaying as Ereignis. (227)

> The leap is the utmost laying-open of the deep sway of beyng, such that we give ourselves over to what has been opened up in this way, that we become insistent and that only through enowning [*Ereignung*] do we first become who we are. (230)

> The leap is the emergence of the willingness to become own to Ereignis … Ereignis cannot be forced intellectually. Rather, the open is to be pre-pared-for through thinking – the open that, as time-space (the flashpoint), makes the aperture of beyng accessible to and stable in Da-sein. (235)

> The leap is the knowing leaping-into the flashpoint of the site of what claims us [*Anfall*], that first [move] that, in the leading word, springs open the sheltering-hiding of Ereignis [*Er-eignung*]. (237)

> How should the intimating gain the slightest room there [locked in the abandonment of being], *that withholding is the foremost and utmost gifting of beyng, indeed its originary deep sway itself*? It takes place as the withdrawal, which draws into the stillness in which truth – according to what is own to it – comes anew to the decision on whether it can be founded as the

clearing for self- sheltering. This self-sheltering is the revealing of the with-holding, is letting-belong to the strangeness of another beginning. (241)

But the full grounding [Ergründung] of the ground must venture the leap into the ab-ground, take the measure of ab-ground itself, and endure it.

Ab-ground as staying-away of ground in the sense just mentioned is the first lighting-up of the open as "emptiness."

But how is emptiness to be understood here? Not in the sense that forms of ordering and frameworks for calculating what is extant of space and time are unoccupied – and not the absence of what is extant in space and time – but rather the timing-spacing emptiness [die zeit-räumliche Leere], the originary gaping-open in hesitating self-withhold-ing. But does this [hesitating self-withholding] not have to bump up against a claim, a seeking, an intention to go there, so that it can be a self-withholding? For sure, but both always hold sway as Ereignis, and now the only thing that is at stake is to determine what is own to emp-tiness [das Wesen der Leere]. What that says is: to think the ab-ground character of the abground, how ab-ground grounds. In fact, that always needs to be thought only from within and out of the ur-ground, namely Ereignis, and in carrying out the leap into its turning. (380–1)

From Über den Anfang (GA 70):

You cannot get to beyng from things/beings, because then an already designed (worked-out, entworfenes] being, unknown in how it came to be, will simply be passed on again.

Every attempt to come to beyng by way of metaphysics is a pretence and a sham. (110)

From Das Ereignis (GA 71):

To experience the beginning-start in its starting ... Setting up Da-sein [is] coming up to that (Ereignis) and abiding in the start and saying eve-rything from within and in favour of this experience [Er-fahrung]. (288)

Now some quotations from the essay "Was heißt Denken?" in Vorträge und Aufsätze (GA 7):

There is no bridge from the sciences to thinking, but only the leap. There where it brings us is not only the other side, but a wholly other place. (133)

For what announces itself only by appearing in self-hiding – we match this by only turning toward it and, with that, giving ourselves the task of letting what shows itself come forth into the unconcealment [coming out of hiding] that is own to it. (134)

For example, we do not learn what swimming means via a treatise or paper about swimming. What tells us what swimming means is the leap into the stream. In this way we first learn the element in which swimming must move. But what is the element in which thinking moves? (138)

Now I will gather those word-images and fit them into the three aspects listed above.

1. The whereunto: Unto where does the leap go?
   - We belong to beyng in its **full swaying as Ereignis**.
   - The open, as the flashpoint, makes the **aperture of beyng** accessible to and stable in Da-sein.
   - **Withholding** is the foremost and utmost gifting of beyng, indeed its originary deep sway itself.
   - This self-sheltering is the revealing of the withholding, is letting-belong to the strangeness of **another beginning**.
   - **Ab-ground** as staying-away of ground in the sense just mentioned is the first lighting-up of the open as "emptiness."
   - Timing-spacing **emptiness** is the originary gaping-open in hesitating self-withholding.
   - The self-withholding always holds sway as Ereignis, and now the only thing that is at stake is to determine **the deep sway of emptiness**.
   - There where it brings us is not only the other side, but a **wholly other place**.
2. Not the way: What are the ways that do *not* work for the leap?
   - The leap lets **everything familiar** behind, expecting **nothing directly from beings**.
   - Ereignis cannot be forced **intellectually**.
   - There is no bridge from the **sciences** to thinking, but only the leap.
   - You cannot get to beyng from **things/beings**, because then an already designed being, unknown in how it came to be, will simply be passed on again.

- Every attempt to come to beyng by way of **metaphysics** is a pretence and a sham (110).
3. The way: What are the ways that do work for the leap?
   - The leap is the utmost **laying-open** of the deep sway of beyng, such that we **give ourselves over** to what has been opened up in this way.
   - The leap is the emergence of **willingness to become own** to Ereignis.
   - The leap is the **knowing leaping-into the flashpoint** of the **ekstasis** [standing outside oneself], that first [move] that springs open the sheltering-hiding of Ereignis [*Er*-eignung] in the **word that hints**.
   - But the full grounding [*Ergründung*] of the ground must **venture** the leap into the ab-ground and **take the measure** of ab-ground itself and **endure** it.
   - What is at stake is to **determine what is own to emptiness**.
   - That is: to think the ab-ground character of the abground, how ab-ground is the no-form no-thing "baseline" that is lasting. In fact, that always needs to be thought only **from within and out of the ur-ground**, namely **Ereignis**, by **carrying out the leap into its turning**.
   - To **experience** the beginning-start in its starting … Setting up Da-sein [is] coming up to that (Ereignis) and **abiding in** the start and saying everything from within and in favour of this **experience**.

With these words about the leap, we tie Heidegger's words intimately to our project.

How can we gain access to all that has been said here in part 4? How to experience it? To become aware and know it with awareness? How to think it? And how to say it? One place where we hear concrete strategies, if you will, is in this quotation from Bohm. I repeat it here as a closure for our work. Read it this time as a meditation, as a kind of opening to the non-dual dynamic of radiant emptiness-awareness. Let each word sink in poi-etically. See what happens.

> The first step would be to stop doing anything and to let the dust [being stirred up entirely by my own concepts] settle. Then I would look

without trouble. Similarly, if the brain [or should one say "mind"? – my comment] can refrain from "trying" to resolve its conflicts, these will vanish of their own accord, spontaneously and naturally, leaving the "emptiness" in which clear perception takes place … We must be intensely aware of how the mind is working, without attempting to do anything about it. This awareness is enough. Real awareness already is action, without the need for a "choice" by the "self" to do something … No choices, decisions, or efforts are needed … To really see deeply the nature of this illusion [of the dust of concepts hiding what is] is action enough. For in the light of this perception, it [the illusion] has to collapse.[16]

- *Don't **try** to resolve anything. Let the dust of concepts settle and just pay attention.*
- *Be **intensely aware** without attempting to do anything.*
- *"This awareness is enough. Real awareness already is action, without the need for a 'choice' by the 'self' to do something."*
- *"Real awareness already is action."*
- *Then the conflicts of duality "vanish of their own accord, **spontaneously and naturally**, leaving the 'emptiness' in which clear perception takes place."*
- *What is left when the illusions vanish? **Emptiness!***

Finally, let us hear what D.H. Lawrence says about the "how":

An act of pure attention, if you are capable of it, will bring its own answer. And you choose that object to concentrate upon which will best focus your consciousness. Every real discovery made, every serious and significant decision ever reached, was reached and made by divination. The soul stirs, and makes an act of pure attention, and that is a discovery.

It is the same with the study of the stars, or the sky of stars. Whatever object will bring the consciousness into a state of pure attention, in a time of perplexity, will also give back an answer to the perplexity.[17]

- *Intense awareness, pure attention.*
- *The soul stirs, and makes an act of pure attention, and that is a discovery.*

- *Bringing awareness into the state of pure attention … will give back an answer.*
- *And we come to know the non-dual dynamic of radiant emptiness, beyng/Ereignis, dao, buddha mind, the immeasurable field of energy – experienced, thought, and said in Greek philosophy.*

c. Next Steps: Understanding Expanding Horizons

At times we are pushing the envelope in this book. This is in part because it is a bit difficult to say what this book is after, given the dualistic language of metaphysics and science that we have inherited (TI). It is also in part because the matter-at-hand here is counter-intuitive and shatters what we have come to know within Western philosophy. It bursts through the limits of our traditional and inherited paradigms. We need a fresh way of thinking and saying, which I have tried to do.

Here are a number of questions-issues that call for further work:

1. **The dual world that emerges within the non-dual dynamic.**
   It is within the non-dual dynamic of radiant emptiness – from Heidegger's beyng/Ereignis, from buddha mind and emptiness, from *dao* or making way, from the field of no-thing energy of quantum physics – that things/beings manifest-appear, into what we know as separate "things" in a duality. Put bluntly: How do the things/phenomena *in their duality* emerge within the non-dual dynamic of radiant emptiness, themselves understood as seemingly something other than the non-dual no-thing dynamic, while still belonging to and within it? How does the non-dual, at-one dynamic stay no-form and no-thing, as the things-phenomena emerge within it?
2. **The language hurdle.** This dynamic defies logic and definition. What does it say when poi-etic language moves indirectly and intuitively into this no-thing and no-form dynamic? This needs further awareness in experience as well as further deliberation, overcoming the limitations of metaphysical, propositional, conceptual languaging. This needs to be worked out more, especially

regarding how it works in experience and how to use poi-etic languaging within the subject-object language that dominates our world. This includes focusing on how science comes to know language's limitations. Here we focused primarily on the early Greek saying. But we can gain insight into the core non-dual dynamic that we find in early Greek thinking, as well as in Buddhism and Daoism, by going deeper into quantum physics and how it struggles to find the fitting way of saying this seemingly illogical non-real dynamic. A more thorough look at this would be beneficial.

3. **Aristotle and νοῦς.** Here I have barely tapped into Aristotle's thinking on νοῦς. There are significant passages in *De Anima*, the *Metaphysics*, and the *Nichomachean Ethics*. It behoves thinking to expand on this thread in Aristotle's thinking on νοῦς. This would be a book in itself.

4. **Plato and Aristotle in general.** Both of these thinkers dealt with matters belonging to the thread of my book here. Given that there are also many mistranslations of their Greek – in addition to that of the early Greeks – it is essential that we (a) remember not to take translations at face value or as accurate and (b) either do ourselves – or trust those who do – the work of opening up all their works to a refreshing translation that rethinks their philosophy. The thread in the early Greek thinkers – the non-dual no-form no-thing dynamic – runs through both Plato and Aristotle. Note: The whole of Plato and Aristotle does not belong to this hidden and covered-over thread that has been mostly mistranslated, but it is prominently there amidst the more metaphysical and dualistic thinking.

d. Coda

- Even though it is invisible, that is not to say that it is not out there, everywhere.
- Even though it is formless, that is not to say that it is does not let manifest and hold things with form.
- Even though it is emptiness, that is not to say that it is not powerful and all- pervading.

- Even though it is emptiness, that is not to say that it is not filled with potential.
- Even though it is immeasurable, that is not to say that it is not the source for all that is measurable.
- Even though it is boundless, that is not to say that the conditioned world does not appear within it.
- Even though it is not a being, that is not to say that it is not that from within which beings/things emerge.

In sum: Everything but everything is connected, driven by potential.
The many names for it:

- The indefinable and in that sense "nameless" and unmanifest **dao**, within the "mystery" of its dynamic oneness with manifestations/things. The dynamic one-ing of *dao* and its manifestations.
- The formless space of **buddha mind** in its dynamic oneness with the world of forms, sometimes called *samsara*.
- The non-physical and invisible **field of energy** of the quantum world, also known as quantum potential, in its dynamic oneness with the world of forms, for example, particles.
- The no-thing, formless **being/beyng/Ereignis** in its oneness with forms/things (Heidegger).
- The space-that-is-not form in its non-dual dynamic with phenomena/things (Plato's *chora*).
- The unfolding-as-such – emerging out of the hidden – in *aletheia* (Heraclitus and Parmenides).
- The no-thing formless dynamic of growing, emerging, "birthing" *physis* (Heraclitus and Aristotle).
- Unmanifest and no-form minding awareness *nous* (Anaxagoras and Aristotle).
- The dynamic of isness as nothing other than the arising, emerging, unfolding – unfolding from within enfolding (Bohm) – of *eon* (Anaximander and Parmenides).
- The one and one-ing of everything as gathering *logos* (Heraclitus).
- The hiding self-sheltering and disclosing vibrating of non-dual no-form no-thing beyng, the trembling-vibrating of beyng as such.

- The no-thing, no-form, and **non-dual dynamic of radiant emptiness,** which lets emerge and holds all that is, including things/beings-phenomena.

What *is* this dynamic?

Given its no-thing and no-form quality, we cannot produce it or actively make it happen. Rather, it is given to us if we are open to it. We cannot create it, we can only discover it. We – as form – are boundlessly within this non-dual and no-form dynamic. It is both "beyond" us and within us simultaneously, that is as a "one" or one-ing. What is special to us humans is that we are the **aware flashpoint** for knowing this one and we can say it poi-etically.

Everything – both form and the formless – is a blending, melting, melding, fusing, coalescing. Distinguishable but inseparable. Intrinsically and naturally. These words here do not name an action that took place at some point in time. Rather, poi-etically, they say and show the one-ness of the dynamic of it, that it is lasting and timeless, that is, outside the framework of time as we know it.

We know that indigenous peoples feel and are aware of a non-material world in ways that differ from our Western tradition. They have a natural ability to know **it.** It is part and parcel of their existential life and history. They know there is some dynamic or force that is "bigger" than they are, going beyond their limits in space. And it dwells within them. Although we Westerners do not come easily to this awareness, it is available and natural to us. The measuring stick of science as we traditionally know it is not the only yardstick.

Mohamed Omar Salem, in his essay "The Heart, Mind, and Spirit,"[18] looks at the *science* behind this up to now "alternative" evidence:

In many cultures throughout history, the heart has been considered the source of emotions, passion and wisdom. Also, people used to feel that they experienced the feeling or sensation of love and other emotional states in the area of the heart. However, in the past, scientists emphasized the role of the brain in the head as being responsible for such experiences. Interestingly, recent studies have explored physiological mechanisms by which the heart communicates with the brain, thereby influencing information processing, perceptions, emotions and health. (1)

[T]he heart communicates with the brain in ways that significantly affect how we perceive and react to the world. It was found that the heart seemed to have its own peculiar logic that frequently diverged from the direction of the autonomic nervous system. The heart appeared to be sending meaningful messages to the brain that it not only understood, but also obeyed. (1)

[T]he concept of functional "heart brain" [revealing] that the heart has a complex intrinsic nervous system that is sufficiently sophisticated to qualify as a "little brain" in its own right. The heart's brain is an intricate network of several types of neurons, neurotransmitters, proteins and support cells similar to those found in the brain proper. Its elaborate circuitry enables it to act independently of the cranial brain – to learn, remember, and even feel and sense. The heart's nervous system contains around 40,000 neurons, called sensory neurites. (2)

Research has also revealed that the heart communicates information to the brain and throughout the body via electromagnetic field interactions. The heart generates the body's most powerful and most extensive rhythmic electromagnetic field. The heart's magnetic component is about 500 times stronger than the brain's magnetic field and can be detected several feet away from the body. (2)

- *We Westerners have long placed consciousness in the brain. But if the heart's magnetic field is stronger than that of the brain, what does that tell us? Note that in Tibetan Buddhism it is in the heart that we gain access to the mind. "Gain access to," because buddha mind – being without form – is not localized. It is either nowhere or everywhere.*

There is now evidence that a subtle yet influential electromagnetic or "energetic" communication system operates just below our conscious awareness. (2)

- *Could it be that what is here named – scientifically – "just below our conscious awareness" is actually the awareness that we have been talking about, just that the scientific view does not know it? And that our usual TI ways do not know it?*

A very interesting research finding has been that the heart is involved in the processing and decoding of intuitive information ... Previous data suggests that the heart's field was directly involved in intuitive perception, through its coupling to an energetic information field outside the bounds of space and time. (3–4)

- *The intuition named here might be the non-conceptual awareness at the centre of this project.*

It has long been thought that conscious awareness originates in the brain alone. Recent scientific studies suggest that consciousness emerges from the brain and body acting together ... As has been shown, a growing body of evidence now suggests that the heart plays a particularly significant role in this process. The above findings indicate that the heart is far more than a simple pump. In fact, it is seen now as a highly complex, self-organizing information processing centre with its own functional "brain" that communicates with, and influences, the cranial brain via the nervous system, hormonal system and other pathways. The involvement of the heart with intuitive functions is another interesting piece of information. However, as persons with transplanted hearts can function normally, the heart can be considered here as a medium or tool, for an underlying more sophisticated integrating system that has the capacity to carry the personal identity of the individual. These new visions might give better understanding to the concept of mind as a multi-component unit that is not only interacting with the physical environment through demonstrable means, but also has the capacity to communicate with the cosmic universe through non-physical pathways ... This gives rise to the concept of the spirit as the non-physical element, or the field, of the mind that can communicate with the cosmos outside the constraints of space and time. (4)

- *A scientific way of saying the non-dual dynamic of radiant emptiness as awareness!*

The research collected in this article is a scientific affirmation of what this book is about.

How we can come to know it in experience? Notes, not directives.
It is impossible to come to know it with logic, concepts, or rational thinking. It is possible only through direct, lived experience and sayable only in a non-conceptual, poi-etic language. It is not a thing, even though things are one with it. It is not physical, even though physical things are one with it. It is not measurable, even though measurables are one with it.

All beings-things, for example, with form, are one with the no-thing and no-form non-dual dynamic of radiant emptiness-awareness, while it seems that we humans are the only beings who can be aware of this formless emptiness-awareness.

We have inherited a kind of amnesia regarding it. So coming to know it in experience, or to have knowing awareness of it, requires remembering. Not the kind of remembering that is at play when we remember someone's birthday or remember to bring milk home. This re-membering is experience, going all the way into (German: er-fahren) and dwelling in *it* in such a way that we experience it directly – and then come to know it as something that has always been there. It is only that we have allowed it to be covered over and hidden with veils and illusions and a warping of concepts. This covering-over tells us that "it" is not natural.

Dwelling *in dao*, buddha mind, the field of energy, beyng that is not a being, the dynamic of radiant emptiness – is re-membering or becoming aware of what has always been there. It is most natural for us, and our remembering coming-aware is also the most natural thing.

When we are alert to what is happening beyond the physical and the measurable, we come to know something about it –

- by paying attention to experiences that are real but not visible to us and not conceptual.
- by not dismissing our authentic experiences simply because culture does not attend to them – does not know them in direct experience.

- by being open to what comes our way, acknowledging our experiences that empirical science cannot touch. Grief, love, ecstasy, friendship are things that we know. And we simply and directly know hunger, thirst, the love we have for our children – and even "falling in love"! By looking into people's eyes and from people's gestures and the tone of their words, we come to know stuff about them, directly and intuitively. So it is with "it"!
- by being open to what emerges into our awareness, letting go of concepts that warp our vision and of blinders that block the feel of the way things are.
- by directing our attention to the heart, listening intuitively.

***

If this project becomes successful, then certain things will happen:

- We will begin to learn how to experience, think, and say that dynamic that is no thing and has no form. But it is possible. It is part of our natural ability.
- Something that we were not aware of will emerge from the background and into the forefront of our awareness and experience.
- We will be transformed.
- We will continue to value Heidegger's contribution to retrieving Greek thinking, learn to hear its originary-starting power, and over time put it into practice.
- Over time – maybe in twenty years – this book will become more useful; and Heidegger's thinking will continue to be appreciated.

Notes

Suggestions, Guidelines

1 Aristotle's *nous poi-etikos* is usually translated into English as "active intellect." When I work through the word *nous* at the end of part 3, it becomes clear that here "mind" works better than "intellect." Also, the word *active* is not wrong, in that this *nous* is indeed active. But the *poi-ein* that is said here encompasses far more than just "active." The entire sentence from the Greek reads: ἔστιν ὁ μὲν τοιοῦτος νοῦς τῷ πάντα γίνεσθαι, ὁ δὲ τῷ πάντα ποιεῖν ... In order to focus on what is at issue here, we can say: ὁ [νοῦς] τῷ πάντα ποιεῖν [νοῦς ποιητικός].

Preamble: Telling the Story of This Book

1 I learned later the reason: the moisture content of the corn stalks, not how dry the stalks *look*, determines the appropriate time to cut for silage. It turns out that the corn stalks in the field in Wisconsin *looked* dry enough to me but in fact still had too high a moisture content.
2 E. Schrödinger: "Quantum physics thus reveals a basic oneness of the universe." https://www.brainyquote.com/quotes/quotes/e/erwinschro 304795.html.
3 Still today, in some curricula, the period from the late fifteenth century to the early eighteenth century is called the modern period, sometimes the early modern period. Sometimes what comes after that is called "contemporary" and sometimes still "modern." What to do?
4 Often called "quasi-legendary," Lao Tzu has traditionally been named as author of the *Tao Te Ching*, which some contemporary scholars write as *Daodejing*. Several points of clarification here:

a. There is little historical evidence of the authorship of this work.

b. Lao Tzu is commonly translated as "Old Master." Thus the "author" of the *Daodejing* could be "some old master."

c. Either way the text itself is not in dispute.

d. Even when the word that tradition uses is *Tao*, it is still pronounced Dao. For a most reliable source for this and other information about the text *Daodejing*, see "Historical Introduction" in *Daodejing*, translated with commentary by R.T. Ames and D.L. Hall (New York: Ballantine, 2003), 1–10.

5 "The religion of the future will be a cosmic religion. It should transcend personal God and avoid dogma and theology. Covering both the natural and the spiritual, it should be based on a religious sense arising from the experience of all things natural and spiritual as a meaningful unity. Buddhism answers this description. If there is any religion that could cope with modern scientific needs it would be Buddhism." I am aware that there is some controversy as to the authenticity of this quotation. https://www.goodreads.com/quotes/501883-the-religion-of-the-future-will-be-a-cosmic religion#:~:text=%E2%80%9CThe %20religion%20of%20the%20future%20will%20be%20a%20cosmic %20religion,spiritual%2C%20as%20a%20meaningful%20unity.

6 "The world is given to me only once, not one existing and one perceived. Subject and object are only one. The barrier between them cannot be said to have broken down as a result of recent experience in the physical sciences, for this barrier does not exist." And "The really-objectively existing world does not exist." https://www.diepresse.com/5527239 /so-offen-ist-die-welt-der-quanten.

7 "Everything we call real is made up of things that cannot be regarded as real." https://quantumawareness.net/2018/06/11/niels-bohr-and-the -buddha-awareness-or-creation/.

8 Anton Zeilinger is part of the East/West dialogue with the Dalai Lama. For example, the conference "Matter and Mind – New Models of Reality" held in Vienna, Austria, in 2012. https://www.theviennareview.at /archives/2012/buddhism-meets-science.

9 Ricard and Thuan, *The Quantum and the Lotus*.

10 Daoism is not mentioned in this question. Here I will focus on Buddhism, while later on Daoism will be the focus – for reasons that will be clear at that point.

11 David Bohm belongs here as well. In part 2 I will use Bohm's words to show how he above all fits here.

12 Erwin Schrödinger coined the term "entanglement," saying that it was "not one but rather *the* characteristic trait of quantum mechanics, the one that enforces its entire departure from classical lines of thought." Schrödinger, "Discussion of Probability Relations between Separated Systems," 555.

13 https://www.zmescience.com/other/feature-post/einstein-christian -15102017.

14 https://www.goodreads.com/quotes/68179-the-scientist-s-religious -feeling-takes-the-form-of-a-rapturous.

15 https://ideapod.com/einstein-thought-buddhism.

Interlude: Heidegger's Words *Da-sein* and *Sein-Seyn-Ereignis*

1 Heidegger's *Gesamtausgabe* is organized according to Heidegger's own wishes, as he in the later years of his life planned for its publication after his death. There are four divisions. The first includes the published works; the second, the lectures from 1919 to 1944; the third, unpublished papers, lectures, and thoughts; and the fourth, notes and sketches. *Beiträge* belongs to the third division.

2 After many of the quotations in this book I will highlight, explain, and sometimes interpret the author's words, in line with the main thread of our entire discourse in this book. My words will appear as bullets and in italics.

3 Paul, *Deutsches Wörterbuch*.

4 See Hofstadter, "Enownment."

5 Note that Hofstadter does not ignore Heidegger's connecting the word *Er-eignis* with *Er-äugnis*. As we just heard, *Ereignis* can be traced back to *Er-äugnis*, from *Auge*-eye. We can say, then, that *er-äugnen* says: to glance, to gaze, to catch sight of something, to bring something unto its "own" through the gaze – or to enown it. On this pathway, one could say *er-eignen* = *an-eignen*. Thus, in its thinking-saying, *Er-eignis* gathers *Er-äugnis*. But *Er-äugnis* gathers in the manner of *an-eignen*. A reminder of how Heidegger says that the many ways to say the issue here is not about diversion or division, but about the amazingly rich and multivalent – that is, the inseparable and non-dual – dynamic of *Er-eignis*.

6 Hofstadter, "Enownment," 29.

7 See Hofstadter, "Introduction," xix. Here he applies the owning or owning-over-to in the fourfold. For Heidegger the fourfold is "the enowning

mirror-play of the onefold of earth and sky, divinities and mortals" (in M. Heidegger, "*Das Ding*" (GA 7:181). En-owning/*Er-eignis* names the work of owning/*eignen* by which the fourfold is thought-said in the dynamic at-oneness or belonging-together mutually; and the dynamic at-oneness is said in the fourfold.

8 Maly, *Heidegger's Possibility*, 111.

Part 1: Shaking Up the Established Views

1 For a detailed and rich laying out of this interplay, see Sallis, *Being and Logos*.

2 See part 3 on *chora*, under *apeiron*.

3 For understanding the revolutionary aspect of Socrates and *logos-mythos-ergon*, I am grateful to one of my mentors, John Sallis. I first heard about this interplay in a course given by Sallis at Duquesne University in 1967. Sallis's exposition of this interplay appears in his *Being and Logos*.

4 B. Ueland, *If You Want to Write* (Minneapolis: Graywolf Press, 1987).

5 Heidegger's term here is *die Technik*.

6 All the words in these last two paragraphs are Heidegger's words to describe the "flight of thinking" (519).

7 Stephen Cope, *The Great Work of Your Life: A Guide for the Journey to Your True Calling* (New York: Bantam Books, 2015), xix.

8 I have listed them in roughly chronological order. The list is not exhaustive but represents the major lineages.

9 Nietzsche, *Philosophy in the Tragic Age of the Greeks*, section 1.

10 Sean Carroll, theoretical physicist specializing in quantum mechanics, gravity, and cosmology, said once that what was discovered in Geneva's Large Hadron Collider (CERN) was not the Higgs particle at all, but rather only "that which it decays into." https://www.youtube.com/watch?v=pLbSlC0Pucw.

11 Nietzsche, *Philosophy in the Tragic Age of the Greeks*.

12 https://www.etymonline.com/search?q=psyche&source=ds_search.

13 Peters, *Greek Philosophical Terms*.

14 Klein, "Aristotle: An Introduction."

15 For a more detailed discussion of this theme, see my book *Five Groundbreaking Moments in Heidegger's Thinking*, 123–36.

16 In a preliminary way we can say that Aristotle sees ἐντελέχεια and ἐνέργεια as convergent. See Aristotle, *Metaphysics*, IX-3, 1047a, 30–1 and 1050a, 21–3), as well as Sachs, *Aristotle's Physics*, 79. We will look further into this matter in a minute.

17 Sachs was a colleague of Jacob Klein at St. John's College in Annapolis, Maryland. Klein, who has been described as one of Heidegger's "star graduate students," heard Heidegger's lecture course *Platon: Sophistes* (GA 19) in 1924, where Heidegger showed how to rethink Aristotle's Greek in today's language. Klein knew Greek very well, and he knew Aristotle. Klein took Heidegger's wisdom regarding Aristotle as a guide for redoing the English ways of translating Aristotle's Greek. He understood well Heidegger's question: How does one translate the Greek in Greek philosophy? See Klein's articles "Aristotle: An Introduction"; and "Aristotle (I)."

In his Introduction to his translation of *Aristotle's Metaphysics*, Sachs tells how, along with Heidegger, Klein was an "outstanding reader" of Aristotle who "led me [Sachs] to see that a new way of translating him [Aristotle] was necessary and possible. Jacob Klein, in his extraordinary brief essay 'Aristotle: An Introduction,' helped me begin to encounter Aristotle's thinking directly and genuinely."

18 J. Sachs, *Aristotle's Metaphysics*, xxxiv–xxxv.

19 Glossary in Sachs, *Aristotle's Metaphysics*, li–lii.

20 Sachs, *Aristotle's Metaphysics*, 179. Bold by me.

21 I suggest that this exciting invitation from Nietzsche lasts until he gets to Parmenides. For it is there that Nietzsche's fresh and open way of thinking stalls.

22 Nietzsche, *The Birth of Tragedy Out of the Spirit of Music*. I have made several changes in the translation, wherever I thought it appropriate.

23 Broad, *The Oracle*.

24 ὁ ἄναξ οὗ τὸ μαντεῖόν ἐστι τὸ ἐν Δελφοῖς, οὔτε λέγει οὔτε κρύπτει ἀλλὰ σημαίνει. The word ἄναξ is a reference to "lord" and is used in conjunction with the gods. I use the word *sublime* in order to cover the same notion as "divine" but without personalizing something like "god." The word μαντεῖόν has a similar bent. -εῖον = the place of, and μάντις = the diviner, foreboder, seer, prophet, soothsayer – all of which suggest "intimating saying." Gathering all of this together, I translate ὁ ἄναξ οὗ τὸ μαντεῖόν ἐστι τὸ ἐν Δελφοῖς as the "The sublime, whose place for intimating saying is at Delphi."

25 Nietzsche, *The Birth of Tragedy Out of the Spirit of Music*, 75.

Part 2: Enacting the Retrieval from "Here" to "There"

1 This project of mine – to see what possibilities there are in early Greek thinking, inspired and guided by the openings that Heidegger has

provided – did not start "yesterday." Here is a list of essays I have
written on the theme of Heidegger and Greek philosophy:
1. "Translating Heidegger's Works into English: The History and the
   Possibility," *Heidegger Studies* 16 (2000): 115–38.
2. "Through Substance Metaphysics and Objectifying Subjectivity to
   Another European Beginning," *Call to Earth* 1, no. 2 (2000): 15–19.
3. "From Truth to Aletheia to Opening and Rapture," *Heidegger Studies* 6
   (1990): 29–42.
4. "Reading and Thinking: Heidegger and the Hinting Greeks," in
   Reading Heidegger: Commemorations, ed. J. Sallis (Bloomington: Indiana
   University Press, 1993), 221–40.
5. "The Transformation of 'Logic' in Heraclitus," in *Heidegger on
   Heraclitus: A New Reading*, ed. K. Maly and P. Emad (Lewiston: Edwin
   Mellen Press, 1986), 89–102.
6. "Reading Heidegger Reading Heraclitus – Fragment 112," in
   Heidegger on Heraclitus: A New Reading, ed. K. Maly and P. Emad
   (Lewiston: Edwin Mellen Press, 1986), 135–51.
7. "Parmenides: Circle of Disclosure, Circle of Possibility," in *Heidegger
   Studies* 1 (1985): 5–23.
8. "Man and Disclosure," in *Heraclitean Fragments: A Companion Study to
   the Heraclitus Seminar*, ed. J. Sallis and K. Maly (Tuscaloosa: University
   of Alabama Press, 1980), 43–60.
2 *Vorträge und Aufsätze* was first published in 1954. The word ἀλήθεια was
   added in preparation for the *Gesamtausgabe* when it was published in
   2000. It is from the marginal notes that Heidegger added over the years
   after 1954. In part 3 we will appreciate the significance of this asterisk
   added by Heidegger.
3 *Ge-birg* as range of mountains, a massif, "a geologically distinct mass of rock
   or a series of connected masses forming the peaks of a mountain range"; *ein
   einziges* as unique, one and only, unsurpassable, singular, incomparable.
4 Some of the information here is from the "Editor's Introduction," in *The
   Essential David Bohm*.
5 *The Essential David Bohm*, 1.
6 Bohm, *Wholeness and the Implicate Order*, xii. Hereafter WIO.
7 WIO, 219.
8 Editors' Preface to the David Bohm Interview in *Omni*, vol. 9, no. 4
   (January 1987), 69–75. Also available at http://www.fdavidpeat.com
   /interviews/bohm.htm. Hereafter Bohm Interview.
9 WIO, 19.
10 WIO, 9.

11 Bohm and Hiley, *The Undivided Universe*, 389.

12 WIO, 62.

13 Descartes, "Treatise on Man," 108.

14 Descartes, *Meditationes de prima philosophia*, 229, 223.

15 collinsdictionary.com.

16 WIO, 220.

17 WIO, 223. A prime example of this non-local and non-causal relationship is entanglement.

18 WIO, 223.

19 John Muir, *Nature Writings*, ed. W. Cronon (New York: Library of America, 1997), 245.

20 Lynn Margulis, "Living by Gaia," in *Talking on the Water: Conversations about Nature and Creativity*, ed. Jonathan White (San Antonio, Texas, Trinity University Press, 2016), 57.

21 WIO, 218.

22 The question is: Are all of these "benefits"? For sure, the people who proposed, designed, built, and used the engineered river saw them as benefits. But are they all "benefits"? Are there any "non-beneficials"?

23 "Dead zones are deadly: Few or no organisms can survive in their oxygen-depleted, or hypoxic, waters. Often encompassing large swaths of ocean (and even lakes and ponds), dead zones become oceanic deserts, devoid of the usual aquatic biodiversity ... Dead zones appear annually, May through September, in the Gulf of Mexico, after tons of nutrients from fertilizer use and sewage in the Mississippi watershed wash downstream into the Gulf. Excess nutrients spark an algal explosion, giving rise to a dead zone." https://www.nationalgeographic.com /environment/article/dead-zones.

24 The word *metaphysics* is used in many loose ways today. I found the following book titles to illustrate this: *The Metaphysics of Evolution; Ten Metaphysical Secrets of Manifesting Money; It's All About Love: Metaphysics Demystified, A Handbook for Life; Heart-Centered Metaphysics; Theology as Revisionary Metaphysics; The Kemetic Tree of Life Ancient Egyptian Metaphysics and Cosmology for Higher Consciousness; An Ontological Search for Man in the Contemporary World: A Critical Re-Thinking in Existential Metaphysics*. Needless to say, these various uses of the word *metaphysics* do not fit with the philosophy that is here named "metaphysics."

25 "The Nature of Reality: A Dialogue Between a Buddhist Scholar and a Theoretical Physicist," with Alan Wallace and Sean Carroll. https:// www.youtube.com/watch?v=pLbSlC0Pucw.

26 Bohm Interview.
27 Bohm Interview.
28 *The Essential David Bohm*, 150–1. Bold print by me.
29 WIO, 243.
30 *The Essential David Bohm*, 31–2. Bold print by me.
31 WIO, 30.
32 Bohm Interview.
33 Bohm Interview.
34 *The Essential David Bohm*, 232–3.
35 *The Essential David Bohm*, 73.
36 *The Essential David Bohm*, 123.
37 WIO, xi.
38 "Der Geist liebt das Feste, Gestaltete, er will sich auf seine Zeichen verlassen können, er liebt das Seiende, nicht das Werdende, das Wirkliche, nicht das Mögliche." Hermann Hesse, *Narziss und Goldmund*, in *Gesammelte Schriften*, vol. 5 (Berlin: Suhrkamp Verlag, 1958), 68.
39 WIO, 36.
40 WIO, 43.
41 WIO, 60.
42 Lao Tzu, *Daodejing: "Making This Life Significant": A Philosophical Translation*, trans. Roger T. Ames and David L. Hall (Ballantine Books, 2003).
43 Lao Tzu, *Tao: A New Way of Thinking*, trans. Chang Chung-yuan (New York: Perennial Library, 1975).
44 Heidegger, "Zum Einblick in die Notwendigkeit der Kehre," 2–3.
45 This is not the only place where Chinese Daoists combine Daoism and Buddhism. I gave a lot of thought to using this quotation, for the simple reason that it is not useful for active practitioners to mix teachings and methods from various schools. But I use the quotation here to give a mirror to the way in which the nondifferentiated "wonder" of *dao* and the differentiated manifestations of *dao* can be understood as a non-dual dynamic.
46 For a fairly uncomplicated explanation of the five buddha eyes, see https://www.baus.org/en/publications/dr-shens-collections/the-five-eyes/. Note that this is from a Chinese Buddhist.
47 I create this chart from a longer list of contrasts from Simpson, *The Leader Who Is Hardly Known*, 100. Simpson's work is grounded in Daoism.
48 Noting that there is no correct translation of the title *Daodejing*. The translators have chosen "Making This Life Significant" as their translation of the word, putting it as part of the title of the work. "But

with deliberation we choose to underscore the human project that has prompted the articulation of Daoist cosmology and is inspired by it" (13).

49 As opposed to "non-action," which is the usual English translation of this word.

50 Simpson's *The Leader Who Is Hardly Known* is a fine example of this Daoist teaching.

51 *Tao Te Ching*, trans. D.C. Lau (Penguin Books, 1963).

52 Jung, "Introduction," 101.

53 One could legitimately add to this list: the fourfold, clearing (*Lichtung*), regioning-nearing (*die Gegend-die Nähe*), and the "it" of *Es gibt*.

Part 3: Retrieving, by Refreshing, What the Greek Words Say and in Saying Show, Shaped by Heidegger

1 Heidegger's words for these two ways are the "first beginning" and the "other beginning." In some sense the traditional and inherited way (the first beginning) started with the Greeks, especially Plato and Aristotle. However, it is also the case (as I try to show, although briefly) that both Plato and Aristotle include elements of the refreshing and retrieving way (the other beginning).

2 Lao Tzu, *Tao: A New Way of Thinking*, 3.

3 Lao Tzu, *Daodejing*, 31.

4 Lao Tzu, *Daodejing*, 31.

5 Lao Tzu, *Daodejing*, 33.

6 Quoted in Simplicius *Phys.* 24, 13; DK 12 A 9, and Hippolytus *Ref.* 1, 6, 1–2: DK 12 A 11. From Kirk and Raven, *The Presocratic Philosophers*, 105–10. The following quotations are from these pages.

7 W. Kranz, *Wortindex*, which comprises the second half of volume 2 in H. Diels, *Die Fragmente der Vorsokratiker*. Diels prepared volume 1: *Die Fragmente der Vorsokratiker* (Berlin: Weidmannsche Buchhandlung, 1903). Diels also prepared an Appendix (*Anhang*), which appeared as volume 2, issue 1 (1907), whereas W. Kranz authored the *Wortindex*, which appeared as volume 2, issue 2 (1910).

8 In 1941 (*Grundbegriffe*, GA 51) Heidegger takes this whole fragment to be authentic and by Anaximander himself. In 1946 in the *Holzwege* essay (GA 5) he says he is inclined to consider only κατὰ τὸ χρεών· διδόναι γὰρ αὐτὰ δίκην καὶ τίσιν ἀλλήλοις τῆς ἀδικίας as from Anaximander himself. However, he adds that the first part of the saying, although probably not from the hand of Anaximander, should not be simply excluded, but rather kept as an indirect witness to Anaximander's thought by

virtue of the strength and saying-power of his thought (GA 5:341). For my purposes here the philological question – significant as it might be – has no bearing, in that the earlier part remains "Anaximandrian" if not by Anaximander himself. The first and the last parts of this German rendition by Heidegger come from GA 51:101; the middle part (that part alone that Heidegger later considers to be by Anaximander himself) is between the ellipses and comes from GA 5:372.

9 Peters, *Greek Philosophical Terms*, 20.
10 The last three sentences are obviously Heidegger's translation of *Timaeus* 50e. In the text of GA 40 the Greek text appears after the first two of these three sentences: ἄμορφον ὂν ἐκείνων ἁπασῶν τῶν ἰδεῶν ὅσας μέλλοι δέχεσθαί ποθεν. ὅμοιον γὰρ ὂν τῶν ἐπεισιόντων τινὶ τὰ τῆς ἐναντίας τά τε τῆς τὸ παράπαν ἄλλης φύσεως ὁπότ᾽ ἔλθοι δεχόμενον κακῶς ἂν ἀφομοιοῖ, τὴν αὐτοῦ παρεμφαῖνον ὄψιν. The German edition makes no mention of the fact that this is a translation from the Greek and gives no explanation for putting the Greek in the middle of the text. The editor's mistake?
11 This paragraph appears in brackets in the *Gesamtausgabe* edition. According to the editor's comments, this indicates that Heidegger added this paragraph when he prepared the lecture course for publication with Max Niemeyer Verlag in 1953.
12 Sallis, *Being and Logos*, 18. Italics by Sallis.
13 Sallis, *Being and Logos*, 16.
14 Sallis, *Being and Logos*, 16.
15 Sallis, *Being and Logos*, 46. The words quoted in this paragraph are from this page.
16 Sallis, *Being and Logos*, 178.
17 Ballard, *Socratic Ignorance*.
18 Heidegger's translation of these lines goes like this: *Denn nicht hat dich Schickung, eine arge, vorausgesandt, aufzubrechen zu diesem Weg – fürwahr nämlich abseits der Menschen, außerhalb ihres (ausgetretenen) Pfades ist der – sondern Satzung sowohl als Fug auch* (GA 54:6).
19 Peters, *Greek Philosophical Terms*, 158.
20 Peters, *Greek Philosophical Terms*, 159.
21 Marcovich, *Heraclitus*, 433.
22 Diels, *Die Fragmente der Vorsokratiker*.
23 Kirk and Raven, *The Presocratic Philosophers*, 106. There this phrase τινὰ φύσιν ἄπειρον is translated as "some other apeiron nature." Hmm ...
24 Peters, *Greek Philosophical Terms*, 166–7.
25 H.G. Liddell & R. Scott, *A Greek-English Lexicon* (Oxford: Clarendon Press, 1940).

26 Peters, *Greek Philosophical Terms*, 167.

27 Diels, *Die Fragmente der Vorsokratiker*.

28 https://en.wikipedia.org/wiki/Metrodorus_of_Lampsacus_(the_elder).

29 Peters, *Greek Philosophical Terms*, 127–8.

30 Google search of the term *nous*: https://www.google.com.

31 John Burnet's translation. http://philoctetes.free.fr/parmenides.pdf.

32 Kirk and Raven, *The Presocratic Philosophers*, 270.

33 "Der Gedanc bedeutet: das Gemüt, das Herz, den Herzensgrund, jenes Innerste des Menschen, das am weitesten nach außen und ins Äußerste reicht und dies so entschieden, daß es, recht bedacht, die Vorstellung eines Innen und Außen nicht aufkommen läßt." Note how this mirrors the non-dual dynamic.

34 Klein, *Lectures and Essays*, 186.

35 Peters, *Greek Philosophical Terms*, 135.

36 Peters, *Greek Philosophical Terms.*, 65.

37 Peters, *Greek Philosophical Terms*, 133.

38 Peters, *Greek Philosophical Terms*, 133.

39 Peters, *Greek Philosophical Terms*, 134–5.

40 Peters, *Greek Philosophical Terms*, 122.

41 https://iep.utm.edu/anaxagor/#H4.

42 The word here is the superlative of λεπτός. It is often translated as "thin" or in the superlative: "thinnest." The word does mean thin with regard to physical things. But from Homer onward, it means fine in the sense of fine-tuned, refined, or delicate. Especially in connection with the words about non-physical aspects, for example, especially, νοῦς.

Part 4: Bringing the Book to a Close

1 L. Strauss, "Progress or Return," in *An Introduction to Political Philosophy: Ten Essays by Leo Strauss*, ed. Hilail Gilden (Detroit: Wayne State University Press, 1989), 292.

2 Klein, *Lectures and Essays*, 186.

3 Klein, *Lectures and Essays*, 65.

4 G. Smetham, "The Self-Aware Emptiness of the Quantum Universe," *Scientific GOD Journal* 3, no. 1 (2012): 83–131.

5 H. Maturana and F. Varela, *Autopoiesis and Cognition: The Realization of the Living* (Dordrecht: Reidel, 1980), 13.

6 https://deutsch.tergar.org/die-buddha-natur-wir-lama-so-wie-wir-sind.

7 *Oxford English Dictionary*.

8 https://www.etymonline.com/word/aware#etymonline_v_19017.

 9 https://www.dwds.de/wb/gewahr.
10 https://www.scienceandnonduality.com/article/are-consciousness
    -and-awareness-the-same.
11 https://www.themindfulword.org/2016/timeless-awareness-time.
12 Rudolf Bauer, *Timeless Awareness as Dzogchen: A Phenomenological View*,
    www.academia.edu., 2016.
13 https://en.wikipedia.org/wiki/Quantum_entanglement.
14 J. Nwanegbo Ben, "Consciousness and Quantum Physics in the
    Interpretation of Reality," *Philosophy Study* 10, no. 1 (January 2020): 38.
15 Ben, "Consciousness and Quantum Physics," 39.
16 *The Essential David Bohm*, 232–3.
17 D.H. Lawrence, *Sketches of Etruscan Places and Other Italian Essays*
    (Cambridge: Cambridge University Press, 2002), 62.
18 M.O. Salem, "The Heart, Mind and Spirit," https://www.studocu.com
    /cl/document/universidad-de-santiago-de-chile/biologia/heart-mind
    -and-spirit-mohamed-salem/51158836, 1–4.

Bibliography

Part A: Works by Heidegger

This is a list of all the volumes of Heidegger's *Gesamtausgabe* that are mentioned in this work. The *Gesamtausgabe* is published by Vittorio Klostermann Verlag, Frankfurt am Main, Germany. References here are listed as GA (*Gesamtausgabe*) followed by the volume number, title, editor, and date of publication.

Some of these texts exist in earlier, separate editions. Bibliographical information for these separate editions of Heidegger's texts – as well as the texts listed in Part B – can be found in the notes as well as in the bibliography.

GA 2   *Sein und Zeit*, ed. F.-W. von Herrmann, 1977, 2018.
GA 5   *Holzwege*, ed. F.-W. von Herrmann, 1977, 2003.
GA 7   *Vorträge und Aufsätze*, ed. F.-W. von Herrmann, 2000.
GA 8   *Was heißt Denken?*, ed. P.-L. Coriando, 2002.
GA 11   *Identität und Differenz*, ed. F.-W. von Herrmann, 2006.
GA 12   *Unterwegs zur Sprache*, ed. F.-W. von Herrmann, 1985, 2018.
GA 13   *Aus der Erfahrung des Denkens*, ed. H. Heidegger, 1983, 2002.
GA 14   *Zur Sache des Denkens*, ed. F.-W. von Herrmann, 2007.
GA 15   *Seminare*, ed. Curd Ochwadt, 1986, 2005.
GA 16   *Reden und andere Zeugnisse eines Lebensweges*, ed. H. Heidegger, 2000.
GA 19   *Platon: Sophistes*, ed. I. Schüßler, 1992, 2018.

GA 33   *Aristoteles, Metaphysik Θ 1–3. Von Wesen und Wirklichkeit der Kraft,* ed. H. Hüni, 1981, 1990, 2006.

GA 40   *Einführung in die Metaphysik,* ed. P. Jaeger, 1983, 2020.

GA 45   *Grundfragen der Philosophie. Ausgewählte "Probleme" der "Logik,"* ed. F.-W. von Herrmann, 1984, 1992.

GA 51   *Grundbegriffe,* ed. P. Jaeger, 1981, 1991.

GA 54   *Parmenides,* ed. M. Frings, 1982, 1992, 2018.

GA 55   *Heraklit,* ed. M. Frings, 1979, 1987, 1994.

GA 65   *Beiträge zur Philosophie (Vom Ereignis),* ed. F.-W. von Herrmann, 1989, 1994, 2003.

GA 70   *Über den Anfang,* ed. P.-L. Coriando, 2005.

GA 77   *Feldweg-Gespräche (1944–45),* ed. I. Schüßler, 1995, 2007.

GA 81   *Gedachtes,* ed. P.L. Coriando, 2007.

GA 97   *Anmerkungen I-V,* ed. P. Trawny, 2015.

Part B: Other Major Texts Referred to in This Work

Aristotle. *See under* Sachs, Joe.

Ballard, Edward. *Socratic Ignorance.* The Hague: Martinus Nijhoff, 1965.

Bauer, Rudolf. *Timeless Awareness as Dzogchen: A Phenomenological View.* www.academia.edu, 2016.

Ben, J. Nwanegbo, "Consciousness and Quantum Physics in the Interpretation of Reality," *Philosophy Today,* 10, no. 1(January 2020).

Bohm, David. "David Bohm Interview." *Omni,* vol. 9, no. 4, January 1987.

– *The Essential David Bohm.* Edited by L. Nichol. New York: Routledge, 2003.

– *The Undivided Universe: An Ontological Interpretation of Quantum Theory.* Co-authored by B.J. Hiley. New York: Routledge, 1993.

– *Wholeness and the Implicate Order.* New York: Routledge, 1980, 2002.

Broad, William. *The Oracle: The Lost Secrets and Hidden Messages of Ancient Delphi.* New York: Penguin Press, 2006.

Descartes, René. *Meditationes de prima philosophia.* In *Oeuvres,* vol. 7. Edited by C. Adam and P. Tannery. Paris: Leopold Cerf, 1904.

– "Treatise on Man." In *The Philosophical Writings of Descartes.* Translated by J. Cottingham et al. Cambridge: Cambridge University Press, 1984.

Diels, Hermann. *Die Fragmente der Vorsokratiker,* 2 vols. Berlin: Weidmannsche Buchhandlung, 1903–7.

Grimm, Jacob, and Wilhelm Grimm. *Deutsches Wörterbuch,* vols. 1–26. Leipzig: S. Hirzel Verlag, 1854–1960; completed edition, vols. 1–33. Munich: Deutscher Taschenbuchverlag, 1984. The version that I used is online at https://woerterbuchnetz.de/?sigle=DWB&sigle=DWB&mode =Vernetzung&hitlist=&patternlist=&lemid=GG10082#0.

Heidegger, Martin. "Zum Einblick in die Notwendigkeit der Kehre." In *Vom Rätsel des Begriffs: Festschrift für Friedrich-Wilhelm von Herrmann zum 65. Geburtstag*, ed. Paola-Ludovika Coriando. Berlin: Duncker and Humboldt, 1999.

Hofstadter, Albert. "Enownment." In W.V. Spanos, ed., *Martin Heidegger and the Question of Literature: Toward a Postmodern Literary Hermeneutics*, 17–37. Bloomington: Indiana University Press, 1979.

– "Introduction." In his translation of M. Heidegger, *Poetry, Language, Thought*. New York: Harper and Row, 1975.

Jung, C.G. "Introduction." In *The Secret of the Golden Flower: A Chinese Book of Life*, trans. R. Wilhelm. New York: Harcourt Brace Jovanovich, 1965.

Kirk, G.S., and Raven, J.E. *The Presocratic Philosophers*. Cambridge: Cambridge University Press, 1957.

Klein, Jacob. "Aristotle: An Introduction." In Klein, *Lectures and Essays*, ed. R. Williamson and E. Zuckermann, 171–95. Annapolis: St. John's College Press, 1985.

– "Aristotle (I)." In *The New Yearbook for Phenomenology and Phenomenological Philosophy*, vol. 3, ed. B. Hopkins (2003), 295–313.

Kranz, Walther. *Wortindex*. In H. Diels, *Die Fragmente der Vorsokratiker*, vol. 2. Berlin: Weidmannsche Buchhandlung, 1910. *See also* under Diels.

Lao Tzu. *Tao Te Ching*, three translations:

– *Daodejing: "Making This Life Significant": A Philosophical Translation*. Translated with commentary by R.T. Ames and D.L. Hall. New York: Ballantine Books, 2003.

– *Tao: A New Way of Thinking*. Translated with introduction and commentary by C. Chung-yuan. New York: Harper and Row, Perennial Library, 1975.

– *Tao Te Ching*. Translated by D.C. Lau. London: Penguin Books, 1963.

Maly, Kenneth. *Heidegger's Possibility: Language, Emergence, Saying Be-ing*. Toronto: University of Toronto Press, 2008.

– *Five Groundbreaking Moments in Heidegger's Thinking*. Toronto: University of Toronto Press, 2020.

Marcovich, Miroslav, *Heraclitus: Greek Text with a Short Commentary*. Mérida: Los Andes University Press, 1967.

Nietzsche, Friedrich. *The Birth of Tragedy Out of the Spirit of Music*. Translated by I. Johnston, rev. ed., 2008, www.holybooks.com.

– *Philosophy in the Tragic Age of the Greeks*. Translated by M. Cowan. Chicago: Regnery, 1962.

Paul, Herrmann. *Deutsches Wörterbuch*, 9th ed. Tübingen: Max Niemeyer, 1992.

Peters, F.E. *Greek Philosophical Terms: A Historical Lexicon*. New York: NYU Press, 1967.

Ricard, Matthieu, and Trinh Xuan Thuan. *The Quantum and the Lotus*. New York: Crown, 2001.

Sallis, John. *Being and Logos: Reading the Platonic Dialogues*, 3rd ed. Bloomington: Indiana University Press, 1996.

Sachs, Joe, *Aristotle's Metaphysics*. Santa Fe: Green Lion Press, 2002.

– *Aristotle's Physics: A Guided Study*. New Brunswick: Rutgers University Press, 1995.

Salem, M.O. "The Heart, Mind and Spirit." https://www.studocu.com/cl/document/universidad-de-santiago-de-chile/biologia/heart-mind-and-spirit-mohamed-salem/51158836.

Schrödinger, Erwin. "Discussion of Probability Relations between Separated Systems." *Mathematical Proceedings of the Cambridge Philosophical Society*, vol. 31.

Simpson, Steven, *The Leader Who Is Hardly Known*. Oklahoma City: Wood N' Barnes, 2003.

Index of Greek Philosophers, Words, and Fragments of Heraclitus

General Index

New Studies in Phenomenology and Hermeneutics

General Editor: Kenneth Maly

Gail Stenstad, *Transformations: Thinking after Heidegger*
Parvis Emad, *On the Way to Heidegger's "Contributions to Philosophy"*
Bernhard Radloff, *Heidegger and the Question of National Socialism: Disclosure and Gestalt*
Kenneth Maly, *Heidegger's Possibility: Language, Emergence – Saying Be-ing*
Robert Mugerauer, *Heidegger and Homecoming: The Leitmotif in the Later Writings*
Graeme Nicholson, *Justifying Our Existence: An Essay in Applied Phenomenology*
Ladelle McWhorter and Gail Stenstad, eds., *Heidegger and the Earth: Essays in Environmental Philosophy*, Second, Expanded Edition
Richard Capobianco, *Engaging Heidegger*
Peter R. Costello, *Layers in Husserl's Phenomenology: On Meaning and Intersubjectivity*
Friedrich-Wilhelm von Herrmann, *Hermeneutics and Reflection: Heidegger and Husserl on the Concept of Phenomenology*, translated by Kenneth Maly. Published in German as *Hermeneutik und Reflexion. Der Begriff der Phänomenologie bei Heidegger und Husserl*
Richard Capobianco, *Heidegger's Way of Being*
Janet Donohoe, *Husserl on Ethics and Intersubjectivity: From Static to Genetic Phenomenology*
Miles Groth, *Translating Heidegger*
Graeme Nicholson, *Heidegger on Truth: Its Essence and Its Fate*
Kenneth Maly, *Five Groundbreaking Moments in Heidegger's Thinking*
Richard Capobianco, *Heidegger's Being: The Shimmering Unfolding*
Kenneth Maly, *A Refreshing and Rethinking Retrieval of Greek Thinking*